Praise for Mel Watkins's

STEPIN FETCHIT

"[A] spryly entertaining telling . . . shading in the details of [Perry's] deeply problematic [career] as fully as [he] deserve[s]."

—*San Francisco Chronicle*

"Watkins's book succeeds in humanizing Perry . . . vividly detailing the demeaning and even dangerous racial landscape that Perry navigated."

—*The News & Observer* (Raleigh, NC)

"Nobody is better suited to write the definitive Fetchit biography than Mel Watkins. . . . [He] offers a convincing defense of Fetchit's career, arguing that the comedian was both a subversive force and a victim of his times—and damn funny, something new viewers are only starting to discover."

—*Los Angeles Magazine*

"Readers get a rare view of the man who was renowned and reviled for his late 1920s and 1930s portrayals of Hollywood's stereotypical image of Blacks."

—*Ebony*

"This biography is valuable for the way in which it draws parallels between the high-minded black attitude toward negative stereotypes of Fetchit's own period and the altered attitudes of today."

—*The New York Observer*

"Excellent. . . . Mel Watkins has given us not only Stephin Fetchit's story . . . bu[…] picture industry. . . . *Stepin F*[…]

[…]*ues Book Review*

Mel Watkins

STEPIN FETCHIT

The Life & Times of Lincoln Perry

Mel Watkins, a former editor and writer for *The New York Times Book Review*, is the author of *Dancing with Strangers*, a Literary Guild Selection, and of the highly acclaimed *On the Real Side: A History of African American Comedy*. He lives in New York City. Mr. Watkins can be contacted at www.ontherealside.com.

ALSO BY MEL WATKINS

African American Humor

Dancing with Strangers

On the Real Side: A History of African American Comedy

STEPIN FETCHIT

STEPIN FETCHIT

The Life and Times of Lincoln Perry

Mel Watkins

Vintage Books
A Division of Random House, Inc.
New York

FIRST VINTAGE BOOKS EDITION, NOVEMBER 2006

Originally published in hardcover in slightly different form in the United States by Pantheon Books, a division of Random House, Inc., New York, in 2005.

The Library of Congress has cataloged the Pantheon edition as follows:
Watkins, Mel, [date]
Stepin Fetchit : the life and times of Lincoln Perry / Mel Watkins.
p. cm.
Includes index.
1. Fetchit, Stepin. 2. Motion picture actors and actresses—United States—Biography.
3. African American motion pictures actors and actresses—United States—Biography.
I. Title.
PN2287.F425W38 2005
791.4302'8'092—dc22 200504183

Vintage ISBN-10: 1-4000-9676-6
Vintage ISBN-13: 978-1-4000-9676-3

Author photograph © Herb Riddick / Sandra Symon
Book design by Iris Weinstein

www.vintagebooks.com

Printed in the United States of America
10 9 8 7 6 5 4 3 2 1

For Step, Crackshot, Butterbeans, Moms, Mantan, Dusty, Kingfish, Hattie, Pigmeat, and all of the early-twentieth-century black comedians who, under the most repressive conditions, satirized and labored to humanize the nation's distorted image of African Americans

Now get this—when all the Negroes was goin' around straightening their hair and bleaching theirself trying to be white and thought improvement was white, in them days I was provin' to the world that black was beautiful. Me. *I opened so many things for Negroes—I'm so* proud *today of the things that the Negroes is enjoying because I personally did 'em myself.*

—Stepin Fetchit, 1971

ACKNOWLEDGMENTS

I want to thank the New York Public Library—particularly the Schomburg Center for Research in Black Culture and the Library for the Performing Arts at Lincoln Center—for their vast resources and their intelligent guidance in searching out needed information. My special thanks to the late Flip Wilson and Matt Robinson, who not only provided essential insight into Stepin Fetchit's personality but also fired my enthusiasm for undertaking the project.

Finally, thanks to all those who graciously sat for interviews and filled in gaps in the information that I so desperately needed, and, as always, to the friends and cohorts who helped either materially or spiritually as Step's story slowly unfolded: my sisters in Ohio, my agent B. J. Robbins, and friends Robert Tate, Al Bright, and George Davis are among them. Special thanks to Elisabeth Dyssegaard, whose patience and editorial suggestions were instrumental in shaping the book.

STEPIN FETCHIT

CHICAGO: NOVEMBER 1976

(A Re-creation)

The frail, dark-skinned old man arose late to the swoosh and thud of wind kicking at his shuttered bedroom window on this raw, steel-gray day. Outside the modest two-story brick residence, which was set in a row of single-family homes on the city's South Side, gusts swept most anything not tied or nailed down out into the street and sent it rolling along the cobblestone pavement. On mornings such as this, there was no doubt as to why Second City citizens referred to the piercing, bone-numbing gales as simply "the hawk."

It was after ten when the old man unraveled the covers, shivered at the draft that whipped between window and sill, and wearily pulled himself up into a sitting position. Head tilted slightly forward, he blinked and dug the ridges of his knuckles and forefingers into his eye sockets. Then, as if drifting back to the twenties and a Hollywood movie set, he ran his hand ever so slowly along the near-bald ebony crest of his head.

As he stirred from heavy sleep, his face momentarily settled into a heavy-lidded, near-bemused expression. That quixotic look had once been as familiar to Americans as Babe Ruth's minced-step home-run trot or little Shirley Temple's cherubic smile. Some forty years earlier, when fans had flocked to his films by the millions, it would have elicited knee-slapping howls, wry grins or, at the very least, tight-lipped simpers of amused acceptance from nearly everyone. During the seventies, however, in an America radically transformed by the civil rights movement and the new black militancy, it was most frequently greeted by a wary flash of recognition, an exasperated frown or, even more often, abusive condemnation.

The familiar gesture and sleepy-eyed expression had become symbols, emblems of an attitude, an impotent posture, and a history of sidestepping, accommodation, and groveling that African Americans desperately sought to erase—not only from public view but also from their own memory. The old man, unfortunately, was a living reminder of that spurned history. And that fact, the near-universal disdain with which he was now viewed, rarely strayed far from the mind of this once-revered relic.

This morning, however, public infamy was an unobtrusive spook. The old man was much more attentive to the gnawing pain that for the last four or five years had accompanied his daily awakening. The spasms that pinched his spine and radiated down into his thighs and spindly, slightly bowed legs silenced most other concerns. Nearly as aggravating was the faint headache that pulsed beneath his gleaming pate. The annoying throbbing ringed his brow as if someone were periodically constricting then loosening a silk sash—the expensive type that not too long ago hung with the dozens of silk robes (not to mention thousand-dollar custom-made cashmere and silk suits, mohair overcoats, and exotic haberdashery) that had lined the closets of his palatial homes.

Deliberately, he pushed his legs over the side of the bed, then slowly stood and padded across the floor with a stoop-shouldered, halting gait befitting a former star who had built his reputation on the improbable billing of "The World's Laziest Man."

The small second-floor bedroom was piled high with old newspapers and boxes filled with mementos—posters, playbills, photos, and reams of faded, yellowed magazine clippings that he had meticulously collected and hoarded over the past fifty years. Pulling on an oversized terry-cloth robe, he padded toward the hallway. Neither his wife, Bernice, nor his hosts, the old show-business friends who owned the house, were about; today he had the tiny bathroom to himself. Later, he made his way down the steps and, after preparing a cup of instant coffee, slouched down into a chair at a wobbly kitchen table.

By late afternoon, Bernice had returned. The old man had retreated to their bedroom. It was his customary routine when he was not out lobbying to have someone publish the autobiography that he still dreamed of writing or producing a television documentary of his life. On rare occasions, he even ventured out onto the road for an engagement at some small-town lodge, social club, or strip joint where curious, predominantly wizened fans still flocked to see him. In those venues he was still a viable attraction. At those appearances, the audiences were often exclusively white, as black Americans had turned a deaf ear to his previous accomplishments and generally regarded him with no more respect than that bestowed on Aunt Jemima or those venerable uncles, Tom and Ben.

Sitting hunched over a small table, he riffled through a pile of photographs and clippings, some dated as far back as the twenties. There were reviews of his early movies, including the silent film *In Old Kentucky,* and his breakthrough role as Gummy in the 1929 talkie *Hearts in Dixie.* Then there were the hundreds of feature stories and personality pieces clipped from national magazines and Hollywood tabloids, as well as notices and announcements of appearances at venues as prestigious as New York's Cotton Club and Roxy Theater or as obscure or seedy as a Clinton, Iowa, Elks social club or a bottomless dive in Madison, Wisconsin. Among the photographs were shots of him and his original stage partner, "Johnnie" Lee; posed publicity shots in which he straddled the nose of a propeller plane while exclaiming, "Is you gwine bust?" or mugged with his friend and former costar Will Rogers; and scores of group celebrity photos with him—beginning as a spry twenty-five-year-old hobnobbing with glamorous chorus girls (a former wife among them) and a Who's Who list of black and white athletes, musicians, and actors that included Rudolph Valentino, Jack Johnson, Shirley Temple, Rex Ingram, Will Rogers, John Wayne, Louis Armstrong, Mae West, John Ford, Cab Calloway, Flip Wilson, and Muhammad Ali.

Lost in the reverie, for a time he was lured back to those more benevolent times. The money, women, lavish parties, cars, frantic adulation, and, yes, even that special sense of the gratification he'd derived from his majestic sham—it all flashed before him, swelled up in his mind. For a moment his eyes brightened and a sly grin lit his face. It too would have been recognizable to many of his former fans, at least to the observant ones who had peered beyond the indolent mask and spied the crafty con artist that lurked beneath it.

The surge of elation, however, was fleeting. And the old man turned to more recent clippings and articles. A few were always kept on the bureau by his bedside along with the legal papers he had filed against CBS and the producers of the 1968 television documentary *Black History—Lost, Stolen, or Strayed* for defamation of character. He never read them without seething or, if there was an audience, bursting into a frenzied, defensive harangue. Still, as if caught up in some Sisyphean ritual, he repeatedly returned to them. Today, alone, he read and silently fumed.

"The white man's Negro, the traditional, lazy, stupid, crapshooting, chicken-stealing idiot," he mouthed the words to himself, shaking his head. "Hollywood's Uncle Tom"; "an embarrassment to blacks"; "a mockery of upstanding Negro citizens"; "the willing accomplice to Hollywood's systematic denigration of the black man." The now-familiar phrases echoed in his mind and, had someone else been present, they would have noticed the veins at either side of his forehead distending and swelling. Caught up in the masochistic rite, the old man was unmindful.

The edema, when it came, was sudden, a slash of excruciating pain on the right side of his skull. It jolted him to his feet and, staggering one step backward, he clutched at his head as his eyes rolled back in their sockets. No one heard the feeble cry he uttered as he struggled to call out to his wife. But when, an instant later, blackness descended and he lurched forward, smashing into the table, the crash reverberated throughout the house. His jaw hit the table's edge, upending it and sending papers and photographs flying about the room.

When Bernice rushed in, he was unconscious. Sprawled on the floor, his left arm lay rigid at his side; his right arm was curled above his head. She shrieked when she saw his face. His mouth was twisted into a grotesque, gaping hole. He was breathing laboriously.

The medics arrived twenty minutes later. Once there, they whisked their comatose patient into an ambulance, which screeched away with lights flashing and sirens blaring.

Inside, Bernice at his side, he lay perfectly still. Partially revived now, eyes open but unmoving, he stared vacantly at the vehicle's roof. He could not speak or move his jaw; it would be months before they discovered that it was broken. Nor could he move his left arm or leg. For now he was only capable of weakly flexing the fingers of his right hand, which he did from time to time as Bernice pressed them between her own palms.

His thoughts were elsewhere. Again he drifted back to the past—to brighter times, the carnival days before *his* world had been devastated, turned upside down. In that world, his folksy, Old South trickery and backwoods buffoonery had functioned flawlessly. In perfect synch with his audience, he had instinctively known how to wring laughter from their fears and prejudices as well as their stunted dreams and muted anger, how to connive, thrive, and brilliantly hold the spotlight.

Oddly, his thoughts were fixed on the nonsensical tune that he and his partner Buck Abel had sung and danced to when they played the black theater circuit, billing themselves as "Step and Fetch It." The smile that struggled to break through his deadened facial muscles was not apparent to Bernice and the medical attendants, but he had been transported. It was as if he were back in the limelight, center stage, basking in the applause and adulation that he knew he had earned and fully deserved.

Curiously at ease, he silently hummed a whimsical jingle that the most ardent vaudeville buff would have been hard-pressed to identify.

The vehicle screeched to a halt. Hauling the stretcher from the ambulance, the medics wheeled their semiconscious patient through the doors of Cook County Hospital. Behind the old man's half-closed, glazed eyes, the doggerel floated through his mind.

"The Step 'n' Fetchit! Step 'n' Fetchit! Turn around, stop and catch it . . . Turn around, stop and catch it . . ."

CHAPTER ONE

In the late 1800s, Key West, Florida, still bore a faint resemblance to the barren wilderness described in settlers' colorful tales about the island's fierce Calusa Indians or the marauding pirates who had kept the eighteenth-century French and Spanish pioneers at bay for decades. The four-mile-long sand and coral island had officially become part of the United States in 1826. Only ninety miles from Havana, Cuba, it was the southernmost settlement in the continental United States and still had the untamed aura of a frontier outpost. By 1860, as the nation moved inevitably toward the Civil War, it had become the wealthiest city per capita in America despite not having a rail link to the Florida mainland. At the time, its economy relied on shipbuilding, sponging, cigar packing, and the harvesting of snail, shrimp, lobster, and stone crab.

The island's prosperity was fleeting, however. Still, the mid-nineteenth-century boom along with the island's natural beauty and reputation as an exotic getaway made it a haven and magnet for adventurers, artists, eccentrics, and tourists, as well as for a growing number of West Indians for whom it was a doorway to the United States. Among the latter group were Joseph H. Perry, a skilled Jamaican cigar wrapper, cook, and would-be entertainer, and Dora Monroe, a Bahamian seamstress who grew up in Nassau. They were married in 1898 and, leaving Nassau, arrived in Key West in 1902.

In addition to being something of a womanizer and traveling man, Joseph Perry was, by many accounts, a fair hoofer, singer, and an aspiring minstrel stage performer. He was a gregarious, cocky man who took great pride in his Caribbean background and his status as a subject of the British Crown—a fact of which he regularly boasted, particularly when dealing with African Americans.

Joseph and Dora had three children. Their second child, Lincoln, would go on to far surpass his father's wildest aspirations.

Lincoln Perry was born on May 30, 1902, in Key West. He later claimed that his father named him for four presidents; his full name was Lincoln Theodore Monroe Andrew Perry. According to one account, "he was born as an American by a few hours only," since his parents arrived in the Keys just prior to his birth. His older sister, Lucille, had been born two years earlier, and his younger sister, Mary, who later changed her name to Marie, was born a year and a half later. Lincoln and his siblings rarely discussed their childhood or family life publicly, and since no personal letters or firsthand accounts related to that period have been found, the actor's early years in Key West and his adolescent years in Tampa after the family moved to the mainland are shrouded in mystery.[1]

Apparently, Lincoln Perry did not suffer from a lack of confidence. Like many other Caribbean immigrants, the Perry family reportedly displayed an assertiveness that, at the time, was most often held in check by former African American slaves and their descendants. Years after he reigned as a Hollywood star, Perry suggested that his youthful self-esteem was derived from his Caribbean background.

"I'm a descendant of the West Indies," Perry told a reporter. "I had talent all my life." Far from being "lazy and stupid . . . the white man's fool" that many made him out to be, he insisted that he was "the first Negro militant."[2]

It was a defense of his by-then-tainted reputation and an affirmation of pride in his West Indian heritage. Perry's attitude reflected a culturally based rift between American-born and Caribbean-born blacks that in the early twentieth century frequently sparked heated clashes.[3]

Despite the mumbling, ostensibly cowering screen character that he later immortalized as Stepin Fetchit, Lincoln Perry displayed his aggressive racial and cultural pride in offscreen relationships with both whites and blacks throughout his career.

Ironically, when his double-talk and roundabout public statements are scrutinized, when his extravagant spending, cavalier lifestyle and frequent clashes with the producers and moguls who controlled the Hollywood studio system are put into context, Perry surfaces in sharp contrast to the image inspired by previous knee-jerk assumptions. Uneducated, but shrewdly intelligent, he parlayed his considerable talent and folk wit (the equivalent of today's street smarts) into screen stardom during a period of blatant racial oppression and intolerance that make conditions in the twenty-first-century "hood" look like a model of racial harmony and equality.

He was far deeper and much more volatile and complicated than the portrait of a shallow, ingratiating buffoon drawn by many historians and critics. Pronouncements of religious fervor aside, he was no choirboy. Hot-tempered, prone to violent outbursts, egotistical, and, at heart, a bit of a scoundrel—he was as confounding as any black star who took to the stage and screen in the twentieth century. But when the character he created on stage and in pictures is considered as a carefully molded *caricature* that burlesqued mainstream America's contemptuous vision of Negroes, Perry also emerges as a cagey self-publicist and brilliant comic actor. Perhaps most surprisingly, when his on-set hassles with studio executives are viewed in the context of the era's twisted racial arrangements and his pioneer achievements in the film industry are weighed objectively, he rears as a prideful, race-conscious agitator for equal treatment in the entertainment field. He was, and still is, largely misunderstood. If not quite the "militant" that he sometimes claimed, he was a sly provocateur. "I didn't fight my way in," he once said, "I *eased* in." At the time, it was realistically the only way of bucking the system.[4]

Pride and Caribbean heritage aside, the racial tenor of early-twentieth-century America dictated that Perry and his family exercise some caution around white Americans. Like many American Negroes, they often resorted to a bit of subterfuge and trickery developed in Southern slave quarters as well as the West Indies—a survival tactic that would be sustained long after slaves were freed. It was perhaps best described by the old saw "Got one mind for white folks to see; 'nother for what I know is me." The tactic found its most frequent expression in what slaves had called "puttin' on ole massa." Lincoln Perry was an expert at it.

At the peak of his Hollywood stardom—when nearly every black shoeshine boy in America began copying his lazy drawl and slow, shambling gait, and motion-picture-cartoon representations of Negroes were invariably modeled on the character he created—Lincoln Perry doggedly adhered to that bit of black folk wisdom. He misled interviewers with fanciful anecdotes about his past, distorting and reshaping facts regarding his childhood as well as other aspects of his personal life in nearly all comments to the press, and, until his last years, generally bedeviled any attempt to expose the real person behind his carefully concocted public persona. For Perry the ruse was also an expression of the waggish delight he took in mocking America's middle-class mores by confounding and often outfoxing assumedly "superior" adversaries.

The rambling, circuitous accounts of his past with which he regaled reporters were often calculated misdirections, reflecting a roguish temperament and sly, double-edged wit that, despite his stature as one of America's best-known comedians, most observers were reluctant to concede he possessed. Throughout his life, Lincoln Perry remained an enigmatic, chameleonlike, conflicted figure—an entertainer whose name and reputation would assume mythic proportions, while the man behind the myth remained as illusive as a shadow. Even today, while most are familiar with the name Stepin Fetchit and may even have used it in a derogatory manner, very few have ever actually seen the actor perform onstage or in motion pictures. (Scenes in which he appeared have been deleted from most of the few movies available on tape or shown on television.)

What generally surfaced in the media was the specter of a self-indulgent profligate and malcontent whose antic conduct—much like the often outrageous stunts of latter-day comics and Bad Boys Richard Pryor and Martin Lawrence—seemed driven by some self-destructive, deep-seated internal demon. The assessment was in part correct. In addition, however, like Madonna, Howard Stern, Britney Spears, J. Lo, Paris Hilton, and many other present-day celebrities, he realized that even bad press sells—that notoriety can and often does confer power.

There is little doubt that at an early age Perry was a cutup and prankster. "Ah was terrible bright, but Ah never studied," he once told a reporter, insisting (as he commonly did with the mainstream press) that his remarks be rendered in stilted stage dialect. "Ah was a bad example. Ah was a thug, allus stealin'." Even his self-dubbed childhood nickname, "Slop Jar," suggests that early on he had an outsider's irreverent, somewhat satirical view of both himself and his life circumstances.[5]

Still, he developed a keen interest in religion at an early age, which lead a childhood friend to insist that "Step was always a church fanatic." It was Dora Perry who initially fired that religious fervor. Unlike her husband, she was a pious woman and a devout Catholic who reportedly insisted that her children attend church regularly. Lincoln adored his mother and seems to have followed her instructions or given the appearance of doing so without much complaint. Long after her death, Lincoln's connection to the church remained one of the most stable elements in his life.[6]

Dora Perry apparently exerted tremendous influence over her son, but outside of her religious convictions she remains a vague figure. The paternal side of Lincoln's background, however, is a little less shadowy. He spoke glowingly of his father on the few occasions that he talked about his childhood and seemed to have been genuinely impressed by the elder Perry's talent as well as his itinerant lifestyle, which contrasted sharply with the religious and family values esteemed by Lincoln's mother.

A free spirit and sportin' man, Joseph Perry often took to the road. Leaving the tedium of family life and his cigar-wrapping job behind, he frequently journeyed to Miami and the surrounding areas to search for more invigorating work as an entertainer. Later, he moved his family to the Tampa area, where the Rabbit Foot Company, a famed black minstrel troupe, was based. Despite the distress his jaunts may have caused his wife or the burden and hardship they may have placed on the family, he was idolized by his son. From an early age, young Lincoln displayed an urge to follow in his father's footsteps.

"His mother wanted him to be a dentist," Joseph Perry told a *Los Angeles Times* reporter during a rare interview in 1929. "She sewed for the wife of a dentist and tried to have the boy work as an errand boy for the dentist and absorb the idea of some day becoming a dentist himself, but he would have none of it. And his mother was heartbroken.

"My boy was always tapping his feet. He would sit down to eat a meal and under the table his feet would always go tap, tap, tap.

"His mother threatened him many times and ordered him to stop. But I always told mammy, 'You hush up and let him tap, because that tapping is going to get him somewhere some day.'"[7]

Although there is no evidence that young Lincoln Perry spent much time fretting over it, the disparity between the lifestyles and values extolled by his mother and those of his father was extreme. Throughout his life, Lincoln Perry seems to have displayed an exceptional ability to accept and, in his own life, effortlessly embrace behavior that most others considered conflicting or contrary. He apparently admired and was drawn to both his father's love for show business and the secular life, and his mother's piety and regard for middle-class respectability. This despite the fact that at the turn of the twentieth century many pious Americans scornfully viewed the entertainment profession as Satan's domain. Among the Negro middle class, scorn was even greater if the entertainers happened to be minstrel performers. Just as many churchgoing blacks vigorously denounced the blues as the devil's music, the Negro elite typically condemned minstrelsy's ethnic comedy as reprehensible and distorted—a detriment to racial progress.

The minstrel show craze that had swept mainstream America in the mid-nineteenth century was waning by the 1900s, but it had left its mark on the face of black entertainment. With few exceptions, the entertainers who worked the traveling medicine shows, carnivals, tent shows, and circuses in the early twentieth century not only reprised much of the material introduced by white minstrel performers but also "corked up" and appeared in blackface.

According to some historians, minstrelsy's traditional semicircular format, which featured a staid moderator and comic end men, Tambo and Bones, who clowned and bantered with him, was created around 1840 by the John Luca troupe, a family of black traveling performers. But it was Dan Emmett and a group of white entertainers billing themselves as the Virginia Minstrels who formalized the presentation and brought it to the New York City stage in February 1843. Performed by white men in garish blackface makeup, the three-act minstrel show quickly became the nation's most popular form of entertainment.

Only a few black performers broke the color line before the Civil

War. William Henry "Juba" Lane, who joined the Ethiopian Serenaders in the 1840s and toured Europe and the United States with the formerly all-white company, was among the first and most popular. The success and acceptance of pioneers like Lane, who was later touted as the father of modern tap dance, set the stage for other black performers, and just prior to the Civil War, a few all-black minstrel troupes began surfacing.

America's first professional black musicians and entertainers, many the sons and daughters of former slaves, cut their teeth on the minstrel stage. Although they were spurned by most respectable colored folk and their performances condemned by some black critics, black minstrelsy soon established itself as the cornerstone of African American performing arts.

Early blackface stars included Billy Kersands, the reputed originator of such popular dances as the Virginia Essence and the Buck and Wing; Ernest Hogan, whose popularity soared with release of the song "All Coons Look Alike to Me" in 1896; James Bland, the performer and composer who wrote Virginia's state song, "Carry Me Back to Old Virginny"; and the comedy team of Bert Williams and George Walker.

Joseph Perry probably watched and patterned his own act after those charismatic entertainers. Talking to his son at home or, when the boy was old enough to accompany him, taking him along on an excursion to watch or perform in one of the tent shows or carnivals that passed through the Tampa area, the elder Perry would have certainly eagerly praised the accomplishments of those pioneers.

Kersands, Hogan, and Bert Williams had altered and subtly humanized the Negro stage characters (originally known as Sambo and Zip Coon) popularized by white minstrel performers. But their updated versions (the shiftless rural rube and bombastic, dandified city slicker), still had firm roots in a mainstream stage tradition that openly satirized the behavior of America's former slaves. As a star of the *Ziegfeld Follies* and one of America's most acclaimed performers, Williams candidly admitted that on stage he portrayed "the shiftless darky to the fullest extent"; beneath his character's artless exterior, however, there was a droll, scantily concealed wit that belied the surface befuddlement.[8]

Young Perry never saw any of these artists perform live onstage, but given his father's love of entertainment and the theater, as an impressionable teenager, he no doubt admired the era's black stage clowns. He may have even begun dreaming of emulating them.

During the youngster's early years, the entertainment field rapidly opened up for Negro performers. The twenty-year period from 1890 to 1910 was a golden age for the black performance arts. African American entertainers not only regularly appeared in road shows and carnivals by then, but were also making inroads in vaudeville and the off-Broadway theater.

The stigma of minstrelsy and blackface entertainment, with its stereotypical comic figures, however, still haunted black theatrical performances. To the aspiring Negro middle class, the derivative comic caricatures that had replaced minstrelsy's Sambo and Zip Coon were no less offensive.

The black masses did not generally share that sentiment. Billy Kersands, Ernest Hogan, and Bert Williams were genuine heroes for many ordinary working-class black folk.

"It goes without saying that minstrels were a disreputable lot in the eyes of a large section of upper-crust Negroes," the famed turn-of-the century blues composer W. C. Handy wrote. "But it was also true that all the best talent of that generation came down the same drain. The composers, the singers, the musicians, the speakers, the stage performers—the minstrel shows got them all."[9]

For most blacks the entertainment world offered one of the few available avenues to success, financial reward, and prestige. Along with athletes like jockey Jimmy Winkfield (the 1901 and 1902 Kentucky Derby winner), lightweight champion Joe Gans (1902–1908), and heavyweight champion Jack Johnson (1908–1915), stage performers became symbols of a life beyond the confines of domestic servitude, sharecropping, and underpaid manual labor. On occasion, they were even able to dance lightly around the rigid Jim Crow laws that literally kept blacks in their places.

Negro folk culture was also enjoying increased popularity. Black America's syncopated music and dance were quickly gaining acceptance with mainstream audiences, and, while still largely excluded from first-rate venues, black performers were increasingly in demand. Joseph Perry was aware of the ferment in America's popular culture, and he no doubt communicated and shared his interest with his gangling young son who, at an early age, had displayed a knack for dancing and clowning, and an urge to command the spotlight.

Still, had his family remained intact, the young Perry—a clever child who reportedly did very well in school—may have chosen a different direction for his future. His mother's illness and untimely death, however, permanently altered the course of Lincoln's life. Despite a brief flirtation with education at a Catholic boys' school, without his mother's influence, Lincoln drifted more toward his father's lifestyle.

Even so, during the spring of 1914 no one imagined that twelve-year-old Lincoln Perry was destined to become one of the nation's most popular entertainers. And since, in the fledgling silent-film industry, blacks were nearly always portrayed on-screen by white actors, there was little or no reason to suspect that this somewhat unruly, sleepy-eyed schoolboy would emerge as Hollywood's first black screen star, and perhaps the most controversial and, to many, infamous figure in the history of black entertainment.

CHAPTER TWO

Dora Perry realized that her husband's vagabond ways made him unsuitable for the role of a single parent. In Tampa she had worked for a prosperous Negro family as a seamstress, and when she became ill, she asked if they would provide a foster home for her children. The family agreed. After Dora Perry's death in 1914, Lincoln and his sisters lived with their father for only a short time before they were taken into the middle-class home of a local dentist.

Piecing together the events of Lincoln Perry's life during this period is particularly difficult since nearly all available information is derived from the often-contradictory "facts" he related to journalists and a few friends in later years. It is clear, however, that the Perry children were soon separated.

By his own admission, Perry was expelled from numerous schools after moving into the foster home. Although bright, he seldom studied and was always in trouble. "I'd steal anything, even if I had to throw it away. I couldn't seem to help it. Sometimes I used to get down on my knees myself, and pray to God to keep me from stealing." In 1915, convinced that the wayward child needed more supervision, his adoptive parents sent him off to St. Joseph's College, a Catholic boy's school near Montgomery, Alabama.[1]

Josephite Fathers in Alabama had reportedly taken a sincere interest in the plight of local Negroes during the postslavery era. And, in 1901, St. Joseph's College had been founded by the Very Reverend T. B. Donovan; its stated object was "to educate young colored men to be catechists and teachers." Lincoln Perry was accepted at the school, but his stay was brief.

Wheelock Bisson, who would later become a Memphis physician, was a close friend of young Perry's at St. Joseph's and was one of only a handful of people who offered recollections of Lincoln's adolescence. "He always liked to go to church," Dr. Bisson told an interviewer in the 1970s. "But he was the kind of boy who, when the collection plate was passed around, would put ten cents in the plate and take out twenty cents change. I remember one night while he was an altar boy in church. He went to sleep while the priest was preaching. So in his sleep, he made a loud rectal noise. He woke up and pointed his finger behind him at an old man with a long white beard who was in the church choir. So the priest put him and the man on probation for a month."[2]

Perhaps because of his fascination with religious study or, just maybe, because Perry was well liked, the sisters and school officials generally ignored his occasionally errant behavior. But during the summer of 1916, he stretched their tolerance nearly to the breaking point. "The people who had adopted me and sent me off to this school, something happened to them," he later said of that summer. (His foster parents were reportedly unable to continue paying his tuition at St. Joseph's.) "And so this priest told me I could work my way through school."[3]

The summer job apparently went well for a few weeks, then, according to his old friend Wheelock Bisson, Perry became involved with a rather ghoulish prank.

"They got him a job at the Catholic hospital in Montgomery as an orderly," Dr. Bisson recalled. "The first world war was going on at that time, and one of the patients in the hospital was a soldier whose foot was frostbitten. Gangrene had set in. When his foot was cut off, Step was given the foot to burn up in the incinerator. Step cut off the swollen, gangrenous big toe of the foot and put it in his pocket. He used the toe, when he was off duty, to frighten little children in the community."[4]

We can only speculate about what—except perhaps the insatiable need for attention displayed by many performers—may have led Perry to undertake such a grisly act. But when hospital officials got word of his bizarre behavior, they immediately informed him that his services were no longer needed. Despite the noticeably rancid smell of Lincoln's pocket and complaints from the horrified children who had seen the gruesome body part, however, sisters at St. Joseph's interceded and tried to have Lincoln reinstated. Their attempts failed. Lacking enough money for tuition and no doubt embarrassed by the extreme reaction to his unconventional prank, young Lincoln decided to leave school. He followed in his father's footsteps. By the end of the year, fourteen-year-old Lincoln Perry was on the road, learning the ropes as a blackface entertainer.

There is little verifiable information about Lincoln Perry's earliest days as a tent-show performer. He seldom went on record about his earliest experiences, and he was rarely mentioned by other performers from the same period. Moreover, on the few occasions when he did comment on details of his career before the 1920s, the facts, when checked, often proved erroneous. Several times, for instance, he cited the Royal American Shows as the carnival he joined in Montgomery at age fourteen. But records show that a troupe with that name did not appear until 1923. If Perry did join the outfit, it would have been as a twenty-one-year-old veteran of seven years on the road.[5]

It is more likely the inexperienced teenager struggled to find work as an entertainer before joining a large professional outfit like the Royal American Shows. And in fact, on another occasion he admitted that he joined a small traveling show in Montgomery after leaving St. Joseph's. "I hung out in Alabama and worked for an old Arkansas medicine show," he recalled. "He had a show in a tent, and me and him sold herbs and iron medicine." Hiring a novice teenager as a part-time performer in one of these small, fly-by-night enterprises would not have been unusual at the time. In fact, medicine shows provided an avenue for many of the era's greatest performers to break into show business. Bessie Smith, W. C. Fields, Tim "Kingfish" Moore, Buster Keaton, Bill "Bojangles" Robinson, and Red Skelton were all medicine-show performers at some time during their early careers.[6]

Small medicine shows traveled from town to town with one or two acts and set up shop in the back of a wagon. Larger shows performed in tents and often had a small band, a song and dance man or buck dancer, a comedy sketch team, a blackfaced comedian, or even a contortionist, juggler, or magician. At the turn of the century, these shows were among small-town America's most popular forms of entertainment. Performers had to be versatile since they were called upon to sing, dance, participate in comedy skits, and play instruments. The entertainers were there to draw crowds, but, since the shows were free, it was the responsibility of the pitchman, or so-called doc, to hawk the tonics or "snakeoil" that kept the outfit afoot.

In those days, before food and drugs were regulated by the government, "anybody could compound some type of medicine and offer it for sale," the early-twentieth-century vaudevillian Tom Fletcher wrote in his memoir *100 Years of the Negro in Show Business*. "In the summer they would pitch tents on vacant lots in large or small towns and put on shows to draw the crowds so they could sell their medicines." The owners of these shows, often outright scam artists, spent very little on entertainment since their sole source of revenue was the elixirs and "medicinal" concoctions they pandered.

"The cheapest and best talent they could get were colored musicians and entertainers, playing banjos, guitars and other string instruments," Fletcher wrote. For young, unproven performers, like Perry, those shows provided an unusual chance to break into show business and learn the ropes.[7]

Some contemporary writers claimed that the youngster eventually left Montgomery with the Rubin & Cherry carnival company, for whom he sang, danced, and, as a roustabout, helped with the chairs and canvases. When the show arrived in Toledo, Ohio, the story goes, Perry quit and attempted to join the army. After being rejected, he worked in a munitions factory for a short time. He then hoboed to Macon, Georgia, where he took up with another traveling show in November 1918.[8]

Perry also claimed that he toured with a "plantation" show owned by "Diamond Tooth" Billy Arnte, a veteran performer on the black theatrical circuit. He said that, for a time, he was billed as Rastus the Buck Dancer. Arnte was "one of those biggety guys," Perry later told a Hollywood fan magazine writer. He "threw things at Step, and Step quit." After leaving, Perry claimed, Arnte sent his wife to "Vamp" him into returning to the show. The young performer resisted the temptation and moved on to larger carnivals and traveling shows. With one, the Cotton Blossom Minstrels, he was billed as "the buck champion of the world." The show offered "$10,000 to Anyone Dead or Alive Who Could Beat Him."

In an unusual show of modesty, Perry added, "That is, they advertised me that way out in the woods. In the towns they didn't say nuthin'."[9]

Other descriptions of Perry's early life on the road claim that at one time or another he was a stable hand, bootblack, laborer, and race tout who followed the ponies from one fair to another. By all indications, the scrappy teenager was forced to learn how to survive by his wits.

Few firsthand reports confirm Perry's recollections of his early years on the road. It is possible, however, to glean something about the nature of his tent-show experience from memoirs and vivid accounts by other black entertainers who worked the black theater circuit in the early twentieth century.

Clearly, the world of itinerant black performers was not a place for the thin-skinned or the fainthearted. In his autobiography, W. C. Handy documented numerous instances of the hazards of traveling with Mahara's Minstrels at the turn of the century. They included being stoned by white mobs, shot at by cowboys as their train passed through Orange, Texas, being forced to hide overnight in the Mississippi woods to avoid a lynch mob, and having one of their band members jailed, then lynched, by an angry mob in Missouri.

On another occasion, after performing at a Mississippi town dance, his band's departure was halted and they were literally kidnapped by a local plantation owner.

"We finished the engagement and were about to catch a train for Memphis when a white man in a dangerous temper came to the platform and ordered us to accompany him to another town," Handy recalled. "There was no refusing. He was not bargaining with us to fill an engagement. Neither was he making a request. He was *telling* us."[10]

In nineteenth-century America, particularly in the Deep South, blacks were usually at the mercy of the whims and caprice of most any white man they met. Being waylaid, insulted, or attacked was not uncommon, and performers, whose attire and demeanor set them apart, were often targets for insults and violence. The comedian Bert

Williams, for instance, forlornly described an encounter he and his partner, George Walker, had with a white mob in a small Louisiana town. They were stopped by a group of surly white men who apparently resented both the duo's dapper apparel and the way they carried themselves. The performers were stripped of their money and clothes, given burlap sacks, and run out of town. They were, Williams suggested, fortunate.[11]

Conditions did not improve much during the first two decades of the twentieth century, although work opportunities increased with the debut of the Theater Owners' Booking Association (aka the TOBA or TOBY). Established around 1907 by F. A. Barrasso, a white Memphis businessman, the agency offered an organized option to the traveling carnivals, circuses, medicine and tent shows that had provided most engagements. Most of the circuit's theaters, although sometimes managed by blacks, were owned by whites. But, except when a section was roped off for nonblack audiences, they catered primarily to Negroes.

The TOBA and several other black theater agencies—including one started in 1913 by Sherman Dudley, a black comedian and former minstrel—offered an extensive network of theaters that showcased the talents of a rapidly expanding group of black artists. In addition, social clubs and fraternal organizations like the black Shriners and Elk's Club sponsored "indoor circuses" that performed for Negro audiences in select cities.[12]

Most agencies did not pay for traveling expenses after the first booking, and minor, marginally paid acts barely broke even. Occasionally, agencies arranged lodging and eating facilities for top entertainers, but most performers were left to their own devices. When traveling in the South, that loomed as an enormous problem.

"The greatest difficulty was in finding places to stay while in different cities," Tom Fletcher recalled. Entertainers depended on boardinghouses or private homes in the Negro sections of the towns, but many Southern Negroes, wary of city ways and the questionable reputations of stage folk, declined to offer them accommodations. Others, anxious to mingle with moderately famed performers or to supplement meager incomes, eagerly welcomed the entertainers. It was a catch-as-catch-can situation, and traveling showmen were often forced to sleep on the floors of the town halls and theaters at which they appeared or, when authorities permitted, in train depots or even the local jail. Even when they were taken in by a local Negro resident, the arrangement was often troublesome.

"The colored people where we had to lodge were not well equipped to take care of anybody outside of their own families," Fletcher wrote. "Being on their own only a short time, very few of them could afford outsiders a place to sleep. The meals were okay because nearly all of the people had their own farms and smoke houses, curing their own meat and also enough space to store some vegetables."[13]

Lodging and eating aside, Negroes traveling through the rural South often faced far more treacherous circumstances.

"The towns in most Southern states were pretty rough to us," Fletcher wrote. "Colored musicians were considered an amusing night entertainment in towns where there [was] no colored population, except possibly just a few families whose parents had been slaves there and who had stayed on. No attention was paid to these few Negroes because it was taken for granted that they 'knew their place,' but the townspeople made it very clear that no other colored people were wanted there." Signs reading NO NIGGERS ALLOWED or NIGGER, READ AND RUN were a common sight in the rural South. Often the latter signs had an addendum: IF YOU CAN'T READ. RUN ANYWAY.[14]

Some Southern theaters were owned or managed by outspoken racists who, while profiting from black performers and patrons, displayed outright contempt for them. Ethel Waters, for instance, described Charles P. Bailey, the owner of Atlanta's 81 Decatur Street Theater, as a "tough-bitten old Georgia Cracker" in her autobiography, *His Eye Is on the Sparrow.* He was among the most powerful men in Atlanta during the teens and twenties and, according to Waters, with the help of local police, ran his theater like an "antebellum plantation." He terrorized performers, threatening and harassing female stars like Bessie Smith, whom he once beat and had thrown into jail. After a heated disagreement with him, Waters was forced to leave her fee and costumes behind and sneak out of town.[15]

Many towns had curfews that barred Negroes from the streets after dark unless they had an official pass; even performers leaving the theatre after a show were required to have a pass to avoid arrest. For theater owners, it was a sweet arrangement, since it effectively gave them total control of the members of a troupe that they engaged. For Negro entertainers, it was virtual peonage.

Owners were not above bending the law to their own purposes. That sometimes meant conspiring with locals to force performers to stay and complete an engagement against their will. Doll Thomas, a minstrel-show performer and later a projectionist at the Apollo Theater in Harlem, recalled an early experience in Atlanta. After witnessing the humiliation of a fellow actor who was excoriated when he attempted to enter the front door of the theater, Thomas decided to quit and leave town. "A week later," he recalled, "I went to the railroad station, put my money down and said, 'Give me a ticket to New York.' The red-faced cracker looked at me and said, 'Ain't no niggers leavin' here. We don't allow them out.' The man refused, absolutely refused, to sell me a ticket."[16]

Not surprisingly, for many Negro performers, the black circuit tour and the acronym TOBA soon came to mean "Tough on Black Asses."

Nor is it very surprising that the nearly six-foot-tall, rail-thin, ostensibly languorous teenager who fled St. Joseph's College to try his hand as a novice on the black theater circuit would survive and prosper in that environment. His boldness, charm, ability to wheedle favors from nearly anyone he met, and his willingness to defy authority—even if it meant stepping outside the law—were often called upon as he traveled through small-town America in the late teens and early twenties.

Some of his most serious encounters during those early years on the road resulted from his reversion to a youthful penchant for larceny when he found himself in desperate financial straits. Most often he emerged from run-ins with local authorities relatively unscathed. "Every time Ah went into a store to swipe something Ah prayed the Lord to get me out of jail and He always did," Perry once admitted. "Once a Mason got me out of jail. Just shows how the Lord works. An' the district attorney was goin' to send me up for ten years."

There were, however, some very close calls.

One occurred when Perry and a girlfriend found themselves broke and stranded in a small Southern town. Caught stealing, they were thrown in jail.

There, Perry got "the third degree," Herbert Howe wrote in a *Photoplay* feature story. When the actor resisted revealing the whereabouts of the stolen goods (a small cache of jewelry, which was actually hidden in his undergarments), all his teeth were knocked out. During the interview with Howe, Perry flashed a broad smile to show the journalist his sparkling new dentures.

"He got out of jail by offering to show the officer where the stuff was hid," Howe wrote. "He got the officer to escort him and his girl into the woods, then returned the rings." Afterward, the sheriff released him as agreed. Perry and the girl trudged through the woods all night long before catching a freight train the next morning.[17]

Perry and other entertainers were traveling America's back roads as the country's racial tensions peaked; the period from the mid-teens to the early 1920s was among the most severe the nation had witnessed since the Civil War. According to Walter White's *Rope and Faggot* (1929), 145 Americans (99 black) were victims of lynch mobs in 1915—the highest number since the late 1800s. Deaths from lynchings decreased, but race riots rose dramatically and racial violence actually increased during the next few years. The number of fatalities from "civil disorders" in the nation far exceeded deaths from lynchings.

In 1917 and 1918, deadly racial disturbances broke out in East St. Louis, Illinois; Houston; and Philadelphia and Chester, Pennsylvania. The following year, twenty-six riots were reported, most occurring during the so-called Red Summer of 1919. Charleston, South Carolina; Chicago; Longview, Texas; Washington, D.C.; and Elaine, Arkansas, were among the cities in which the bloody clashes erupted.

White reaction to the mass migration of over a half million Southern blacks to large cities in the North during World War I and the return of thousands of black servicemen from Europe prompted the increase in racial confrontations during this period. Northerners feared the competition for jobs and objected to the influx of Negroes into their previously all-white neighborhoods. Southern whites, who at first seemed pleased at the mass exodus, began to fear the loss of its primary labor force and ultimately used legal as well as extralegal means to prevent Negroes from escaping. Nearly all whites resented the new aggressiveness and budding sense of entitlement displayed by black servicemen who returned with expectations of more equal treatment. Those veterans soon discovered that not much had changed on the home front. As one New Orleans white man put it: "You niggers are wondering how you're going to be treated after the war. Well, I'll tell you. You're going to be treated exactly like you were treated before the war!"[18]

Even earlier, however, the increasingly tense atmosphere had been exacerbated by the 1915 release of the controversial silent film *The Birth of a Nation.* Based on Thomas Dixon's 1905 novel, *The Clansman,* a melodramatic tract that pitted saintly Aryan Southerners and docile, contented slaves against unscrupulous Northern white carpetbaggers and ignorant or venal Negro freedmen, D. W. Griffith's technically innovative picture opened to rave reviews in 1915. At its conclusion, hooded, night-riding Klan members, presented as knightly defenders of decency and Old South ways, gallop in to save the day.

The stereotypical presentation of blacks and the glorification of the Klan sparked protests from liberal whites and black leaders from the militant Monroe Trotter to accommodationist Booker T. Washington. But the movie was highly praised by most critics, including Thomas Dixon's college friend President Woodrow Wilson. "It is like writing history with lightning," Wilson said after the movie was screened at the White House. "And my only regret is that it is all true."[19]

When the film premiered at theaters, riots were reported in some cities, but the furor only heightened its appeal. *Birth* became the first legitimate cinema blockbuster.

Beyond heated critical disagreement and disturbances at theaters, the release of *The Birth of a Nation* and its apparent sanction of white vigilante justice had more lasting social consequences. When the film opened in Atlanta in June 1915, an entire street was burned down by former Ku Klux Klan members during a wild celebration—an ominous portent of future events. The modern Klan, which had fallen into decline, was revived during the ensuing months and, by the end of the decade, had again risen to national prominence. Griffith's film demonstrated that motion pictures had considerably increased the scope and impact of the mass media in shaping Americans' opinions and behavior. And with the advent of sound movies and commercial radio in the mid-1920s, media influence would be vastly extended.

Birth had made African American leaders aware of the power of motion-picture portrayals of Negroes and of the need to monitor mass-media images. But blacks would not only generally be excluded from decisions involving the nature and content of most mainstream media, but also severely restricted with regard to their appearances in the new media for more than two decades.

Before Griffith's film, the fledgling film industry had been ignored by black audiences and most black performers. There was little impetus for the relatively small African American audience who could afford the entrance fee to buck protocol and buy a ticket at a segregated theater. For many Americans, in fact, early silent pictures were considered little more than a passing fad.

Prior to 1905, most films were quasi-documentaries in which Negroes were generally filmed au naturel and shown in scenes selected to reinforce current stereotypes. Filmmakers reaffirmed popular conceptions of black life in short movies like *Watermelon Contest* and *Dancing Darkies* (both released by Biograph in 1896), which, respectively, depicted Negro youngsters slavering over watermelon and feverishly dancing to banjo music. In Edwin S. Porter's ambitious cinema adaptation of Harriet Beecher Stowe's novel *Uncle Tom's Cabin* (1903), the Biograph comedy *A Nigger in the Woodpile* (1904), the Lubin Company's *How Rastus Got His Pork Chops* (1908), white actors portrayed black characters. The policy was in part a concession to Southerners who claimed to be affronted by the appearance of genuine Negroes on the screen. When shown in the South, the pictures were preceded by advertisements assuring patrons that black roles were actually played by whites, even though the most myopic viewer would have immediately recognized the films' blackfaced apparitions as cartoonish imposters.

In 1914, the famed stage performer Sam Lucas became the first black to appear as Tom in the many film versions of *Uncle Tom's Cabin*. Bert Williams, one of the nation's premiere stage comedians, also made his motion-picture debut in 1914 in the independently produced *Darktown Jubilee*, which many historians consider the first all-Negro-cast movie.[20]

In contrast to the usual ragged outfit he wore on the Follies stage, Williams appeared in top hat and a zoot suit and without blackface makeup in *Darktown Jubilee*. The change of image was apparently too radical for moviegoers, and, when the film opened at a Brooklyn theater, rowdy whites in the mixed audience greeted it with catcalls. A riot nearly ensued, and the film was subsequently boycotted by distributors.[21]

Williams returned to the screen in 1916, starring in two short films, *Fish* and *A Natural Born Gambler*, which were shot in the Bronx, New York. Although he appeared in blackface, in each picture he portrayed a clever, independent black character the likes of whom were seldom seen in films of the time. The movies were not widely distributed and only halfheartedly promoted. Williams, to whom Perry would later be compared, had not been able to establish himself in movies even though many mainstream critics ranked him among the early twentieth century's best comedians.

Those experiences dampened Negro enthusiasm about the prospects of motion pictures. Still, by 1916 the black actor Noble M. Johnson and his brother George P. Johnson (an Omaha mailman) had quietly formed the Lincoln Motion Picture Company. *The Realization of a Negro's Ambition* (1916) and *The Trooper of Troop K* (1917) were the independent company's first two film releases. But, like Williams's movies and the efforts of a few other independent black film companies, the Lincoln company's motion pictures suffered from inadequate distribution and promotion. The company folded in the early 1920s; its efforts to realistically portray serious, ambitious Negroes went largely unnoticed by black audiences and the Negro press.

From the viewpoint of most blacks in show business, attempting to pursue a career in motion pictures during the mid- and late teens was about as unrealistic as seeking political office in the South. As the black minstrel and vaudeville performer Tom Fletcher pointed out in his memoir, the foremost goal for the era's black performers was to reach the New York City theater stage.

Lincoln Monroe Perry's ambitions probably did not exceed that goal. He may have dreamt of nearing Bert Williams's vaudeville and Broadway stage success. But as a teenager struggling to survive the lean times, narrow escapes, and frequent humiliations encountered by itinerant black performers, it is unlikely that Perry regarded silent flicks and the motion-picture industry with anything except wonderment and mild curiosity.

CHAPTER THREE

By the mid-1920s, Lincoln Perry had moved up the ladder from medicine and tent shows, carnivals, and small-town venues to engagements at larger, urban TOBA and black-circuit theaters. It was a substantial accomplishment for a performer just out of his teens, but the ambitious entertainer had his sights set even higher.

And while the TOBA theatrical circuit was far less hazardous than the carny or tent-show tour, it too had its pitfalls.

At its peak in the 1920s, the TOBA was composed of more than forty theaters throughout the country. They included larger theaters like the Lafayette in New York, the Royal in Baltimore, the Lyric in New Orleans, the Howard in Washington, the Earle in Philadelphia, the Grand in Chicago, the Palace in Memphis, and the Lincoln in Los Angeles. The tour also featured stops in smaller venues in such cities as Richmond, Birmingham, Raleigh, Louisville, Atlanta, Pittsburgh, Columbus, Peoria, Nashville, Houston, Indianapolis, and St. Louis.

A few of the TOBA theaters were grand in scale and well kept. Most were not. Since they served Negroes, who were considered second-class citizens, many provided second-rate accommodations for audiences and squalid working conditions for performers. Ethel Waters recalled: "Of all the rinky-dink dumps I played, nothing was worse than the Monogram Theater in Chicago." It had paper-thin walls and was near the el, so "you stopped singing—or telling a joke—every time a train passed," then continued when the noise died down. "You dressed away downstairs with the stoker," where you had to stoop over to get into costume, "then you came up to the stage on a ladder that looked like those on the old-time slave ships."[1]

Waters was not the only Negro artist to complain about the TOBA's shoddy conditions and devious financial practices. At the height of their careers, such stars as Louis Armstrong, the Buck and Bubbles and Miller and Lyles teams, the actor Clarence Muse, and Stepin Fetchit all balked at and publicly voiced complaints concerning the TOBA's creative accounting or alleged outright thievery.

In addition to contending with unscrupulous managers and owners who sometimes cut or withheld agreed salaries once an act or troupe arrived for a show, according to Muse, performers were forced to sign a TOBA management agreement which assured that only the most overwhelmingly successful acts might show even moderate profit.

When booking an act for the tour, Muse wrote in a 1928 *Baltimore Afro-American* article, the TOBA demanded that artists sign a contract that placed nearly all responsibility for advertising and liability for an engagement's attendance and financial success on the performers. If a single member of a troupe was unable to appear or if a revue did not draw enough for a theater manager to satisfy agreed-upon salaries after a fifty-fifty split of box-office revenues, the manager was contractually free to radically reduce an outfit's pay. This arrangement, of course, opened the door for false box-office counts and shifty bookkeeping practices. Some troupes were forced to place one of their entourage at the door to assure that ticket sales were correctly reported.

And while TOBA management provided most acts with an advance and railroad tickets for the first leg of a tour, the advances had to be paid back in full before funds for any subsequent stop were forwarded. It amounted to a kind of theatrical sharecropping arrangement (Muse called it a "pawn broker system") in which artists were continually indebted to the TOBA. The inequity was heightened since—the success or failure of a particular appearance notwithstanding—TOBA management exacted a $50 fee for each engagement booked.[2]

For bottom-tier or average entertainers, like Perry, it often required a frantic attempt to pick up engagements by forming temporary affiliations with new partners or a knack for quickly altering acts to fit the needs of a specific theater owner, troupe, or spontaneously formed fly-by-night show. A flair for the extemporaneous and a willingness to accept last-second calls or travel at the drop of a hat were practical realities—the price of the ticket.

It was a situation that an entertainer with the audacity and reckless ambition of a Lincoln Perry could manipulate better than most. He was no stranger to adversity. And by 1926, when he left Chicago on a tour that would eventually take him to the West Coast, his spirits must have been high. In addition to the tour, he had obtained a job as an entertainment reporter for the *Chicago Defender,* one of the nation's leading black weekly newspapers. He was probably earning no more than a few dollars for his reports—initially called "Lincoln Perry Writes" and, later, "Lincoln Perry's Letter"—but his byline in the weekly paper surely raised his stock among other performers. And besides providing news about the black entertainment circuit and a promotional platform for his work, which he frequently used, it documented events on the otherwise largely uncharted course of his prescreen career.

It was in his *Defender* column that Perry identified his first stage partner as the dancer and comic Johnnie (aka Johnny) Lee, who later teamed up with the writer-comic Flournoy Miller and, during the 1950s, portrayed the bogus lawyer Algonquin J. Calhoun in the television version of *Amos 'n' Andy.* According to Perry, he and Lee had parted by 1920.

Perry expressed genuine excitement about the chance meeting he had with his former partner in 1927, but also alluded to the rough times they had experienced and suggested that during his late teens he considered permanently quitting show business. "Jonnie [*sic*] and I have been all through the bad end of the game together," Perry wrote in his entertainment column. "I was indeed glad to see him after seven years, when our act broke up to allow me to carry out my desire to become a priest."[3]

The split took place in New Orleans, Perry indicated. He claimed to have committed himself to studying for the clergy for a year, but was unable to support himself. "Ah decided Ah could still be good and be in show business" he told a reporter, "that was my alibi for goin' back, understand?"[4]

It is possible that after a few years of hustling on the chitlin' circuit, Perry regretted his decision to leave St. Joseph's College, but there is no verification that his alleged flirtation with the priesthood was ever seriously weighed. Despite the apparent sincerity of his religious beliefs, the tale may have simply been a ruse concocted for publicity. Perry's fondness for his former partner, however, was apparently heartfelt. And in later *Defender* columns he wrote glowingly of Lee and Johnson, the act that Johnny Lee formed with his wife Baby Johnson in the late twenties.

After he established himself as a popular actor, Perry spoke more openly, if not necessarily more precisely, about his early days on the road. He offered several specific accounts of how the name Step and Fetchit originated.

"It was this way," he told a reporter, "some of the papers have it all wrong. You see, I used to hang around the tracks; was everything from stable boy to tout. It was at a Texas race track that I saw Step and Fetch It, the racer. I had lost on every race and didn't have a dollar in my pocket, but I did have on some classy togs and a stud that sparkled like 'nobody's business.' Before the next race came on a friend who was with me wanted to bet me that Lawn Martin would win the race. Lawn Martin had never been beaten on that track, but as I looked over the list I saw the name 'Step and Fetch It.' . . . Here's a horse that can beat Lawn Martin, I told my friend."

Perry claimed that he bet his clothes and pin against $150 of his friend's cash, and the horse Step and Fetch It won the race by a neck. The young vaudevillian considered it an omen.

"I was a dancer and singer and after that I teamed with a fellow," he continued. "We took the name of the horse. He was called 'Step' and I was called 'Fetch It.' Our act was good but we split up and I was billed with a minstrel show as 'Rastus the Buck Dancer.' But I didn't like that name so I called myself 'Jolly Pard,' then later 'Skeeter Perry.'

"Then hard times came to 'Skeeter Perry.' He was put in jail and it seemed like his residence there was to be permanent. I ain't ashamed to tell you that I really prayed. I told the Lord if He'd just let me out I'd go straight if I starved.

"I've seen some pretty tough days since then but I never forgot my promise. At times I made as low as fifteen dollars per week, but I always stayed straight. So God knew I meant what I said and then I began to get some good. I got on a vaudeville circuit and was soon pulling down one hundred per week. I took the name 'Stepin Fetchit.'"[5]

The chronology of events recounted in that interview is questionable. And what actually happened between 1920 and 1926 is uncertain. Perry may have parted with Lee to pursue a religious calling or, perhaps, given his sometimes unruly behavior and later run-ins with the law, because he was incarcerated. In fact, it's not difficult to imagine that it was a combination of both—that is, a stint of jail time during which he seriously considered returning to the Catholic Church.

Whether the name Step and Fetch It was actually adopted after Perry saw a racehorse with that name is also debatable. By the 1920s, blackface acts were cropping up with names like Buck and Wheat, Moonshine and Sawdust, and Molasses 'n' January. At about the same time on the TOBA circuit, black acts like Pen and Ink, Dots and Dashes, Dis 'n' Dat, Sleep 'n' Eat, and Brains and Feet were thriving. The colorful Texas racetrack tale was not verified, although years after the actor rose to fame in the 1930s, the name was indiscriminately applied to horses, yachts, and even some slothful public servants.

After resuming his career in the early 1920s, Perry did appear with stage duos called "Skeeter and Rastus: The Two Dancing Crows from Dixie" and, later, "Step and Fetch It: The Two Dancing Fools from Dixie." By the mid-1920s, according to reports of TOBA bookings in black newspapers, Perry and Buck Abel were touring the circuit with the simpler billing "Step and Fetch It."

In a December 1926 newsletter, Perry reported from Tulsa that Abel "was on the sick list and compelled to confine himself to a medical treatment at the hospital in McAlester, Okla." Almost immediately, Perry recruited Ed Lee, a performer who had formerly been the owner and manager of an act called Lee's Bathing Beauties. "After a successful engagement in Muskogee, Okla., we are now completing a very successful week's run here [in Tulsa] at the Dreamland Theater," Perry wrote. "Our act alone is packing them in every night." The partnership between Perry and Ed Lee must have immediately clicked since two weeks later, with Buck Abel still hospitalized, Perry reported from Kansas City that he had talked to "the manager of the western Orpheum circuit." He advised readers to "look out for 'Step and Fetch It' in the big game soon."[6]

Despite numerous setbacks, Perry had gained some credibility as a journalist in the black press and was apparently on the brink of cracking the elusive big-time vaudeville circuit. His reputation was on the rise, just as black entertainment in general was experiencing a tremendous boom on the East Coast.

The mainstream resurgence of interest in African American culture and entertainment had exploded in 1921 with the Broadway debut of *Shuffle Along*, a musical comedy that received rave reviews from both black and white critics. It was based on the 1907 musical *The Mayor of Dixie,* which Flournoy Miller and Aubrey Lyles originally created and starred in at Mott's Pekin Theater in Chicago. Music and lyrics were written by Noble Sissle and Eubie Blake, and included the hit songs "Love Will Find a Way" and "I'm Just Wild About Harry." The groundbreaking musical, which satirized small-town politics in a fictional black town, featured stunning new dance numbers and broad ethnic comedy sketches.

It took New York by storm and ran for over five hundred performances on Broadway before beginning a precedent-setting road tour that broke the color barrier at previously all-white theaters across the country. Miller and Lyles and Sissle and Blake had hoped to bring "authentic Negro artistry to Broadway," and, in fact, the show tremendously enhanced the popularity of syncopated black music, or jazz, and introduced black dance routines that influenced Broadway musicals for years to come. That influence was acknowledged in the 1922 *Ziegfeld Follies,* which featured a white songstress belting out a tune entitled "It's Getting Dark on Old Broadway."

Ev'ry cafe now has the dancing coon.
Pretty choc'late babies
Shake and shimmie ev'rywhere
Real darktown entertainers hold the stage,
You must black up to be the latest rage.
Yes, the great white way is white no more,
It's just like a street on the Swanee shore;
It's getting very dark on old Broadway.[7]

Shuffle Along was the first in a string of successful black musicals that opened on Broadway during the twenties. The music and dance routines showcased there and in subsequent productions not only had a tremendous impact on Broadway musical productions but also helped set the carefree tone and lifestyle that swept the nation during the "Roaring Twenties," or "Jazz Age." Among the best of the black musicals were *Dinah* (1923), Miller and Lyles's *Runnin' Wild* (1923), *Africana* (1927), *Blackbirds of 1928*, and *Hot Chocolates* (1929). They spotlighted such performers as Ethel Waters, Fats Waller, Josephine Baker, and Bill Robinson, and introduced dance sensations such as the Black Bottom and the Charleston.

These popular black Broadway musicals helped ignite the Harlem Renaissance, which spurred a tremendous expansion of black artistic expression, producing some notable literary figures as well as a raft of heralded entertainers. They also fueled the growing white infatuation with Negro lifestyles and nightlife.[8]

In Harlem, speakeasies and nightclubs like Connie's Inn, the Bamboo Inn, the Lenox Club, and Small's Paradise thrived, featuring such renowned entertainers as Bill Robinson, Louis Armstrong, Lena Horne, Fats Waller, Cab Calloway, Ethel Waters, and Duke Ellington. While those clubs showcased the era's premiere black performers, they also generally excluded black patrons and indulged timeworn stereotypes of Negroes as either comic foils or carefree primitives. Waiters danced the Charleston in the aisles as they served food and drinks; blackfaced vaudevillians provided comic relief; beautiful Negro women (nearly always of light or near-white complexions) slithered about in scanty costumes in chorus lines onstage; and at the famous Cotton Club, Duke Ellington's orchestra played swinging jazz compositions advertised as "Jungle Music" in a sumptuous African setting. Audiences for the exotic displays included such downtown celebrities as Mae West, Gene Tunney, Jack Dempsey, Sophie Tucker, George Raft, Tallulah Bankhead, Hoagy Carmichael, Helen Morgan, and Benny Goodman.

Harlem nightlife had become a magnet for celebrities and the well heeled, as well as for ordinary blacks and whites who were intrigued by its extravagant exoticism or, as one contemporary journalist wrote, sought to "go on moral vacation."[9]

During the Jazz Age, black entertainment soared in popularity and mainstream fascination with black life, reflecting the era's bizarre

Negrophilia, continued to escalate. But while in music and dance the attraction was to more complex, stylish, and hipper urban artistic expression, in comedy very little had changed. The comedy in *Shuffle Along*, for instance, rehashed rural, blackface Sambo or darky characters and minstrel-like routines. It mirrored the low humor usually offered in TOBA routines at black theaters across the country. A typical example occurs when one of the black mayoral candidates is told that his opponent has stopped stealing chickens. "Is he dead?" the mayoral hopeful incredulously responds.

Still, Miller and Lyles updated the stereotypes by introducing overtones of the trickster idiom and a touch of urban flair to their comic routines. Their stage characters—a scheming city slicker and a feisty but gullible underdog—bristled with energy and theatrical flourish. The urban dandy or quasi-black trickster figure and the contrasting naive, somewhat dim straightman developed by the comic team emerged as the most popular black comic figures on the TOBA and vaudeville stages. Throughout the decade, nearly every hit black show on Broadway featured similar comedy duos. Miller and Lyles's version of minstrelsy stage Negroes remained the cornerstone of African American humor until at least the 1950s.

The influence of those Broadway shows and the growing popularity of black entertainment was not confined to Harlem, and as images of bathtub gin parties and flapper-clad revelers, uninhibitedly dancing the Charleston, spread, black entertainment found new audiences, and white patrons found their way to black nightspots across the nation. The Eighteenth Amendment and Prohibition era notwithstanding, black cabarets, after-hours clubs, and theaters flourished on Beale Street in Memphis, 47th Street on Chicago's South Side, and Central Avenue in Los Angeles.

Typically, these cabarets and theaters showcased black revues featuring a curious mixture of Harlem Renaissance New Negro–type performers and slightly altered, but familiar, minstrel throwbacks. The sophisticated sounds of bands led by musicians like the debonair Duke Ellington, the elegantly cool Count Basie, or the more frenetic Cab Calloway stood in stark contrast to comedy interludes spotlighting blackface buffoonery by comedians like Sandy Burns or Pigmeat Markham. The slick tap routines of hoofers like John Bubbles (of Buck and Bubbles) or Bill Robinson were often preceded by a raucous dose of sidesplitting coonery from comics like Crackshot Hackley, Andrew Tribel, or Dusty Fletcher.

Switching stations on the radio dial, one might have leapt from the lush, big-band compositions of Fletcher Henderson or the swinging sounds of Louis Armstrong to the farcical patter of the black duo Frye and Moss or a team of ersatz Negroes served up by white entertainers Freeman Gosden and Charles Correll on the *Sam 'n' Henry* show. That show, renamed *Amos 'n' Andy,* would become the nation's most popular radio program.

By 1927, like nearly every other aspiring young black performer, the savvy, ambitious Lincoln Perry had surely sensed that future stage success entailed reprising some variation on the characters and comedy themes established by the era's black pioneers. But when he arrived on the West Coast, he had not begun billing himself as Stepin Fetchit, "The World's Laziest Man."

In fact, although he had assumed the role of the gullible, shiftless rural rube in the "Step and Fetch It" act, he claimed that, initially, he didn't know if he was "Step" or "Fetchit." "See, I didn't know which one I was, until one night I got sick, you savvy," he told the writer and producer Matt Robinson, "and they made the announcement at the theater that 'Step' would be there but 'Fetchit' couldn't make it. That's the onliest I knew which one I was."[10]

Moreover, as he later freely admitted, he didn't think people would pay very much to "see someone do nothing." The routine that became his specialty was inspired by a former partner, who "was so lazy, he used to call a cab to get across the street." During the mid-1920s when his partner occasionally missed a show or owners could not afford two performers, he would approach the manager or owner and assert, "No, it's not two of us. It's just one of us, the Step and Fetch It." Or, when pushed, he would rhetorically ask, "What you need him for?" It was, he insisted, just one of the tricks of the trade.[11]

From January to April 1927, Lincoln Perry dispatched columns to the *Defender* from Kansas City; Pocatello, Idaho; Portland, Oregon; and San Francisco before he and his partner arrived in Los Angeles.

Those early "Letters" established the general rambling tone of his columns. They not only detailed his whereabouts, offered behind-the-scene news about other acts on the TOBA circuit, and described typical vaudeville bills, but also revealed an ostensibly thoughtful and serious side of his personality. Perry's journalistic style ranged from straightforward reportage to florid, often fawning passages in which the performer voiced his concerns about black entertainers' ethics and professionalism. The prose was frequently interlaced with pious biblical references or highlighted by catchy rhymes reflecting his songwriting ambitions.

A February 1927 newsletter, for instance, described the show in which he appeared in Pocatello. "We're in a five act unit," he wrote. "The juggling act is No. 1, the whistling act is too [*sic*], but none can do the stunts Bob Mills, our one-arm pianist, do. Then we in fourth spot, take the stage and let our hoofing get it, because we always give the best that's in old 'Step and Fetch It.' The closing act is real refined and very much artistic. Three dancers, one a New York Jew, and two are Spanish. A few encores and curtain bows and that's our unit."[12]

An earlier column included a poem inspired by the death of Nathaniel Sterman, a tuba player with the Lincoln Theater orchestra in Kansas City.

When death comes to snatch a trooper from our side,
Don't it make you think about the day that you and I must die?
Whether a musician or performer, young or old in age,
We'll someday leave (never to return) for some orchestra, pit or stage.
So while fighting hard for fame (as it's fortune we all crave).
Let us nourish the clear conscience that portrays us to our grave.
And in our line of entertainment do it well and do it hard,
But omit the many no account things that keep us from our God;
Because it is no harm to entertain in an artistic way,
But art and talent is mistaken by some of us today.
So as Salem Tutt Whitney said about resolutions for the New Year—
Let's be professional and artistic and above all on the square.[13]

Although he had not yet appeared in films and was not among the black circuit's most successful acts, the ambitious performer was already indicating that he intended to assume an important position among the Negro entertainment elite. The reference to Salem Tutt

Whitney—who, in addition to having a successful career as an entertainer, songwriter, and cofounder of the "Silas Green from New Orleans" troupe, was a regular columnist for the *Defender*—was a clear indication of the esteemed company in which Perry wished to be included.

With regard to actors' artistic integrity, and, ironically, their public image, early in his career Perry often took the high moral ground in *Defender* columns, reprimanding his peers for detrimental behavior that he himself would later display. For instance, in a February 1928 letter, he commented on Universal Pictures's remake of *Uncle Tom's Cabin* (1927), in which Charles Gilpin was originally cast for the lead role then dismissed for his supposed drinking and "aggressive reading" of the part. Gilpin, considered "America's greatest black actor" at the time, was replaced by James Lowe.

"Gilpin," Perry wrote, "only increased in the producer's mind the belief that the race artist would be hard to get along with and that he would allow his pride to encourage him to misuse the advantage he possessed for personal gain."

Perry credited Lowe for confirming the ability of race actors but also criticized him for making "the road harder" for them. "I don't mean to condemn the action of these two Race professional history makers, but to remind that our action, although not intentional, plays sometimes two-thirds of the parts in our 'nonadvancement' and the victory for us lies first in the phrase 'Conquer oneself and the rest is easy.'"[14]

On other occasions, Perry advised actors that "if they intend to be in the profession they should become professional." And, in an item acknowledging the death of Bob Robinson, a musician with Curtis Mosby's orchestra, he warned colleagues against the danger of excessive womanizing and drinking. His death, Perry wrote, should be "a particular warning to many of us who have been watching death creep up on this boy for quiet [*sic*] a while to stop and consider that there is an end to this existence." Girls, partying, and drinking, he claimed, shorten our lives and "hamper and smother the real ability that's in us."[15]

Shortly after completing his first film, *In Old Kentucky*, while commenting on the groundbreaking nature of his work with Carolynne Snowden, Perry was still advising Negro actors on proper off-screen decorum and urging black newspapers to avoid exaggerating the race's accomplishments in films.

"Although Miss Snowden and I have a very prominent part, and I think we will get all screen credit for the picture, neither of us were starred," he wrote. He maintained that they had "positions never before attained by Race performers in a white production" and claimed that Snowden was the race's "greatest prospect" for stardom. Still, he objected to race papers calling them movie stars.

"When a director or a producer reads such things they have reason to think us as ignorant as the southern whites try to picture us," he continued. "Such things encourage the whites to believe that we are still lacking and will accept a camouflage as quickly as we will a reality."[16]

The avuncular, advisory tone that Perry assumed in many of his "Letters" was often balanced by a more flippant, playful voice. After reaching San Francisco in March 1927, for example, he began a letter with the following: "As I haven't written for a week or so I thought I'd write, so all could know, that 'Step and Fetch It' is on the go out on the coast in Frisco. Frisco is not what I thought it would be, but still it's all right with me, with its sunny weather all the year round, its Golden Gate and Chinatown."[17]

In May, "Step and Fetch It" arrived in Los Angeles, and Perry, teamed with Ed Lee, began an engagement at the Pasadena Theater. He advised his *Chicago Defender* readers to send all correspondence to his home at 1302 Central Avenue, Los Angeles, California.[18]

Shortly afterward, however, Perry announced that he had begun working as a single: "I will close with 'Step and Fetch It,' yours truly himself, minus the partner, playing the Meralta Theater," he wrote. "Use your own judgment, because it is a poor head that would praise its own face. Have not had to pick anybody out of the aisles yet, but have been extended an offer from the Public Theater."[19]

Fetch It of "Step and Fetch It" had begun a radical transformation. Perry was nearly ready to permanently step out on his own. When, in his own flamboyant fashion, he assumed center stage, the pleas for moderation and words of wisdom offered to his colleagues would resound like an ironic chorus highlighting his every excess.

CHAPTER FOUR

By 1927, Los Angeles's Central Avenue was a thriving, vibrant thoroughfare that stretched south from downtown Los Angeles to the area now known as Watts. It was not only home to the growing Negro working- and middle-class community that was developing in the sprawling, segregated city but also the center of the West Coast black entertainment world. Like 47th Street in Chicago (about whose "glory and glamour" a former resident gushed, you felt "a sense of pride" just "being on the street") and Lenox Avenue in Harlem (which left Cab Calloway "awestruck" when he initially saw it in the twenties), Central Avenue was a cultural showplace and social center that attracted blacks from all walks of life. Dubbed "the Stroll" by entertainment insiders, it was perhaps best known as the home of a string of theaters and hot nightspots that bristled with the excitement and glamour of the Roaring Twenties and featured many of black America's most celebrated entertainers.[1]

"As the sun set," Steve Isoardi wrote in *Central Avenue Sounds,* "the bustle of shoppers, shopkeepers, clerks and businessmen was replaced by the swagger of the night crowd, fresh from an afternoon with the barber or hairdresser and dressed in the sharpest clothes fresh from the cleaners. . . . Each night the Avenue became a social and cultural Mecca, attracting thousands of people throughout Southern California to its eateries, theaters, nightclubs, and music venues. A nonstop, vibrant club scene." It was one of the few integrated settings in Southern California and, by the mid-twenties, area residents as well as the black-owned weekly newspaper, the *California Eagle*, would glowingly refer to Central Avenue as "Brown Broadway."

"I've been to all those places that are supposed to be swinging, like Kansas City, Chicago and New York," said Fletcher Smith, a former pianist with the Lionel Hampton and Billy Eckstine bands. "But they don't swing like Central Avenue. It was one of the swingingest streets in the world, man, when it was jumping."[2]

In the early twenties, the Bluebird Inn at 12th and Central, and Frank Sebastian's Cotton Club on Washington Boulevard near La Cienega were reportedly the preferred nightspots among whites clamoring to view extravagant sepia revues. Although exceptions were made for the famous or well heeled, neither club encouraged Negro patrons. Those clubs featured many of the era's best black bands and revues and the most beautiful showgirls. They also attracted a stream of celebrities from the Hollywood Hills who came south to view the exotic entertainment. "They slummed on Central Avenue," one resident recalled. John Barrymore, Rudolph Valentino, Mae West, Roscoe "Fatty" Arbuckle, Tom Mix, Mary Pickford, George Raft, Clara Bow, and Charlie Chaplin were among the Hollywood elite who occasionally partied there.

Dance halls, burlesque houses, theaters offering movies and live performances, cabarets, circus sideshows, and speakeasies spread south along Central all the way to present-day Watts, which at the time was still a rural area virtually unrestricted by curfew laws. But according to the jazz saxophonist Marshall Royal—a Los Angeles native who as a teenager played at the famous Apex Club and later was a member of both the Lionel Hampton and Duke Ellington bands—the "hub of the musical entertainment business, inasmuch as the blacks were concerned, was at 12th and Central." It was there that the brothers John and Benjamin (Reb) Spikes, both musicians, opened Spikes Record Shop in 1919. That store soon became a favorite gathering place for area musicians who met to exchange stories and discuss jobs and craft. Lincoln Perry, who lived a block away, was at the center of the ferment.[3]

During the spring and summer of 1927, Perry pressed ahead with his stage career as a solo act and as part of the Step and Fetch It team, appearing at Central Avenue nightspots as well as other venues in and around Los Angeles. When not performing, he apparently shadowed the Central Avenue club and theater scene. His "Lincoln Perry's

Letter" appeared nearly every week in the *Defender* and included reviews of and items about acts playing at all the major nightspots. Those columns ranged from reports on headliners and future screen stars like Carolynne Snowden—the featured act at Sebastian's Cotton Club who was often seen "going to and fro in her big yellow Packard"—to items about lesser-known local performers like the dancer Chick Johnson or Tommy Harris of the comic duo Tolliver and Harris, who, despite their popularity on the West Coast, never achieved national prominence.[4]

In May, for instance, Perry noted the appearances of "Reb Spikes' red hot orchestra at the Follies," "Joyce and Foster at the Orpheum," and a forty-person revue—which featured Tommy Harris and "Kid" Tolliver—opening for "an eight week run" at the Capitol. He was often effusive in his praise, noting, for instance, that "Blondy Robinson at the Hippodrome" was "the greatest single [act] I have seen in the West."[5]

Both Perry and Buddy Brown, another *Defender* entertainment writer, were avid promoters of the West Coast scene and paid particular attention to race-conscious performers like bandleader Joe Sheftell. "Joe has made a great reputation for himself as a race man out here," Brown wrote. "He is one man who is not afraid to air his views before anyone, no matter what his creed or color. We should have more performers like him."[6]

Perry frequently peppered his column with folksy advice for black performers. "I get many letters from professionals in the East asking my opinion about coming out here," he wrote in his May 7, 1927, "Letter," "and in answer to all I wish to say: 'Come, if you can come right and ready.' But there are many performers out here, both white and of our group, who want to get back East and can't. The result is they have to do something for a living after playing the legitimate stuff out here, which is mostly Friday, Saturday and Sunday, and they take what they can get, at whatever price they can get; and if 'Josh' don't, 'Joseph' will."

Promoting his own career, Perry also detailed his own engagements during this period. By June of 1927, he was appearing at the Jazzland cabaret with Ragtime Billy Tucker, a versatile vaudeville performer and producer who had managed to get his foot inside the studio doors. In June, Perry unassumingly reported that he and Tucker had made "a visit to the Metro-Goldwyn studio."[7]

Billy Tucker is "running around in his Chandler prior to a picture date he has with Metro-Goldwyn, Inc., to furnish a company of Race artists in a cabaret scene, which will last about fifteen days," Perry wrote from the studio lot.

A few weeks later, "Perry's Letter" began with an explanation of why he had not returned to the East Coast. "Well, the whole thing in a nut shell is the West Coast, Inc. has a lot of work out here and it's all open to me, so I have decided to play it all," he wrote. He advised readers that he and Tucker intended to open a dancing school and booking agency.[8]

In his July 2, 1927, "Letter," Perry wrote that he intended to "offer acts in the near future," and continued, "in other words, I am going to forsake vaudeville and take to presentations." Certainly by early July, Perry had decided that a major shift in his career was at hand. And, if "presentations" is taken to mean motion-picture work, he seems to have been suggesting that he intended to pursue a career in movies.

The Tucker-Perry partnership was brief, but the association seems to have had tremendous impact on Perry's career goals. The dance school and booking agency that the pair considered never materialized, but Perry's brief flirtation with "Metro-Goldwyn, Inc." (by then, actually Metro-Goldwyn-Mayer) had made a lasting impression. And within the next few weeks, he would return to the studio and audition for a part in an upcoming picture. It was a fortuitous choice for a performer who was not an elite attraction on the TOBA circuit.

Perry's apparent optimism and enthusiasm notwithstanding, prospects for black actors attempting to crack the mainstream movie industry color line in the mid twenties were still dim. In contrast to the Broadway stage, where blacks were making inroads, studio pictures remained almost exclusively white.

Before the advent of sound films later in the decade, only a handful of Negro actors—among them Noble Johnson, Madame Sul-Te-Wan, George Reed, and child actors like Ernie Morrison—had managed to find regular work in studio pictures. Johnson's light complexion and sculpted features enabled him to win parts as Mexicans, Native Americans, and half-breeds in a host of movies from the late teens to the forties; he supplemented his Hollywood movie roles with work in all-black cast pictures produced by his own Lincoln Company. Madame Sul-Te-Wan, equally distinctive in appearance, made her film debut in *The Birth of a Nation,* appeared in a 1920 L-KO Studio black-cast comedy series, then sporadically found work as a maid or in such exotic roles as voodoo priestess in a dozen or so later films. Reed also appeared in *Birth* and played "Nigger Jim" in the 1920 version of *Huckleberry Finn*; subsequently, he was typecast as a porter, stable hand, or butler in scores of films. Morrison, aka "Sunshine Sammy," was a featured child star in early releases of Hal Roach's *Our Gang* series.

The *Gang* series, in fact, was one of the brightest spots in Hollywood studio films at this point in black cinema history. In 1922, following Morrison's debut, one-year-old Allen "Farina" Hoskins joined the Gang as a regular. Hoskins, who according to Hal Roach was "one of the finest natural actors we had in the Gang," made the transition from silent to sound films and went on to appear in 105 *Our Gang* comedies.

But even the handful of exceptional Negro actors who worked with some consistency in silent pictures had difficulty supporting themselves in the film colony. Morrison, for instance, left Hollywood after a row over salary, and late in her career Madame Sul-Te-Wan admitted that "I get bitter sometimes because I don't work long enough to buy a handkerchief."[9]

Despite some highly publicized exceptions—including Sam Lucas's breakthrough as the first black actor to appear in a full-length feature in 1914, Reed's role as Nigger Jim in 1920, and Roach's *Our Gang* juveniles—feature roles for Negroes in Hollywood films were still minimal when Lincoln Perry visited the MGM lot in 1927. And since studio honchos had little faith in the acting ability of blacks and were concerned about backlash from Southern white audiences if Negro characters were featured, white actors were most often recruited to step in and don blackface. Blacks, even experienced East Coast actors, were mostly relegated to extra or atmosphere work or cast as servants.[10]

Negro butlers, maids, stableboys, bootblacks, and chauffeurs were not only the most frequent black on-screen roles offered by Hollywood films in the twenties, but, often, real-life servants were called in to portray them. Casting directors usually sought suitable types rather than capable actors, which meant that parts were often dispensed as favors. Early in the decade, so-called studio Negroes like Harold Garrison,

Jimmie Smith, and Oscar (Cutie Pie) Smith (who were not related) functioned as liaisons between studios and the black community. They combed Central Avenue and the streets of southeast Los Angeles in search of "actors" or extras who best represented the type needed for a specific studio cattle call.[11]

The consequence of the peculiar relationship between the Hollywood Hills film colony and Los Angeles Negroes, who were isolated by zoning laws and herded into the city's southern basin, was that Negro servants had more access to the studios than most serious, legitimate performers. Oscar Smith, for instance, gained access as a retainer. He came to Paramount after World War I as Wallace Reid's valet. In gratitude for his loyalty, Reid stipulated in his will that Smith "be given a shoeshine stand in perpetuity." Smith appeared in several studio films during the twenties, including *Beau Sabreur* (1928) and *Thunderbolt* (1929). Garrison—who in releases to the black press was identified as an "assistant director" for the 1929 film *Hallelujah!*—was known to friends and to whites at the studio as "Slick-em," and was described as an "erstwhile bootblack on the Metro-Goldwyn lot" by a contemporary fan magazine. Despite their inflated reputations on Central Avenue, Smith and Garrison were considered little more than gofers by many within the studios. Still, they made optimum use of their service-entrance access, exacting as much power, influence, and exposure as possible from their tenuous footholds.[12]

Their ambivalent, quasi-servile relationship with the film colony was by no means extraordinary. In general, for blacks in and out of show business in early-twentieth-century America, segregation and racial bias made service jobs prime employment opportunities. For Negroes working as domestics, valets, porters, and chauffeurs, feigning a passive, accommodating demeanor was a tried and proven way of increasing job security and placating employers, even though the pretense affirmed the mainstream view of Negroes as an unambitious, contented lot. The façade not only elicited favors but ultimately brought some measure of status within the black community. Domestics' access to white society's material comforts were most often envied, and tales of employers' gullibility and arrogance were a prime source of black folk's private humor.

Rufus Thomas, the black disc jockey and blues singer, mirrored a common attitude among blacks when he recalled how he dealt with patronizing white customers as a waiter in Nashville during the twenties. "During that time, the white fellow was most boastful . . . he'd say all these things. But he'd pay well, pay well. At the end of the night, I had the money. I won't say he was broke, but he'd splurged and I had the money. And so you ask yourself: 'Hell, who's the fool or who's stupid?' "[13]

In Hollywood's fantasy world, of course, the rewards for accepting a subservient position were potentially much greater than cash. Getting a foot inside the studio door as a bootblack or as a movie star's manservant or maid could have led to a part in a picture and from there, who knew—possible celebrity and fame, even stardom, in America's most glamorous industry. The old Negro stereotypes still prevailed in Hollywood, and to many members of the film colony, being black equated to being inherently funny as well as being naturally suited to servile positions. So by the mid-1920s, in addition to atmosphere work in Tarzan movies and background cabaret scenes, Negro players had gained some acceptance in films as domestics—parts in which casting directors assumed they were required only to be themselves.

The assumption, however demeaning, was an advantage to performers who dreamt of seeing themselves on the silver screen. Libby Taylor advanced from being Mae West's real-life maid to playing a cinema maid in several pictures, among them her employer's *Belle of the Nineties* (1934). Louise Beavers and even future Academy Award–winner Hattie McDaniel worked as maids before they emerged as Hollywood's best-known portrayers of the comic Black Mammy character in the thirties and forties. Although unconfirmed, it was alleged that Perry had briefly taken a job as a porter at MGM prior to his film debut in 1927.[14]

"From 1915 to 1920 roughly half the Negro roles reviewed in *Variety* were maids and butlers," the film historian Thomas Cripps wrote, "and 74 percent of them were known in the credits by some demeaning first name. In the 1920s servile roles reached 80 percent of all black roles."[15]

Many of the era's black filmmakers struggled to change this one-dimensional portrait of Negro life. By the late teens, the Lincoln Motion Picture Company was producing pictures that countered the prevailing image of blacks as laggards and comic buffoons. Traverse

Spraggins's Frederick Douglass Film Company, which was based in Jersey City, also emerged in the teens and released an adaptation of Paul Laurence Dunbar's *The Scapegoat* (1917). Both companies focused on African American achievement and consciously depicted Negroes who might be seen as heroines and heroes by the community. The Harlem-based Reol Motion Picture Corporation, which employed performers from the Lafayette Players, followed the same pattern.

The race film industry expanded rapidly, and, like the race record industry, which emerged about the same time, it slowly but inevitably succumbed to the control of nonblack interests. Soon independent white-owned companies began dominating the market. In 1927, several dozen companies were vying to supply films for the nearly seven hundred movie houses in Negro communities where black audiences were starved for on-screen representation. Black-cast pictures were transformed into a largely commercial venture that often exploited the same stereotypes established in Hollywood.

Remarkably, one black filmmaker survived the mainstream takeover of race movies and continued producing motion pictures until the 1940s. Oscar Micheaux—who was born in Metropolis, Illinois, in 1894 and acquired land in Gregory, South Dakota, where he was a farmer, rancher, and novelist before turning to motion pictures—came to the film industry with an inventiveness, determination, and con man's spirit that sustained him when other black filmmakers faltered. Lorenzo Tucker, the leading man that Micheaux dubbed "the black Valentino," recalled that Micheaux "was so impressive and charming that he could talk the shirt right off your back."[16]

Micheaux's interest in filmmaking was apparently ignited when Lincoln company founders Noble and George Johnson approached him in 1919 hoping to acquire the movie rights for his 1917 novel *The Homesteader.* When Micheaux insisted on directing the film, however, the Johnsons withdrew their offer. According to cinema historian Thomas Cripps, the Johnsons left their meeting with the young novelist convinced that he was an "upstart, a mountebank, and an untrustworthy hustler." Micheaux was determined to maintain control of the film, however, and pursued the project with his usual irrepressible energy. Soliciting financial aid from his South Dakota neighbors (mostly farmers and ranchers), he produced the film independently. *The Homesteader* was released in 1919.[17]

Much of Micheaux's success accrued from the unorthodox distributing and marketing tactics he developed while promoting and selling his early self-published novels. He visited black communities throughout the country, convincing theater owners to book or back his movies, seeking out prominent people, and speaking at schools and churches, where he met the working class. Flamboyant, jaunty, and blessed with a bit of the trickster instinct, he charmed and inveigled, creating widespread grassroots support for his pictures.

His filmmaking approach was nearly as unorthodox as his marketing techniques. "He was his own writer, his own choreographer, his own cameraman. I can't think of anything he didn't do," said Honi Coles, the famed tap dancer and former Apollo Theater stage manager. He "would walk into a place and take his camera out and start rolling—without asking anybody. Next thing you knew, you were in a picture somewhere, but nobody seemed to mind." Despite impromptu techniques and shoestring budgets, Micheaux produced an impressive array of movies. They ranked with the best of the independently produced race pictures and were distinguished by Micheaux's willingness to directly challenge American racial assumptions.[18]

In the mid-twenties, black-cast pictures seemed to offer the most promising future for aspiring black performers. More black film companies were emerging and some—like the Colored Players company, which released *The Scar of Shame* in 1927—were beginning to produce films that approached the quality of low-budget studio releases. In addition, more critics in the black press were touting race films as a positive alternative to the timeworn stereotypes offered in Hollywood pictures.

By 1927, however, the silent-film era was rapidly drawing to a close. Within a year or two, sound movies would revolutionize the industry and drastically alter the studio perception of Negro actors. *The Jazz Singer* was among the first pictures to utilize the new technology; its October 1927 release marked the beginning of a new era in motion pictures. The film—starring Al Jolson, a minstrel and vaudeville singer who was fascinated with the "new rhythm" and "primitive appeal" of Negro voices—was a tale of a cantor's son struggling against his religious background. Its somewhat sentimental plot was boosted by the partial addition of sound and a score featuring Southern songs and jazzy rhythms derived from Negro life.[19]

By the summer of 1927, studio executives were aware of the impending technical innovation and, perhaps, even of the looming shift in the status of Negro performers. A positive change was at hand. It's possible that Lincoln Perry also had inside information; through his status as an entertainment reporter and his friendship with blacks like Ragtime Billy Tucker who had studio connections, he may well have received some hint of the coming change.

As late as July 1927, however, his *Chicago Defender* columns offered little indication that he was making any headway in the motion-picture industry. Early in the month, his stage partnership with Billy Tucker was abruptly dissolved. Perry's *Defender* columns suggested the separation was amiable. "Ragtime Billy Tucker and his Darktown Follies are supposed to open at the Hippodrome for a week soon," Perry wrote in his July 9 "Letter," suggesting that Tucker was about to begin a vaudeville tour as a single.[20]

Of his own activities, Perry reported only one appearance during the month. Presumably, by midsummer his attention was focused on the studio audition for his first role as Highpockets in *In Old Kentucky.*[21]

During a 1929 interview, Perry described his encounter with studio executives during his MGM audition:

> One day a friend said to me, "Step, why don't you try out for pictures. Metro-Goldwyn-Mayer needs a boy in "In Old Kentucky."
>
> I went out to the studio and entered a room filled with aspirants to the role. When the man asked my name, I said "Stepin Fetchit." He smiled. "Is that your name?"
>
> "Sure," I replied.
>
> He soon came back and said the director wanted to see me. I slouched into the office and flopped in the chair nearest the door. You see, I put on that pose for their benefit.
>
> Well, the director liked me so they offered me one hundred per week to play the part. I told them, all right, and he told me when to report for work.
>
> When I get back to my room, I started thinking. I had sold myself too cheaply. I was making one hundred on the stage. Why quit that if I wasn't going to get more? The day before we were to begin work, I went to the studio and told them, "Nothin' doing for one hundred per week."

"How much do you want?" they asked.
"One hundred per day," I said slowly.
They laughed and I started out the door.
Well, we finally agreed upon seventy-five per day.[22]

Lincoln Perry's older sister Lucille related a slightly more colorful rendition of the actor's initial audience with director John M. Stahl.

He said he just stood there looking like he didn't know where he was or why he was there and he was scratching his head, which he had shaved clean, and he was just looking around like he was lost. I guess he looked so sad and lost and everything that he got their attention.

So, one of the directors, he pointed at Step and yelled, "Say, You!" And Step, he looked all around the place acting like he thought they couldn't have been talking to him, but knowing all the time that they were, and they called him again. He turned around all slow and wide-eyed and pointed to himself and said, "Is you talkin' to me?" And the dumber he acted, the more they laughed, because nobody had ever seen anybody *that* slow and ignorant. So they told him that he had the part.[23]

In August, Perry announced that he had gotten the role and Carolynne Snowden was working in the picture with him. From Metro-Goldwyn-Mayer studio, he wrote that he was on a set where "Lon Chaney, Henry Walthal and Marceline Day" were shooting a scene in a garden for "one of Mr. Chaney's latest pictures, 'The Hypnotist.' " Perry indicated that he had a four-week guaranteed contract "to play a very prominent part" at a salary "that has only been exceeded by Chas. Gilpin and [James] Lowe and Noble Johnson."[24]

In a disarmingly modest manner, the legend of Stepin Fetchit, movie star, had quietly begun taking shape. Soon, Lincoln Perry the man, as well as the journalist and vaudevillian, would be entirely consumed by the ever-broadening shadow of Stepin Fetchit, the enigmatic star and soon-to-be racial pariah.

CHAPTER FIVE

During the summer and fall of 1927, much of the buzz around Hollywood studio lots concerned the emergence and rapid evolution of sound movies, or "talkies." In 1926, Warner Brothers released *Don Juan,* a swashbuckling silent film that incorporated sound effects and a synchronized score. And with the release of *The Jazz Singer* in 1927, Warner suddenly became Hollywood's hottest studio. Fox and other major studios scrambled to meet the challenge and get into sound pictures. Both Fox and MGM would sign with Movietone, a sound track company formed by William Fox and Case Research Laboratories.[1]

For black entertainers, the emergence of talkies had equally dramatic consequences. Reportedly initiated by Bill Foster, a black producer who for more than a decade had struggled to make his mark in the film industry, rumors concerning the Negro's particular suitability for sound pictures had begun circulating. Foster claimed that "tests proved one great outstanding fact—the low mellow voice of the Negro was ideally suited for the pictures." In addition to his musical comedy attainments, "the peculiar ability of the Negro" altered the ground rules of Hollywood stardom, Foster insisted, so that "he fits right into the new age."[2]

Foster's claims, however suspect, were later echoed by the esteemed black writer, teacher, and NAACP director James Weldon Johnson as well as the black press. In correspondence with Foster, Johnson asserted, "I myself have noticed that their voices record better than white voices."

"It is significant that with the coming of talkies, the first all-Negro feature pictures were attempted by the big companies," a black entertainment writer added. "White America has always made much of the fact that all Negroes can sing and dance. The movie of yesterday, to be sure, let him dance, but his greatest charm was lost by silence. With the talkie, the Negro is at his best, and no one who has seen 'Hearts in Dixie' or Al Christie's 'Melancholy Dance' will disagree with the assertion that the Negro's voice can be a thing of beauty."[3]

By 1929 even fan magazines like *Motion Picture Classic* had jumped on the bandwagon. "With the advent of the talking pictures, a new race has come to the screen. Practically every studio with a sound stage is experimenting with at least one feature all-Negro picture," a Hollywood reporter wrote. "The Negro is exceptionally adapted to the sound screen. The humorous drawl, the pungent philosophies, the rich gift of music and of dance make this race a boon to the singies and talkies. Whether this is merely an experimental epidemic or the start of a new feature of the screen remains to be seen."[4]

The speculation was given further credence by the era's enthusiastic embrace of black syncopated music, jazz singing and choral groups, and the discovery that the voices of many silent film stars were too weak for talkies. In response, Hollywood studios began the first serious consideration of black-oriented movies and, almost immediately, began cranking out a stream of all-black shorts featuring prominent African American entertainers.

"Like a string of Chinese firecrackers, all-black two-reelers exploded erratically," the movie historian Thomas Cripps noted. "These films brought the best Afro-American vaudeville, vernacular dancing, and the more commercial forms of jazz." The shorts, which were relatively inexpensive and could be produced quickly, were the forerunners of today's music videos. They brought the nation's most successful and popular black entertainers to the screen.[5]

The black entertainment community was, naturally, elated. Although there were a few very vocal dissenters, critics and pundits generally waxed optimistically about the expected new opportunities. And in contrast to much previous commentary that had criticized the film industry's neglect and strongly suggested that East Coast theaters offered black professionals the most promising work, some critics began urging performers to go West. "Los Angeles is the western mecca of Race performers and things theatrical on the coast," a *Chicago Defender* article claimed. "It is still in its infancy as regards our group, but bids fair to become the haven of refuge, the saving grace and welcoming city of opportunity to those who grow tired of the competitive struggles back East. A hint to 'good' performers—'head West.' "[6]

It was against this backdrop that Lincoln Perry hustled to complete *In Old Kentucky*. A screen adaptation of a nineteenth-century racetrack melodrama with a plantation setting, it rivaled *Uncle Tom's Cabin* as a popular vehicle for both blackface and Negro performers.

Initially a three-act play, which featured pickaninny songs and buck dancing, *Kentucky* surfaced in the late 1890s and was a favorite among early traveling theatrical troupes. D. W. Griffith had released a screen version with white actors in blackface in 1909, and, in 1928, Harlem's Lafayette Players would arrive in Los Angeles with an elaborate touring company stage production. Later, Bill "Bojangles" Robinson would reprise the Stepin Fetchit role in a 1935 Fox remake that starred Will Rogers. In the 1927 version, which starred James Murray and Helene Costello, Perry was credited on screen as Stepin Fetchit and was cast as the stable hand Highpockets; the part of the house servant, Lily May, was played by the beautiful dancer, producer, and Sebastian's Cotton Club star Carolynne Snowden.

Although Snowden had bit parts in previous silent films, she regarded her *In Old Kentucky* role as a major career advancement. In August, she closed a sixty-eight-week-long engagement at the Cotton Club to devote herself full-time to the film. And a September news report indicated that she intended to put all "her nerve into her work in pictures," where, "as the only Negro girl doing important roles in big cinema productions," she believed she "occupied a unique position." During production of the film in late August and September, Perry also avoided stage engagements. His *Defender* column appeared only once between mid-August and completion of the film.[7]

In that lone September "Letter," Perry indicated that the picture was near completion and that upon its release he intended to take a trip to the East; where he would see his father and sister and attend the New York City premiere. He seemed in good spirits and very much at ease. In fact, the twenty-five-year-old entertainer demonstrated that he had not abandoned his adolescent love of monkeyshines and pranks.

"Tommy Gates and Archie Grant worked on my set in the Metro-Goldwyn-Mayer studio one day this week," he wrote, "and we were having a wonderful time until I told Tommy that his employment was only to keep me company for the day, and he wanted to leave without pay. Well it was only my joke, because the director soon appeared and in less than an hour and a half the scene was shot and everyone headed for Central Avenue."[8]

That carefree, prankish spirit seems to have dissipated by the time the picture was completed, however, and his *Defender* column a few weeks later suggested that his spirits had dampened. Perry claimed that he was "under the watchful care of a psychological specialist from South America" and was "in the midst of physical retreat."

Perry did not specify the nature of his malady, and it may have accrued in part from the stress of completing his first major cinema role. His short "retreat," however, apparently had no long-term effects, as he also reported that on September 30 he had joined a group of local artists who greeted Doc Straine's "Chocolate Scandals" musical company, which had left New York City and arrived in Los Angeles for the opening of the Lincoln Theater, the Avenue's newest showplace. The Lincoln would open the following week at Central and 23rd Street. Featuring new motion-picture releases, live stage acts, and fine furnishings, it provided a theatrical showplace for Negro artists and patrons. For a considerable time, the Lincoln was the Avenue's most luxurious, modestly priced theater and was known on the Stroll as the "West Coast Apollo."[9]

The Lincoln's grand opening was cause for celebration among the Avenue's artists. "Every musician, every performer and Race film actor was at the station with private automobiles to convey Doc Straine and his bunch," Perry wrote, "and an orchestra composed of some of the best in town blasted the musical welcome. Then the big parade wended its way down Central Ave. to the Lincoln Theater, where everyone had the joy of meeting and shaking hands with old friends." In a not uncommon bit of West Coast boosterism, Perry added, "Hurrah for the spirit of the musicians and performers of this city, and may its spirit become the spirit of the profession the world over."[10]

While waiting for the release of *In Old Kentucky*, Perry busied himself performing and reporting on the Central Avenue scene. The grand opening of the Lincoln Theater, of course, was the most exciting news on the strip; without "fear of contradiction," Perry wrote, it was "the greatest Race theater in America in beauty, architecture and comfort." Curtis Mosby's Dixieland Blue Blowers and Doc Straine's troupe were the headline acts for the opening, which also featured an appearance by Farina of the *Our Gang* film series and an address by A. Philip Randolph of the Brotherhood of Sleeping Car Porters. In his review of the show, Perry lauded the comic performances of Straine, Sam "Bilo" Russell—who "made himself the hit of the show"—and his former partner Johnny Lee.[11]

Even as Los Angeles's black entertainment community celebrated the opening of its fashionable new theater, however, it was shocked by news of the death of one of the era's most beloved artists. Florence Mills had gained national recognition with her role in *Shuffle Along* in 1921. In 1926, she starred in Lew Leslie's *Blackbirds,* an all-black revue that opened at the Alhambra Theatre in Harlem, then played in Paris. A 276-performance run at the Pavilion Theatre in London followed, during which the Prince of Wales reportedly saw the show more than a dozen times. By 1927 the diminutive Mills was not only a popular favorite among African Americans but had also become an international star whose fame rivaled Josephine Baker's popularity in Paris. Weeks after returning to New York, she checked into a hospital for an appendectomy; fans and performers were shocked when she died of complications on November 1, 1927. Her Harlem funeral attracted massive crowds—some estimates reported over 150,000—at the time, the largest such gathering in the community's history.

Grief over Mills's death was felt as deeply in Los Angeles. During the following weeks, prominent artists hosted several benefits. The old Globe Theater at Central and 35th was later renamed the Florence Mills Theatre as a tribute to the star.

Mills's tragic death also inspired numerous journalistic tributes in both the mainstream and black press. Among them was Lincoln Perry's extended paean in a November 1927 *Defender* column.

A telegram came to the Lincoln,
And when it was opened and read
Brought sadness among the profession.
'Cause it reported "Florence Mills is dead."

Yes dead! Amidst fame and achievement
And an illuminous [sic] *future ahead,*
She our pride and advancement
Chose "the rest of the weary" instead.

Instead of a trip back to Paris,
And additional fame across the sea,
She boarded death's ship to cross Jordan
With her contract for eternity.
I'll be back, she not long ago told Paris
And when saying "Au revoir"
Death wouldn't disclose his secret
That Paris would see her no more.
Allowing her to sign other contracts
And arrange other things to do,
When he (death) knew he had a contract
That he intended to hold her to.

Well, we too have a similar contract
Which although against our wills
Dread death will demand us to carry out
As he did our Florence Mills.
We know not the place nor the hour,
But like Florence Mills whom we laud,
Can be meek and humble in all success
Which is very pleasing to God.[12]

In Old Kentucky was released amid the pall of grief that lingered after Florence Mills's death and the frenzied optimism that had swept the Avenue over the prospects offered by the Lincoln Theater's opening. Given the circumstances, it is not surprising that at first the picture did not prompt the bombshell effect among black audiences or the West Coast black entertainment community anticipated by the studio or its featured black performers, Snowden and Perry.

According to Perry, on October 26 the film premiered at "an exclusive motion picture house" on Wilshire Boulevard with both him and Snowden in attendance. "What a thrill it was," a brimming Perry wrote, "to sit in a million-dollar theater and watch and laugh at myself taking a featured part in a featured picture! Miss Carolynne Snowden and myself closed the picture with a love scene, which is something that has never happened before in a big ofay production. Then after the showing of the picture, yours truly was congratulated with the warm and unprejudiced hand-shake of the big officials of a firm under whose standards plays by such as Lon Chaney, Norma Shearer, John Gilbert, [and] Jackie Coogan are produced." Perry was effusive in his praise of Snowden—citing her deft handling of a crying scene—and MGM, "the biggest of the best," and did not restrain his self-congratulatory instincts. After expressing his surprise at having "really earned such a reception," he added, "Ain't that a grand and glorious feeling."[13]

When released, the picture was moderately successful, but most notices were middling. Perry's positive contribution to the effort, however, was affirmed in *Variety.* "Much mush stuff," the critic wrote, "but the M-G. finish to the film and a colored comedian hold up the picture. He's just a lazy, no good roustabout, wheedling money out of the colored help, but he's no mean pantomimist."[14]

For Snowden, who had won bit parts in studio movies prior to *In Old Kentucky* and been touted by the black press as a rising star, the picture's tepid reception was a major disappointment. She continued to thrive on the cabaret circuit and later resurfaced in minor parts as a maid and appeared in several of the studio's two-reel musical shorts. But Snowden was soon eclipsed by such emerging hopefuls as Ethel Waters, Nina Mae McKinney, and Hattie McDaniel. She never achieved the motion-picture eminence predicted by her admirers.

And, despite the *Variety* notice received for his performance in his first picture—unprecedented for a Negro actor in a supporting role—and his accurate assessment of the unique nature of his on-screen love scene with Snowden, the still relatively unknown Perry was not immediately elevated to feature-player status in films or allotted exceptional treatment at the studios. Nor was the red carpet rolled out for him by the Stroll's entertainment community.

Interestingly, what emerges from reports of the West Coast entertainment scene was that when his first picture was released the soon-to-be star, Stepin Fetchit, was clearly not among the nation's or even the Los Angeles area's most popular or celebrated black comic performers.

After Bert Williams's ascent as a *Ziegfeld Follies* star, only a handful of black comedians had attained even marginal mainstream prominence on the national level. In fact, the most popular Negro comic figures in America during the late twenties were Amos Jones and Andy H. Brown, the fictional duo whose continuing exploits aired on radio via the clever ethnic ventriloquy of Freeman F. Gosden and Charles J. Correll. Among black performers, Flournoy Miller and Aubrey Lyles—largely due to their Broadway successes with *Shuffle Along* (1921) and *Runnin' Wild* (1923)—were probably the best-known comics in mainstream America. And, although acclaimed more for his dancing than for the comic patter that spiced his vaudeville act, Bill Robinson was not only America's preeminent black stage performer but also its most revered. After seeing him perform live for the first time, Perry observed, "To my great delight, I can join the band of those who hail Bill Robinson as the world's greatest single and the dean of tap dancing." Among black audiences on the TOBA circuit, such future stars as Butterbeans and Susie, Crackshot Hackley, Moms Mabley, Tim Moore, Mantan Moreland, and Pigmeat Markham were rapidly establishing themselves as the tour's favorite comics.[15]

Even in South Los Angeles, there were several comedians performing in Central Avenue theaters and nightspots who drew considerably larger audiences than Perry. Tommy Harris of the comic duo Tolliver and Harris had been a local favorite since the early twenties. Harris, the *Defender*'s "Coast Dope" column claimed, was "the biggest name on the Coast as a comedian."[16]

Sam "Bilo" Russell, also a huge favorite, regularly teamed with the producer, writer, and comic Sandy Burns; their act, Ashes and Bilo, was billed as "The World's Funniest Comedians" on the TOBA circuit. "Ashes [Burns] was a straight man, and Bilo was the real, real funny one," Marshall Royal, the alto saxophonist and Central Avenue denizen, recalled. "He was actually the funniest comedian I'd ever seen in my life."[17]

Perry's first partner, Johnny Lee, had also quickly established a reputation on the Avenue with his stint at the Lincoln. "The truth is the light, so here am de truth. [Lee] and his wife, Baby Johnson, are receiving great compliments from the patrons, the directors and the studios and in this week's show is proving his versatility," Perry wrote in his

Defender "Letter." "All I can say is that the right man's going to catch him soon."[18]

Given the abundance of black comic talent available nationwide and on nearby Central Avenue, the selection of Perry for the prime role of Highpockets in MGM's *In Old Kentucky,* and his subsequent mercurial rise to Hollywood fame, baffled many of his peers. When examined more closely, however, his success was not that surprising.

Most important, Perry was simply a better *actor* than most of his more celebrated peers; as a result, the indolent comic character that he developed was more suited for silent pictures. In contrast to either the slapstick or the highly theatrical *caricatures* developed by nearly all of his contemporaries, Perry's stage *character* was infinitely more believable, eerily realistic and, consequently, more provocative and empathetically engaging to moviegoing audiences.

Pigmeat Markham and Moms Mabley introduced comic stage types that had rarely been seen on the black circuit. But their signature characters—Pigmeat's thorny, irrepressible judge (from his "Here Come the Judge" routine) and Moms's feisty old lady—remained highly stylized creations that were personally identified with their originators. They worked well in short variety films where the entertainers played themselves, but, without drastic alteration, were not easily integrated into the plot line of a full-length motion picture. Markham did surface later in slapstick roles as the stereotyped frightened coon. But Mabley, whose act featured inclusive, often blue, patter about subjects specifically geared to the tastes of black-circuit theater audiences, was rarely seen in pictures and did not appear in a feature Hollywood film until *Amazing Grace* in 1972.

Most of the other popular black-circuit funnymen worked in duos; and, for the most part, the era's comic teams thrived on presenting familiar blackface caricatures—slapstick gags and *shtick.* They relied on outlandish farce as opposed to character-based comedy. The stage routines of Ashes and Bilo, Miller and Lyles, Tolliver and Harris, Butterbeans and Susie, as well as Mantan Moreland, Johnny Lee, and Tim Moore (all of whom usually worked with a partner) fit loosely into the latter category.

The stage routines of these duos may have worked on-screen if the studios had chosen to feature them in the type of comedy vehicles written for Laurel and Hardy or, later, Abbott and Costello, but in mid-1920s Hollywood such projects were unthinkable for race actors. In 1929, when the studios boldly attempted casting Negroes in feature roles, Miller and Lyles did appear in a loosely adapted screen version of their Broadway hit *Shuffle Along* called *Jimtown Speakeasy* and released by MGM. The comedy short and its sequel *Jimtown Mayor* were undistinguished box-office failures, as was a 1929 Pathé comedy series featuring Buck and Bubbles. Mainstream America was simply not receptive to all-black, low-comedy screen showcases.

The "Step and Fetch It" stage act had also relied heavily on a variation of the contrasting comic figures—scheming city slicker and slow, gullible rube—that prevailed at the time. The role of the slick, conniving city boy was filled by Perry's various partners; Perry assumed the part of the slow-talking country boy. By the late twenties, Perry had altered the traditional rural Negro character in a subtle but striking fashion.

Bert Williams had slyly turned the dim-witted stereotype inside out—humanizing the caricature by revealing innate wisdom and an emotional core. He limited the deprecative aspects of the character to the surface elements of slow movement and speech; the latter, although rendered in dialect, was nevertheless coherent and witty. His jokes depended on word play or lampooning traditional institutions and were delivered, as one critic noted, in the persona of "a wise fool or more often the fool's upstairs neighbor, the common sense philosopher." In that guise, he could deliver lines that reflected the character's subtle wit: "Somebody made a great mistake when dey gived de cat nine lives and de chicken jes one" or "Don't loaf 'round the corners and 'pend on the Lord fuh yo' daily bread. De Lord ain't runnin' no bakery." Underneath the slumped shoulders, molasseslike movements, sad-sack gaze, and broken speech, the character had, in Williams's words, "a philosophy that has got something."[19]

Although not as talented as Williams, Perry was an extremely gifted comedian. The inequity with regard to most appraisals of his career is that he is often singled out as the *inventor* or lone perpetuator of what, in retrospect, was generally regarded as a deplorable stereotype. In reality, Perry was not imitating white purveyors of racist stereotypes, as many critics have asserted. He was working within the parameters of an established and accepted comic representation that, at the time, dominated the era's theatrical world. He stands out from the hundreds of black comedians who were working variations of the same character only because, ultimately, he was far superior to most of them.[20]

Onstage, Fetchit avoided the folksy wit that Williams favored. Instead, his character's torpid physical presence and halting, meandering speech became the focus of the interpretation. Perry isolated those elements and, with the deft touch of a master pantomimist, honed them to near perfection before arriving in Los Angeles in the mid-twenties. Although he sometimes sang and spiced his act with nonsensical doggerel ("The Stepin Fetchit! Turn around, stop and catch it . . ."), the comedy derived primarily from the combined near-hypnotic languidness of his stage entrance and the contrasting light-footed dance steps that followed. Occasionally, he spiked his heavy-lidded, hangdog demeanor with a surreptitious wink, a subtly ironic grin or, more infrequently, a barely audible quip or joke.

Every movement was meticulously controlled. In much the same way in which some heavy comedians—the 1950s vaudeville team, Patterson and Jackson (billed as Two Tons of Fun), or, in the 2000s, Cedric the Entertainer—play their hefty stature against agile dance steps, Perry skillfully contrasted his absentminded coon lethargy with the silken finesse of his dancing. Onstage, he would come meandering out, scratching his head, looking utterly confused and lost. Mouth agape, eyes half closed, shoulders slouched, arms dangling, he would slip into a practically incoherent monologue; delivered in a whining monotone to no one in particular, most often it had little meaning beyond the visual impression of confusion.

Then, suddenly, the gangling actor would spring into a spirited dance routine that, when first encountered, often astounded audiences. His facial expression changed subtly, the half-closed eyelids lifted, eyes momentarily widening to reveal a flash of energy, near-arrogance, that the simpleton mask had intentionally concealed.

If Williams's sluggish stage character was the indolent philosopher or wise fool, then Perry's lazy man was the scheming slacker, the dolt as trickster.

In motion pictures, Perry's slouching, hesitant, incoherent darky pose was seized upon while the contrasting aspect of his act—the smooth vaudeville entertainer—and the man who enacted it were nearly always ignored. True enough, Perry's unique take on the sluggardly rural black comic trope was compelling in and of itself. Few other actors came close to duplicating it on the stage or screen at that time or later. The comedian who most closely approximated it, Nick, or Nicodemus, Stewart (aka Nick O'Demus), would surface in films in the 1930s. Years later he was cast as the stuttering, nitwit janitor Lightnin' on the *Amos 'n' Andy* television show.

By the late 1920s, however, Perry had already mastered the darky presentation and marked it with his own distinct imprint; it was perfectly suited for motion pictures. As some early reviews suggested, the actor's on-screen presence was spellbinding—particularly in the silent-film medium where eccentric personal magnetism and exaggerated facial expressions and body language were key.

A reporter would later describe Fetchit's screen interpretation of the comic ploy as "a lazy pantomime" in which the "Negro comic has a total indifference to the laws of enunciation." Fetchit called it "audible pantomiming" and described its origin and intent to the journalist.

"It's a new art, born with talking pictures," Fetchit later claimed. "I made my start in Hollywood on the silent screen, when pantomime was all important. When speech came along, film comics were up against a new program—to fit their funny gestures to words, or fit the words to gestures, however you like to look at it.

"I decided to go ahead pantomiming just as I had always done. I picked out the important words in the lines I had, the ones important for laughs, or that gave cues to other actors; I consciously stress them—the rest of the speech doesn't matter. I mumble through the rest, gestures helping to point the situation."

Fetchit's stylized presentation was original and unique, and while he admitted that it was based on the "rhythm" of regional Southern Negro speech and mannerisms, he rightly claimed that the portrayal depended on pantomime. He even advised audiences not to "strain to hear everything," but to relax as he did, and enjoy the fictitious character.[21]

Directors John M. Stahl and Paul Sloane (who would take the helm of Perry's breakthrough picture *Hearts in Dixie* in 1929), the Fox production director Winfield Sheehan, and, later, Hollywood studio kingpin and Twentieth Century-Fox founder Darryl F. Zanuck quickly recognized the motion-picture potential of Perry's stylized performance. Stahl recruited Perry for several projects after *In Old Kentucky*, and it was Sloane and Sheehan who insisted that Perry be cast as Gummy in *Hearts in Dixie*. After leaving Warner Brothers and merging with Fox, Zanuck was instrumental in advancing the black actor's career.

In addition to Perry's compelling presence on-camera, the actor was apparently much more adept at dealing with the studios off-camera than most of his contemporaries. His tough-mindedness and ability to wrangle with studio executives had been demonstrated when negotiating his initial contract with MGM, and in the following years, those qualities repeatedly surfaced in interactions with studio heads, directors, and producers. He was hard-nosed and irrepressibly ambitious—"as intelligent and shrewd as the twentieth century businessman," one reporter wrote.[22]

In a Hollywood environment that insistently ignored or trivialized contributions by blacks, Perry relied on charm and sly aggressiveness to hasten his acceptance and expand his roles. And, like maverick filmmaker Oscar Micheaux, he was not above using conniving and wily misrepresentation when dealing with the studios' white executives.

Not content with reveling in the light of the unprecedented notices for his initial full-length film performance and unmindful of the black acting community's casual reaction to his success, Perry did not simply return to the stage to await the next studio cattle call. He continued writing his *Defender* column, and applied his energy to skillfully orchestrating the next stages of his career as he scrambled for small parts in pictures and sparingly accepted engagements at local clubs and theaters.

One of his most important contacts was the director John M. Stahl, who had admired the actor's work since he auditioned for *In Old Kentucky*. Stahl had began producing his own films, and for a brief period merged with Tiffany Productions—a small B-movie company founded by Robert Z. Leonard and his wife, the actress Mae Murray—to form Tiffany-Stahl Productions. During 1928, Perry had small parts in three action-dramas produced and released by Stahl or his associated company.

In the December 31, 1927, issue of the *Defender*, Perry's "Letter" opened with an inspirational greeting. And as with his other pious advisories from the 1920s, it reared in stark contrast to the excesses of his own behavior two years later.

The letter, a sermonlike riff worthy of an evangelist, chided readers for focusing on the holidays' surface materialism and gaiety, urging a return to their true spiritual meaning—that "peace that the world with all her riches cannot give, that is only obtained by the true spirit of Christmas." Arguing that "our misfortune and failure in the past were only the offspring of our follies, carelessness and neglecting of our duties toward God," Perry concluded that "no matter how much we accumulate," our "future progress and happiness in this and eternal happiness in the life to come" depended on the peace that comes with an acceptance of God.

Perry provided an update on his activities in films. "Carolyn [*sic*] Snowden and myself have been busy at work on a picture entitled 'Clash,' starring Antonio Moreno and Claire Windsor, and intend to start work on our picture as soon as plans are completed. I think we will have a female director from the Fox studio. I have also worked with William Collier, Jr., under the direction of King Baggot and Christy Cabanne."[23]

The movie that Perry identified as *Clash* was apparently retitled *Nameless Men*. Both Perry and Snowden had roles as servants in the crime drama. Perry also had a minor role as a porter in *The Tragedy of Youth*, a tale of infidelity involving a wayward wife whose affair drives her husband to attempt suicide. The picture featured William Collier and the future Academy Award–winning actor Warner Baxter. A third Stahl production—*The Devil's Skipper*, a horror story starring the well-known character actor Montagu Love—reunited Perry and Snowden as a married slave couple.

Perry's roles in those 1928 Tiffany-Stahl silent-movie releases were not exceptional and caused little stir among mainstream critics or the black movie community. They were hardly distinguishable from minor comic appearances by race actors or entertainers in dozens of films released at the time. And they paled when compared to the excitement generated by the sound-mixed, two-reel comedy shorts that the studios had begun producing.

In addition, the first of a series of sound-mixed musical shorts featuring headline black entertainers had appeared, and blacks in show business were understandably intrigued. By 1928, RKO had released two of the best of these two-reel musicals. Both were written and directed by Dudley Murphy, a previously unheralded independent filmmaker with an ardent fascination for black life.

The first, *St. Louis Blues,* featured the music of W. C. Handy and J. Rosamond Johnson. Bessie Smith, at the peak of her career, was cast as a misused cabaret singer, and the dancer Jimmy Mordecai played a hustler and gigolo in this spare, gritty story of black street life. *Variety* gushed over its authenticity and described the film as "pungent with tenseness and action and replete with Aframerican local color." Thomas Cripps called it "the finest film of Negro life up to that time."[24]

Later in 1928, *Black and Tan,* a sultry, fantasylike drama enacted in a seedy nightclub, was released, starring Duke Ellington and the vampish Fredi Washington. Washington was cast as the lovesick heroine who works to support her musician lover (Ellington). She collapses and ultimately dies as Ellington plays the title composition. The *New York Amsterdam News* praised Ellington's "half-savage, half-tender" musical score and the "stark realism" of the film's depiction of Harlem life. This short, with its haunting, tragic overtones, is still compelling viewing, particularly for lovers of Ellington's music.[25]

The upsurge of short two-reel films notwithstanding, there was a temporary slowdown in activity involving Negroes in full-length Hollywood features during the transition from silent to sound movies in 1928. In a May *Defender* column, Perry commented on that situation as well as on his own temporarily stalled picture aspirations. "In the picture world things have not been so favorable," he wrote. "The first happening at Warner Brothers studio, where $13,500 that was intended for the Race was turned over to white extras under cork.

"Then it is rumored that M.G.M. casting department has been ordered not to hire any more Negroes, which, I hope, is just a rumor, and about which I hope to say something definite in my next article."[26]

Perry's next "Letter," in fact, did not address the subject, and in retrospect his assessment of the big-studio situation seems to reflect his personal predicament as much as the overall status of blacks in films. He had seemingly reached a crossroads in his career.

"At Tiffany-Stahl production," he announced, "I am expecting an option on my contract to be ignored and am arranging a vaudeville trip." He also mentioned that he had written a film script "for Carolyn [*sic*] Snowden, a Farina type, and a Highpockets with a white cast," which he was attempting to sell.[27]

In reality, although there was a brief hiatus in full-length films, Hollywood executives were gearing up to exploit the black presence on the screen more than in any previous era. Two-reel shorts featuring performers like Louis Armstrong, Bill Robinson, Mamie Smith, Duke Ellington, and Miller and Lyles were released the following year, and behind the scenes executives at two major studios were already contemplating production of their first full-length, all-black-cast extravaganzas.

Perry's disenchantment with film prospects was short-lived. Two weeks later, his *Defender* "Letter" reported that he was writing "on the train on my way to Sacramento, Cal., where Universal Studios is shooting some of the exterior scenes of the screen version of the 'Showboat,' in which I am portraying the role of 'Joe.'" Both the filming and release of the Broadway hit's first movie adaptation would be delayed by a series of problems involving sound and musical rights as well as production costs, and Perry offered some interesting background details about the off-camera difficulties that plagued the picture.

"Universal had to cut some of the best and emotional parts in the screen version on account of the censor," he wrote. And after pointing out that great precautions were being taken to assure that the director Harry Pollard didn't near the production costs of *Uncle Tom's Cabin,* a previous film whose budget reached $2 million, he continued: "The 'Showboat' was originally intended to be a feature sound and talk picture. But Flo Ziegfeld, who has proved that the screen version would be an infringement on the stage rights of his play, has left the symphonizing and screen version unsettled. Of course, if it is not settled by the time they are ready to begin synchronizing and preparing the dialogue, why Universal will substitute the songs with other folk songs, and the original of yours truly will substitute for 'Old Man River,' as we are at present using it for a theme song while working."[28]

Although "Old Man River" was retained, *Show Boat* was released without the rest of Jerome Kern's score or Oscar Hammerstein II's lyrics as a part-silent, part-talkie film with music but little dialogue. The black actress Gertrude Howard won the supporting role of Queenie in the integrated cast; the part of the tragic mulatto Julie was portrayed by white actress Alma Rubens. According to one critic, the substitute score, featuring "forgettable tunes written by entrepreneur Billy Rose," contributed to the picture's lackluster reception.[29]

Perry was also cast in another Universal Studios picture in 1928. He was credited as the "Negro Man" in *Kid's Clever,* a silent comedy about a young inventor struggling to find love; like *Show Boat,* it was released early in 1929. While none of the pictures significantly advanced Perry's career, they were among his numerous film credits in 1929, a year that witnessed the release of two of the most important movies in black cinema history. As the critically acclaimed costar in one of those releases, Perry would quickly be catapulted into Hollywood stardom.

CHAPTER SIX

By the summer of 1928, William Fox at the Fox Film Corporation and Louis B. Mayer at MGM had signed off on two groundbreaking all-black-cast projects—*Hearts in Dixie* and *Hallelujah!*—intended to depict and contrast Southern Negro country and urban lifestyles and, by fully utilizing the new sound technology, to exploit the increasing audience demand for black music in pictures. From preproduction planning and publicity through the pictures' 1929 releases and their critical aftermath, however, the films were surrounded by controversy.

Melodramatic back-lot intrigues, the studio's wavering endorsement, incidents of segregation and racism during location shootings, claims and counterclaims of racist stereotyping in the scripts, and black critics' heated discussions and polarized opinions all contributed to the furor. Still, the films would emerge as milestones in black cinema history, and, ultimately, the controversy surrounding them would have unprecedented impact on the evolution of black themes in movies, influencing the depiction of Negroes in Hollywood motion pictures for decades. Given the black community's high expectations for the projects, the most startling immediate result of their release was Lincoln Perry's sudden rise to star status at the Hollywood studios.

Fox began first, with plans for a black-cast, two-reel musical. Under the guidance of production director Winfield Sheehan, those plans, however, were quickly expanded. After filming began, the studio hired

Walter Weems, a former minstrel performer, to develop a longer script and geared itself to produce a first-of-its-kind, full-length feature that combined traditional Negro spirituals with a dramatic story line and plantation setting. Sheehan and Fox executives attempted to cast a veil of secrecy over the project, literally shutting the doors of the sound stages. Nevertheless, buzz about the ambitious production began spreading throughout the industry.

Perhaps influenced by early rumors, during the summer MGM finally reversed its decision to pass on a proposed film by King Vidor, an acclaimed director with an avid interest in social issues who for years had pitched the idea of bringing an "authentic" depiction of Southern Negro life and music to the screen. Despite fears that the picture would attract too many Negroes to the theaters and keep whites away, terms were set and Vidor quickly began preliminary preparations for filming *Hallelujah!*

That summer, as gossip about the two blockbuster black films began filtering down to the Central Avenue entertainment community, Lincoln Perry conveniently found himself at work on the Fox lot. After finishing *Kid's Clever* for Universal, he had landed a supporting role as a janitor in *The Ghost Talks,* a Fox film directed by Lewis Seiler, and had begun rehearsals for what was his initial appearance in a sound film with dialogue. In his *Defender* column, writing from the "Fox rehearsal hall," he announced that Lincoln Theater chorus-line star Baby Mack had been "given a contract and will be my next teammate in William Fox's first 100 per cent talking picture." Earlier the white actress Madge Bellamy had taken a test in "brownskin make-up" to audition for the role "Baby Mack landed," he continued, "so you can realize by that how outstanding the part will be."[1]

Even though he was working on the Fox lot, Perry's column did not refer to Fox's proposed full-length Negro musical during the summer and early fall. It is likely, however, that he had not only heard of but also actively lobbied for roles in both the Fox and the MGM all-black-cast projects even before word reached the black community. In his column, he indicated that he had spoken with King Vidor and was appraised of the director's location scouting and casting efforts for *Hallelujah!* "King Vidor made a mysterious trip to Georgia, taking one race boy with him, but keeping secret his intentions," he wrote. "It is rumored that Ethel Waters has been selected for his feminine lead. I had but one interview with him, and I think this trip is just for exterior shots and for completion of the writing of the script."[2]

Perry's initial silence about *Hearts in Dixie* and his upcoming role in the film may have been motivated by the veil of secrecy with which Fox studio executives tried to shield their project. Whatever the cause, during September and October, Perry avoided the subject in his letters, focusing on Central Avenue happenings and his first experience with dialogue while completing *The Ghost Talks.*

Referring to his role in *Ghost* as "the biggest chance I've been given by the Hollywood producers," Perry wrote that the film "will also give me a chance to learn the secret of the talking picture performance which is a proposition that has the best actors of Hollywood in doubt." In the same letter, he gave his present employer a self-serving plug. "This is my first picture on the Fox lot," he wrote, "and I am very glad of the opportunity because William Fox studio made such stars as Janet Gaynor, Charles Farrell, Delores Del Rio, and Victor McLean."[3]

In early October, while shooting *Ghost,* he offered more details about his reaction to the transition from silent movies to spoken lines in a sound picture. "I have just completed my first week before the camera as a talking picture artist, and I guess many imagine it a great thrill to see one's self on the screen as in silent pictures. But I thought I would scream when the director assembled the cast in the projecting room and gave each not only an eyeful but an earful of his or her ability. The talking picture industry has been worrying many and most of the stars of Hollywood that have not had stage experience, but after one week of it I can say that it's nothing but a test of one's real acting and speaking ability. Many will be made and many will lose. But I personally prefer the silent pictures as one can do more acting and more justice can be done to a story."[4]

Only a month later, however, after *Ghost* was completed, Perry wrote that *The Ghost Talks* "was indeed the greatest engagement of my recent screen experience."[5]

The low-budget comedy, which starred Charles Eaton, Helen Twelvetrees, and Joe E. Brown, was released in February 1929 and, except for Perry's appearance, barely triggered a critical ripple. Still, the actor's optimistic appraisal of his ability to move from silent to talking pictures was immediately justified when the film opened in theaters. the *New York Times*'s Mordaunt Hall reported that "Stepin Fetchit is excellent as the negro [*sic*]." And *Variety*'s critic cited Perry for his contribution to the picture's "best gag."[6]

Earlier, however, as the shooting of *Ghost* drew to a close, word-of-mouth buzz on the Fox lot about Perry's performance had a more dramatic effect on the actor's career. Winfield Sheehan and the newly assigned director for *Hearts in Dixie,* Paul Sloane, both of whom were admirers of Perry's work, were still wrestling with cast assignments for their proposed blockbuster film. Charles Gilpin was originally chosen for the feature role of Nappus, a tenant farmer struggling to eke out a living on near-barren Southern soil. Meanwhile, Sheehan and Sloane had witnessed Perry's work on Fox's *Ghost* and were impressed with the actor's ability and hypnotic screen presence. Perry was handed the plumb role of Gummy, Nappus's malingering field-hand son. Some film historians contend that it was studio executives' recognition of Perry's potential star appeal that influenced the decision to expand the picture into a full-length feature.[7]

In November, soon after Fox and MGM began issuing publicity releases to the press, interest and heady anticipation of a new era of heightened Negro participation in Hollywood pictures soared in the black community. "Production schedule for Fox-Movietone entertainments has reached a new high point according to an announcement by Winfield Sheehan, vice-president of Fox films," the *California Eagle,* a black weekly newspaper, announced early in the month. *Lonesome Road* (still the working title for *Hearts*) was "ready to start under the direction of Paul Sloane, with Charles Gilpin, celebrated Negro stage actor, who created a furore [*sic*] in Eugene O'Neil's 'Emperor Jones,' playing the leading role. Gilpin has just arrived in Hollywood and, having what critics call 'the most dramatic voice on the stage today,' is expected to give an inspired performance via Fox-Movietone."[8]

The picture's title had been changed by mid-November and the *Eagle* announced that Fox studios had begun shooting in Bakersfield, California, on November 25. "Among those who left the city last Sunday morning for location scenes, in Wm. Fox's 'Hearts in Dixie' allcolored cast picture, were some of Los Angeles' most renowned choristers, under the very able directorship of Mrs. A. C. Bilbrew. They will supply the chief background for the plantation scenes—cotton pickers—then return to the studio to complete the sound arrangements."

The article noted that Charles Gilpin, and other cast members, "including Big Zack Williams and Step'n Fetchit did not accompany the troupe," and concluded with an uninhibitedly enthusiastic endorsement of the project. "Mr. Paul Sloane, the director, Jimmie Townsend, the casting director, and all others interested in putting this initial effort over, are thus far pleased with their efforts. They have a wonderful supporting cast, very accurate background and everything else needed to put a picture across. It's over! They carried it over."[9]

Earlier in November, when Perry reported that he had won the part of Gummy in his *Defender* letter, hints of behind-the-scene intrigue as well as the barely concealed competition between *Hearts* and *Hallelujah!* producers had begun to surface. Before rather humbly expressing gratitude, Perry took a swipe at MGM and its project, scolding King Vidor for ignoring Los Angeles actors and going to the East Coast to cast his film. "King Vidor left Hollywood to assemble a cast for his all-Colored picture [and] spoke very poor of the Race artists and actresses out here," he wrote, "but Fox studio has assembled a cast for an all-Colored picture, which will be a superproduction entitled 'Deep River,' in which I will share honors with none other than the incomparable and beloved Charles Gilpin of 'Emperor Jones' fame. Mr. Gilpin was the only artist selected for the cast that was not listed among Los Angeles artists. I consider this a great opportunity to be costarred with America's greatest Race artist, and far be it from anyone to think that I considered myself equally cast on account of this picture, but it is due to my work in Fox's first 100 per cent talkie that obtained me this opportunity, and I assure the gang that I will try to show the pleasure I feel at being placed so high by the greatest performance of my career."[10]

The ever-ambitious Perry—who was quickly becoming a resourceful, even ingenious self-promoter—may have helped his own cause with a grandiose advertisement he took in a trade paper during the summer of 1928. The film historian Thomas Cripps wrote that Perry had placed an ad describing himself as "a convincing, unexaggerated original or modern Negro . . . that will meet with the approval of the Board of Censorship and the patrons of the North and South." That image had been shaped on the road in "southern towns that wouldn't allow other members of his race to enter."[11]

It was soon obvious that Fox Movietone (the name adopted for the film company's new sound picture studios) had long-term plans for the young actor. In a December issue featuring Christmas greetings from various entertainers, the *California Eagle* included an item on Perry which announced that he had signed a new contract with Fox. "Step 'N Fetchit [is] truly one of the greatest colored actors ever to appear on the silver" screen and "is numbered among the higher salaried actors," the story reported. "He enjoys the novel distinction of being one of the few people of any race enjoying a Movietone contract. He is under contract for six months for Wm. Fox." Perry had signed the first extended contract offered a black performer by a major Hollywood studio. In addition, the agreement made Perry the "highest salaried colored actor since Bert Williams."[12]

On the set of what was now called *Hearts in Dixie*, however, problems were building. Winfield and Sloane quickly lost patience with Charles Gilpin and his alleged "crankiness and carelessness." The outspoken and occasionally temperamental actor—who previously had clashed with Universal Pictures executives and lost the role of Tom in the 1927 version of *Uncle Tom's Cabin*—was soon dismissed despite his stage reputation. Fox attempted to sign the sixty-two-year-old character actor George Reed for the part. But Reed—a dependable performer who appeared in more than a hundred films during his career—refused to accept the role, perhaps fearing the unfavorable black fan reaction accorded James Lowe after he replaced Gilpin as "Tom" two years earlier. Finally, Clarence Muse was selected.[13]

One version has it that Muse accidentally met Sheehan on the Fox lot while looking for atmosphere work at a cattle call. He was offered an audition and eventually not only won the part of Nappus but was also retained as background adviser on the project. In a 1972 interview, however, Muse said that he was in New York when he received a telegram from Hollywood, asking him to play the role of Nappus in the Fox picture. "My only love was theater, though, so I sent back a ridiculous price for my services, since I wasn't interested," he recalled. "But they agreed to my terms of $1,250 a week, which, at the time, was a hell of a lot of money. I went for 12 weeks and stayed forever."[14]

With Muse in tow, the set was further disrupted in December when word was leaked from an unnamed studio source suggesting that "all was not so well between Fox and [its] new protégé." The story appeared in several black papers, including the *Chicago Defender*, which ran the article under the headline "Actor Too Proud to Work in Films With Own Race." The reporter, citing anonymous sources, aired rumors about Perry's disruptive behavior on the set during a shot in which he was "cast to represent a lazy roustabout lying along a fence, whose duty in one scene was to rise regretfully and yawn. He did his part so well that he always fell asleep and failed even to do the rising and stretching parts of his assignment, this accusation said, even after the other actors had built up to this bit of business."

The on-set discord, the article claimed, was set off by Perry's dissatisfaction with appearing in an all-black picture. "According to the studio's version, the trouble began when Fetchit decided he did not belong in a picture made wholly by members of his Race. He does not like to be surrounded by black actors. He prefers to be an actor in a white cast, it is said."[15]

The reference to Perry's overzealous rendering of the lazy roustabout seems frivolous and suspiciously akin to the kind of self-promotional anecdote the actor would concoct about himself during the next decade. But the anonymous studio executive's remarks and the allegation that Perry was opposed to working with Negro actors, their validity notwithstanding, were potentially damaging to the actor's heretofore doting relationship with both Fox and the black community.

Perry swiftly responded to the allegations in a letter written to Negro critic Maurice Dancer and published by the *Pittsburgh Courier* a month after the original story appeared.

> Dear Sir:
>
> I was very much grieved to read an article of yours during the month of December in which I was made to appear as trying to snub my own race and associate with white actors.
>
> In this story which was evidently picked up by your representative on the Fox lot, I am quoted as saying that I don't like to be surrounded by colored actors, but prefer to be an actor in a white company. This makes it appear that I am trying to high-hat my own race, which is untrue. I

know my place and that story has made me do a lot of explaining among my friends, besides the harm it will do me among people of the race around the country that happen to read it.

What I really said was that I much preferred to work as comedy relief in a company of white people rather than an all-colored picture because in the former company I have no competition as to dialect and character, and, therefore, have a much better chance for recognition.

I know that mistakes happen in writing stories and I am not writing for a retraction. That would only spread the story; the less said the better. What I would appreciate, however, is that, in the future, whenever your man has anything to say about me, personally, he would see me and get the real story and in that way avoid any bad impression.

Thanking you in advance for same, I am

Very truly yours,
Stepin Fetchit[16]

Ultimately, the story was submerged in the wake of publicity that followed *Hearts in Dixie*'s completion and release. That incident, however, signaled the beginning of Perry's erratic relationship with Hollywood studios as well as the vacillating love-hate kinship he shared with the Negro community during the remainder of his career. And while Perry's increasingly hectic performance schedule is most often cited as the reason for the discontinuation of his journalistic efforts with the *Chicago Defender*, his departure was probably hastened by that story and its attendant flap. "Lincoln Perry's Letter" did not appear in the *Defender* after 1929.

On the Fox set, problems continued until a few weeks before the *Hearts* release date. After the film was previewed in early February, director Paul Sloane announced that additional retake scenes would be necessary. "About thirty people worked three days" to reshoot the scenes on the weekend of February 8–10, the *California Eagle* reported.[17]

Ultimately, the picture's story line was rather thin. After a languishing opening shot in which the camera pans a cotton field filled with wearily serene blacks picking and chopping, and crooning a spiritual, the scene switches to the sand flats where at day's end the mournful sound of the choir gives way to a jazzier beat as tenant workers release themselves in a frenzy of dance amid makeshift shanties. Gummy (Perry) is among a group of adult revelers and pickaninnies (the latter included four-year-old Matthew Beard, later "Stymie" in the *Our Gang* series) who take part in the spirited celebration. It is against these contrasting rhythms of dirge and revel that the story of the righteous old patriarch Nappus (Clarence Muse), his daughter Chloe (Bernice Pilot), her shiftless husband Gummy, and his two grandchildren, Chinquapin (Eugene Jackson) and Trailia (Mildred Washington), slowly unfolds.

After Gummy's wife and daughter contract a mysterious illness, Nappus calls a doctor (the film's only white actor) to attend them. But when the doctor arrives, Gummy has already brought in a hoodoo woman (A. C. Bilbrew) to perform a regenerative ritual over his dying wife and daughter. Gummy, who claims he is unable to work because of miseries in his feet but is still able to cut a mean step when dancing, courts and weds Violet (Vivian Smith) after Chloe's death. At first, Violet tolerates his malingering. Once they are married, however, she insists that he give up his trifling ways and go to work. When he asks why she has changed, she tells him, "You can't feed a fish after catching him." Finally, the once free-spirited Gummy (who delivers such lines as "I ain't askin' you is you ain't, I's askin' you is you is") grudgingly slips into the pattern of grueling, dead-end labor that rules the lives of the other fieldworkers. A note of optimism is introduced by Nappus, who sees salvation in the city, where he determines to send his surviving grandchild, Chinquapin, to acquire an education and escape the plight of his ancestors.

Hearts opened in February at the Gaiety Theater in New York City. Describing it as "the first authentic screen record of the Old South—throbbing with emotion—epic in its simplicity," a studio ad promised that "All the happy-go-lucky joy of living, laughter and all-embracing gusto of plantation life has been re-created with brilliant realism."[18]

In contrast to the veil of secrecy surrounding the Fox project, MGM assertively broadcast progress on its black-cast production. Studio promotional hype and the resultant prerelease buzz drew attention. But it also created a carnival-like atmosphere that ultimately undermined or, at minimum, muddied public perception of King Vidor's original conception. Vidor, who grew up in Galveston, Texas, had been exposed to black culture as a youth when he met Negro workers at his father's sawmill. "The sincerity and fervor of [the Negro's] religious expression intrigued me, as did the honest simplicity of their sexual drives," he said of his vision. "In many instances the intermingling of these two activities seemed to offer strikingly dramatic content." Vidor's determination and near-zealous commitment to actualizing the dream of authentically portraying the lives and culture of Southern Negroes on-screen was reflected in the fact that he had agreed to reinvest much of his guaranteed salary to assure the picture's completion. Nicholas Schenck, chairman of the board of Loew's, MGM's parent company, finally signed off on the project, saying, "If that's the way you feel about it, I'll let you make a picture about whores."[19]

By the fall of 1928, filming had begun. Vidor had already piqued interest among black actors and journalists, particularly those in the Northeast, when he announced that he would conduct auditions in Northern cities to recruit authentic types for the film. "Black performers fought each other for the good roles in the brief season of Northern city tryouts," wrote Thomas Cripps. "Negroes hurried from New York and Chicago nightclubs, from the ranks of black workers, and from 'on the street' to auditions."[20]

Vidor vigorously courted the black community to ensure the picture's acceptability. James Weldon Johnson, the author and lyricist who was then general director of the NAACP, was consulted, and Harold Garrison, an occasional actor and part-time casting agent for the studios, was brought aboard as background adviser and "assistant director." On location in Texas, Tennessee, and Arkansas, Vidor made more conciliatory nods to the black community, enlisting the aid of Negro church officials, employing a local authority on baptism, and casting members of a local church as extras to enhance authenticity while shooting the picture's crucial baptismal scene. In addition to these interracial overtures, all noted in publicity releases, Vidor readily made himself available to black journalists.

Generally, the black press enthusiastically touted the project. A *New York Amsterdam News* story typified the prerelease buzz. The article opened with a quote from Vidor: "We are trying to do for the Race what we did for the doughboy in the 'Big Parade'—show in a film story a sort of cross-section of an entire people," he said, referring to his own epic 1925 World War I drama, which was hailed as "one of the finest [movies] ever made in Hollywood." Ignoring the imminent release of *Hearts in Dixie,* the reporter hailed Vidor's unfinished project as "the first all-Race film drama in history" and "one of the most elaborate film plays of the year."[21]

Black critics were particularly pleased with the cast, which was primarily selected from the ranks of Negro stage performers. Although Vidor was unable to sign either Paul Robeson or Ethel Waters for the lead roles, he did assemble a cast of outstanding theatrical performers. Daniel L. Haynes (who starred in the New York stage productions of *Rang Tang* and *Show Boat*) and seventeen-year-old Nina Mae McKinney (a dancer who had been featured in the chorus line of *Blackbird of 1928*) were ultimately cast in the central roles; stage comedian Everett McGarrity and blues singer Victoria Spivey were also tapped for key supporting parts.

Haynes contributed to *Hallelujah!*'s early promotion with an article that echoed the black film community's eager anticipation of the picture's release. "Now after years of heart-breaking struggle, yet always years of hope, which have made the Negro eager to express the thoughts in his heart, his chance has come," the former journalist and preacher-turned-actor wrote. "I cannot say what our race owes King Vidor and Metro-Goldwyn-Mayer—there are not words forceful enough for that. 'Hallelujah!' will, as Moses led his people from the wilderness, lead ours from the wilderness of misunderstanding and apathy."[22]

The white press also weighed in, fueling the media frenzy with reports of the cast's exotic behavior on the lot and at location shootings where curious Southerners ogled the unprecedented spectacle of a troupe of Negro actors shooting a highly publicized movie and being treated as professionals by a white director. Dixie reporters often overlooked breaches of Southern race etiquette because they were convinced that Vidor and his Negro crew were set on portraying "the negro living in the environment that he is accustomed to and loves so well." Other journalists, those who had praised Vidor for his attempt to portray authentic Negro life, viewed "the cast on the set as no more than a motley of blacks 'clustered about the card tables, gambling, crapshooting, losing, winning, calling drawly greetings to one another, shuffling nervous dancing feet between scenes.' "[23]

In the latter vein, Louella Parsons, Hollywood's most influential columnist, described the cast as "Dusky belles, tall young black skinned boys, plump mammies and pickaninnies . . . swarming about the Metro-Goldwyn-Mayer lot, giving it the appearance of a California Harlem, or a real 'down south' plantation."[24]

From the outset, *Hallelujah!* was beset by production and cast switches as well as on-set difficulties and intrigues. Unlike the Fox Movietone sound process used for *Hearts,* which permitted recording on location, scenes for *Hallelujah!* were shot without sound, then sent back to Hollywood to be synched at the studio—a meticulous process that severely tested the moviemaking skills of Vidor and his editors. And when the teenage newcomer Nina Mae McKinney replaced the more experienced stage actress Honey Brown as leading lady in the part of the seductive Chick, some black critics protested. According to the film's black musical director, composer Eva Jessye, however, it "was clear from the beginning that Honey Brown was not the type to enact the role of Chick even before Nina Mae appeared on the scene. One has but to see Honey Brown make a gesture, toss her head, pirouette across the floor to realize that she is the modern, sophisticated type of girl who differs not one whit from the white."[25]

The picture's meager pay scale and location shooting in the segregated South also heightened tension on the set, according to Jessye.

"You may believe me when I say that the salaries paid the cast were ridiculous," she wrote in a four-part series of articles that promised to reveal the "unvarnished truth about the salaries, and the conditions under which this pioneer group labored for more than seven months." Jessye, who made "less than one hundred dollars a week," insisted that "it was common knowledge that several leading characters received not more than fifty dollars weekly."

"The whole cast was engaged at a lump sum that one small-sized Hollywood star would consider not half enough to worry along on," she asserted. Still, they put pride aside and "gave all they had to the creation of the picture," hoping that it might "open the way for the Negro in the talking screen."[26]

The cast, however, did object to parts of the script, which was based on Vidor's original story and written by Wanda Tuchock, a white MGM scenario writer "who knew nothing about Negroes." The script initially distributed among the black cast was riddled with references to "darkies" and "niggers." Ironically, while the dialogue would probably not have raised an eyebrow on the set of a gritty twenty-first-century gangster movie purporting to depict real life in the "'hood" or even an irreverent Hollywood comedy like *Barbershop,* the *Hallelujah!* cast was appalled.[27]

While rehearsing dialogue, for instance, William Fountaine, who played the menacing "Hot Shot," reportedly gasped when he saw the suggested line, "A big coon like you ought to be carrying dat donkey 'stid a riddin' him."

"O, my God! You don't mean for me to say that, I know," he reportedly yelled. "Not me. Why man, I wouldn't dare to go back to Harlem."[28]

Although much of the dialogue was altered by the black actors, Jessye concluded that, to "true Southerners" like "Vidor and his scenario writer, Negroes are 'niggers,' and thus it was perfectly natural to express themselves." The hostile reactions of local whites who came to view location shots in the Southern swamps and cotton fields were also "perfectly natural." Both Nina Mae McKinney and Daniel L. Haynes were threatened with violence, and Vidor reportedly refused to let Haynes wander away from the troupe without a guard. "One poor ignorant soul actually pulled a gun on Haynes because he 'had gone to college,'" a contemporary fan magazine reported.[29]

Spectators' anger sometimes erupted into scene-stopping outbursts. During a shoot at a Mississippi cotton gin, for example, the gin's notoriously racist owner seethed when Vidor showed too much consideration for actors toiling in the noonday heat. When Vidor calmly told them to take a break, the "red-neck" Mississippian burst onto the set and yelled, "Come on theah, you niggahs!" He then stared at Vidor "in utter disgust," according to Jessye, "as if to say, 'Watch me and learn how to talk to them.' . . . He shifted a wad of tobacco, spat, and looked evilly and defiantly at the 'Hallelujah' crowd, his eyes saying as plainly as if he had spoken, 'Yes, and you'all is niggers too.'"[30]

The cast persevered, however, ignoring segregated traveling, sleeping, and eating accommodations; the initially self-deprecating dialogue; threats and derogatory jeers from hostile Southern spectators; as well as annoying indignities such as black actors being served smaller, less appetizing lunches than the white crew. The project also survived such internal disasters as Nina Mae McKinney's threat to quit after a grip called her a "nigger" and Daniel L. Haynes's narrow brush with death during filming in a sawmill when a huge saw broke loose and missed him by inches.

If Walter Weems's *Hearts* scenario, intended to highlight Perry's acting talent, was hastily written and somewhat superficial, the plot of *Hallelujah!* was convoluted and steeped in melodramatic conflict. Viewing black folk culture through his own Southern Gothic vision, Vidor produced an intense, brooding portrait of Negro sensuality and religious ritual that was fueled by pulsating spiritual and secular music.

The plot followed the travails of Zeke Johnson (Daniel L. Haynes), a God-fearing tenant farmer who is charmed by the beautiful dance-hall vixen Chick (Nina Mae McKinney). Caught up in the flashy but gritty world of ghetto nightlife, he is lured into a crap game and fleeced by Chick and her lover Hot Shot (William Fountaine). A brawl ensues in which Zeke wrestles a gun away from Hot Shot and accidentally shoots his own brother. Zeke escapes and, driven by guilt, takes to the road as an itinerant preacher. He is so successful and compelling that Chick is drawn to one of his revival meetings and, intoxicated by the frenzied crowd, hypnotic music, and Zeke's fiery oratory, is converted at a mass baptism. Deserting his plain country girl (Victoria Spivey), Zeke again takes up with Chick. But after they run off together and settle into country living with Zeke working in a sawmill, Hot Shot returns to disrupt their lives. Chick leaves with her former lover, and Zeke pursues them. In a final confrontation, Chick dies and Hot Shot is strangled by Zeke. King Vidor's passionate tale of sex, religion, obsession, and murder was amplified by the music of the Dixie Jubilee Singers as well as jazzy secular music. When released, it was easily the most penetrating and controversial portrait of Negro life ever attempted by a major Hollywood studio.

In August, *Hallelujah!* opened at both the Lafayette Theater in Harlem and the Embassy downtown, which roused some protests from blacks. "It is believed by many that the reason for the simultaneous premiere was to keep our people from mingling with the whites on Broadway," J. Winston Harrington wrote in the *Chicago Defender.* The comedian Aubrey Lyles of Miller and Lyles was among those who led a protest against the "Jim Crow" event. Still, the Uptown opening, "Harlem's first world premiere," was a gala affair. Hosted by Bill "Bojangles" Robinson, it featured appearances by cast members as well as Illinois Congressman Oscar De Priest, the first Negro elected to Congress in the twentieth century. "We are standing on the threshold of civil and cultural emancipation in America," De Priest claimed. "Tonight we have seen how far our race has progressed culturally and artistically since the Emancipation Proclamation."[31]

There were dissenters, of course, but when *Hearts* and *Hallelujah!* were initially released, black and white critics generally applauded the movies. It appeared that the pictures might indeed signal the beginning of a new era in black filmmaking.

Opening in February at New York City's Gaiety Theater, *Hearts in Dixie* was hailed by many as a breakthrough film, one of Fox Movietone's most impressive all-talkie pictures. In the *New York Times,* Mordaunt Hall called it "a delightful Movietone production" which "cleverly captured" the "spirit of the Southern negro [*sic*] of a year or so after the Civil War . . . a talking and singing production that is gentle in its mood and truthful in its reflection of those days down yonder in the cornfields." It is a film, he continued, "in which all the voices are modulated and wherein the humor is so effective that laughter was not enough last night. The audience had to applaud."[32]

Most mainstream critics applauded the film's use of the new sound technology, or "the double novelty of Negro players and movietone." Some strung their praise in a net of contemporary stereotypes, saluting the film's depiction of blacks as "lighthearted, ready with its songs, dances and laughter" or nodding to the vivid portrayal of Negroes' "simplicity" and "love of a good time." Others noted both "flashes of their joys and ambitions" and hailed the "dearth of pseudo-Nordic coating." Very few white critics took note of the absence of attention to the oppressive Jim Crow system that kept Nappus and his fold on the bottom rung of the Southern social order.[33]

Black critics were ambivalently congratulatory. In the *Pittsburgh Courier*, Sylvester Russell wrote that *Hearts in Dixie* "was perfect of ancient tradition and shown beautifully on the screen, a vibrate talkie with fine voices in song, music and chorus. Clarence Muse was an artist, but with a touch of Uncle Tom." The *Chicago Defender* review reported that the picture was "novel to be sure, with its Dixie cotton field settings and its complete gathering of darkie players"; while rapping the "slackness in action," it praised a "bit of appreciable dancing by Stepin Fetchit." The *Chicago Whip* preferred Stepin Fetchit's languor to Muse's "overacting," but found "that the picture, in the cotton scenes and acted in the Southern dialect and customs, was degrading." Similarly, in the *Baltimore Afro-American,* Maurice Dancer observed that Hollywood still clung to "the old tradition that the American public still wants to see our people singing in the cotton fields and dancing bare-foot in the sand."[34]

Walter White, who later, as executive secretary of the NAACP, emerged as one of Stepin Fetchit's most outspoken detractors, was among the most vocal black critics of *Hearts.* Clarence Muse, the cast's most respected actor, was among those who stepped forward to counter White's criticisms. "This is a game we must build ourselves into," he argued, suggesting that it was unrealistic to expect Hollywood's first all-black feature to have no stereotypes. He urged Negro fans to support the film and demonstrate enough audience support to justify future investment in black projects. Later, Muse would directly address the underlying problem faced by blacks in Hollywood pictures in *The Dilemma of the Negro Actor,* a 1932 pamphlet in which he discussed the difficulties encountered by performers who wished to display their talents in a serious way for black fans.[35]

Although overwhelmingly positive, the critical response to *Hearts in Dixie* varied considerably, with some pundits questioning and theorizing about its use of sound technology or its handling of black themes such as the fieldworkers' passive acceptance of their grueling, poverty-stricken existence. Others pondered its effect on the future of blacks in films. Concerning the performance of Lincoln Perry (aka Stepin Fetchit), however, consent was nearly unanimous.

The positive reaction to his performance was established early on in a mildly unfavorable *Variety* review of the "slowly paced . . . Southern

Negro study" that singled out the actor's work. "Popularly," the critic wrote, "the entertainment appeal rests in Stepin Fetchit, a funny guy who was the redeeming figure of Fox's 'The Ghost Talks.' "

In the *Times,* Mordaunt Hall cited Fetchit as a comedian ("the sluggard of the tale") whose performance inspired not only laughter but also applause. The *Los Angeles Times* praised the actor's "inimitable work" in the picture. Sylvester Russell, in the *Pittsburgh Courier,* called Perry "a master of naturalness" while chiding him for using "the slang Stepin Fetchit, which could be better applied to horses and dogs." The *Chicago Defender,* in its muted critique of the film, noted the comedian's "appreciable dancing." And after working with Perry, Clarence Muse called the comedian "the greatest artist in the world."[36]

Motion Picture magazine professed that the film was not only "thoroughly successful" and "delightful entertainment," but also one of "the most important contributions to the cinema," and added that "conspicuous in a group of excellent actors are Clarence Muse and a coal-black comic listed on the program as Stepin Fetchit." *Photoplay* placed the film in its "Best Picture of the Month" category and cited Stepin Fetchit as one of five in its "Best Performance of the Month" listing. "At the risk of giving that colored boy, who glories in the classic monicker of Stepin Fetchit, a bigger opinion of himself than he now possesses," the reviewer wrote, "we are going to say that you ought to see that boy throw his feet around in 'Hearts in Dixie.' This is the lad who has usurped the leadership of colored society in cinema circles. He stands outside the theaters in Hollywood and when one of his race goes by he points to himself on the posters and yells: 'Look ahere, big boy, that's me!' " The movie itself, according to *Photoplay*'s critic, "gives you on the screen a grand explosion of plantation life with its joys and sorrows, its ignorance, its superstition and religious frenzy. It's all very real and understandable."[37]

The most admiring review of Perry's performance, however, came from none other than Robert Benchley, the actor, screenwriter, author, Algonquin roundtable wit, and drama critic for both *The New Yorker* and *Life* magazine. "Of course, entirely outside the main story (what there is of it) is the amazing personality of Stepin Fetchit. I see no reason for even hesitating in saying that he is the best actor that the talking movies have produced. His voice, his manner, his timing, everything that he does, is as near to perfection as one could hope to get," Benchley asserted. "When Stepin Fetchit speaks, you are there beside him, one of the great comedians of the screen."[38]

As social and racial attitudes shifted during the next few decades, both black and mainstream critical views of *Hearts* and Fetchit's performance would shift drastically. Typically, revisionists reviews would echo the sentiments expressed by the British film critic Peter Noble in 1948. In retrospect, Noble saw the film as an "ambitious, probably well-meaning pioneer effort" and hailed its introducing the "wholly delightful actor, Clarence Muse" to the screen. His "charming performance, fine dignity, grand voice and noble bearing more than compensate for the appearance of Stepin Fetchit in one of his more nauseating 'lazy but lovable vagabond' parts."[39]

Noble's conflicting appraisal of Perry's performance—"lovable" yet "nauseating"—reflects a dilemma confronted by nearly anyone who watches the film today. The actor's Deep South drawl and lazybones languor are simultaneously funny and unsettling. But if the skewed Old South setting with its distracting stereotypes is momentarily put aside, the brilliance of Perry's portrayal of Gummy is undeniable. *Hearts* is, after all, the picture in which the underlying logic and rebellious nature of his trifling, overtly slothful character is most clearly defined. The old slavery-based pretense of illness or physical malady to avoid insufficiently rewarded, backbreaking labor is established quickly by shots contrasting worn and weary cotton pickers with the jubilation demonstrated at a nighttime celebration where Gummy shucks off his "miseries" and leads the revelers in spirited dance. Gummy, who has spent the day lolling barefoot in a chair, lights up the screen in this and other sequences, revealing a joyousness and energy that is unmistakably associated with his having avoided the day's grueling labor.

In addition, Perry's role offered an unusual opportunity for him to flit between comedy and near-tragedy, both of which he handled masterfully. His acting ability is tested with the sorrow and grief he is required to display as his wife dies. Later, his comic skills emerge as he shrewdly sidesteps work, flirts and sets out to find a new mate, then jousts with his new wife as she cajoles and ultimately forces him to give up his malingering ways.

Finally, for today's viewers, *Hearts* is one of Perry's most accessible movies, since he had not yet totally committed himself to the whining, nearly indecipherable speech pattern that he later made a central part of his cinema characterizations. Here, as Robert Benchley suggested, his timing, movement, and voice are all perfectly synchronized. In scenes where he flirts and playfully raps to Vivian Smith, he even displays a bit of rural smooth-talking rarely seen in his later films. Although Gummy's transformation from fun-loving, trickster-idler to woe-begotten, hardworking field hand is too sudden, in *Hearts* Perry demonstrated that he was an immensely talented comic actor.

With its sultry erotic overtones, fervent religious depictions, and violent clashes, *Hallelujah!* also holds up well for today's viewers. And when it opened in August 1929, reviews were even more glowing than for *Hearts.* Mordaunt Hall reported that it was "a most impressive audible film," comparing its finale with Eugene O'Neill's *Emperor Jones* before straying onto some fatuous observations about humor that issues naturally "unto the negro [*sic*], whether it deals with a hankering after salvation, the dread of water in baptism, the lure of the 'come seven, come 'leven' or the belated marital ceremonies." He was also impressed with the "capital work" of Daniel Haynes, the "clever performance" of Nina Mae McKinney, and King Vidor's evident "familiarity with the ways of the dusky sons of Ham." The *Los Angeles Times* critic thought it "barbaric, weird . . . oddly fascinating and sometimes oddly repellent." Other mainstream critics were less patronizing. The *New York Post* deemed it "truly great," and Richard Watts called the film "one of the most distinguished and exciting motion pictures ever made." The Hollywood film community took note of the rave reviews, and King Vidor received an Academy Award nomination as best director for his efforts.[40]

Some Negro critics objected to Vidor's focus on the black community's sordid side—variously attacking the picture's seamy depictions of black urban life, its focus on "primitive" aspects of black religious fervor and the near-slanderous portrait of a black preacher's yielding to the temptation of the flesh. The black press eagerly reported on the ongoing debate, with columnists heatedly expressing pro and con opinions long after the film's release. In the *Baltimore Afro-American,* for instance, Ralph Matthews ridiculed "the darker brothers" who objected to Vidor's portrait of black life and reported that the Negro audience "laughed long and loud" at a Baltimore screening in 1930. "He realizes that the thing is himself; although it is exaggerated, and can't help laughing at himself," Matthews wrote, adding that "Zeke, the traveling evangelist, was, if anything, an improvement over the swallow-tail jacklegs who inhabit the storefront gospel emporiums along Druid Hill and Pennsylvania Avenues."[41]

Overall, however, most Negro critics echoed the upbeat appraisal offered by boosters like Haynes and Congressman De Priest, hailing the picture's artistic achievement, serious intent, and importance for the future of black participation in Hollywood films. Significantly, W. E. B. Du Bois—editor of the NAACP's *Crisis* magazine and the era's leading black intellectual—endorsed the picture. While dismayed over *Hallelujah!*'s lack of attention to white complicity in the Negro's plight and critical of its "lurking comedy," he praised the "scenes of religious ecstasy," writing that they "rise to magnificent drama, unexcelled in my experience and singularly true to life."

Upon release, the support of eager Negro and curious white audiences resulted in both pictures doing fairly well at the box office. They were not megahits, however, since restricted theater bookings below the Mason-Dixon line kept them from doing top-dollar business. Still, for blacks the promotional clamor, and the completion and generally positive reception of the films, ignited further expectations. Many critics and intellectuals urged Hollywood to continue the effort to produce serious all-black-cast movies. They envisioned Hollywood films that not only showcased top black stars, but also offered multilevel depictions that ventured beyond comedy, song, and dance to engage more varied and complex aspects of Negro life. That optimism was soon doused.

In part, Hollywood's failure to follow through on the promise of *Hearts* and *Hallelujah!* derived from the Great Depression and the financial crisis that rocked America's economy after the stock market crash of October 1929. Like nearly every other enterprise, during the early 1930s the Hollywood film industry was forced to tighten reins. Shooting schedules, salaries, ticket prices, and office budgets were cut. "Negroes, in such a shabby corner even in good times," a film historian wrote, "became the first victims of the rollback of production induced by the Great Depression." Reaffirming the old adage "Last hired, first fired" as venues and profits shrunk, "the studios dropped blacks." Moreover, as studio heads assumed even more control in an attempt to assure profitability, projects were streamlined and molded to appeal to traditionally safe and sound markets.[42]

Unfortunately for the black film community, black-cast pictures were not only still viewed as controversial and risky, but they also had the inherent problem of limited bookings in the South. Negro audiences' anticipation of "great triumphs for the dark-skinned artists on the audible screen" had already begun to fade.

And by May 1930, an article in the *Baltimore Afro-American* would assert that the "advent of a new era" hailed by *Hallelujah!* and *Hearts in Dixie* had ended. "With the exception of a few minor shorts, no move is being contemplated by the big motion pictures concerns toward the making of feature pictures starring Negroes," the report claimed. Admitting that some attributed the situation to a "prejudice on the part of motion pictures officials," the story ultimately placed blame with "Southern attitudes toward the Negro." The accusation was supported by a long and, given the times, surprisingly candid statement from an unnamed studio executive.

> It is thoughtless as well as unfair to brand the motion picture companies as prejudiced because they are turning out no more Negro pictures. We are in the game to make money, not to make friends or enemies. We produce whatever it pays to produce, regardless of color or creed of the subject. In order to realize adequate profit on a production distribution must be nation-wide. It does not suffice that the East, West and North accept Negro pictures, and the South refuses to accept pictures wherein the Negro is starred. . . .
>
> The story of the picture has no bearing on the situation . . . even the Octavus Roy Cohen pictures are rejected by the South. I understand that twelve Cohen stories were contracted for by a well known company. The first "short" went over very well. On the second one the profits dropped approximately fifty per cent. . . .
>
> It is a deplorable state of affairs, but the South is the South and will tolerate no representation of the Negro as independent, well-dressed,

> handling money, in a position of dignity . . . in any case above the depths of ignorance, subjugation, and poverty which they consider his place, and where they have apparently determined to keep him.[43]

The anonymous source in the *Afro-American* story shunted all responsibility for curtailed production of all-black features to Southern racism, but two weeks later the *California Eagle* suggested that for at least one studio Negro actors' unruly behavior was at issue. An item in the paper's "Theatricals" column reported that a Fox studio executive "very positively declared that his organization had had enough of colored casts in the making of 'Hearts in Dixie' and would not attempt any further experiments with an entire colored unit!" Although the picture was admittedly financially successful and had been shown "in all parts of the country" with no "adverse criticism," the article continued, "Fox refuses to make further pictures of the kind."[44]

The much-ballyhooed new era of major-studio black-cast feature films had stalled. At the studios, executives resumed doling out cookie-cutter servile and/or comic-relief roles in integrated films and accelerated production of musical shorts in which black performers played themselves. "There is no indication that Negroes will be cast in any but the usual roles," a black entertainment writer concluded in the spring of 1930. It would be six years before Warner Brothers Pictures began production of a new black-cast feature, *The Green Pastures.*[45]

As Hollywood returned to traditional business as usual, the anticipated rise to stardom of featured players from *Hearts* and *Hallelujah!*—with one prominent exception—was also diverted.

Daniel L. Haynes, who had been touted by both the black and white press as a talented actor and singer, was able to garner only small, sometimes uncredited roles in a half dozen pictures after *Hallelujah!* His next screen appearance was in the minor role of a death-row convict in *The Last Mile* (1932), a prison melodrama starring Preston Foster. And in 1935, reunited with director King Vidor, he played the house servant William Veal who was pitted against the rebellious field-worker Cato (Clarence Muse) in an Old South epic that starred Margaret Sullavan and Walter Connolly. His last film appearance was in the role of a taxi driver in *Fury* (1936), an exploration of small-town injustice directed by Fritz Lang and starring Spencer Tracy.

Nina Mae McKinney also had her difficulties in Hollywood. Studios preferred heftier black women to serve as comic foils. As with such glamorous black actresses as Carolynne Snowden who preceded her or Lena Horne who followed, McKinney did not fit that rigidly stereotyped on-screen image.

Still, during the early thirties, she was briefly embraced by the Hollywood crowd. "I wouldn't hardly know there was any difference in our color," she gushed to a reporter. "Everyone is jes' wonderful to me. I'm invited to all the movie stars' homes."

A furor arose in 1930, however, when a *Motion Picture Classic* article alleged that she had turned her back on her own people. "I'm nice to them, and I speak to them on the street and everything. But you have to be so careful not to get common. If you start going out with them, pretty soon they think they're just as big as you are," she reportedly said. The article also portrayed the actress as "primitive, joyous, greedy. Crazy for admiration. Crazy for money. Crazy for men."

McKinney bluntly denied the allegations that she had rejected her own race and that she was man-crazy, but confirmed her ambitious nature, insisting that "I don't like men. I've got my mind on jes' one thing—mah career. I want to make a lot of money, and take care of my mother and my future." As predicted by the fan magazine reporter, however, McKinney's filmland stardom was short-lived.[46]

After her role as Chick, the sultry actress signed a highly publicized five-year contract with MGM but worked in only three feature films during its duration. She was showcased in a lavish production number called "Harlem Madness" in the musical comedy *They Learned About Women* (1930) and was cast as a waitress who befriends a doomed, exiled white hooker in *Safe in Hell* (1931), a melodrama in which Clarence Muse and Noble Johnson also had minor roles. In *Reckless* (1935), which starred Jean Harlow and William Powell, she was seen briefly in a minor role as a singer.

Although she appeared in several musical shorts during the early thirties—most notably in *Pie, Pie Blackbird* (1932) with Eubie Blake and the Nicholas Brothers—she left the film colony frustrated in 1935 and pursued a career in Europe. Touring with her own cabaret act, she was often billed as the "Black Garbo." She was also featured in several stage productions and costarred with Paul Robeson in the *Sanders of the River,* a seminal English film released in 1935. When war broke out in the late thirties, she returned to the States, where she starred on the club circuit and appeared in nearly a dozen independently produced black-cast race films. In 1949, when McKinney returned to Hollywood to take a supporting role in *Pinky* (a somewhat controversial "passing" melodrama, which starred Jeanne Crain as a light-skinned Negro and featured Ethel Waters as her grandmother), her once beguiling beauty and sultriness had lost their luster. McKinney successfully carved out a career as a singer and featured player in independent black films, but the motion-picture stardom that she so desperately sought never materialized.[47]

Clarence Muse, a writer and composer as well as an actor, had a longer and more productive Hollywood film career than any of the 1929 black-cast picture stars, appearing in nearly 150 films from 1929 to 1979. As one of Hollywood's most enduring character actors, his roles ranged from a featured part as "Nigger Jim" in *Huckleberry Finn* (1931) to supporting roles in *Porgy and Bess* (1959), *Buck and the Preacher* (1972) with Sidney Poitier and Harry Belafonte, *Car Wash* (1976) with Richard Pryor, to his last appearance in *The Black Stallion* (1979). During an interview filmed just before his death in 1979, Muse attributed his longevity to a willingness to take on supporting roles. Hollywood stars usually enjoyed only short-lived popularity, he claimed, but there was always a need for character actors. In his 1948 book *The Negro in Films,* Peter Noble wrote that Muse was "one of the outstanding character actors in Hollywood—a man who ranks with the Lionel Barrymores, Frank Morgans and Hume Cronyns."

Despite his versatility as screenwriter, playwright, and composer and his longevity as an actor, Muse never achieved true star or celebrity rank in Hollywood. Throughout his career, he distanced himself from the film colony's hoopla and glitter, working quietly as a dependable screen presence as well as behind the scenes in various capacities. He was also an active lobbyist for black equality in the Hollywood system and a staunch defender of black actors who were criticized for accepting servile roles in the thirties and forties.[48]

Of the *Hearts* and *Hallelujah!* stars, only Lincoln Perry rose to prominence as a featured box-office draw in Hollywood pictures.

Perry would ride the crest of his rave reviews in *Hearts* to unprecedented popularity as a black film actor. By the spring of 1929, the cocky but ostensibly pious and race-conscious vaudevillian and entertainment reporter had been reborn as the unpredictable cinema star and celebrity Stepin Fetchit. For much of the next decade, "Step," as most of his friends and close associates called him, would reign as the most controversial, enigmatic, and highly paid black performer in Hollywood.

CHAPTER SEVEN

Stepin Fetchit's role as Gummy in *Hearts in Dixie* established his nationwide motion picture fame, but he had begun exhibiting the prickly temperament and flamboyance commonly associated with the Jazz Age's most popular film stars months before the movie opened. His behavior after the film's release, therefore, did not come as a surprise to many of Central Avenue's regulars.

Despite frequent sanctimonious calls for professional discretion and piety in his *Chicago Defender* column, Fetchit had established a reputation among the Stroll's late-night revelers. The Negro actors, musicians, entertainers, showbiz hangers-on and hustlers who set the tone for the Stroll's sporting life knew him as one of its flashiest, most glib players—an aggressive, wily, if somewhat moody and enigmatic hell-raiser who frequently haunted after-hours joints until dawn. Moreover, it was no secret that during his early vaudeville days the lean, sleepy-eyed actor's personal behavior had flirted with and frequently slipped beyond the line of propriety.

On the Avenue, Fetchit had a reputation as an aggressive, charming, if egocentric bon vivant who was as quick-tempered as he was quick-witted. Having fended for himself since his teens, he was well versed in the ways of hustling to survive in a segregated society and, like many of the era's Negroes, had honed and developed a deceptive trickster manner designed to outwit or disarm adversaries. During the fall of 1928, with his motion-picture star swiftly rising, however, he seemingly tossed caution to the wind and openly vented the less inhibited, outspoken, side of his personality. His outbursts and demands for preferential treatment increased dramatically. The twenty-six-year-old actor was emerging as Central Avenue's most temperamental, extravagant, and notorious Bad Boy as well as one of its most insistent and colorful Romeos.

By mid-1928, Central Avenue's reputation as Brown Broadway, the center of black entertainment and nightlife on the West Coast as well as the heart of Los Angeles's Negro community, was also peaking. The newest jewel on the Avenue's growing chain of classy venues was the Somerville Hotel (later renamed the Dunbar) at the corner of Central and 41st Street.

Envisioned and financed by John Alexander Somerville—a Negro dentist and businessman who like other prominent black artists and leaders had been consistently denied lodging at segregated hotels in downtown Los Angeles—the four-story, one-hundred-room establishment opened its doors in June. It was one of the few first-class hotels west of the Mississippi that accepted nonwhite guests. Among its amenities were a barber shop, a beauty parlor, a pharmacy, and a flower shop. The lobby "was decorated with murals, tapestries and exquisite furnishings," and a patio with a gushing fountain faced the 41st Street entrance. Its dining room, which included a balcony for an orchestra, seated nearly a hundred diners. The hotel, often called the "colored Ritz," opened in time to host the 1928 NAACP national convention; James Weldon Johnson, Charles Chesnutt, and W. E. B. Du Bois were among the prominent early guests. The elegant showplace, which featured many of the era's top race performers in its lounge, became a central meeting place for affluent Negro residents as well as for entertainers and celebrated visitors.[1]

After the stock market crash of 1929, Somerville was forced to sell the hotel; it was bought by a group of blacks headed by Louis Lomax and renamed in honor of the poet and author Paul Laurence Dunbar. During the thirties, its popularity again soared; blacks often proudly described it as a cross between the Cotton Club and the Waldorf Astoria. Over the years, its main lounge would feature such nationally renowned black artists as Fats Waller, Herb Jeffries, Duke Ellington, Louis Armstrong, Billie Holiday, Cab Calloway, and Count Basie. Stepin Fetchit was among the first celebrities to reside at the original

Somerville Hotel; during the fall of 1929, he reportedly rented a "suite" with "extra rooms for secretary and chauffeur."[2]

The Somerville also stimulated the growth of Negro-owned businesses and hastened southern expansion of the black community along Central Avenue. An immediate result of its presence was the opening of the Apex Club, which the saxophonist Marshall Royal described as "probably the most exclusive, classy club that ever was on Central Avenue." The Apex was opened next to the Somerville at 4015 Central by the drummer and bandleader Curtis Mosby during the fall of 1928. Its "Grand Opening" featured Carolynne Snowden and the big-band sound of Mosby's Dixieland Blue Blowers. Although the club was a bit pricey for ordinary Central Avenue residents, it soon became a favorite among the Negro upper middle class, both local and visiting black entertainers, and whites from the movie colony. "It drew all the notables from Hollywood," Royal attested, among them, "Fatty Arbuckle, the Talmadge Sisters," as well as popular Western stars "Tom Mix, Buck Jones, and Hoot Gibson."[3]

While the Apex was a gathering place for blacks and whites, there were restrictions on public intermingling at the club. "Strict etiquette," for instance, was observed regarding interracial dancing according to the white *Photoplay* journalist Herbert Howe. Explaining why he declined to accept an offer to dance with Nina Mae McKinney when interviewing her at the club, Howe lightly scoffed at the segregated policy, writing, "My complexion was off, but what with my deepening coat of tan and a natural kink in my hair it won't be long, hey, hey!"[4]

The club prospered for several years, but the stock market crash had begun to take its toll on nearly all Americans, and the black community, its businesses and entertainers, were among the hardest hit. "Admitting their white brothers have been caught in the year of theatrical depression and nation-wide employment," *Variety* reported, "the Negro show producers, theater operators and players have apparently been caught deeper, though being less in numbers."[5]

Times were so bad, Groucho Marx once quipped, that "the pigeons started feeding the people in Central Park." Along the Stroll, dwindling crowds and the growing number of locks and bolts appearing on the doors of previously thriving clubs and businesses signaled the impact of the financial collapse. As the bright lights dimmed, most local performers had to scramble to find work. And by the fall of 1930, gossip about the imminent closing of the Los Angeles Apex began circulating. Describing the Avenue's plight, the *California Eagle* columnist Harry Levette observed, "For months with Nite Clubs dark and half the shops closed, the famous block where formerly you could stand still and see all the gay fraternity, resembled the 'Valley and the Shadows' of gloom."[6]

Ultimately, the financial crunch forced Mosby to sell most of his interest in the Los Angeles club in 1931, but he opened a second Apex club in San Francisco within the year. Back in Los Angeles, the old Apex was reopened under new ownership as the Club Alabam in September. Shortly afterward, the irrepressible ex-heavyweight boxing champion Jack Johnson was hired to manage a nearby cabaret. Johnson was no novice at running nightclubs. He had opened the Club Deluxe at the corner of 142nd Street and Lenox Avenue in Harlem in 1920, and, when mobster Owney Madden took over the cabaret and reopened it as the Cotton Club, Johnson stayed on to manage the famed speakeasy for a time. The ex-champ, who was also an amateur cellist and bass fiddler, was one of Central Avenue's most charismatic and beloved personalities. And a few months after the Alabam opened, he was tapped to preside over the Showboat, the Dunbar Hotel's new cabaret and lounge. With Johnson as impresario, that club and the new Alabam helped revitalize the area near Central Avenue and 41st Street. Several smaller nightspots were also attracting crowds, and soon the area emerged as one of the Avenue's most vibrant centers. To insiders, it was known simply as "The Block."[7]

It appears that "Brown Broadway will take on its old name and aspect," Levette wrote of the revival. "The dizzy white lights are dancing daringly again, lightsome, lilting, laughter is tinkling from lips curved merrily in happy faces of white, brown, cream or rich orange as the gay, many colored gowns of women of all races flutter like so many tropical butterflies."[8]

In addition to its big band and chorus line, the Club Alabam continued to headline the era's best black entertainers. "Everybody who was anybody in the thirties played at the Club Alabam," Haven Johnson, a Los Angeles–born organist and songwriter, recalled. Like the adjacent Dunbar, the Alabam survived the thirties financial crisis. The Block also remained one of the Avenue's most popular areas throughout the thirties, attracting integrated crowds that included both working- and middle-class Negroes as well as black entertainers and Hollywood's most celebrated stars. According to Avenue lore, it was the comedian and film star W. C. Fields who, after a night of heavy drinking at the Alabam, "integrated" the Dunbar Hotel when he passed out and slept in the lobby.[9]

As one might expect, Fetchit was a regular visitor to the Block. After the Alabam opened and Johnson took charge of the Showboat, the actor was among the clubs' most famous celebrity regulars. During the twenties and thirties, he and Johnson often hung out together.

"We was both celebrities," the actor said, "and I used to sit in his corner when he was fighting." Fetchit claimed that they "became friends" after Johnson discovered that they had been taught by the same priest. "Jack Johnson had noble ideas," Fetchit said, referring to Johnson's demands for equal treatment and his flouting of Jim Crow laws. "We had no inferiority complex," the actor continued. "Jack always wanted to show that all men were created equal, so he goes to Newport News society and married a white woman out of the society register."[10]

In the early twentieth century, Paul Robeson, Jack Johnson, and Stepin Fetchit were, for various segments of the society, the most notorious of America's Negro celebrities. An All-American football player, Columbia University law graduate, Phi Beta Kappa, and preeminent actor and concert performer, Robeson was ostracized, blackballed, and for a time exiled by white America because of his outspoken stance against segregation and advocacy of socialist ideology. Johnson, the first black heavyweight champion, would inspire America's search for "the great white hope" not only because of his position atop the boxing hierarchy, but also for his irreverent mocking of the nation's miscegenation laws and refusal to adopt the humble demeanor that the country expected of Negro celebrities. Despite the solace that Fetchit's screen character may have provided the mainstream, the actor's lavish lifestyle, decidedly uppity attitude with studio executives, and demands for what was previously "white only" star treatment forged an ambivalent love-hate relationship with both whites and blacks and kept him at the center of a media firestorm.

Still, for some, the Fetchit-Johnson friendship seemed bizarre. The two celebrities, however, had much more in common than readily meets the eye. Most obviously, they shared a knack for self-promotion, put-on, and an apparent pleasure in slyly twitting mainstream America's mores and the media's willingness to publicize, if not necessarily swallow, their most outlandish tongue-in-cheek tales of Negro bravura, witlessness, or chicanery. Their high self-regard, disrespect for the societal limitations imposed on Negroes, crafty manipulation of the press, fondness for tweaking America's racist consciousness, and love of the sporting life and lavish living, also bonded them. Had their conversations been recorded as they savored their own sly, Brer Rabbit–like flouting of Jim Crow restrictions and mocking of bigotry during late-night sprees at the Apex Club, the Showboat, or other Avenue hot spots, an earthier, more colorful chapter in African America's clandestine struggle against segregation might have been unveiled. Unfortunately, it was primarily their escapades and public scandals that made headlines.

In the 1920s and '30s, Negro readers often turned to the *California Eagle* and Harry Levette's popular "Behind the Scenes with Harry" column for updates on Central's nightclub scene as well as activities on studio lots. Levette was among a very short list of Negro writers with free access to the studios and emerged as one of the black press's most revealing sources for the latest gossip and scuttlebutt. Most often he focused on the positive achievements of black performers, but he could dish dirt with the kind of titillating spin that now, some seventy-five years later, is regularly employed in the pages of the *National Inquirer,* in the *New York Post*'s "Page Six" column, or on *Access Hollywood* or E! television. His column, which with slight revisions also appeared in the *Chicago Defender* and the *Afro-American* in Baltimore, was frequently peppered with spicy reports on the off-stage or off-camera doings of the Stroll's race professionals.

"Listen my children and you shall hear some wild tales that make your 'Scene Peeper' blush," he once promised readers. "Dark doings after dark! Weird parties that out-Hollywood Hollywood—fights—mistreated jobs—ofays, browns, blacks and yellows, strange jealousies, zipping cars, faithless hubbys—trifling wives—curling 'hop' smoke—

'queer' love affairs, etc. Oh boy, this goin' to be good when your shocked 'Scene Peeper' exhibits the latest and choicest 'key-hole reel,' calls names, rings door-bells, and points out places. Stand by for a load of this."[11]

As the "Scene Peeper," Levette's coverage of black performers often mirrored contemporary mainstream tabloids and fan mags that hyped and fed off the escapades of the movie colony's white stars. Levette's column frequently included items about the fast-rising comic actor Stepin Fetchit.

"Although we were friends, Step used to feel mistreated when this column condemned his misbehavior back in 1928 and made 'hot copy' of his frequent escapades," Levette later wrote of the period. "In fact he consulted Atty. Curtis Taylor concerning the matter. 'Should I sue that guy Levette for slander or should I beat him up?' he asked. But Taylor with a wise twinkle in his eye answered the angry star thus: 'Well I doubt if he has enough gold and bonds for you to sue him, and as he is pretty husky, you might have bad luck trying to beat him up, so Step, if I were you I'd just be a good fellow and all the writers will let you alone.' "[12]

Fetchit did not attempt to sue or confront Levette, but neither did he adhere to his attorney's advice and curtail his increasingly unpredictable behavior. The young actor was already raising eyebrows and frequently receiving bad press for his tardiness on movie sets and penchant for speeding along Central Avenue and around the Fox lot in one of his three new roadsters; in addition, his comments about preferring to appear in films without other black performers had rankled some race professionals. And like many of the era's prominent male entertainers (as well as some females), black and white, he was particularly fond of partying and cavorting with the stream of beautiful, mostly young and light-skinned Negro chorus girls who migrated to Los Angeles with dreams of motion-picture or stage stardom. During the spring of 1929, he publicly expressed what appeared to be heartfelt remorse over the conflict between his fondness for the sporting life and his desire to be a good Catholic.

"Ah'm spoiled, been sportin' round, foolin' round with women, been a little thug," he told *Photoplay* writer Herbert Howe. "Full of impurities, yes-suh. You know—messin' round with women an' all that . . . understand what Ah'm talkin' 'bout?

"You see Ah'm a good church member. When Ah marries it's for *life.* An' on the other hand, Ah can't be goin' round committin' impurities. It's hard, it sure is hard. But nuthin' is impossible to the Lord," he bemoaned. "Ah'm pure now . . . but will Ah be? That's the question. Ah've been pure before but Ah went back. If Ah goes back again Ah'm goin' to marry."[13]

His avowal of distaste for the good life was no doubt tongue-in-cheek, but marriage apparently loomed as a major consideration in the actor's life during that time. In the same interview, he admitted that he had recently been engaged. "But Ah ain't engaged no more," he lamented. "I dunno. Ah says it wasn't intended."[14]

Fetchit was even briefly linked romantically to Nina Mae McKinney in 1929. But that highly volatile match had quickly soured. "He proposed to me," McKinney told a reporter. "But he don't save his money. He says the Holy Virgin will take care of him. I say, 'Ya? . . . The Holy Virgin is goin' turn on you some day, big boy!' "[15]

In addition, during the fall of 1928, the actor had met and apparently became involved on more than a casual basis with an aspiring seventeen-year-old entertainer who had recently arrived in Los Angeles. The affair lasted about six months. But neither the relationship nor the actor's alleged verbal promises to teenager Yvonne Butler—who was later variously described as a chorus girl, movie extra, and beauty contest winner—were initially widely publicized. Months later, however, his former relationship with Butler would ignite the first major scandal of the actor's career.

Although working on his feature role as Gummy in *Hearts* and a bit part as a janitor in another Fox film, *Thru Different Eyes*—a courtroom drama involving murder and infidelity that starred Warner Baxter—by early 1929, Step's prodigal ways were gaining momentum. During this time, the actor began establishing a reputation for high jinks and high living that quickly became part of Hollywood lore. His extravagance and unruly conduct stirred criticism from the Negro press and ridicule from many whites.

The *New York Times* would later describe it as a "gaudy African style which makes the antics of Brutus Jones [from *The Emperor Jones*] pale into reticence by comparison." Fetchit defended his behavior, suggesting that successful Negro stars were entitled to the same wealth and lifestyle enjoyed by their white counterparts. Years later, an *Ebony* magazine article supported the actor's contention. The "gaudy exhibitionism, which became standard in Fetchit's life as a top movie star," the anonymous writer claimed, was "an accepted part of the pattern that made what was perhaps Hollywood's most colorful era."[16]

The writer's characterization of Fetchit's exorbitance as well as the social background in which it occurred was both accurate and revealing. When the popularity of silent pictures soared in the mid-teens, the fledgling movie industry gave birth to a new American phenomenon, the screen idol. Early filmmakers had begun by shooting novelty scenes focused on ordinary, mostly anonymous, real-life people. But with the introduction of scripted and edited silent pictures, actors—previously considered little more than incidental hired help—were thrust to the forefront.

"Overnight the obscure and somewhat disreputable movie performers found themselves propelled to adulation, fame and fortune," the former child actor Kenneth Anger wrote in *Hollywood Babylon*. "They were the new royalty, the Golden People." And from the late teens to the early thirties, the "Golden Age" of Hollywood films, many of the nouveau riche performers who rose to the top adopted lives of spectacular opulence. Dizzy with their escalating popularity and wealth or, perhaps, fearful that their sudden luminance might just as quickly fade, some plunged themselves into lives of flighty, near-egomaniacal extravagance. Their wealth and heady sense of power, moral license, and untouchability as America's newest and most sought-after idols were openly flaunted.

In part, their rebellious behavior was bolstered by the era's chaotic social setting.

Following World War I, America was consumed by a wave of conservatism. Involvement in a foreign war initially intensified the country's desire to preserve its traditional, rural ideals, and, in the late teens and early twenties, the nation struggled desperately to reaffirm Puritan roots that were being threatened by increased industrialization and migration to the cities. The resurgence of the Ku Klux Klan, the appointment of J. Edgar Hoover as the director of the newly created antiradical division of the Justice Department (1919), and passage of the Volstead Act, which enforced the Eighteenth Amendment (1920), prohibiting the sale and consumption of alcohol, were signs of the time.

"The genteel middle-class cultural structure, which had ruled over American ideals for nearly two centuries," one historian wrote, "raised itself to new heights of rhetoric, energy, repression and control."[17]

But America's mood was shifting. Writers, artists, scholars, and bohemians of various persuasions began openly criticizing postwar repression and the ideals on which it was based. This opposing trend was encouraged by innovations in mass production (Ford's assembly lines), advances in transportation (affordable automobiles and airplane travel), and electronic technology (the advent of commercial radio and sound movies) as well as accelerated urban migration and a related push for women's rights and distrust of rural ideals. Led by intellectual dissenters like H. L. Mencken, the move toward a less parochial, if more materialistic, era quickly gathered momentum. The designations "Jazz Age" and "Roaring Twenties" reflect the enthusiastic way in which much of America eagerly embraced a less inhibited urban lifestyle and modern outlook.

"The decade of the nineteen twenties was at one and the same time the gaudiest, the saddest, and the most misinterpreted era in modern American history," the historian Bruce Catton wrote.[18]

A period of tremendous change, it was defined in many ways by its excesses and the urgent quest for new moods of personal expression. Perhaps the most striking example of the latter involved the shifting role of women. Inspired by innovators like Amelia Earhart, who flew solo across the Atlantic, and Margaret Sanger, who risked public infamy by promoting birth control, women of the era demanded liberation from Victorian-era constraints. Lipstick, bobbed hair, one-piece bathing suits, short skirts, public smoking and drinking were all gaining acceptance in urban America during the twenties. In many circles, even discreet promiscuity no longer meant ostracization from polite society. On the screen, whereas Mary Pickford and Lillian Gish had represented restraint, purity, and innocence, the twenties' heartthrob Clara Bow brimmed with youthful rebellion. Known as the "It Girl" and described as "the hottest jazz babe in films," the bubbly, outspoken Bow captured the era's devil-may-care attitude. She and vamps like Theda Bara and, later, Jean Harlow set the tone for the flappers who came to symbolize the Roaring Twenties.

In addition, the era was marked by an obsession with celebrity and the glamorous lives of the rich, famous, and, frequently, notorious. "The most famous people in America were a strange assortment—movie stars, gangsters, Channel swimmers, professional athletes, imaginative murderers, and eccentrics of high and low degree," Bruce Catton wrote. "Before 1920, moving-picture actors and actresses were outsiders; now they were at the top of the ladder, living in the limelight as no one ever did before or since."[19]

Perhaps not before, but by the end of the twentieth century, a similar obsession swept America. Television shows documenting the lives of the rich and famous flourished. The exploits and excesses of such celebrity athletes, entertainers, and film stars as Britney Spears, Madonna, Robert Downey, Jr., P. Diddy, J. Lo, Phil Spector, Kobe Bryant, Eminem, and Michael Jackson, or self-anointed celebrities like the Hilton sisters or previously anonymous reality-show participants, dominated the headlines and gossip columns. In like manner, gangsta rap and the adulation of real-and-quasi-thugs-turned-entertainers inspired a new wave of popular homage to attitude, rebellion, and irreverence within the culture.

The phenomenon, however, was unprecedented in the twenties. And, for a primarily rural American audience reared on homespun, small-town values, it initially evoked awe if not outright shock. Prohibition and the popularity of illegal alcohol catapulted high-profile gangsters like Al Capone into the era's spotlight; their fame and notoriety would later inspire a raft of gangster movies with tough-guy heroes played by such actors as Edward G. Robinson, George Raft, James Cagney, and Humphrey Bogart. In sports, the prodigious feats and rowdy behavior of baseball's swaggering "King of Swat," Babe Ruth, would quickly establish him as a national icon. (When questioned about why he was paid more money than the President, Ruth shot back, "I hit more home runs than he does.") Still, it was Hollywood's incandescent new stars—with their bigger-than-life on-screen presence, as well as their opulence, glamour, and sometimes reckless libertinism off-screen—that most intrigued Americans.

Douglas Fairbanks, Jr., Lillian Gish, Wallace Reid, Clara Bow, Roscoe "Fatty" Arbuckle, Theda Bara, Rudolph Valentino, Harold Lloyd, Buster Keaton, Mary Pickford, John Gilbert, Gloria Swanson, W. C. Fields, Greta Garbo, and Charlie Chaplin are names that provide a representative short list of the preeminent twenties screen stars. And at the height of their careers, nearly all inhabited a world of ostentatious splendor befitting royalty: a bevy of Negro or, even more preferred, Filipino servants; imported wines and champagne (at the height of Prohibition); flashy jewelry and couture fashions; and the finest chauffeur-driven automobiles—Valentino's custom-built Voisin tourer, Mae Murray's canary-yellow Pierce-Arrow or white Rolls-Royce, Gloria Swanson's leopard-skin-upholstered Lancia, Fatty Arbuckle's custom-made $25,000 Pierce-Arrow—were accepted symbols of their success.

Their palatial estates and home furnishings reflected similar glitz and cupidity. "The Hollywood in-crowd," Kenneth Anger wrote, "whooped it up in an atmosphere of staggering luxury." There were "Spanish-Moorish dream castles" like Valentino's Falcon Lair, with its all-black-marble-and-leather bedroom; Marion Davies's hundred-room oceanfront Santa Monica home, with its all-gold salon, movie theater, and vast "marble bridge-spanned" swimming pool; Barbara La Marr's "all-onyx bathroom" and huge sunken bath with gold fixtures; Harold Lloyd's forty-room fortress with fountains to rival Tivoli; Gloria Swanson's black marble bathroom and golden bathtub; Tom Mix's "rainbow-colored fountain in his dining room"; John Gilbert's fleet of boats (his schooner, the *Temptress;* his motorboat, the *Vampire;* his sailboat, the *Harpie;* his dingy, the *Witch*) and "his Cossack servants and private balalaika orchestra"; Clara Bow's exotic Chinese Den; and Charles Ray's "solid gold doorknobs."[20]

The riches, glamour, and gay, uninhibited lives of Hollywood's newly crowned elite provided an unending source of material for such high-profile Los Angeles–based journalists and provocateurs as Louella Parsons and Hedda Hopper or, in New York, the powerful, fiery, often vindictive Walter Winchell, who many contend initiated the so-called culture of celebrity. Along with lesser-known contemporary gossipmongers and muckrakers, they built lucrative careers monitoring the conduct of the era's most powerful, wealthy, and famous personalities—glamorizing their successes, exposing their mishaps and trysts, and headlining the slightest hint of scandal.

Scandal, of course, was the hottest commodity for the tabloids. And during the Jazz Age, banner headlines broadcast a steady stream of celebrity encounters involving adultery, illegal drug and alcohol use, suicides, and mysterious deaths.

The most famous and, perhaps, most lurid of the era's scandals occurred in San Francisco at a celebration for Fatty Arbuckle, the 260-pound silent-film-comedy star, who had signed a new $3 million contract with Paramount. In September 1921, on the third day of a boozy weekend party in a luxurious hotel suite, the screams of twenty-five-year-old actress and model Virginia Rappe brought friends running to the bedroom where she had retired with Arbuckle. After the drunken Arbuckle stumbled from the room, the bruised, hysterical actress was rushed to a hospital. Five days later, she died of "internal injuries."

Arbuckle was jailed and brought to trial in November, as rumors about drunken orgies, rape, and murder swept the country. After two trials resulted in hung juries, the actor was acquitted in April 1922. Still, Paramount put his unreleased films on the shelf and canceled his hefty contract; he occasionally found work as a writer and director, but his acting career was over. A virtual outcast in Hollywood, he turned to alcohol and, in 1933, died disillusioned and broke in New York.

The Arbuckle incident was among a series of scandals that rocked the film colony in the twenties and ultimately led to the hiring of a watchdog, Will H. Hays, to redress Hollywood's image and calm the public outcry over decency and morality. Hays was appointed president of the Motion Picture Producers and Distributors of America in 1922 and charged with overseeing both the on-screen content of motion pictures and the off-screen behavior of the stars. Despite his announced intention of ridding films of improprieties and inserting morality clauses into the contracts of actors, very little changed immediately. Producers and directors made token efforts to comply with the Hays dictates concerning picture content, but during the remainder of the decade it was generally business (and pleasure) as usual with regard to the stars' private lives.

Their extravagant lifestyles and not infrequent indiscretions and capers continued to dominate the pages of tabloids, the gossip columns of major newspapers, and such fan magazines as *Photoplay, American Film,* and *Screenland.* The era's most publicized scandals involved some of Hollywood's biggest names, among them the 1922 murder of famed director William Desmond Taylor and the discovery of photographs and other evidence suggesting that drug use and his simultaneous affairs with screen stars Mabel Normand and Mary Miles Minter may have provoked the foul play; the disclosure of megastar Wallace Reid's morphine addiction and his subsequent death in a private sanitarium at age thirty in 1923; Charlie Chaplin's disastrous marriages to sixteen-year-olds Mildred Harris (1918) and Lillita McMurray (1924) and his ongoing fascination with teenage girls; the alleged cover-up surrounding the death of director Thomas H. Ince on William Randolph Hearst's yacht in 1924, and the insinuation that it was connected to a botched attempt to shoot Chaplin, who was reportedly having an affair with Hearst's companion, Marion Davies; screen idol Rudolph Valentino's marriages to two alleged lesbians and questions surrounding his masculinity and the cause of his untimely death at age thirty-one in 1926; rumors alleging wild orgies and rampant promiscuity by the "It Girl," Clara Bow, which were reinforced in a detailed account (sold to tabloids by the actress's private secretary in 1930) of a torrid rendezvous in the Chinese Den of Bow's Beverly Hills home.

"Oh, the parties we used to have!" Gloria Swanson said of the era. "In those days the public wanted us to live like kings and queens. So we did—and why not? We were in love with life. We were making more money than we ever dreamed existed and there was no reason to believe it would ever stop."[21]

The merrymaking and carousing, of course, were not confined to the plush mansions and boudoirs of Beverly Hills. The stars' reveling often spilled down from the Hills into the basin area and the Negro community. As in Harlem, it was trendy and fashionable for whites to rub shoulders with the sepia crowd whose syncopated music and supposed exotic lifestyle had inspired much of the Roaring Twenties passion and élan. Hollywood's elite often partied at Sebastian's Cotton Club on Washington, an exclusive spot at the edge of the black community where Negroes entertained and served but were rarely welcomed as customers. The more daring ventured a little farther south to the Dunbar Hotel and the Apex (later the Club Alabam) at 41st Street, where with some restrictions they could actually party *with* blacks. The boldest motored down to the far southern end of Central where the Plantation Club and more gutbucket speakeasies offered not only an unrestricted taste of black life in the raw but also freer access to illegal drugs and alcohol.

And by the late twenties, as more Negroes found work in the film industry, some of the studios' immense budgets began trickling down to Central Avenue's black entertainers. For some of the headline stage performers who starred in musical shorts and a few featured players (although they made a mere fraction of the fortunes paid stars like Valentino, Arbuckle, Bow, and Chaplin), shades or facsimiles of the Hollywood high life were within reach.

In the late twenties, Clarence Muse and Stepin Fetchit were the highest-paid Negro actors in the movie industry. And while Muse generally lived a low-key, contemplative life far removed from the Hollywood party scene, Fetchit eagerly embraced both the scene and the spotlight. He came closer to approximating the ostentatious lifestyle of Hollywood's elite than any other black actor. It was not by accident.

Fetchit remains one of the most enigmatic of black performers, but one aspect of his personality seems unambiguous. Beginning with his his first rave review, and continuing throughout his movie career, he rarely questioned his star status; despite public disclaimers, he viewed himself as the equal of the film colony's more celebrated white screen legends. But unlike most of the era's black actors, he not only assumed entitlement to equal treatment and access to amenities other stars received, but consistently demanded it. "If I am a good actor," he wrote in an open letter to the *Chicago Defender* in 1930, "I want the respect and recognition that is given to good actors."[22]

That assertive attitude, combined with his promotional flair and unrelenting ambition, set him apart from nearly all of the era's black actors. Widely cast as the primary collaborator in perpetuating Hollywood's racist image of Negroes as his career ebbed, he was often viciously satirized by the white press and condemned as a toady or Uncle Tom by blacks. But ironically, it was his assertiveness and insistence on respect and star treatment within and without the studios that, along with his contentiousness and egotism, accelerated his fall from grace within the industry. At the time, that attitude certainly marked him as "difficult"; in fact, in the eyes of many studio executives, he had become impossible, the ultimate "uppity" Negro.

Years after his film career ended, Fetchit insistently claimed that his artistic integrity and independence accounted for his troubles in Hollywood. "I was an artist. A technician. I went in and competed among the greatest artists in the country," he said. "There was no white man's idea of making a Negro Hollywood motion picture star, a millionaire Negro entertainer. Savvy?"[23]

By 1929, the actor had begun assuming the role of a Hollywood superstar. During an interview for a July *Motion Picture Magazine* article, in which he bragged about his luxurious lifestyle, he curtly dismissed critics. "I don't need no insurance," he asserted. "When I die, jes' throw me out in the street." Asked about his lavish spending, he reportedly said, "Ah ain't never goin' to save a dollar. A man who puts a dollar in the bank depends on that for safety. If a man can't depend on God he can't depend on no little old silver trinket."

Fetchit's outspoken rejection of the principles of moderation and thrift advocated by Booker T. Washington, the era's most prominent race leader, merely amused or mildly rankled most Northern whites; but they clearly frustrated and angered Southern whites and some blacks. Fetchit's prodigal, live-for-the-moment ways, for instance, prompted the more accommodating bootblack and sometime actor Oscar "Cutie Pie" Smith to characterize the actor as "Jes' a plain damn fool!" That assessment was shared by more than a few of the conservative Central Avenue entertainment crowd—for them, Fetchit was violating one of the Negro middle class's most sacred taboos. He had become the nation's most visible and odious example of publicly acting "nigger rich."[24]

Negro press claims that he "went Hollywood" or "that he couldn't stand prosperity" and criticisms of his "eccentricities" and "big head," however, were ignored by Fetchit. His meteoric rise to stardom and hefty $1,500-to-$3,000-per-week salary seemed to surprise him as much as it did his detractors, and he embraced it with what in some ways appeared to be boyish, guileless enthusiasm. "When his name appeared on the posters advertising 'The Ghost Talks,' " a fan magazine reported, "Step spent the better part of two days standing in front of a billboard gazing at it. 'Oh boy!' he kept saying. 'There I is! That's me! In great big letters. Oh, boy!' "[25]

He was soon living large. When "picture after picture featuring him smashed box-office records" and his popularity was at its height, he not only kept a suite at the Dunbar but rented the biggest house on Central Avenue. He owned several automobiles "of the biggest and costliest models and had a different chauffeur in a different uniform in each car. The uniforms were a cross between those worn by a Swiss admiral and the Emperor Jones. And on the back of each car there was a big sign bearing the name of Stepin Fetchit, which at night blazed out upon the startled world in big electric lights." Some avowed that his name appeared on the rear-mounted spare tires just above an inscription reading WILLIAM FOX STAR.[26]

The actor regularly showed up at studio lots or cruised Central Avenue in a cavalcade of automobiles. He drove one of the cars, among them a custom-built Cadillac roadster; chauffeurs drove the other two. "Step told me that he would drive one car for awhile, then get out, greet fans and friends, and switch with one of his drivers," said Keter Betts, a musician who met the actor in the fifties.

Despite his frequent problematic behavior, Fetchit remained a practicing Catholic nearly all of his life and claimed to have donated 10 percent of his earnings to the church for years. Still, he apparently had no reservations about playing to the crowds when attending services. His excursions to Sunday masses—friends and admirers often filling each car—were said to be among the Avenue's more eye-catching spectacles on sleepy Sabbath mornings.[27]

"Lots of men will go to church with me," he told a reporter, "jes' because they like to be seen with Stepin Fetchit. The priest can reach people through me that he'd never get to talk to otherwise. Why some of the worst characters on Central Avenue have been to mass with me!"[28]

Fetchit readily admitted that he had a passion for flashy, unusual cars and, during his heyday, owned twelve luxury automobiles. "Every time a fellow got hold of any kind of car that was hard to get rid of, he hunted me down," he recalled. "I was the first one to have a $16,000 pink Rolls-Royce," he said, confirming that it "had a neon sign on the back" with his name on it. Forever the showman, he added an unusual bit of pageantry to his colorful cruises along the Stroll in 1930. "I used to carry a trumpet instead of a horn," he told an *Ebony* magazine reporter. "When the chauffeur wanted his horn, he'd just hunch the footman, who'd blow the trumpet. Man, people liked that!"[29]

In many publicity photographs and in all of his films except the last, Fetchit was presented in tawdry, ill-fitting attire—coveralls; oversized shirts and coats; short, high-water pants. It was the image with which he would later be permanently associated in the minds of most Americans. That image, in fact, no more reflected the actor's actual deportment than did debonair Charlie Chaplin's tattered on-screen tramp attire or the elegant Bert Williams's buffoonish onstage rural rube attire. Like many of the era's screen idols, Fetchit attired himself in royal fashion.[30]

His lavish wardrobe included dozens of custom-made suits; many were cashmere and imported from India. Some, he claimed, cost over $1,000 and were bought from Rudolph Valentino's tailor after the actor's death in August 1926. "Clothes make the man," he advised a reporter, adding that "Cecil B. de Mille was a cashmere man, too."[31]

The purchase and retailoring of Valentino's suits, and the comparison of his taste to that of legendary Hollywood director Cecil DeMille suggest that early in his career Fetchit perceived himself among the ranks of the film colony's elite. Whether motivated by ego or, as he later argued, a sense of history as the first black film star, the actor saw himself as a reigning superstar who was due all the perks that came with that status.

The mainstream press, however, generally viewed him as a parvenu, an upstart old-school Negro entertainer attempting to rise above his class. It was the twenties, after all, and although Fetchit had been compared to the legendary Bert Williams and hailed as "the best actor that the talking movies have produced," he was still black. Despite the country's fascination with Negroes' "exotic" lifestyle and music, even wealthy or famous blacks were expected to maintain a low-key posture and stay in their places.

In the spring of 1930, when an anonymous studio executive justified postponement of future all-black motion pictures with the claim that audiences would "tolerate no representation of the Negro as independent, well-dressed, handling money, in a position of dignity," he was referring to Southern filmgoers. Racist attitudes, however, were not confined to the South. They were a part of the nation's social fabric. Generally, the Northern media and most Northerners shared many of the same biases.

Consequently, whereas the excesses and escapades of elite mainstream stars (unless obviously criminal) were usually greeted with a casual wink or a mild reprimand, the success and extravagant lifestyle embraced by Fetchit or black celebrities like Nina Mae McKinney and Jack Johnson often elicited mockery from the mainstream press. In some instances, news stories either subtly or directly suggested comparison between black male celebrities and minstrelsy's Zip Coon or Jim Dandy—the pretentious urban Negro stage caricature who was portrayed as an uncouth simpleton despite his wealth, finery, and flashy attire. The effect was often achieved by simply imposing fractured Southern Negro dialect on the speech of blacks in news reports.

In 1910, for example, two versions of heavyweight champion Jack Johnson's response to questions about the use of his considerable boxing earnings were published in the *New York Times*. A news article reported that Johnson had said that bonds "do not pay as much interest as some stocks, but they sure pay." The following day, however, a *Times* editorial about the same incident offered a more colorful rendition of the boxer's response. The latter alleged that he'd said he would invest the money in "Gov'munt bonds; they don't bring so much, but they's gilt edged."[32]

In the case of Stepin Fetchit, the media's comic portrait and ridicule was, in part, the result of the actor's own promotional ploys. Perhaps realizing that sustaining an eccentric, oddball public profile would make his crossover popularity and lavish lifestyle more acceptable to white America, in typical trickster fashion he often urged reporters to blur the line between his real-life and screen personas. "He is shrewd beneath his happy negro [*sic*] humor," a reporter wrote in 1929. "When I left him he said, 'Ah talk to you like Ah never talks in the studio. Make it light, make it funny, 'cause that's what folks want from me.' "[33]

During the late twenties and throughout the thirties, the press enthusiastically obliged. Mainstream journalists not only presented his quotes in a broken coonlike dialect but also regularly lampooned the actor's ostentatious ways as an example of a tasteless African style and portrayed his lavish spending as childlike, Zip Coon caprice. "When Stepin Fetchit bought tickets for the prizefights," a *New York Times* reporter wrote, "he bought them by the bunch. And he saw to it that he sat in the centre of a block of friends. Wherever he went there was a chorus of dark acclaim, because everybody that called 'Hi Stepin!' got a bit of pasteboard entitling him to a ringside location.

"Stepin had thirty-six suits and so many shirts that his neighbors just stepped in and borrowed one whenever they felt like it. Once he held a seventy-five-dollar telephone conversation with his mother in the East trying to come to a decision on the purchase of a thirty-six-dollar dress by his sister."[34]

The article, in that instance, was a curious mixture of fact, fiction, and, one assumes, tongue-in-cheek hyperbole. The most glaring error is that Dora Perry, the actor's mother, had died when Lincoln Perry was a fourteen-year-old schoolboy—prior to his vaudeville career and, no doubt, long before he had even seen $75.

On occasion, the derisive overtones were more pointedly racial, as in "Step Tells All," a *Motion Picture Magazine* article that characterized Fetchit as "the Court Jester at Fox studios" on the heels of his performance in *Hearts in Dixie.*

"That's Step. Nothing fancy. Nothing educated or emancipated," Elisabeth Goldbeck wrote in the fan magazine. "He typifies his race. All the traits and talents that legend gives to colored people are embodied in him. He has their joyous, child-like charm, their gaudy tastes, their superstitions. And as for singing, dancing, and strumming a mean banjo—he does them all. And would probably steal chickens if he hadn't promised the Lord never to do anything illegal again."[35]

By the summer of 1929, despite some occasional bad press, Fetchit had reportedly become "the idol of Central Avenue" and was "having a hard time keeping the women away from him." But in addition to his freewheeling spending habits and notorious reckless driving, his romantic conquests, legal problems, and frequent public fracases were mounting. They led to a series of high-profile incidents that were ripe for exploitation by the tabloids and fan magazines as well as the mainstream and black press.

During the spring of 1929, while apparently still involved with the aspiring teenage starlet Yvonne Butler, Fetchit began courting Dorothy Stevenson, a seventeen-year-old Jefferson High School student. The stunning teenager had moved from New Orleans to the West Coast five years before meeting Fetchit and lived near Central on 14th Street, not far from the actor's reported address during 1927 and 1928. Little information about their courtship or any formal announcement of an engagement appeared in the press; but only months after the relationship began, the *Los Angeles Times* reported that the couple was to be married on June 27 at St. Patrick's Roman Catholic Church in Los Angeles.[36]

After the ceremony, Fetchit was "said to have broadcast his wedding to all Hollywood by driving up and down the boulevards in one of his three Cadillacs, the car being decorated with signs announcing his marriage." The actor's wedding surprised most everyone, including some journalists who were following his career. A profile appearing in the *Baltimore Afro-American* in early July, for example, reported that Fetchit was living with his father and sister in a "charming bungalow" at 1609 East 40th Street. There was no mention of Miss Stevenson, even though the account stated that the actor was "to be married."

"I want a house full of children," Fetchit reportedly told interviewer Ruby Berkley Goodwin. "I'll have plenty to take care of them with, so the girl that doesn't want to mother children doesn't want me."[37]

Goodwin's generally flattering portrait of Fetchit appeared in the same issue of the weekly that featured a farcical news report on one of the actor's early public brawls. That story reported that Fetchit and John "Bubbles" Sublett of the Buck and Bubbles dance-comedy team had engaged in a "knock-down, drag-out, house-and-alley battle that had half of California's 'Harlem' excited"; it also included one of the few mentions of Miss Stevenson as the actor's fiancée. The account, written more like a slapstick scenario for a Rastus, Topsy, or Sambo silent-film comedy skit than a news report, is a example of the colorful exaggeration that characterized coverage of Fetchit's high jinks by both the mainstream and the black press.

> Screams, yells, sounds of crashing glass and china, thuds of heavy objects, such as furniture or bodies falling, suddenly emanated from Stepin Fetchit's residence at 1609 East 40th Street, last Sunday afternoon late.
>
> In the midst of the bedlam, out the front door burst the long, lean form of Bubbles leaping like a greyhound with Stepin curving down the driveway from the back of the house and right behind Bubbles throwing full bottles of home brew at him, which exploded as they struck with

> reports like French howitzers. One of those struck the long legged runner on the right fore'arm [*sic*] cutting a ragged gash but never slowing his pace.
>
> Step's liveried chauffeur then speeded out behind Bubbles in Step's expensive limonsine [*sic*]. For a while it too was out distanced by the speeding Bubbles, but as the driver was on mercy bent he succeeded in convincing the dancer that he only wanted to take him to a hospital and get his arm "sewed up."
>
> Thoroughly wrathy now, he craved revenge on his erstwhile host, so he refused medical attention but bought a half dozen pints of Avenue "panther sweat" and drinking and raving announced that he was getting ready to go back and clean out the Step domicile. Friendly policemen finally took him in hand and sent him home.
>
> The brawl started through a joke that Step suggested Bubbles help him play on his fiancee, Miss Dorothy Stevenson, a 17-year-old Los Angeles girl. They were to stage a fake quarrel over her affections but it seems that Bubbles was too good an actor and Step, detecting a note of sincerity in Bubbles' statement, grew angry and the battle began in real earnest.
>
> Other frightened guests fled to the streets and Step's sister tried to prevail on Bubbles to jump the back fence and avoid Step, who was in the driveway armed with a case of home brew.[38]

Presumably, the Baltimore paper's interview took place and the Associated Negro Press (ANP) news story appeared prior to Fetchit's wedding. Given the lapse of time between events and published reports in weekly newspapers like the *Afro-American,* it is probable that the alleged clash between Fetchit and Bubbles occurred at a premarriage celebration.

Although he didn't recall the occasion for the party, John Bubbles confirmed that he and "Step" had a run-in at the actor's house "around that time."

"They was wild times," Bubbles said during a 1979 interview in his Los Angeles home. "We partied a lot when I was in Hollywood. See, Step had a big contract with Fox, and I was working over at Pathé with my partner in a new comedy series. We was on top of the world, thought the party would never end.

"Yeah, there was a little rivalry between me and Step, but it was all in fun. He liked playing jokes . . . always messin' and playin' with somebody, you know. It started out like that, a joke. But I guess we got a little hot and it got a little outta hand. I got mad, and we got in each other's face. But, you know, the papers blew up everything we did." He paused and smiled. "Yeah, didn't they say something about me outrunnin' Step's limousine? Step must a put 'em up to that. Nah, I sure don't remember us runnin' down the streets like fools. Wasn't even no hard feelings. I was back at Step's house for another party a week or so after all that mess happened."[39]

Almost immediately after his encounter with Bubbles, Fetchit found himself at the center of another media storm. In mid-July the *Afro-American* ran a story headlined "Says Fetchit Jilted Her; Sues for $100,000." The article reported that just weeks after his marriage to Dorothy Stevenson, Fetchit had "been named defendant in a suit for alleged breach of promise to marry, filed by Yvonne Butler, 17, in which the girl asks $100,000 damages."[40]

Shortly afterward, the *Los Angeles Times* announced that Fetchit had agreed to a compromise settlement of the breach-of-promise suit in superior court. Since she was underage, Miss Butler appeared in court with her mother, Aletha Weston. The compromise agreement required that the actor pay the plaintiff $5,000 in damages—$2,500 cash and $50 a week for fifty weeks.[41]

The Yvonne Butler affair would haunt Fetchit for several years. But with the compromise temporarily behind him, in the late summer of 1929 it seemed that he was on the verge of bringing some stability into his life. Newly married and having recently signed an optional two-year contract with Fox (reportedly for $1,000 to $3,000 a week plus expenses), Fetchit was the wealthiest as well as the most popular and acclaimed black motion picture actor in the nation. During the summer, a *Los Angeles Times* article had reported that Fetchit was "now in possession of a contract which makes him the highest salaried colored actor since Bert Williams." The article went on to suggest that "studio folk" were comparing the actor, whose "name shines in electric lights," to Williams, the legendary *Ziegfeld Follies* star.[42]

Earlier in the year, Fetchit had completed *Innocents of Paris,* a Paramount release, and *Fox Movietone Follies of 1929*, his fourth film for the William Fox studios. He and Carolynne Snowden had minor roles in *Innocents,* a musical that is remembered primarily because it featured Maurice Chevalier in his Hollywood film debut. When it was released in May, *Variety* dismissed it as "skimpy," an "ordinary little talker," and called it "unfortunate for Chevalier." In most reviews, neither Snowden nor Fetchit were mentioned.[43]

Movietone Follies enjoyed a more positive reception. Like *Innocents of Paris,* it was a musical comedy with a theatrical setting. The film starred John Breeden, Lola Lane, and DeWitt Jennings and was among the first Hollywood films to include color sequences. It generally received glowing notices for its comedy and Broadway musical numbers when released in May. With a more substantial role in this film, Fetchit, as Swifty, a theater callboy, was singled out for his outstanding performance. Calling it a "pioneer effort" by Fox, the *Variety* critic wrote that "Stepin Fetchit, colored comic and hoofer, rates number two for notice," adding that "his sleepy characterizations caused many laughs." *Photoplay* noted that "Stepin Fetchit furnishes his usual brand of unexcelled comedy." And while *Motion Picture Magazine* panned the film, it did spotlight Fetchit's work, crediting his dance as "the one really snappy episode of the picture."[44]

The *New York Times* review was even more approbative. "That dusky comedian, Stepin Fetchit, who made his debut in 'The Ghost Talks,' and subsequently scored in 'Heart's in Dixie,' goes remarkably well in this current film," Mordaunt Hall wrote. "His particular brand of lazy comedy fits in splendidly. During one sequence he is called upon to dance. And Mr. Fetchit's feet are like chained lightning as he performs before an audience seen on the screen."[45]

With the high praise for his last picture and mounting national popularity, Fetchit's stock at Fox was seemingly on the rise in June 1929. That summer was also one of the busiest periods of the young actor's accelerating career. In addition to his marriage and ongoing promotional activities, he was not only hard at work on two more Fox films, *Big Time* and *Salute,* but was also reportedly attempting to expand his involvement in filmmaking. In July, he told a reporter that he had written a script that Fox studios had bought; according to the actor, he was slated to star in the production. The film script, which Fetchit mentioned on several occasions, was never produced, but he would continue efforts to both produce and write films throughout the thirties.[46]

He was also active on the stage. His August appearance in a Franchon and Marco musical revue at Los Angeles's Loew's Theater received an upbeat notice in *Variety.* "Fetchit's main appeal to a professional audience is his dancing. Old Negro shuffling with no attempts at wings, floor sweeping, or the modern intricacies in taps," the critic wrote. "Step doesn't try to break a leg, although plenty animated when becoming the minstrel. Otherwise he's mumbling 'Lonesome Road,' the spiritual which climaxes Universal's 'Show Boat,' for an entrance and only gets away from his established lethargy to shuffle."

Working in a suit with top hat and cane, Fetchit told gags, danced and sang his "national anthem, 'California, Here I Come,'" the reviewer reported. "House enjoyed it and wanted more, but Step's idea was that it was time to park the body, and said so. In lieu of the screen rep he has worked up for himself, Step can do a neat seven minutes in anybody's picture house."

If you had passed the stage door, the writer noted, you would have seen "a big car with a chauffeur and page boy up front, the latter wearing everything but neon tubes. Merely a tip to Central Avenue that Step is on his way."[47]

The actor was at the height of his popularity, a hit both on stage and screen. Fetchit's film roles had elevated him to a position that few African Americans had occupied. He had become a pop cultural icon—the most acclaimed Negro screen actor as well as the first acknowledged black film star in the nation's history. In 1929 and 1930, he ranked with the fictional radio duo Amos and Andy (portrayed by the white entertainers Charles Correll and Freeman Gosden) and the black stage team of Flournoy Miller and Aubrey Lyles (of *Shuffle Along* fame) as the nation's best-known and most popular interpreters of the comic-stage Negro. The actor's meandering, high-pitched voice and nonsensical retorts ("you'se a garbage mouth falsifier" or "I ain't askin' is you ain't, I'se askin' is you is") were echoed by fans nearly as often as "I'se regusted" or "Ain't dat sump'thin," signature quips from the Correll and Gosden, and Miller and Lyles teams. And like *Amos 'n' Andy,* Fetchit's racially based buffoonery had cross-cultural appeal.

By the thirties, however, the actor was beginning to pose a dilemma for industry insiders. His unpredictability, demands for star treatment, and increasingly cavalier attitude had begun rankling some studio executives. During the filming of *Salute,* tensions mounted.

"Fetchit came to Annapolis where he was engaged in making a motion picture which had the U.S. Naval Academy for its background," Ralph Matthews wrote in the *Baltimore Afro-American.* "Although all the actors were given specific orders not to leave the lot, Fetchit became restless and ran away to Washington, D.C., where he got broke and found it necessary to call upon the manager of the Fox Theater to get enough money to get back to Annapolis. The story broke in the capital's dailies and Fetchit came in for a reprimand."[48]

Fetchit later recalled the Annapolis shoot as an example of the precedent-setting early status he achieved as a black star in Hollywood. "John Ford, the director, is one of the greatest men who ever lived," he told a journalist in 1971. "We was at the U.S. Naval Academy in 1929 making a picture called *Salute,* using the University of Southern California football team to do us a football sequence between the Army and the Navy. John Wayne was one of their football players. And in order to be seen by the director at all times, because Ford wanted to make him an actor, John Wayne taken the part of a prop man. That director made him a star. And on that picture, John Wayne was my dresser! John Ford, he was staying in the commandant's house during that picture, and he had me stay in the guest house. At *Annapolis*!"[49]

Wayne and Fetchit remained friends long after their first encounter. The actors also remained among director Ford's favorite performers. In fact, in later years, Ford's admiration for Fetchit would prove indispensable to the actor's career.

Meanwhile, reviews of Fetchit's work in *Salute* and *Big Time* were mixed.

The former, an adolescent romantic comedy set against the famed Army-Navy football rivalry, was released in August and didn't appreciably improve his esteem in the eyes of studio honchos. The film starred George O'Brien as cadet John Randall and Frank Albertson as his brother, Midshipman Paul Randall.

"It's football, but more important than that—there's laughs, and plenty of 'em, with Frank Albertson outgrossing Step Fetchit," the *Variety* reviewer wrote. "Step Fetchit rings in as the servant in Paul's household who follows the boy to the Naval school and becomes a rubber for the grid squad. From spots in the picture it listens as if the sound boys will have to be careful with Step. The colored boy is mumbling so freely he can't always be understood. But they laugh when they see him so maybe it doesn't make much difference." The *New York Times* reviewer was less impressed with the picture but shared *Variety*'s complaint about Fetchit's inaudibility. "Stepin Fetchit plays a small comedy part," Mordaunt Hall wrote, "and although he is quite good, his work would be much more appreciated if his groaning utterances were distinct."[50]

Big Time, a romantic tearjerker that starred Lee Tracy and Mae Clarke, was later described as "a predecessor to 'A Star Is Born.'" Released in September, *Variety* called it a "penetrating study of a self assured 'ham hoofer' actor type, always from a sympathetic side." Its "sentimental sequences," the critic wrote, were relieved by the "capital low comedy sketch by the colored actor Stepin Fetchit who has now earned featuring by his distinctive style of handling the dumb darky role." In the *New York Times,* Mordaunt Hall singled out Fox's black comedy star in a one-line plaudit: "Stepin Fetchit contributes many a laugh with his lazy tones and his treacherous memory."[51]

After traveling to New York to promote *Big Time* in September, Fetchit returned to Los Angeles and reportedly began writing songs to accompany a new stage act that he planned to unveil during a nationwide tour between film assignments. He also began another Fox picture, the third film adaptation of Booth Tarkington's popular play *Cameo Kirby,* which was being shot near Sacramento.

While much of the nation trembled with the spreading effect of the October stock market crash, Fetchit's future seemed secure. As America's most popular black motion picture actor, he was earning more than he had ever imagined and was apparently happily married to a beautiful new teenage bride.

At the Fox studios, however, the rumblings of discontent were growing.

In addition to his demanding on-set demeanor and an aptness for tardiness and unexplained absences, which often delayed filming, studio heads were concerned with Fetchit's pattern of helter-skelter, erratic driving on and off the lot, which not only endangered their highly paid star but also jeopardized others. The latter concern was reflected in an unusual clause that was inserted into the actor's contract with Radio-Keith-Orpheum, promoters of the actor's upcoming national vaudeville tour. "Fetchit will tour the country," a news story reported, "in one of the three special made Cadillacs which he uses. According to the contract, he is not allowed to drive any of these cars."[52]

Word of Fetchit's difficulties at Fox was aired in a short, easily overlooked item that surfaced in Harry Levette's "On the Movie Lots" column in mid-November: "Rumors are flying thick and fast about great changes to be made at Fox Studio, affecting Stepin Fetchit."

For Fetchit, the ax would fall quickly and with surprisingly little fanfare.[53]

CHAPTER EIGHT

In December, the William Fox studios quietly notified Stepin Fetchit that the option on his contract would not be renewed. Surprisingly, the abrupt termination of his association with Fox did not seem to affect the actor's confidence or ego—not on the surface, at least.

When he headed for the East Coast and an abbreviated vaudeville tour in December, Fetchit assured friends and the press that he would soon be back in pictures. Instead of reining in his wild behavior as Fox had requested, however, his rebellious, devil-may-care attitude seemed to soar out of control. What in the past had most often been extravagance, puckish jesting, or calculated showmanship suddenly escalated to peevish outbursts and outright belligerence. Being an extremely proud man, he would have never admitted it, but his increasingly bizarre behavior may well have stemmed from an underlying anxiety over his stalled film career.

Whatever the cause, by early 1930 the more contentious side of the young actor's erratic personality took center stage. It was during this period that Step's reputation as Hollywood's black Bad Boy was emphatically established. He was involved in a stream of disastrous incidents—career blunders, marital problems, automobile accidents, public brawls, and various other disputes—that kept his name in the headlines as well as on trial dockets in courts across the country during the next two years. The highly publicized episodes, which ranged from the comical to the tragic, reshaped the actor's colorful public image.

Attention gradually shifted from his comedy and acting abilities and triumphs in pictures to the media's near-obsessional fixation on his eccentric, often buffoonish exploits off-camera.

One of the earliest signs of his public meltdown surfaced while he appeared in a Philadelphia theater. Just before New Year's, at the outset of his vaudeville tour, he was arrested for drunken driving. The offense was minor, but because the Keith-Orpheum contract stipulated that Fetchit could not drive, his court appearance drew some media attention. At the trial, the arresting officer testified that after being stopped the actor was staggering when he stepped out of his automobile. Fetchit, of course, denied that he had been drinking. He offered a unique explanation for his erratic driving. "I stay up every night so I'll be sleepy the next day," he told the jury. "It was 3 a.m. when I was arrested and I was sleepy then."

Fetchit's claim that he was simply preparing for his stage act apparently won over the jury. The bizarre excuse was accepted, and Fetchit soaked the incident for all its publicity value. According to one news story, "The screen star fell asleep in the courtroom and had to be awakened to be told the jury had acquitted him."[1]

Freed from his Fox contract, the comic began contacting other studios about motion-picture work in December and January. And a few days after being acquitted in the drunk-driving trial, he landed a role in *Lover Come Back*, a new Columbia picture. He was signed by Harry Cohn, the tough, outspoken mogul who had built Columbia Pictures from scratch during the twenties. The unlikely pairing of the wayward actor and the hard-nosed, demanding producer and executive naturally sparked considerable commentary in the press. "Fetchit, according to stories emanating from the coast, is hard to handle," one news story reported. "Cohn, however, feels that he and Stepin can get along together. All Hollywood recognizes the man's genius, even though it is generally admitted that he is temperamental."[2]

When Fetchit reported to the Columbia Pictures lot in late January, he no doubt felt vindicated by his speedy rehiring by another major studio. But the romance between the headstrong actor and Cohn—whose bullying and occasional vulgarity were legend—lasted only a few days after shooting began.

By the first week in February, the brief association between Stepin

Fetchit and Columbia Pictures had been abruptly terminated. A February 6 release from the Associated Negro Press reflects the black press's growing impatience with the actor's behavior.

> As a sort of exclamation to the escapades in which Stepin Fetchit has featured since he became a star performer in the movies, came the announcement that he had been fired by Columbia. The official announcement reads:
>
> "Stepin Fetchit is out over at Columbia. He had been cast in an important role in 'Lover Come Back,' which Erle C. Kenton is directing, but after two days his temperament got the best of him. Harry Cohn, rather than put up with him, let him out and scrapped the film that had been shot up to the time Fetchit went 'haywire.' Clarence Muse, well-known colored actor, steps into the role."
>
> Of course, this announcement does not give Fetchit's side of the story, which your correspondent is presently trying to obtain. But there have been frequently circulated stories of his irresponsibility and some of his feats have landed him in the police station.
>
> It is generally regarded as a step forward to have Clarence Muse selected to take the Fetchit role. Although Muse is not the comedian Fetchit is, he is a much more finished actor.[3]

In the *Pittsburgh Courier*, the story was treated rather flippantly; it was accompanied by a photograph of the actor seated in one of his roadsters wearing a pilot's cap and goggles. The picture ran beneath a banner headline reading "Now He Can Drive All He Wants To."

Weeks later, the *Baltimore Afro-American* published an even more stinging indictment of the actor's behavior:

> Stepin Fetchit, who was engaged by Columbia Studios to play one of the most important roles in "Lover Come Back," was given the air after two days of "shooting" and replaced by Clarence Muse, one of our most clever comedians.
>
> "Step," it seems, developed temperament, and despite his relative success in the film colony, he still has to learn that the man who "pays off" is the only one who can afford such a liability as "sometimeness." This same temperament has endowed him with a mania for speeding up

> and down the coast boulevards and drawing successive reprimands from judges.
>
> The colored actor's chance in Hollywood will probably be killed by the slightest indiscretion of one or two fellows who become intoxicated by success in a comparatively small way. The action taken by the Columbia people in Fetchit's case is described by Walter Winchell as "one cure for inflated skulls," but in the plain old Harlem lingo, "big heads."[4]

Reaction to the Cohn-Fetchit fiasco signaled a critical shift in Negro press coverage of the controversial actor. Black newspaper reactions to Fetchit had run hot and cold since his *In Old Kentucky* debut. Frequently, his pioneering efforts in the industry were praised, and he was applauded as a credit to his race. And from that supportive viewpoint, as with the equally controversial prizefighter Jack Johnson, the actor's excesses and extravagances were accepted as colorful or amusing idiosyncrasies. The mumbling, indolent character that Fetchit played in films, however, set him apart from the macho ex–heavyweight boxing champ. Whereas Johnson, despite his braggadocio and rebellious Bad Nigger image, had been a legitimate, much-admired sports hero for most blacks, Fetchit's stage and screen character had consistently irritated elements of the Negro community, particularly the aspiring middle class. And as the young comedian's behavior came under fire from the studios and the mainstream media, the black press more frequently voiced disapproval of Central Avenue's Bad Boy. Fetchit's quarrel with Cohn and his subsequent firing stirred heated reactions in the mainstream press as well. On the East Coast, even Broadway's powerful syndicated columnist Walter Winchell felt obliged to take a swipe at the actor's impertinence.

At the time, the possibility that Fetchit may have been reacting to some racial slight or instance of unprofessional treatment by the director or studio was not seriously weighed in the black press even though in the past the actor had been cited for protesting such treatment. The *Pittsburgh Courier*, for example, had reported that, "according to stories emanating from the Coast," Fetchit is "hard to handle. He has ideas of his own and despite his droll mimicry, has defied producers who attempt to ridicule his race. Clean and wholehearted fun fits in his scheme but anything else is taboo." And more than a year after the fact, in describing the Cohn-Fetchit encounter, the *Baltimore Afro-American* reported that the comedian "got into trouble when he refused to say certain lines assigned to him by a prejudiced producer, which Fetchit claimed was a reflection on his race."[5]

The waffling Negro press view of Fetchit's behavior reflected the extremely sensitive nature of race relations in early-twentieth-century America. The black media often expressed concern over the derogatory portraits of Negroes in films. But, fearing backlash and disruption of the precarious foothold that race performers acquired in the industry, it was reluctant to criticize the studios or forcefully and consistently support actors who balked at the roles offered. The situation put Fetchit in a no-win position. He was criticized for the offensive parts he took, but if he complained and was rebuked by the studios, he was castigated as a troublemaker. It was a dilemma that would haunt Fetchit and nearly every other black actor during Hollywood's early years.

For months after the run-in with Cohn, Fetchit exercised considerable restraint in commenting on the incident. One seemingly far-fetched report claimed that he had been let go by the Columbia group "because he refused to say, 'Rusty, I'm all wet.' Asked why he refused to repeat the lines, Fetchit sidestepped the question, jokingly responding, "I thought those words might offend many of my old friends down in 'Bam.'" According to the reporter, Step "seemed unworried over his release."[6]

Later, however, he wrote a somewhat sanctimonious confessional that appeared in several black newspapers. And while he insisted that he was not attempting to defend himself, he did obliquely suggest that his troubles at the studios may have stemmed from underlying racial or ethical conflicts.

"First I respect no man or amount of money if it is not surrounded with principles that are considered good in the eyes of God and I will not accept a position or any amount of money or honor unless I can demand respect and the dignity that goes with it," he wrote.[7]

In February, however, Fetchit seemed more intent on reviving his flagging career and getting back into pictures than explaining why he had been fired by two major studios during a seven-week period. *Cameo Kirby*, his last Fox film, was released early in the month, but few reviews even noted his appearance. When he was mentioned, the notices were less than favorable. The *New York Times* critic, for example, dismissed his performance in one line: "Stepin Fetchit, the negro [*sic*] performer, is slower and more indistinct than ever." With the Negro press more frequently echoing mainstream criticism of his lackadaisical work habits and "irresponsible" lifestyle, prospects for a new contract with another studio seemed dim.[8]

The ever-optimistic Fetchit, however, remained outwardly upbeat. "They can't keep a good man down," he beamed to friends who worried about his future. "I'll get another and better job within a few days."[9]

Fortunately for the struggling actor, there were still a few producers and directors who both admired his unusual comic talents and were willing to risk dealing with his temperament. Hal Roach—who guided the early careers of the legendary comedians Harold Lloyd, Stan Laurel, and Oliver Hardy and was a pioneer producer during Hollywood's "Golden Age of Comedy"—was among them. And near the end of February, the trade papers and Negro press announced that Fetchit had signed a multiple film contract with Hal Roach Studios. That announcement, it turned out, was premature.

"Stepin Fetchit was a very funny guy," Roach told the authors and film historians Leonard Maltin and Richard W. Bann before his death in 1992. "That's why we tried to use him, because he was a *skilled* comic. . . . the colored people in those days got as big a kick out of Stepin Fetchit as anybody. They used to come to the studio every single day, you know, dozens of them, wanted to see him and so on."[10]

Roach was impressed enough with Fetchit that he offered him a contract to star in a series of eight comedy shorts at a salary of $350 per week for the first block of films, which were to be shot after the studio's summer break. Roach was also the creator and producer of the extremely successful *Our Gang* comedy series (renamed *The Little Rascals* when it debuted on television in the 1950s), and as a pilot for the proposed series, Fetchit was cast in *A Tough Winter*, an *Our Gang* short that began shooting around the end of February. Although the film did not reach theaters until June, in March, publicity stills of Fetchit and nine-year-old Allen "Farina" Hoskins, the Gang's black child star at the time, were being released to the press.[11]

While waiting for the Roach Studios contract to be finalized during the spring of 1930, Fetchit appeared to be frantically looking for roles or projects to revive his career and replace the considerable income lost with the termination of his Fox contract. In addition to a Los Angeles stage appearance in the musical comedy *Up and At 'Em,* he found film work at Pathé Studios as well as with the colorful independent director and producer James Cruze. In his first Pathé assignment, Fetchit had a minor role in *Swing High,* a middling musical set against the backdrop of circus aerialists that starred the exotic former Broadway star Helen Twelvetrees. Working with the maverick director Cruze—whose Bad Boy reputation was even more notorious than Fetchit's—he was cast as Spot and provided comic relief in *The Big Fight,* a dramatic account of mobsters' attempt to fix a championship boxing match.

Despite his career woes, while working on *The Big Fight* the actor seemed to be in good spirits. In one of a few favorable write-ups to surface during this time, a *Chicago Defender* portrait of Fetchit and his family—including his "pretty," "auburn-haired and slender" seventeen-year-old wife; his motherly maid, Mrs. Jones; his "handsome red-haired chauffeur," Fred; his "teasing brown secretary"; and his pet whippet, Queenie—described the actor's household and "palatial home" in glowingly harmonious terms. In addition to expressing interest in expanding his family, Fetchit was reportedly busily at work on new songs and a screenplay entitled *The Dancing Fool,* which he hoped to produce himself. "It is the star's desire," the journalist wrote, "to expel the cotton scenes in his future pictures and instead bring out the modern Negro as he is in the North or the larger southern cities." Given the priorities of Hollywood producers during the thirties, it is doubtful that studios ever seriously considered the project. Despite Fetchit's continued efforts, an independent production never got off the ground.[12]

Meanwhile, both on- and off-camera the actor's troubles were growing. In March, Fetchit's reckless driving had again been spotlighted when he was involved in a serious automobile accident. The crash had sent his passenger, "Daddy" Lane, a "well-known stage character, and aged veteran of movies," to the hospital. Lane was released after being examined, but two days later he collapsed and died from complications. A news article reported that "two ribs had been cracked and other internal injuries suffered which were not discovered at his first examination." There was no report of Fetchit being held responsible for the tragedy.[13]

In early April, barely a week after the auto accident, Fetchit was involved in a row with his brother-in-law. Typically, the press treated the incident with comic irreverence. "Ah suttinly intends to pros-cute him," Fetchit reportedly said, " 'cause . . . well, jes imagine mah embarrassment . . . befo' the eyes of all mah friends!"

"The fracas resulted from a fight a week ago," another news story reported. Fetchit had objected to Johnson's "butting in" on a quarrel between him and his wife and reportedly "knocked him under a piano with an iron pipe" during a party at the actor's home. The two met at a friend's house the following week, and when the comedian left, Johnson followed. Fetchit claimed that Johnson brandished a gun, then chased him into a neighbor's backyard, where he hid in a chicken coop. Johnson then pummeled the actor with a "deadly weapon" (a makeshift club) while he was ensnared in the coop. Afterward, Johnson "walked away leaving the comedian helplessly entangled in wire."[14]

The chicken-coop encounter again emphasized Fetchit's unfortunate knack for ludicrous public display and provided an early hint that, despite the harmonious façade displayed to the *Defender* reporter, domestic problems were brewing. Still, the incident was little more than a farcical exclamation point on the black actor's rapid fall from favor in the spring of 1930. Fetchit, however, was not the only black Hollywood star to experience a precipitous decline.

The industry's frenzied pursuit of Negro projects and actors, which had blossomed with the introduction of the talkies, abruptly ceased. And with the shunting of Negro performers to appearances in musical shorts and minor supporting roles in features, the black community's hopes for a "new era" of Hollywood films also came to a sudden halt.

As a result, the brief mainstream press romance with the high-profile performers who had emerged with the release of *Hallelujah!* and *Hearts in Dixie* gradually turned sour. Nina Mae McKinney, the curvaceous vixen who was embraced by the industry and its elite stars more than any other contemporary black performer, is a case in point. On some levels, McKinney broke the color line in Hollywood; before her no black performer had been courted with such uninhibited exuberance. Immediately after the release of *Hallelujah!* she was hailed as "the greatest acting discovery of the age" by Irving Thalberg, MGM's second-in-command and one of the most powerful and respected producers in Hollywood. She quickly became a media darling as well as a frequent guest at Hollywood's most elite affairs.

The tag line to a July 1929 *Photoplay* feature story gushed that "she may be black but she's got a blonde soul—and Hollywood says Nina May [*sic*] is a great acting discovery." In Herbert Howe's slavering, somewhat sexist and patronizing article, the "copper-colored maiden" was portrayed as an ambitious ingénue who was destined to drive both Hollywood and Paris "mad with the rhythm of the tom-toms beating in her blood."

"All Hollywood is wonderful to Nina," Howe wrote.

"They invite me to all their parties," McKinney chimed in. "I been to Miss Swanson's an' Miss Davis' an' Mistah Vidor's an' John Gilbert's. Oh Lordy, Mistah Gilbert!"

"I like Nils Asther too—but Mistah Gilbert most of all."

McKinney was being touted as a fast-rising star who combined the exoticism of Josephine Baker with the exuberance, sensuality, raw sex appeal, and liberated spirit of Clara Bow, the "It Girl."

"When I marry it's goin' be for money," she told Howe. And when he suggested that she might consider marrying for love, she allegedly shot back, "I can't. . . . No, suh, he's got a wife! Anyway, what does love get you?"[15]

By the spring of 1930, however, Hollywood's love affair with the "bronze" Lolita had noticeably cooled. Shortly after signing with MGM, she shot *They Learned About Women,* a mediocre musical that was universally panned. But McKinney's charismatic performance as a chorus-line singer in the "Harlem Madness" sequence was cheered by most critics. She was given a serious acting role in the 1931 picture *Safe in Hell,* but after all was said and done, the film colony's infatuation with the young starlet seems to have been more libidinal than professional. Despite the initial hype and hoopla, she found herself relegated to musical shorts and offers of minor roles in features; there was no room for a Negro siren or leading lady in Hollywood feature films during the thirties.

Her predicament was most clearly signaled in an April 1930 *Motion Picture Classic* feature story "Black—and *Potentially* Blue," an article that was both an exposé of "the little brown Cleopatra's" naïveté and gullibility as well as an inadvertent indictment of the film colony's racism.

"Nina Mae imagines that she has made the jump from the black world to the white," Elisabeth Goldbeck wrote. "She has a long contract with Metro-Goldwyn-Mayer. But what can she do all this while? An occasional number in a revue. Perhaps one more all-colored picture before the vogue is entirely over."

Referring to McKinney's "illusory success," Goldbeck predicted that the actress was in for a rude awakening. "No wonder she has accepted the illusion of Hollywood's friendliness. Hollywood epitomizes all the things that Nina wants. And she has what it takes to get them—for a while. But the bubble is going to break. The white people are going to tire. And Nina Mae will be left wondering: 'What did I do, To be so black—and blue.' "[16]

Despite the negative publicity and the fan magazine's blunt warning, McKinney continued to aggressively pursue and assume the posture of a celebrated motion-picture star. She hobnobbed with the rich and famous, usually accompanied by her mother, a young woman "of light skin, who might have Spanish blood" and who reportedly was only "thirty-two" years old; the actress's mother apparently condoned her libertine ways. Rumors about McKinney's off-camera escapades increased as the pair reveled in their transient fame and submerged themselves in the era's party-scene decadence. By the early thirties, even the black press began to tire of her divalike aloofness.[17]

"The town can quiet down now," Harry Levette facetiously quipped in an October 1930 "Behind the Scenes" column, "Nina and her mama have left town." A few weeks later, he was more explicit: "Her last few months here she was far from being hot copy. Even her scandals and escapades failed to bring surprise any more. There are some untold tales though that would bring undesirable publicity, at least to others, if not to the ex-star of 'Hallelujah.' "[18]

Although her cabaret act flourished, McKinney remained little more than an exotic curio in Hollywood.

Fetchit's career prospects seemed equally dismal in the early thirties. His rejection, however, was strictly professional, not social. As a black male actor, Fetchit had never been welcomed into the film community's inner circles. And unlike Jack Johnson, McKinney, and performers like the popular dancer "Snake Hips" Tucker (who raised eyebrows with what one columnist called "a black and tan domestic triangle" and was dismissed at one studio for allegedly passing a suggestive note to "a blonde while working in a motion picture"), Fetchit apparently did not seek acceptance in integrated social situations. In that regard, he was more of a staunch "race man" than many of his less maligned contemporaries. McKinney, for instance, was invited to sit alongside MGM honcho Irving Thalberg and his wife Norma Shearer at the premiere of *Hallelujah!*; she also attended the postpremiere parties. Whereas at the *Hearts in Dixie* premiere, Fetchit reportedly sat upstairs in the gallery, "where I belong," he said. Later, he celebrated with cronies on Central Avenue.[19]

After completion of the *Our Gang* short and the Pathé and James Cruze features, Fetchit found movie roles increasingly hard to come by. For a short time, he tried resurrecting his stage career by accepting engagements on the Theater Owners' Booking Association circuit. His act was generally well received on the TOBA.

"Although it was a bit difficult for members of the audience to catch the words of Stepin Fetchit's lazy drawl in his appearance at the Regal Theater this week, due to the large size of the house," a reviewer said of a May 8 Chicago appearance, "the patrons of the house tumbled without reserve for the film comedian."

"Fetchit made the biggest hit with his singing and dancing," the reviewer claimed. "He can't sing nor do much playing, but his attempt is so ludicrous and so much with the genre that it takes with the audience. However, the boy can dance. He put on his Stepin Fetchit shuffle which the audience forced him to repeat until he lazily claimed that 'I'se finished.' "[20]

Later in the month, Fetchit returned to the West Coast to take a comic role in a Pathé Studios Western. Again, the actor found himself at the center of an on-set dispute, the details of which were not revealed. Fetchit was immediately fired and replaced by "Stompen and Sellit" (aka Stomp 'n' Sellit), an "unknown" Step imitator who was hired for $200 a week, which was considerably less than the salary Fetchit had been paid. The short news account announcing his dismissal added that the actor had recently "flopped" on the stage in the musical comedy *Up and At 'Em.* "The boy has his ups and downs, these days," the reporter wrote, "but mostly downs."[21]

With another disastrous movie-set confrontation and his film career rapidly going downhill, Fetchit and his wife left for the East Coast to resume his theatrical tour. Life on the road, however, did not noticeably improve Fetchit's fortunes.

Trouble arose in Philadelphia, when after a week he walked out on an engagement at the Pearl Theater. The theater manager subsequently claimed that "Fetchit was harder to handle than any artist ever playing" the Pearl. The problem seems to have been set off by a dispute between Fetchit and "his white manager over the matter of salary."

"Fetchit, it is said, was to receive $2,500 for his week's work," a news report explained, "but when he became temperamental and failed to draw as expected, one-fourth of his salary was withheld." According to his manager, the actor's slow drawl was "slowing up the show considerably and when he was asked to discontinue it he refused. He was also asked to stop giving away from the stage books of his life, as the patrons rushing up to receive a copy almost caused a riot. He is reported to have refused to comply with the requests."

Although the reported facts seem somewhat at odds—the actor was accused of both failing to attract an audience and nearly inciting a riot by handing out press releases to fans—Fetchit's Pearl Theater appearance was terminated. "When his salary was not forthcoming," the write-up reported, "the star refused to leave, and is still in the city, spending most of his time around the Pearl Theater in hope of obtaining the rest of his money."[22]

Disputes about contractual obligations between performers, particularly Negro artists, and theater managers were by no means unusual during the era. Many Negro entertainers balked at the often sleazy conditions and unscrupulous financial practices of booking agents and theater managers on the black theatrical circuit.

In the case of the Pearl Theater conflict, Fetchit seems to have encountered just such a situation. In this instance, the stubborn, hard-nosed business aspect of his personality apparently reared itself. Fetchit not only refused to finish his Pearl Theater appearance, but also delayed his next scheduled engagement at the Royal Theater in Baltimore when its manager refused to pay the agreed-upon salary. The recalcitrant comedian demanded both back pay from the Pearl and his full salary in advance for the Baltimore performance.[23]

Although the final resolution of the problem was not made public, Fetchit released the white manager who he felt had conspired with the theater owner. The incident and accompanying publicity further confirmed the star's reputation as "difficult" and "hard to handle" in the eyes of both the press and the entertainment industry. Fetchit, however, would later insist that he was simply demanding fair treatment and fighting for equal rights as a black performer.

Shortly after the Baltimore theater debacle, Fetchit and his young wife, who was nearly six months pregnant, arrived in New York City; during the spring of 1930, they temporarily settled in Harlem. Barely eight months had passed since the October 1929 market collapse, but Negroes were already feeling the hardship of massive job losses. Early in 1930, the *New York Herald Tribune* reported that the crash "produced five times as much unemployment in Harlem as in other parts of the city." Historians would later write that "Harlem contained some 200,000 people" and, by 1930, "half of them depended on unemployment relief."[24]

Still, when the Fetchits arrived Uptown, the severity of the situation was largely masked by the glitter of Harlem nightlife. "When it comes to pep, pulchritude, punch and presentation, the Harlem places have Broadway night clubs distanced," a front-page *Variety* story claimed. "From midnight until after dawn it is a seething cauldron of Nubian mirth and hilarity. Never has it been more popular."[25]

Despite the crash's devastating effect on the community, as late as February 1931, a daily newspaper reporter from downtown came away with the following impression of the Harlem scene: "Lighthearted throngs . . . shouting flip greetings at friend and stranger alike . . . the clink of glass and bottle. The agonizing wail of muted trumpet and sax. The throaty sound shout of 'hot' blues singers. Music! Lights! Night Clubs!"[26]

The luster of the Harlem Renaissance and the dream of the "New Negro" still flickered during the summer of 1930. It was readily apparent in the lifestyles of Harlem's entertainers, artists, and wealthy residents like A'Lelia Walker, the millionaire daughter of cosmetic heiress Madame C. J. Walker, and in the ballrooms, theaters, and speakeasies that dotted Lenox and Seventh avenues.

At her lavish apartment on 136th Street, Walker hosted swank interracial soirées for prominent Harlemites such as Walter White, executive secretary of the NAACP, white writer Carl Van Vechten and other bohemians, as well as famed members of the Negro literary set (the so-called Niggerati), plus, according to the *Amsterdam News*, "prominent individuals in both European and American society." The Harlem Renaissance writers who hobnobbed with Walker, although often strapped for cash, were at the height of their productivity and popularity during the summer of 1930. Langston Hughes's *Not Without Laughter*, which had just been released, was the talk of the Harlem literary set at the time.

At the other end of the spectrum, the rowdy rent parties that had become an Uptown tradition were as hip and hot as ever, since, come the first of each month, increasingly more Harlemites were out of work and in need of financial help.

Although Fetchit and his wife settled on 138th Street and Seventh Avenue, at the northwest corner of Harlem's exclusive Striver's Row, where many of the community's middle-class gentry resided, the actor would not have been welcome at Walker's class-conscious literary soirées. But he no doubt frequented many of the area's famed late-night establishments.

The Savoy Ballroom, home of the Lindy Hop, which occupied the entire block between 140th and 141st streets on Lenox and offered a two-hundred-foot-long, fifty-foot-wide polished maple dance floor, was among its most popular attractions. Although the dance hall welcomed everyone, including truck drivers, shoe-shine boys, and porters, and its admission price was no more than a dollar, it also attracted Broadway's and Hollywood's most glamorous stage and screen stars. Celebrities were "a dime a dozen," an *Ebony* magazine article claimed. "Royalty from Europe and other foreign lands make the Savoy a must on their visits to New York."[27]

The Savoy's dual bandstands featured the best, most swinging orchestras. And in 1930, the roster included Fletcher Henderson, Fess Williams, Don Redmond, Claude Hopkins, and Chick Webb, the ballroom's "acknowledged king."

The Lafayette (known as the "Uptown Palace"), Lincoln, and Alhambra theaters were also thriving. During the year, they would feature such stars as Butterbeans and Susie, Tim Moore, Pigmeat Markham, "Peg Leg" Bates, Moms Mabley, Bilo and Ashes, Buck and Bubbles, and Cab Calloway, as well as theatrical and musical productions featuring the Alhambra and Lafayette players, scores of beautiful chorus girls, and the honorary "mayor of Harlem," Bill "Bojangles" Robinson.

While not aggressively enforced, Prohibition remained in effect, so both bathtub gin and the uptown speakeasies, cabarets, and nightclubs that served illegal alcohol were still very much in vogue. And in 1930, many of those clubs offered star-studded bills. In addition to extravagant revues and fabulous chorus lines, the Cotton Club, at Lenox and 142nd Street, headlined Duke Ellington's band, which had returned from the West Coast after a cameo appearance in the Amos 'n' Andy film *Check and Double Check.* Connie's Inn, at 131st Street and Seventh Avenue, which had recently presented the acclaimed all-black musical *Hot Chocolates,* featured Cab Calloway's band. Neither club admitted Negroes (unless they were light enough to "pass" for white) but they were usually packed with film and theater stars as well as foreign dignitaries and downtown whites of all ilk. Those policies had prompted an outraged editorial in the weekly black newspaper the *New York Age* condemning the establishments' insistence on barring "even Harlem's best blacks" while admitting "'slummers,' sports, 'coke addicts,' and high rollers of the white race who came to Harlem to indulge in illicit and illegal recreations."[28]

On Lenox and Seventh avenues, the Lenox Club, the Dunbar Palace (formerly the Bamboo Inn), and Small's Paradise were nightspots that more readily welcomed Negro patrons. And 133rd Street between Seventh and Lenox—a block with so many clubs that it was variously called "Beale Street" or "Jungle Alley"—was home to Tillie's Chicken Shack, Pod's and Jerry's, and Mexico's, speakeasies that catered to Harlem's own luminaries as well as its hippest resident players and late-night revelers. Mexico's was "the hottest gin mill on 133rd Street," according to Duke Ellington, who hung out there. "We called it 'a ninety-nine per cent,' one more degree . . . would bust your top."[29]

It was at the latter establishments that Stepin Fetchit would have found the black performers and show-business cronies with which he enjoyed fraternizing. He reportedtly held court at Pod's and Jerry's during visits to Harlem. Given his quick feet and eccentric dance steps, it's probable that he was also a frequent visitor to the Savoy Ballroom. In fact, with his love of nightlife and the sporting scene, the dozens of clubs and speakeasies surrounding his apartment on West 138th Street were no doubt a constant temptation.

Fetchit, of course, also had professional obligations. After arriving in Harlem, the actor was immediately tapped by producer Charles Davis to appear in *Joy Boat,* an all-black-cast musical revue that opened at the Lafayette Theater, at the hub of Harlem's entertainment circuit, on June 14. The musical was created by Davis and featured a cast of nearly forty performers, including Dusty Fletcher, the popular Harlem comedian who gained prominence with his "Open the Door Richard" routine in the forties. With Fetchit advertised as the "Famed Colored Stage and Screen Star," *Joy Boat* drew packed houses during its one-week run. Davis "assembled a large and excellent cast in support of Fetchit. The result is a thoroughly delightful revue," a *New York Amsterdam News* critic wrote. "Fetchit moves through an excruciatingly funny comedy situation on board a boat, which shows him to be very droll. The drawling and complaining voice and the fast eccentric dancing that proved to be a great hit in 'Hearts in Dixie' brought storms of applause at the opening show."[30]

Joy Boat's short but successful run was no doubt reassuring for Fetchit. The three movies he had shot earlier in the year were also released in June; but, while they confirmed his continuing presence in motion pictures, his performances were mostly ignored or panned in the mainstream media. There is "not a single bit of novelty or newness in the tale," *Variety* said of *Swing High,* noting that even Stepin Fetchit was unable "to wring a laugh." Later that summer, Negro press reviews of the films were more upbeat. The *Amsterdam News* critic, for example, gushed that *The Big Fight* was "a sensationally gripping talkie which, for sheer intensity and drama, has rarely been seen." Fetchit "walks away with the honors in this tense drama of the prize ring."[31]

Fetchit was under considerable pressure. His film career was uncertain and his public image was still slipping. The actor probably felt even more urgency since in Harlem, some three thousand miles away from the film capital, he was surrounded by elite East Coast theatrical entertainers whose star status challenged or equaled his own.

And in July, even he must have been impressed when fifty-two-year-old Bill Robinson—just back from Hollywood after finishing *Dixiana,* his first feature film—pulled off a Step-like promotional coup. Venturing downtown to Times Square, Robinson stopped traffic by racing backward and "outsprinting fast runners, including Bill McAllister, the former 100-yard-dash champ." The dancer, who was "allowed a 25-yard lead," repeated the feat a few days later at Yankee Stadium before a Negro League baseball game between the Lincoln Giants and the Baltimore Black Sox.[32]

Fetchit surely took note of both the publicity stunt and the fact that the popular "Bojangles" was being hotly courted by Hollywood producers. He was also aware that in Hollywood Negro actors were considered interchangeable and that his position atop the studios' short list of black performers was at best tenuous. The competitive challenge and prospect of being displaced, however, may well have energized the already ferociously ambitious actor. In late June, he had reportedly arranged a tryout at RKO's 58th Street Theater "in the hope that customers would like him." He was promised a contract for $1,000 per week if audiences were receptive. "Customers," a news item reported, "seemed pleased enough at the first showing of the comic dancer's act." On July 2, he opened at the RKO Theater.[33]

During the same time, Fetchit began rehearsing for a role in *The Black King,* a satirical portrait of controversial black leader Marcus Garvey. The *Black King* was an unusual career choice for Fetchit, but his interest in the project may not have been purely professional.[34]

Garvey, born in St. Ann's Bay, Jamaica, had arrived in Harlem in 1916 and, a year later, founded the Universal Negro Improvement Association, with its visionary goal of creating an independent black nation. His call for resettlement of American Negroes in Africa struck a note with the era's disillusioned black masses. By the early twenties, the UNIA emerged as the world's largest Negro political organization.[35]

From the beginning, however, Garvey had many detractors. The UNIA's separatist "Back to Africa" doctrine, its leader's West Indian background, and its rejection of the Negro church and attacks on "indigenous black protest organizations" came under fire from established African American leaders. Moreover, his popularity notwithstanding, Garvey was a squat, very-dark-skinned man who some described as "homely" and many others condemned as hotheaded, overbearing, and "arrogant." During the early 1920s, he was an easy target for blistering attacks by race leaders and the press, who mocked him with epithets like "ignoramus," "Jamaican jackass," and "buffoon."[36]

In 1925, the charismatic leader who had built the largest mass black movement in American history was dethroned. Garvey was convicted of mail fraud and sentenced to a five-year term in the Atlanta Federal Penitentiary. He was deported to Jamaica by order of President Calvin Coolidge in 1927.

Stepin Fetchit's opinion of the UNIA was not recorded. But given his own unprecedented success as a film star, it is unlikely that the actor supported any Back to Africa agenda. Still, Fetchit shared the exiled leader's Caribbean heritage and, some contended, his arrogance. And at the time, Fetchit seemed as intent on appealing to the black common man or "average working fellow," as he referred to his audience. Also like Garvey, he often found himself under attack by an elitist Negro middle-class who searingly criticized the slothful character he portrayed on screen and stage, and blanched at his public brawls, rash outbursts, and the demanding manner he often displayed with theater owners and film producers. The actor would have also certainly nodded appreciatively at the pageantry, showmanship, and glitter that characterized Garvey's colorful conventions, street ceremonies, and parades.

Fetchit finally dropped out of the *Black King* project, but his downtown theatrical appearance was a success. In July, he was working a split engagement on stage at both the RKO 58th Street and Franklin theaters. "After attempting to star in a Race revue," an ANP article from New York reported, Stepin Fetchit "is now under RKO direction. The clever comedian is busy this week, both in person and on the screen here." The item went on to point out that two of Fetchit's recently released movies, *Swing High* and *The Big Fight*, had opened simultaneously at Harlem theaters.[37]

Just after the RKO engagements began, however, Fetchit received disturbing news. His father, Joseph Perry, who was living in Los Angeles, had died. Due to stage commitments and the time required for transcontinental travel, the actor was unable to return to the West Coast. Ed Lee and "Diamond Tooth" Billy Arnte, both of whom had worked with Fetchit earlier in his career, were among the pallbearers at the July 10 burial, however; and many of Central Avenue's most celebrated performers, including the entire roster of Arnte's show, turned out for the funeral.[38]

Fetchit had admired his father since childhood, and Joseph Perry's death undoubtedly caused tremendous grief. The elder Perry, himself a vaudevillian, had always encouraged his son's entertainment career and tutored him in the ways of the profession. One of the entertainment business's oldest traditions was that the show most go on, and in this instance the actor adhered to it.

During July, August, and early September, Fetchit pressed ahead with stage appearances; staying close to home in anticipation of the birth of his first child, and in August, billed as "That Dancin' Fool from Dixie," he appeared in Brooklyn at Loew's Fox Theater in the musical revue *Wild Company.* On September 12, he opened at the Capitol Theater on Broadway in *Bye Bye Blues.* "Stepin Fetchit, colored, just has a way with him on the boards," an early review avowed. "His tapping is not extraordinary, but his drawl and use of the broken high hat are. They liked him a lot at the matinee performance."[39]

His successful reception on Broadway was not the only good news Fetchit received on September 12. On the night of his Capitol Theater opening, Dorothy Perry gave birth to a "ten-pound baby boy" at Sloan Hospital in New York. The infant was named Joseph Jemajo Perry; his rather unique middle name was reportedly conceived as an acronym for Jesus, Mary, and John, "because of the intense religious nature of his father."[40]

While Fetchit's Capitol Theater opening was a noteworthy achievement, the birth of his son obviously overshadowed it. He had enthusiastically expressed his desire to start a family in the past; moreover, three years earlier, he clearly indicated that he preferred motion pictures to "theatricals." His ongoing efforts on the stage aside, the actor's acknowledged career goal was to return to films. He was well aware that national recognition as the most popular Negro motion-picture star held the key to stage success as well as salvaging his vacillating image in the press.

Fetchit had ample reason for concern over his increasingly sour relationship with the black press; a *Chicago Defender* announcement of his son's birth reflected how much his stock had plummeted with Negro scribes. The story moved swiftly from a congratulatory account of Jemajo's arrival to a gratuitously damning summary of the actor's career and Hollywood ouster.[41]

As an avid reader and collector of anything written about him, Fetchit probably steamed at the *Defender* story even as he focused on his Capitol Theater engagement, basked in his new role of proud father, and continued writing and developing his own theatrical production, *Hollywood Revue.* One can reasonably assume, however, that he was also anxiously awaiting a call from a major West Coast studio with an offer of a substantial role on the big screen.

CHAPTER NINE

Stepin Fetchit was still appearing at the Capitol Theater when he received the long-awaited call from Hollywood in late September. He was contacted by MGM—the studio that had produced his first film, *In Old Kentucky*—and offered a role in a new film by *Hallelujah!* director King Vidor. The comedian quickly terminated his theatrical appearances and, leaving his wife and newborn son in New York, headed for the West Coast.

The picture, originally entitled *The Southerner,* was an Old South drama focused on the life of a self-exiled hobo who returns to his wealthy family's plantation after years on the road. Academy Award nominee Lawrence Tibbett was assigned the feature role, and Fetchit was cast in a supportive comic role as Hokey, a bumbling servant. The black actress Mildred Washington also had a minor part as a servant. The project got off to a shaky beginning when Vidor was forced to withdraw because of illness; eventually, Harry A. Pollard, who had directed Fetchit in *Show Boat,* took over the project. Despite production changes, at the outset Fetchit was on his best behavior.

In fact, when Fetchit arrived in Los Angeles in early October, even Negro newspaper scribes got on board to welcome the actor back and noted the shift from his formerly flashy, Central Avenue Bad Boy demeanor to what appeared to be a calmer, more subdued lifestyle. "Stepin Fetchit is back in town after a successful tour in the east including Chicago, Philadelphia and New York. His pretty wife and their new baby are still in the east where he will return later," Harry Levette wrote in his *Eagle* column. A few weeks later, the columnist noted that the actor "seems to be in for the simple life these days. He is driving a Ford roadster and does not seem the least embarrassed."[1]

This apparent serenity was short-lived. By the end of October, the hot-tempered comedian was again caught up in a firestorm of controversy.

Legal problems and difficulties on *The Southerner* set arose concurrently. During October, Fetchit was summoned to court to face two lawsuits. The first involved his ongoing disagreement with teenager Yvonne Butler over the compromise $5,000 settlement reached in her breach-of-promise suit. Butler alleged that "after the first installment, Fetchit failed to pay, and went to New York."

In addition, the owners of the apartment Fetchit had rented at 1609 East 40th Street prior to signing his first Fox contract brought suit against him. They charged that "he not only failed to pay them their rent on a furnished house" but "also damaged the place and carried off rugs and other items of great value." The owners "entered suit in the Superior Court against the comedian for the sum of $2,450. He was to have paid $200 a month, but failed to do so."[2]

Trouble was also reportedly brewing at MGM. The comedian "has been showing spells of stubbornness and temperament," one report alleged. "After wasting nearly an hour of the studio's valuable time for him to read certain lines as director Pollard wanted them, he is said to have been given this ultimatum: 'Either go on with your part in ten minutes, or we'll have you put off the set.' "[3]

Shortly after publication of the article, Fetchit's role in *The Southerner* was terminated, even though an Association of Motion Picture Producers agent and high-ranking MGM officials were initially called in to arbitrate the dispute. Previously filmed scenes were used in the finished movie, but in subsequent footage extras were hired to appear "as doubles for Step in long shots." Fetchit's abrupt dismissal on October 29 was reportedly prompted by the actor's unqualified refusal to blubber the word "frugality" in a comic dialect conversation with actress Mildred Washington.[4]

Although he denied the claims, on the surface it appeared that Fetchit's self-indulgence, caprice, and obstinacy had cost him a role in what one writer called "one of the best parts of his career." The actor's position was further compromised by the esteem with which Pollard was held by much of the Hollywood community. Due to his previous experience with high-profile Negro pictures—*Uncle Tom's Cabin* and the 1925 film *California Straight Ahead*—the director was favorably regarded by many black entertainment professionals. In addition, Fetchit's departure had serious implications for other Negro actors.

In a year-end report on the financial status of race actors in 1930, Harry Levette underlined the effect of Fetchit's dismissal by MGM. After pointing out that $12,000 had been paid to "colored actors, extras and choristers during the month of October," making it "one of the best months of the summer and autumn in film productions that used Negroes," Levette reported that "$10,000 more was lost by the failure of M.G.M. studio to make a barbecue picnic scene, and a stupendous cabaret scene in 'The Southerner' just finished."

Stepin Fetchit alone, Levette continued, "is said to have lost $2,100 in salary" when the studio prematurely ended his part in the picture. "Step was said to be getting $450 to $1,500 a week and Ernest Wilson $25 a day as attendant or valet to him." The writer claimed that Fetchit's release and "other unfortunate occurrences" also "caused delay," which may have resulted in "injuring the local colored film colony."[5]

When a reporter specifically questioned him about his run-in with Pollard and MGM the following summer while he was appearing at the Paramount Theater in Seattle, Fetchit was unapologetic: "There's a whale of difference between exhibiting temperament and fighting for a principle. I fought for a principle when the roles that came my way were not my type of thing. I was very frank. Of course, I spoke firmly.

"But there was nothing temperamental or ritzy about my manner. It was simply my opinion—and I still believe that I was right."

Fetchit asserted that when he took the part he understood that he was to be the central comic relief. But when shooting began, he found that the white actors, Cliff Edwards and Roland Young, were in fact the principal comics in the cast. "The three-way distribution of comedy scenes," the reporter surmised, "didn't leave much for Fetchit."[6]

The picture, which faced even more delays and script changes after Fetchit's departure, was not released until June of 1931 (as *The Prodigal*) and was generally panned as a mishmash of comedy, music, and drama that dealt unsatisfactorily with the problems of homeless men during the Depression. As Fetchit later attested, most of the comedy sequences featured Edwards and Young; the film's Negro presence was relegated to typically obsequious plantation tomfoolery and high jinks. In a rare review that even cited Fetchit's abbreviated appearance, the *New York Times* critic Mordaunt Hall wrote simply that the actor "furnishes some lethargic comedy."[7]

While the clash with MGM director Harry Pollard may or may not have temporarily damaged relationships between the studios and the Negro acting community, there is no question about its having a seriously detrimental effect on both Fetchit's immediate financial situation and Hollywood career. Faced with two lawsuits and having lost thousands of dollars in salary, the actor filed for bankruptcy early in December.

"Stepin Fetchit is broke," an item in the *Chicago Defender* reported that month. "The Scribe can remember only a year ago when the lazy-voiced comedian used to have to pull straws to make up his mind which car he wanted to take out and numerous other displays of unlimited wealth. Alas, such is fame and fortune. It leaves as fast as it comes. Step lists his liabilities at $17,444 and his assets at $6,505. And more than half of his assets are tied up in salaries which as yet have not been paid."[8]

Despite his bankruptcy, as he had the prior year, on December 27 Fetchit published Christmas messages and ran large half-column holiday greeting ads in black newspapers. The *Chicago Defender* article was titled "Perry Writes to Clear Up Many Rumors" and ran with a subhead claiming "Stepin Fetchit Refutes Press Stories." At the outset, Fetchit seemed ready to fulfill the headline's promise. "I feel it is time now that I tear down in a few minutes things that false rumors have been trying to build for years," he asserted. The rambling article, however, was mostly a self-serving, frequently pious, promotional harangue.

"I consider my position in life at present as being more able to give defense than in needing defense, as I, with all due respect to humility, know that I now occupy a position that can be envied by any actor, regardless of who he may be or how financially successfully, who cherish [*sic*] a desire to make an impression for something that would aid the glory and honor of God and the salvation of his soul and the souls of many," Fetchit sermonically intoned.

Ironically, Fetchit admitted that as "an actor portraying the character that I do on the screen, I know I never could demand international respect and admiration, or gain any popularity" that would benefit his employees or himself unless he was "clean cut" and free from "scandal" or "suggestiveness."

The actor inferred that the crux of his problem with Hollywood studios was his outspokenness, demands for less offensive roles, and insistence that his talent be recognized. "I don't want to ever be so weak as to think that I have to be a 'yes man' to some one who has only the box office in mind," he wrote, again noting that "If I am a good actor I want the respect and recognition that is given to good actors."[9]

In a similar piece published in the *Baltimore Afro-American* on the same date, Fetchit took a more inspirational approach. Comparing his own career problems with the hardships most Negroes were experiencing as the Depression deepened, he urged readers to be optimistic and confident, regard hard times as "only blessings in disguise," and "remember that sweet is pleasure after pain."

Again the actor danced lightly around rumors concerning the source of his Hollywood woes, hinting that he had shelved his ego and temperament, and was prepared to moderate his behavior. "It's just a matter of too many chests poked out and too many heads swollen," he asserted. "Time had to be taken to squeeze some of the air out of the swollen heads and chests and show many that the world would not cease to exist without them."[10]

Fetchit assured fans that he would return to pictures. His holiday greeting included the disclosure that he had recently been contacted about a project that he optimistically described as "the miracle achievement of the entire show game."[11]

Fetchit's wife and child joined him, and, during January and February, he remained on the West Coast. But when the promised "miracle" project to which he alluded did not materialize, with no other options, he returned to the theatrical circuit. Reportedly on "recess from film work," in February Fetchit opened at Curtis Mosby's Apex Club in San Francisco's Chinatown district. The stage tour wound through northern California for several weeks before he returned to Los Angeles in March.

In early April, the comedian brought his stage act to Central Avenue and 42nd Street. "The inimitable Stepin Fetchit 'tiahed' feet and lazy drawl, will make a personal appearance Sunday, Monday and Tuesday at the Tivoli Theater for the benefit of fans who seldom see the character off the silver sheet," the *California Eagle* reported. "Step, now the proud papa of Jemajo, has been hard at it on various circuits and this week's appearance marks his first engagement in the city since his return from the north where he earned the usual triumphs."[12]

The Tivoli appearance was a huge success. The actor's languorous charisma drew packed houses for each performance as he combined comic patter with adroit dance steps and, playing on his movie star status, talking to audiences about the exotic world of motion picture production. "Stepin Fetchit scored in his first appearance on 'Brown Broadway' in his new vaudeville act," one critic wrote. "For about 30 minutes he sings, dances, chats about his movie career and does a comedy reading act with the audience as subjects. His own piano player accompanies him."[13]

The actor's apparently tranquil domestic life, however, suddenly erupted. In the same issue of the newspaper, it was reported that Mrs. Perry (Dorothy Stevenson) was "contemplating a divorce action" in a front-page article that ran with the subhead "Famous Movie Star Is Accused of Cruelty and Non-Support." The *California Eagle* article alleged that there had been whispers of trouble brewing since the couple returned from the East Coast. According to Stevenson, who was living apart from her husband, the "situation came to a head when Step went to his wife's home, 708 North Alvarado, and took [their] child away with him." She claimed that she had been awarded custody of the child by the courts and reportedly told an interviewer "she would seek a warrant from the district attorney's office charging him with kidnapping."[14]

Echoing the mainstream press's often sensational depiction of controversial white celebrities, particularly down-on-their-luck actors, the Negro press spotlighted the comedian's domestic woes and rehashed the career scrapes that preceded them. Baltimore's *Afro-American*, for example, called the actor a "paradox among movie stars" and noted that although "a fanatic on the scriptures, he has an uncanny faculty for getting into one scrape after another." The report's subhead blared: "Spectre of Ill-Fortune That Wrecked Movie Career Now Invades Stepin Fetchit's Home Life."[15]

The paper also ran excerpts from a statement that Fetchit issued to the press, admitting that he had taken his son while appearing in Los Angeles but had returned the child to his mother. In the seventeen-page release, the actor denied allegations of kidnapping and insisted that there would be no divorce.

"Since through some misfortune my personal affair has become a public matter and for the benefit of the many people who are so misinformed about myself I have desired to issue this statement," the press release began. The rambling response placed the blame for his marital problems on "false friends."

"I guess my wife is now celebrating the return of her son whom she had not seen for eight days. I heard that she intended getting a divorce and I want to tell the world that I don't believe it. If she does I'll never give it to her," Fetchit said, "because 'What God hath joined together no man can unjoin or let no man put asunder.' I wouldn't swap places with the biggest star in Hollywood or the president of the United States or with nobody I know living unless it was for a place on the altar or in a monastery. And I know that I have the girl that I was intended to have and that she is a great girl and a good little scout."[16]

Shortly afterward, Fetchit and his wife apparently agreed to attempt to reconcile their differences. And during the next few months, the actor seemed raptly focused on repairing both his marriage and his sour relationship with film producers and theater managers. In May, after being ignored for eight months, Fetchit was finally offered another motion-picture role. It was only a minor comic part in Allied Pictures' *Wild Horse,* a B-western that featured cowboy star Hoot Gibson; but the actor jumped at the opportunity. The quickie western was completed in June, and, shortly afterward, Fetchit set off on a theatrical tour through northern California and Washington State, taking his family with him.

On the set of *Wild Horse,* the actor had apparently behaved impeccably. And since at this point in his career almost anything other than a disastrous encounter with the studio bosses was rare enough to be considered noteworthy, the black press eagerly trumpeted the news. According to a news report, an Allied studio source avowed that Fetchit "was not late a day during the picture. Besides that he never broke a studio traffic law, never got stubborn or temperamental and all in all gave the directors no trouble at any time."[17]

ABOVE: *Stepin Fetchit (in doorway) as Gummy in* Hearts in Dixie *(Fox, 1929).* SPRINGER/PHOTOFEST

BELOW: *With Bernice Pilot as his wife, Chloe, in* Hearts in Dixie *(Fox, 1929).* SPRINGER/PHOTOFEST

In a typical Fox publicity photo (c. 1929). PHOTOFEST

A rare publicity photo, in which Perry is not "in character" (c. 1930). AP, WIDE WORLD

ABOVE: *Stepin Fetchit entertaining at his "Temple of Rest" on the roof of his apartment building in Los Angeles. Prominent Hollywood guests were often served watermelon, also referred to as "letters from home," to put them at ease According to the press caption accompa nying the photo, "his philosophy is that too much work kills the soul" (1936).*

AP, WIDE WORLD

LEFT: *In this studio publicity photo, according to its caption, "the screen's ac of spades . . . has announced his determ nation to become the first of his race to essay a flight to Africa. . . . To make sur he has no mishaps, Stepin will carry, in addition to his two lucky numbers after which he has christened the ship, a rabbit's foot and a horseshoe" (c. 1934).*

AP, WIDE WORLD

ABOVE: *With Will Rogers in* The County Chairman *(Fox, 1935).* PHOTOFEST

BELOW: *As Scipio, with Lionel Barrymore in* Carolina *(Fox, 1934).*

ABOVE: *With Cotton Club dancer, singer, and Broadway actress Winnie Johnson, and their son, David Martin (1939).*

BELOW: *Winnie Johnson and Canada Lee at the Cort Theater, on Broadway, in a publicity photo for* South Pacific, *in which they were both appearing (1943).* VANDAMN STUDIO/PHOTOFEST

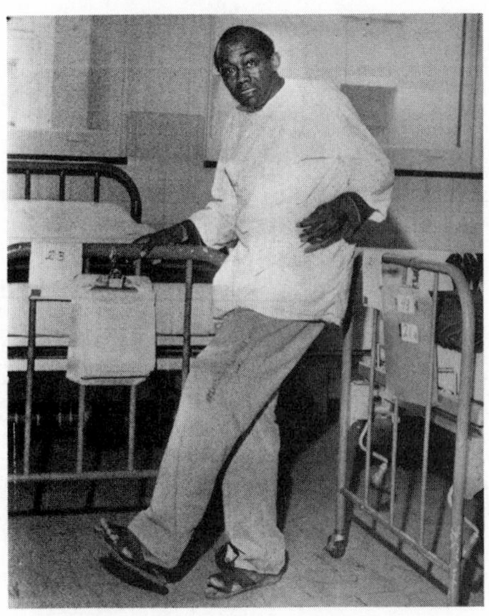

ABOVE: *An Associated Press Wire Service photo of Perry, at age sixty-two, recovering from an operation in Chicago's Cook County Hospital, where, according to the caption, he was a "charity patient . . . Friends who know him well say he made and spent at least $2 million in the days when taxes were low and income and living high in Hollywood"* (May 1964).

PHOTOFEST

BELOW: *With Muhammad Ali (center) and Jodie "Butterbeans" Edwards a few months after Ali's first fight with Sonny Liston* (August 1964).

AP, WIDE WORLD

RIGHT: *At Muhammad Ali's training camp before the Ali-Liston rematch (1965).* AP, WIDE WORLD

BELOW: *Holding a press conference outside the Federal Building in Indianapolis to publicize his lawsuit against CBS, Xerox, Twentieth Century Fox, and the Indiana Broadcasting Company. Perry claimed that his portrayal in the 1968 CBS series* Of Black Americans *was defamatory, in that he was described as "the white man's Negro" (1972).* PHOTOFEST

Still, the actor had not abandoned his flamboyance or flair for publicity. His theatrical tour had reached Canada by mid-June, and "armed with a thousand souvenir photos of himself" produced in Los Angeles "by the Tivoli photo studio," he and his vaudeville act were reportedly thriving. Fetchit kept the press advised of his whereabouts and successes. He also continued attempting to dash reports that his marriage was on the rocks. While appearing at the Royal Theater in Vancouver, British Columbia, he wired old friends at the *Chicago Defender* requesting that the paper "inform the world that he and Mrs. Fetchit [were] enjoying a wonderful trip through Canada," adding that "little Jemajo also coos his love."[18]

When he returned to Hollywood in July, Fetchit was again tapped for a role in a B-picture produced by one of the industry's satellite companies. Mascot Films, a small company that had renewed or extended the careers of a number of Hollywood stars, offered a role in a twelve-part serial starring football legend Harold "Red" Grange. These short, multipart cliff-hangers were popular during the thirties and forties, and were usually shown in weekly installments at theaters in addition to feature films. Each episode ended in some suspenseful, unresolved conflict, a ploy intended to lure patrons back to the theater to witness the outcome.

Desperate to revitalize his career, Fetchit accepted a meager comic role in *The Galloping Ghost,* a melodrama involving gamblers' attempts to fix football games. Serials were not widely reviewed by mainstream critics and, in this instance, even the Negro press generally ignored the film. Fetchit, however, probably hoped that as with stars like Frank Darro, John Wayne, and Boris Karloff, as well as cowboy favorites Ken Maynard, Gabby Hayes, and Gene Autry, the unheralded Mascot serial might help jump-start his film career. In most surviving tape versions of the film, Fetchit appears for only ten seconds in Chapter Six, and has the following less than memorable lines: "I'm sorry Mr. Grange, but that coach is done left for the football field. Yessuh, you might catch him, but he sure drives a fast car."

Meanwhile, the Fetchits surface domestic accord was suddenly exposed as a sham. In late August, his wife filed suit for divorce in a Los Angeles court, citing brutality as cause. A New York newspaper reported that the suit alleged that Fetchit "broke the nose, jaw and chin of Dorothy Perry, his wife, with his fists and a broomstick."[19]

"Mrs. Perry's appearance before the courts was a complete surprise to friends of the couple here as the split in their matrimonial ranks, started several months ago, was thought to be healed," the *Chicago Defender* reported. "The main hitch in the plan of Mrs. Perry to go through with her plans for divorce is the disposition of their child." The *Defender* indicated that Fetchit was now prepared to grant his wife custody. "I am willing to let my wife keep our son," Fetchit reportedly said, "but I must see him at intervals. When I am denied that, then I shall seek other means of possession."[20]

The couple reached an amiable separation agreement, but as a practicing Catholic, Fetchit resisted his wife's demands for a divorce. "I did not get a divorce," he later told a reporter. "The only thing is I live in California and my wife, she lives in Arizona. My little son is with her." The actor's wife had contracted tuberculosis months after their separation and left Los Angeles for health reasons. During the separation, Fetchit attentively supported his wife and child. Mrs. Perry, one report claimed, had "every possible comfort provided by her husband" who called and visited frequently, hoping for a reconciliation.[21]

During the spring and summer of 1931, Fetchit was frequently depicted as a mere flash-in-the-pan by Negro news journals, particularly those that urged blacks to support "serious" artists, or openly blamed him and his wayward behavior off and on the set for his untimely demise.

One writer contended that he "went ritzy" after signing a huge contract, "kept directors waiting," branched out in "a silver Rolls Royce," and according to a Fox source, "began living on a ridiculously elaborate scale." Noting the actor's "irresponsibility and mischievousness," another journalist cited a bizarre, unsubstantiated incident. During a break in shooting, he wrote, "Step went to the barbershop and had his head shaved bald. When the company resumed work an hour later, Step looked like a different person. The director faced the alternative of holding up production for a week while his hair grew back or trying to put hair on his head from the makeup kit. They called out the makeup experts who worked for hours trying to put the hair back. High-powered stars, drawing huge salaries, sat around and twiddled their thumbs. Step's hair-cut cost the company thousands of dollars."[22]

As Fetchit's star faded, imitators like Stompen 'n' Sellit and newcomer Sleep 'n' Eat began garnering more coverage in the Negro press and much more attention from the studios. "At last Stepin Fetchit has an imitator who really does credit to the lazy comedian," a news item said of the latter late in 1930. "The lad, whose real name we haven't as yet discovered, plays an important role with Harold Lloyd in 'Feet First,' under the cognomen of 'Sleep 'n' Eat.'" Six months later, it was announced that the young actor, described as "Stepin Fetchit's successor," was about to appear in Universal Pictures' *The Virtuous Husband.* And the following year—reflecting middle-class Negro disdain for Fetchit's screen achievements—an *Amsterdam News* writer touted an unusual specialty attraction, the relatively unknown Negro dwarf Edgar "Blue Boy" Connor, as the new black comedian destined to replace Fetchit in Hollywood.[23]

Ultimately, it was Sleep 'n' Eat (later billed under his real name, Willie Best), who most effectively emulated Fetchit's soporific film character and was most vigorously promoted as a Step clone by the studios. With his successful appearance in *Up Pops the Devil,* released in May 1931, Best provided studios with a competitive alternative to Fetchit's popular lethargic black screen character.

The Mississippi-born performer had begun his career in a traveling carnival and was discovered on the streets of Central Avenue shortly after arriving in Los Angeles at age fourteen or fifteen. His initial discovery was based largely on his remarkable likeness to Fetchit. Best recalled walking along the Stroll and noticing a white man in a car watching and following him. Thinking it was a police officer, he bolted. Fortunately, he was unable to elude his pursuer, who surprised the actor with the offer of a picture role. The bizarre episode not only foreshadowed his persona on-screen but eventually led to a contract with RKO.[24]

In his early motion pictures during the thirties and forties, Best projected an almost schizophrenic timidity. With his lean, gangling, underfed appearance, from a distance he was a dead ringer for Fetchit. Moreover, he frequently appeared confused and drowsy, displaying a languor that bordered on the comatose. It was unvarnished mimicry, a near mirror image of the character that Fetchit had brought to the screen. In addition to mirroring Fetchit, Best brought his own distinct comic *shtick* to films. His character alternately quaked with fear, giving the impression that someone or something frightful and unseen was threatening or pursuing him even in the most benign situations. His lanky, stoop-shouldered frame was usually coiled in readiness for flight, and his dark, slack-jawed face emitted a sense of perpetual awe. When actually frightened, Best would literally quiver with alarm. As his wide eyes dilated, his pupils would dart about frantically, flashing in pools of white; his lower lip drooped, and sweat popped from his forehead. Shaken and drawn, when some imagined specter loomed or a real villain appeared, he would bolt—his high-stepping, slew-foot gait sending him into haphazard, headlong flight during which he outran everyone and everything, including horses and automobiles. It was a classic comedy bit, one that became a cinema staple by the forties—reenacted countless times by mainstream comics like Lou Costello or Negro comics like Mantan Moreland. Few, if any, however, matched the exaggerated intensity Best brought to that particular bit.

A role as a chauffeur and valet in *The Smiling Ghost* (1941), a routine comedy whodunit that starred Wayne Morris and Alexis Smith, provided an opportunity for Best to display his nervous, petrified coon bit. In one scene, when Morris asks if he is afraid, he replies, "I ain't afraid but my feets ain't goin' stand around and see my body get abused." Later, when Morris and Smith tell him they intend to find a body in the graveyard, Best declines their invitation, saying, "When folks stop breathin' and walkin', I'm through wit' 'em." Finally, after reluctantly entering the cemetery, the trembling Best voices concern about "tramplin'" around on top of the dead. Smith assures him that "there's six feet between you and them."

"Yessum," he replies, "but it's goin' be six miles between us any minute now."[25]

Best never reached the level of popularity or notoriety attained by Fetchit. Although he appeared in over one hundred pictures during a career that spanned three decades and consistently played parts that equaled or surpassed Fetchit's most servile roles, he was never targeted and criticized with the fervor directed at Fetchit. In the 1950s, he became a fixture at the Hal Roach Studios and had minor continuing comic roles in the Roach-produced TV series *The Stu Erwin Show* and *My Little Margie.* Despite rigidly stereotyped parts, Best was considered an able character actor. He built an impressive list of film and TV credits and worked with some of the best talent, including Laurel and

Hardy, the Marx Brothers, Bob Hope, and Shirley Temple. Hope, who appeared with him in *The Ghost Breakers* (1940) and *Nothing but the Truth* (1941), once referred to Best as "the finest actor I knew."[26]

Best, like nearly all of the Negro actors who won parts at Hollywood studios during the early thirties, was noticeably less confrontational in his dealings with the studios than was the outspoken Fetchit. Few balked at or resisted Hollywood's continued refusal to portray urban or professional Negroes, its insistence on confining black actors to stereotyped servant roles and revisiting plantation settings or the annoying on-set indignities such as separate, second-rate dining areas, shabby, cramped dressing facilities, and most often sneering, contemptuous treatment by white crews.

"I often think about these roles I have to play. Most of them are pretty broad. Sometimes I tell the director and he cuts out the real bad parts," Best said of his stereotyped film roles. "But what's an actor going to do? Either you do it or you get out."

The actor was expressing an opinion held by nearly all of Hollywood's black screen players during those trying financial times. The film industry had reacted to the market crash and the Depression by "cutting costs, shutting East Coast plants, trimming low-volume theaters, wages, ticket prices, and office budgets and by using stock shots, postponing building plans, and pruning shooting schedules." The studios' hard-line, cost-cutting, no-nonsense approach and the bleak financial and racial realities of the times no doubt influenced black actors' restrained, accommodating approach. But the lesson learned from Fetchit's unpredictable behavior and aggressive, demanding stance with industry bigwigs—resulting in what was essentially an across-the-board blackballing at major studios—must surely have influenced them as well. The message was clear. Toe the line or leave.[27]

Meanwhile, Fetchit's career had hit rock bottom. The extent of his total estrangement from Hollywood producers at this point in his career would surface later in several Negro press stories.

"Made a dozen pictures and a barrel of money," a brief summary of the actor's career asserted. "Became the studio pest—was never on hand when he was wanted. Became so unreliable that the Hollywood ax was dropped on his unsuspecting neck and he found himself a penniless ex-star."[28]

"You can't argue with these movie producers and get away with it," another columnist offered. "There is the case of Stepin Fetchit, the famous comic, who was unable to agree with his front office over several details to making a picture. 'Step' had told them that unless certain things were done he'd quit the studios. They didn't ask him not to. But instead 'Step' was given a part in a picture at a little boost in salary which looked good on surface, but there was method in those movie producers' madness. The picture had 'Step' picking 'cooties' from a camel, which is about the cheapest thing a man can do. The idea made a few laughs, but it just about killed 'Step' as a popular favorite with his fandom."[29]

The part was the kind normally offered to extras, but it "gave producers the chance to curtail some of the Fetchit popularity," a *Chicago Defender* reporter alleged, "which many figured was what they were trying to do."[30]

"In the North," the African American folk saying advises, "they don't care how big Negroes get, as long as you don't get too close. In the South, they don't care how close you get, as long you don't get too big." And after all was said and done, Hollywood was part of *Southern* California—"more segregated than Georgia under the skin," Fetchit would later contend. Ultimately, Stepin Fetchit had gotten much too big, far too fast, for even the relatively liberal tastes of the nouveau riche bohemians, thespians, vaudevillians, and motion picture moguls who resided in the Hollywood Hills.[31]

Ostracized by the studios, estranged from his wife and child, and nearly broke, the actor groused about his predicament and, perhaps out of frustration, vented his rage against his old friend, actor Clarence Muse.

Early in September 1931, he and Muse were invited along with other Negro performers, including the fast-rising star Hattie McDaniel, to appear at a Boy Scouts of America benefit. Fetchit apparently thought Muse "was getting too much attention" and verbally attacked the veteran actor during the festivities. Onlookers were shocked when he railed that "I am a far greater movie star than Clarence Muse." A shouting match ensued, and, reportedly, "a few moments later the two movie men were engaged in a verbal 'tat-too' that had many of the patrons reaching for the doors." The only thing that kept them from engaging in an out-and-out brawl, a Los Angeles journalist reported, was "the reluctance of 'Step' to replace his verbal attack upon Muse with an avalanche of fists." The breach between the former friends would extend throughout their careers.[32]

Some weeks later, while touring the South with his recently formed orchestra, Stepin's Studio Strutters, the irrepressible Fetchit announced that he was seeking funding and searching for actors for his own independently produced picture. It was hyped as an "all-colored cast" sequel to *Hearts in Dixie* entitled *Skeeter,* a project that he had been pitching to the studios for over a year. "I have been unable to find men willing to cast me in certain types of films," he explained, and "whenever some mention is made of placing me in a picture that contains real class they turn the other way and it is for that reason that I intend to write my own story and produce my own film."[33]

Surprisingly, Fetchit was offered a minor part as "the Hustler" in *Neck and Neck,* which starred Walter Brennan. When no further roles were offered after its release in November, the young actor reluctantly returned to the vaudeville circuit. He continued billing himself as the "Famed Colored Stage and Film Star," but except for an appearance as himself in the musical short *Slow Poke* in 1932, he would beat the bushes in nightclubs, juke joints, and TOBA theaters for two years before being offered another part in a feature-length Hollywood picture.

CHAPTER TEN

Banished from films, Stepin Fetchit began an odyssey that took him far afield of Hollywood's glamour and marquee showcasing in 1932. Appearing as a single act with a lone pianist or backed by Stepin's Studio Strutters band, he crisscrossed the country playing sites that ranged from upscale Keith-Orpheum–circuit venues to the shabbiest TOBA theaters, from off-Broadway theaters to one-night stands in small Midwestern and Southern town halls or burlesque houses where even the cut-rate forty-cent ticket prices for the best seats were stiffer than most locals were willing to pay.

It was a humbling reminder of his early years on the black entertainment circuit. Near the end of his two-year exile in the early thirties, a *New York Times* reporter sardonically wrote that during those lean years, Fetchit "found the corn pones less succulent than the pork chops he used to eat in the back seat of any one of his three limousines back in the pre-Roosevelt days."[1]

Mainstream press coverage of Fetchit's activities on the road during his exile from Hollywood, however, was rare. Once he fell from grace, the white media turned a cold shoulder.

Nor did the Negro press extend much coverage or "love" to a star who little more than two years before it had compared to the legendary Bert Williams and praised as "truly one of the greatest colored actors ever to appear on the silver screen." Fetchit had been effectively removed from the public eye.

While its most popular Negro player languished in the boondocks, the film industry did not miss a beat. There seems to have been a general sigh of relief at not having to deal with the unsettling and, in early-twentieth-century America, controversial presence of a wealthy black movie star—particularly one as strong-willed, confrontational, and confounding as Step.

As critics often claimed, many whites saw Fetchit's screen character as a comforting reaffirmation of prevailing stereotypes. For predisposed viewers, the craven, trifling character he brought to the screen offered superficial support for claims of across-the-board Negro inferiority and justification for a continued paternalistic policy toward blacks. His popularity and prominence may have also reassured many that, segregation and second-class citizenship notwithstanding, colored folk remained a nonthreatening, childlike, contented lot. Motion-picture fantasy, however, collided head-on with off-screen reality for more aware viewers. Fetchit's popularity had availed him of a lifestyle that far exceeded the bottom-rung status expected or, in the South, demanded of blacks by most of white society in early-twentieth-century America. His wealth, flamboyance, and outspoken sense of entitlement clearly belied the image of the humble Negro embraced by mainstream America. It annoyed or, in some instances, outraged conservative whites in Hollywood and throughout the country.

Negro opinion of Fetchit was also dramatically split. Among intellectuals and the middle-class, he was often scorned and vilified as a toady and racial embarrassment because of the very nature of the character he portrayed. Fetchit's nationwide fame was seen as an obstacle to serious consideration of positive Negro achievements. The average white person, an indignant writer claimed in a February 1930 letter to the *Baltimore Afro-American,* was "forced to believe" the portrait of black life that "comes to him in the way of amusements." The Negro's silence regarding the stage and film "clowning of bell boys, porters and waiters for their white spectators," he continued, demonstrate that "we are not only as 'patient as a jackass,' but just about as sensible."[2]

The opinion expressed by that reader was directed toward the *Amos 'n' Andy* show—which in its time far exceeded the popularity of such present-day megahits as *Friends* or *Seinfeld*—but echoed rising criticism of Fetchit and other actors whose comic portrayals of ne'er-do-wells and ingratiating domestics accounted for nearly all Negro roles in

Hollywood films. The debate over the negative consequences of burlesquing and exploiting the lifestyles of uneducated, lower-class blacks was rapidly accelerating. The issue would not disappear. It not only shadowed Stepin Fetchit's career, but has also resurfaced recently with protests over the image of black life projected in some of the glib, self-deprecating lyrics of rap songs or by such movies as *Booty Call, Barbershop,* and *Soul Plane.*

The most serious early protest of the *Amos 'n' Andy* radio show, for example, arose in 1931 when Robert L. Vann, editor of the *Pittsburgh Courier,* one of the nation's largest weekly black newspapers, launched the first nationwide campaign to ban the show from the airways. The newspaper's drive for a nationally sponsored petition fueled the discussion, and the *Courier* reportedly collected 740,000 signatures supporting its position before the campaign fizzled within a year or so. Ironically, while Fetchit and other black performers remained targets of Negro critics, protests over the *Amos 'n' Andy* radio show subsided. The program would remain on the air until the 1960s. Still, the heated exchanges that arose at the height of Vann's petition had stoked a debate that exposed the rift between blue-collar and middle-class blacks on the issue of detrimental media images.[3]

Most supporters of the *Courier* petition, for instance, were more concerned with the effect that negative characterizations had on white America than with their impact on Negroes themselves. Many agreed that caricatures of the black underclass had some basis in reality but felt that excess focus on the lowest stratum of Negro life obscured the progress made by black professionals; they argued that suppressing those crude, comically exaggerated images was essential to uplifting the race and gaining respectability in the larger society.

Still, a large segment of the working-class black community ignored middle-class objections and embraced the overt tomfoolery of black comic presentations. From their viewpoint, the high jinks of most Negro comics were entertaining fantasies—inside humor that allowed them to laugh at themselves as well as at whites. The running gag in Fetchit's early screen appearances, for instance, was that despite his characters' servile position they usually outwitted their white "superiors" and cleverly sidestepped efforts at forcing them into compliance with their boss's unwieldy demands. Many Negro fans apparently recognized that the stylized, over-the-top put-ons enacted by "Highpockets," "Gummy," and "Smoke Screen" were comic parodies of a ruse that slaves and farmhands as well as urban blacks mired in low-paying servile jobs had employed for decades.

In films Fetchit's bumbling ineptitude typically disguised a determination to avoid unwanted tasks. His hesitant, dawdling reactions to commands from whites most often resulted in chores being postponed or assigned to someone else. His seemingly befuddled responses to requests and mumbled, under-the-breath responses to questions usually resulted in a standoff. Exasperated bosses generally left those encounters laughing and shaking their heads in disbelief. Fetchit's Br'er Rabbit–like characters were experts at ducking and dodging, demonstrating that calculated sloth and the pretense of confusion and ineptitude could thwart an employer's demand for hard, unrewarded labor in a dead-end work situation.

In many instances, they were cinema reflections of an old folk ruse that advocated "taking low"—giving the appearance of losing the battle while assuring survival and winning the war. They mirrored the wisdom of ingenious folk characters who wheedled their way out of the most precarious confrontations with white authorities. A typical example was the tale of an underfed slave who, tired of a diet of fatback and grits, resorted to stealing his master's turkeys in order to feed his family. "You scoundrel, you ate my turkey," the master raged after catching him red-handed. The quick-witted slave opines, "Well suh, Massa, you got less turkey, but you sho nuff got mo nigger." The indisputable logic not only humored and placated the "boss" but also avoided immediate punishment. The Harlem Renaissance writer Zora Neale Hurston once colorfully described the tactic as "making a way out of no way. Hitting a straight lick with a crooked stick. Winning the jackpot with no other stake than a laugh."

Many of Fetchit's black fans understood the subversive aspect of the humor and the social circumstances from which it had been derived. For them, the whites bamboozled by Step's fakery were the butts of the joke. Others, no doubt, admired the actor simply as a symbol of success, an example of the wealth and acclaim Negroes could grasp with guile, talent, and a healthy dose of gall even within a Jim Crow society. Many viewed Fetchit as a sort of folk hero who cleverly jeered white gullibility and thumbed his nose at expectations of Negro allegiance to mainstream models of respectability. For them, he confirmed the value of pretense, deception, and a little old-fashioned trickery in deflecting or neutralizing oppressive white control.

The actor posed an unusual problem for the film colony's producers and executives as well. On the one hand, since the era's social customs encouraged and generally demanded diffident behavior from blacks, Fetchit's surreal cinema depictions of an indolent black character were perceived as little more than realistic representations of a common Negro type by most whites—including many of Hollywood's elite filmmakers. Certainly at the outset, in addition to regarding Fetchit as a moneymaking machine, some in the film community saw the actor as something of a pet, a true-to-life personification of the Old South feckless Negro character that had dominated Hollywood films.

Fetchit had contributed to that initial impression in 1927 when he auditioned for the role of Highpockets in MGM's *In Old Kentucky* and caught the director's eye by pretending to be an illiterate farm boy. He sustained the charade when interacting with the white press by demanding that his comments be translated into broken dialect. And even two years later—after the release of *Hearts in Dixie* and despite his growing reputation as a Central Avenue sport and on-set agitator—the Hollywood crowd still insisted on equating the actor and the comic rural buffoon he portrayed on-screen.

As a result, many producers and directors failed to recognize the actor's work as stylized parody—performance. His popularity and acceptance were often attributed to an authentic representation of the servile roles he played, not to his ability to fashion a comic character that often mocked and stretched the limits of those clichéd roles. It may have been a reflection of the era's knee-jerk assumption that Negro achievement in the performing arts was always a guileless, "natural" representation of their true personalities or simply a reluctance to grant star status to a black performer. But the studios' inability to recognize let alone fully appreciate the actor's unique comic burlesquing of America's palliative, fondly embraced image of the inept, harmless darky, meant that Stepin Fetchit and his lucrative contract were expendable. In the eyes of many Hollywood execs, one coon was as good as the other.

Of course, given the temper of the times, one might add that if Hollywood honchos or white audiences had perceived the actor's satirical ruse for what it appears to have been—subversive mocking of an offensive stereotype—it is unlikely that Fetchit would ever have been embraced, endorsed, and promoted by the studios.

As the comedian would later loudly proclaim: "There was no white man's idea of making a Negro Hollywood motion picture star, a millionaire Negro entertainer. Savvy?"[4]

By the time he left Hollywood and took to the road in 1931, the far more affordable, accommodating, and controllable Step lookalike Willie Best had already been brought in to fill the niche the former star had vacated.

Best was not the only performer who benefited from Fetchit's expulsion. The star's exile opened opportunities for dozens of Negro motion-picture actors in the early thirties. The immediate result was the studios' frantic scramble to find an actor who could approach the Negro comic's box-office appeal, preferably someone who was less controversial and publicity-minded. From 1931 to 1933, dozens of performers were recruited in an attempt to copy or reprise what was generally viewed as a stock Negro comedic presentation. Among the most prominent and resilient of the players called upon were Sam "Deacon" McDaniel, Nicodemus Stewart, Fred "Snowflake" Toones, and Mantan Moreland.

Hattie McDaniel's brother Sam appeared in twenty-nine films during Fetchit's hiatus in 1931 to 1932. Stewart was introduced to the screen in 1932 and, in the late thirties, emerged as the actor's most insistently cloying imitator. Fred Toones—"one of the most rigidly stereotyped and at times most embarrassing black actors to work in American Movies," according to film historian Donald Bogle—debuted as an extra in *The Galloping Ghost,* one of Fetchit's last early-thirties movies, and went on to appear in thirty-three pictures during his mentor's absence. Ironically, but perhaps not coincidentally, Toones later billed himself with a diminutive variation of the name Snowball, the character Fetchit played in *Ghost.* After an initial 1933 role as a night watchman in *That's the Spirit,* Mantan Moreland emerged as the undisputed king of Hollywood's comic Negro servants. During a career that spanned four decades, he made over three hundred films; they included the Charlie Chan detective series, in which he appeared in his signature role as the skittish chauffeur, Birmingham.[5]

Along with Willie Best, these actors' dutifully reenacted Hollywood's familiar depiction of the acquiescent, perpetually cowed black male servant. Each added their own personal stamp to the comic portrayal. Only the veteran McDaniel, perhaps perceived as less of a threat because of his advanced age, was given license to mouth an occasional wisecrack that challenged white authority. The comic actors who replaced Fetchit during his early-thirties exile were shackled with minstrelsy-inspired "Yassuh, Boss" characterizations that mirrored those Fetchit had labored to overcome. None were able to effectively resist.

Such old-guard stalwarts as Noble Johnson and Clarence Muse also received increased attention from the studios. Muse, Johnson, and, in rare appearances, Clarence Brooks, Madame Sul-Te-Wan, George Reed, Daniel L. Haynes, and Nina Mae McKinney were the benefactors of a few better-than-average roles, some of which portrayed Negroes as more fully drawn human beings. Brooks, for example, was cast as a doctor facing a moral dilemma regarding treatment of blacks on a Caribbean island in John Ford's *Arrowsmith* (1931). Also in 1931, McKinney and Muse explored more complex human emotions in *Safe in Hell,* another island drama. As the locales of those films indicate, it was apparently easier for studio bosses to justify less stereotypical depictions of Negro characters who lived outside the United States.

The early thirties also saw a rise in exotic films such as MGM's Tarzan series as well as increased production of pictures with sports, Old West, and underworld crime themes. Negro extras portraying hostile or co-opted native primitives and bearers in jungle pictures reaped most of the rewards in the location pictures. And while westerns generally offered only comic sidekick roles that mirrored traditional servant parts in Southern plantation movies, in a few sports and crime movies the depiction of blacks was stretched beyond Hollywood's usual limits. The increase in atmosphere work for Negroes also derived in part from Hollywood's decision to occasionally show blacks in background scenes of pictures with urban settings. Although tentative, it was an eventful step for an industry that, except for servants and entertainers, had largely ignored the existence of blacks in mainstream America. Despite the Depression then, extra work increased steadily during the spring of

1932. Nearly seven hundred actors were hired by the studios in the month of May, a figure that reflected a significant increase over those hired in both the previous month and in May 1931.

The Negro press not only noted the flurry of activity but, on occasion, rhapsodized over the situation. "Say the jigs have it in this man's town right now," Harry Levette wrote in 1932. "The ladies and gentlemen of the histronic [*sic*] profession who are of African descent certainly appear to have monopolized stage and screen work at this present moment. Why it would warm the cylinders of your old heart to run from one theater to another, one studio to another and find from one to a hundred of your own blood brothers and sisters of Aunt Hagar. It may not be so long but right now it is 'gentle readers,' it is."[6]

Levette's enthusiastic outburst aside, in retrospect the most significant development in the evolution of the Negro presence in Hollywood pictures during Fetchit's hiatus was probably the emergence of spunky, somewhat independent, and generally morally upright black maids—servants with attitude.

Two remarkable actresses, Louise Beavers and "Hi-Hat" Hattie McDaniel, topped a list of a dozen or so black women who played these roles. Their performances not only offered a less veiled reflection of Negro retainers' wry, often cynical perception of white employers but also, because of the wit and underlying self-reliance projected by the actresses, countered the nation's stereotypical perception of Negroes as dimwitted and childlike. These roles, of course, drew even more attention to the industry's insistent casting of Negro males as fainthearted comic servants and fueled steadily intensifying NAACP protests regarding the image of blacks in Hollywood pictures.

Meanwhile, Beavers and McDaniel burst onto the screen with a bold assertiveness and almost familial sense of personal connection to their employers that made Stepin Fetchit's otherworldly distance, hesitance, stylized mumbling, and calculated stonewalling appear archaic. Beavers debuted in silent pictures in 1923 and was cast as a maid in nearly two dozen supportive roles during the next seven years. From 1931 to 1933, however, the actress appeared in forty pictures and, along with McDaniel (who appeared in a dozen films during the same period), established the assertive Black Mammy as a central figure in Hollywood films of the thirties and forties.

They were the antithesis of the shrinking-violet types usually portrayed in Hollywood films. Beavers was most often optimistic and cheerful, the strong-willed, quiet, but resourceful black woman who provided unwavering support and commonsense counsel for both employers and her family. McDaniel was typically louder, more outspoken and cantankerous, an often belligerent agitator who cut through sentimental claptrap. These robust take-charge women frequently controlled the households in which they worked. Beavers even managed to exert some behind-the-scenes influence when, with assistance from the NAACP, she successfully lobbied to have the word "nigger" removed from the script of *Imitation of Life,* the 1934 film that ignited her career.[7]

In terms of image, McDaniel and Beavers may have made their most significant contribution by shattering the taboo regarding blacks talking back to whites in motion pictures. Fetchit and other male cinema servants were generally only permitted to express dissent indirectly by scowling, winking, or mumbling incoherent protests or objections beneath their breath. These actresses often confronted whites head-on, openly ridiculing or challenging their actions or decisions. In theaters, black audiences frequently greeted their scathing retorts with cheers.

Finally, however, their unwavering strength and obsessive concern for their employers' welfare were as distorted and unrealistic as the images of dutiful, self-effacing servants they replaced. Each, in fact, spawned new stereotypes. Beavers' sunny screen persona would give rise to the selfless, ever-dependable and much-adored Aunt Jemima image that comforted mainstream America for decades. The tough, no-nonsense character that McDaniel established on-screen would evolve into the shrill, overbearing caricature of Sapphire, a mythical figure that would haunt and confound black male-female relationships into the second half of the century.

Meanwhile, Stepin Fetchit continued his nationwide theatrical tour. In August, he announced that he would begin a cross-country "good will tour" during which he would "look for talent" for his independent cinema project. He convinced several dozen New York area performers to join him and, by the fall, the show was on the road.[8]

His absence from the screen, however, had dulled Fetchit's stage appeal. From the outset, his stage tour frequently sputtered and sometimes stalled completely.

In October 1932, for instance, the ANP reported that the actor's road show had been dissolved after leaving the East Coast. The troupe of fifty performers, including singers, a chorus line, and Stepin's Studio Strutters band, had been scheduled for a series of one-night stands in Pennsylvania towns, but the show did not draw enough to sustain its meager $3,400 weekly expenses, which were allegedly "weighted down" with Fetchit's $500 salary. By comparison, top-flight white performers like Bing Crosby were personally earning $3,500 for a week's engagement in 1932. Even the postscandal Fatty Arbuckle reportedly was paid $1,500 per week for a Southern stage tour during the spring of 1933.[9]

Unfazed by the Pennsylvania closing, Fetchit reorganized his revue and, by the winter, had begun an extended Southern tour. Fetchit's new *Echoes of Skeeter* show focused its appearances in Florida, where the actor had begun his career and still had friends and family. Dates in February and March included the Lyric Theater in Miami and the Grand in Palm Beach. According to a letter penned to columnist Harry Levette, Fetchit and his troupe were appearing in Miami in February 1933 at the time of the attempted assassination of President-elect Franklin D. Roosevelt at Bayfront Park. Step "sent a photo snapped at Hialeah Park races and a verse of his new song to be used in 'Skeeter,' the new picture for which he is gathering material," Levette added.[10]

The large company—including "many well-known vaudeville performers, a large chorus of beautiful dancing girls, direct from a Harlem night club revue and a red hot jazz band"—clearly worked on a shoestring budget, and the scarce reports of Fetchit's activities in the hinterlands were mixed. A few reviews indicated that the troupe was embraced by both whites and blacks, and the "keys to the cities were his but for the asking" in some stops. But others claimed that the troupe was "busted" during his Dixie tour.[11]

Ralph Matthews of the *Baltimore Afro-American* offered a more blunt, if premature, assessment, writing that the comedian "was rapidly fading into oblivion."[12]

By the summer of 1933, Fetchit had returned to Harlem. Rumor had it that the trip back up the coast was made possible by a loan of funds and an automobile from a wealthy Tampa resident for whom his mother had once worked. Whatever the circumstances, both his return and his continuing Bad Boy reputation were quickly confirmed with headline reports of his being arrested and jailed for speeding along Lenox Avenue soon after arriving in the city. Despite the run-in with the law, he wasted no time in lining up a new stage show. In mid-July he began rehearsing for a proposed one-week engagement at Madison Square Garden, then located at Eighth Avenue and 49th Street. Surprisingly, the composer-writer Donald Heywood, who had briefly worked with Fetchit on the aborted *Black King* stage project, was enlisted as musical director. An observer at those rehearsals left a colorful description of the comic actor's stage work.

> Next comes Stepin, he shambles on the platform to a drowsy tune and begins his funny work. Look! The piano man is sho nuff spankin' dose oblongs and Stepin shifts into high.
>
> He throws his hat into the air—swerves to the right—left—he's down on his knees—he's up—dusts off his tootsie wootsies, gives one complete turn and then goes into a coma of nonsensibility murmuring a blah-blah of nothingness—he shambles off of the stage looking here, there and everywhere while the small audience bursts in a combustion of exalted delight. They liked "dat ole lazy Collud boy's" work.[13]

Fetchit's scheduled Garden debut created considerable buzz in New York, but, as with their previous project, the collaboration with Heywood never materialized.

Near the end of July, however, rumors surfaced that Hollywood honchos were again attempting to contact Step. "The studios searched high and low for a substitute before they took Stepin Fetchit back into their good graces," one writer claimed. Fox had decided to recall the actor and offer a plum part in a new picture. The columnist Harry Levette claimed that, following queries about Fetchit's whereabouts, he had supplied a Harlem address. And in early August, Winfield Sheehan, Step's longtime contact at Fox, visited New York. A week later, the studio revealed that it had signed Fetchit to a third film contract.[14]

Initially touted as a three-month pact with optional extensions, it was later redrawn as a long-term contract. There was, of course, some grumbling among middle-class Negroes who had welcomed the actor's demise; for members of the Negro press who had written him off, the new deal also came as a surprise.[15]

The mainstream press also occasionally laced reports of the actor's reappearance with a subtle critical dig. Stepin Fetchit "is back in Hollywood" and has been offered roles in *The House of Connelly* with Janet Gaynor and Lionel Barrymore, and in *Fox Movietone Follies of 1934*, a *New York Times* report announced, adding that "two or three years ago almost every player who dropped into New York from Hollywood had a new anecdote to add to the chronicle of the eccentric Negro comedian who never quite understood why people laughed at him." While hailing his return, the *Los Angeles Times* sardonically teased the actor about the restrictive clauses in his new contract. "Stepin Fetchit isn't going to step and fetch it quite so fast as he used to do," the report asserted. "Fox persuaded him to sign an agreement that he would allow a manager to look out for him and his affairs."[16]

Most critics, however, greeted Fetchit's return with much more enthusiasm. The *Los Angeles Examiner* ran a banner headline, and gossip columnist Louella Parsons wrote that "the man who was the first Negro to attain fame and stardom with the advent of sound pictures" had signed a long-term contract with Fox. She also noted that he had promised not to break the studio lot's speed limit of twelve miles an hour, report to the set on time, listen to his director, and cut out the street brawls. And the *Chicago Defender* cheered: "Step-in-Fetchit is on the way back to Hollywood to work in pictures! Yowsah!"[17]

Harry Levette, a longtime supporter, heralded Fetchit's reemergence in a more moderate voice. "Step has learned a lot of lessons since being out. And small vaudeville engagements, barnstorming in the South and odd-jobbing around did not nearly measure up to that old hot $1,500 a week he used to get," the columnist wrote. "His return will help Negro screen players no little for you can look for a cycle of pictures using numbers of Negroes as before if his first to be started on his arrival, October 11, makes good."[18]

The exile was over. But there was very little overt fanfare along Central Avenue when Fetchit returned to Los Angeles in the fall. In fact, some members of the Negro film community were reportedly staunchly opposed to his return. "While in Hollywood," the *Afro-American* theatrical editor Ralph Matthews wrote the following year, "the colored citizens of Los Angeles looked upon Fetchit as an objectionable necessity which they had to tolerate. I was even advised by some to ignore him altogether because his early capers had brought the entire colony of colored artists into disrepute."[19]

But many performers were well aware that Fetchit's initial popularity and the zealous self-promotion that catapulted him to star stature had helped elevate the status of Negro entertainers in movies and spurred increased casting of blacks in supporting comic roles. His nagging demands for better parts and higher pay may have annoyed those who felt he was jeopardizing their tenuous foothold in pictures, but the result was increased salaries for Negro actors across the board. Moreover, his abrupt dismissal had set off a search for new black talent that opened doors for a fresh wave of actors.

In November, the *Chicago Defender* ran one of the rare press reports that reflected Fetchit's side of the negotiations that preceded his return or credited him for his behind-the-scenes push for better roles.

"Stepin Fetchit, employing the same gameness that drove him out of films and which many figure brought him back to the studios, made certain that he was to have the proper role before agreeing to make his latest release," the writer claimed.

"However, the man who made slow and droll comedy famous on the screen made no bones about asking that he be given better parts. Funny? Yes, Stepin is still funny. That is what he is supposed to do in pictures, be funny. But there is high and low comedy in pictures and on the stage and the latter class is what Stepin wanted no part of when he returned to the movies.

"And his wish was granted. He is making a trio of films for Fox and in two of 'em he holds what may be well termed the leading role."[20]

Still, there were the unusual restrictions that had been inserted into Fetchit's contract to coerce the actor into curtailing his rowdy behavior off the set and toeing the line at the studio. Even though he had agreed to the stipulations, some doubted that the actor was capable of complying with them. It surprised many when, after a slight misstep at the outset, he reversed his Bad Boy image, toned down his flamboyant off-camera behavior, and, for a time, emerged as one of the Stroll's most well-behaved celebrities.

"It is a subdued and chastened Step who has returned to the movies after quite a long spell of idleness," Levette announced. "But just the same he doesn't look back with regret on the time when he was making $2,500 a week."

" 'When I was in the dough they was always tellin' me how I should save my money and not spend it having a good time,' " the actor told Levette. " 'They told me to buy this stock and that stock so I'd be rich. Well, those guys is just as busted as I am and they didn't have a good time.' "

Still, Fetchit promised, " 'I'm a new boy.' " The " 'motion picture business is the parlor end of the show business and I'm gonna stay.' "[21]

Referring to what he called his "before the crisis" or "B.C. period," Fetchit vowed to begin a "new period" and, with not a little hyperbole, compared his own downfall to the Great Depression. "I had a hard time. The birds of the air didn't even so much as sing. Men were all solemn when I passed in the street. Weather was sad looking all the time, summer and winter got mixed up. I hope we never go back to that vile stage in our history again, and I mean my own personal history."[22]

On the lot, however, he would quietly resume pressuring the studio to finance an all-black-cast sequel to *Hearts in Dixie* and would slyly pad his roles by altering his lines and improvising during scenes. He would also continue to badger producers and directors for better, more expanded assignments.

In fact, some recall that Fetchit's temper outbursts, oscillating moods, and demands for star treatment were still readily apparent at the studio. "I avoided him," recalled Sidney Bloomberg, a rare film collector who worked at Fox during the 1930s. "He was like Dr. Jekyll and Mr. Hyde, you never knew which Stepin Fetchit you would meet. If he were alive today, he'd be on Prozac."[23]

The Central Avenue Bad Boy's rebellious spirit had not been entirely extinguished.

CHAPTER ELEVEN

Two weeks after the actor was slated to begin shooting *The House of Connelly* in mid-October, a banner headline on the *Chicago Defender* entertainment page blared "LOST! ONE FILM STAR; NAME, STEPIN FETCHIT."

"Fetchit was booked to appear in a trio of films," the tongue-in-cheek account stated. "If you happen to see him, pass the news that he is wanted at Fox studios."

The humorous, if misleading and gratuitously biting, announcement of Fetchit's third Hollywood sojourn insinuated that the actor was up to his old irresponsible tricks. But, like current teaser headlines in such tabloids as the *Globe* and the *National Inquirer*, and many contemporary press accounts of Step's exploits, it was geared more to exploiting the actor's notoriety and attracting readers than to relating facts. Upon his return, Fetchit was initially a model of reliability.

He had actually reported to the studio only a few days late—over a week before the article ran, explaining that he simply "hadn't felt well." *Defender* editors had apparently opted to run the story anyway, adding a one-line addendum acknowledging that in fact Fetchit had surfaced. Days prior to the *Defender* story a *Los Angeles Times* journalist had reported spotting the actor at Fox "minus the liveried footman, with coat of many colors, who used to wait upon the colored comedian."[1]

The mordant *Defender* story notwithstanding, Fetchit seemed totally committed to avoiding his past mistakes when he arrived in Hollywood. While working on the Gaynor-Barrymore project, which was released as *Carolina,* the actor's behavior on and off the set was reportedly exemplary.

"Step has been living a very quiet life since his return to the movie capitol [*sic*]," Harry Levette wrote in November, "and is seldom seen along 'Brown Broadway.'" Later the columnist added that according to Winfield Sheehan, "Step has been throwing his whole soul into his work and doing his level best." In addition, Fetchit's return coincided with and perhaps, as some predicted, even helped spark a marked increase in work for black entertainers. "Negro stage and nite club performers, movie actors and extras," Levette colorfully observed, "had the best two months at the close of 1933 that the sepia theatrical and screen colony has seen since Mrs. Big Bad Wolf Depression parked herself and all her puppies on our doorsteps."[2]

A self-proclaimed changed man, Fetchit impressed nearly everyone at Fox; his fellow actors, in fact, openly expressed their admiration and occasional anxiety over his magnetic screen presence. During filming of the Old South melodrama, Lionel Barrymore, who was cast as a frustrated, alcoholic patriarch attempting to resurrect past slave traditions and the glory of plantation life, was outspoken in his praise of the actor. "Without even trying, Fetchit can steal a scene from any living man or woman," Barrymore asserted. "The late Bert Williams, at the peak of his form, was never half as good as Stepin Fetchit."[3]

After its release in February 1934, the somewhat controversial film, along with its esteemed star's comments, would ignite a heated debate among critics, fans, and the black entertainment community that dramatically reflected the ambivalent love-hate regard with which moviegoers viewed Fetchit.

Meanwhile, the actor's resurgent career was back on track and soaring. *Carolina* "was an important film for one Stepin Fetchit," a *Variety* report asserted. He had a chance to come back, which "he did so conspicuously that Fox has renewed his contract with a hope that he may even become a star." In addition to an extended contract, his work and attitude on the set of *Carolina* were so impressive that, before the film was completed in January, he was cast in two other pictures. Studio reports "from production boss, Winfield Sheehan, down to the lowly prop man," a California weekly asserted, claimed that Fetchit had set "a new picture assignment record for actors." The "noted Fox sepia comic set the record when he received assignments to three major Fox films." In addition to *Carolina,* Fetchit was cast in *Fox Movietone Follies of 1934* (released as *Stand Up and Cheer!*), a musical extravaganza that featured many of the studio's most illustrious stars, and was tapped for a small uncredited role in *David Harum* with Will Rogers.[4]

Off the set, Fetchit was noticeably absent from the Stroll's nightlife and there were no headline news reports of off-screen escapades. Upon returning to Los Angeles, he had again been served papers for back rent and destruction to an apartment that had occurred two years earlier; in February he quietly paid the $1,404 demanded. During this time, the only story that faintly hinted at any display of the actor's notoriously eccentric behavior was a whimsical item alleging that he had "scouted the hills of Hollywood for a valet and broke out with a Jewish boy." Denizens of Central Avenue, the writer suggested, were humming a new ditty called "Stepin Won't Eat Pork Chops Any More."[5]

There were, however, frequent rumors about Fetchit's continued attempts to expand his roles and steal scenes on studio sets. *Stand Up and Cheer!* director Hamilton MacFadden and at least one actor on the set spoke out about the actor's expansive camera presence.

MacFadden seemed surprised that Fetchit was "an alert, active young man who stands and speaks briskly"—that his mumbling speech, slow walk, and slouching posture were comic "mannerisms reserved for the camera." The director had been warned about the actor's "scene-stealing," however, and later joked that it made him a "terror" to the rest of the actors. Academy Award winner Warner Baxter, who led an all-star cast that included James Dunn, Ralph Morgan, and Shirley Temple, thoroughly agreed. Baxter reportedly "jubilated" when his scenes with Fetchit were completed.[6]

Fetchit had emerged as one of Hollywood's busiest actors, but his initial three appearances in early 1934 provided little indication of the studio's promise to guide his career in a new direction. They neither reflected the actor's demands for relief from stereotypical, low-comedy roles nor satisfied his request for expanded parts. In fact, despite relatively good notices from the contemporary press, his roles in *David Harum* and *Stand Up and Cheer!* would later be listed among his most demeaning screen performances.

In *David Harum,* a vehicle for the popular Will Rogers, he had a minor, uncredited role as the stable groom Sylvester. This tale of a rivalry between upstate New York horse traders was a remake of an earlier, silent film. When released in early March, Fay M. Jackson of the *Baltimore Afro-American* graciously noted that Step "provided much laughter in the character of a stable boy." The *New York Times* critic Mordaunt Hall wrote that it was a "refreshing picture, which, judging by the constant outbursts of laughter, was enjoyed greatly by the audience." Some of that enjoyment stemmed from Fetchit's stereotypical servile role.[7]

During his brief appearance, he is traded for a horse, pushed and shoved about, and subjected to a stream of racial jokes. Many latter-day critics cite the film as a prime example of Fetchit's pandering to white tastes. But while much has been made of the dehumanizing significance of the horse-trading sequences and Rogers's general patronizing treatment of the black actor in the film, little was said of Fetchit's onscreen reaction. As the stableboy Sylvester, he affected a surreal obtuseness which so insistently ignored the slights that they were not only deflected but trivialized. Even Rogers appears to have had trouble maintaining a straight face when confronting Sylvester's deadpan insouciance.

More important than critical responses, however, the picture marked the beginning of an association with Will Rogers that would fuel Fetchit's career for the next two years.

The star-studded *Stand Up and Cheer!* featured Fetchit in a more prominent role as part of an ensemble cast of Fox entertainers. The loosely structured musical comedy revolved around the appointment of a Secretary of Amusement (Warner Baxter); he was charged with assembling a group of performers to distract the nation from its economic woes. Most reviewers agreed that Fetchit and the fast-rising child star Shirley Temple stole this entertaining but somewhat disjointed picture.

"Fetchit clicks on the comedy, ditto the Temple cutie," *Variety* observed. Describing Step as an "eminent African artiste . . . whose voice sounds like a stream of musical molasses running uphill," a *New York Times* critic reported that the actor had "graciously" contributed "his comic talents" to the Fox effort. Fan magazines such as *Photoplay* and *Motion Picture Magazine* also commended Fetchit's efforts.[8]

Contemporary critical reactions to Fetchit's performance in *Stand Up* vividly illustrate the gap between the 1930s and the present day with regard to media tolerance for farcical depictions of racial humor. Most reviews failed to note that Fetchit's character, Shaw, was featured in one of the most bizarre and embarrassing and grating scenes of his cinema career. The surreal scenario depicts the apparently baffled Shaw believing that a talking penguin is comedian Jimmy Durante. As he shambles about the room in pursuit of the creature, Shaw implores: "Mr. Durante! Is dat you? . . . Yessuh, but my goodness how you done shrunk up. . . . Last time I seen you, you was jes as wholesome and standard size as you could be. . . . Don't do nothin' rash, now." When Shaw catches him, the insolent bird mumbles, "In the hands of slavey . . . a black . . ." Despite the insult and ridicule, the stupefied Fetchit character eagerly leaps into an aquarium to help the abusive penguin catch a fish.

In his lone scene with Warner Baxter, Fetchit offered a more typical example of his stage humor when he approached the newly appointed entertainment czar for a job. When the executive learns that his name is George Bernard Shaw, he quips, "You're a little sunburned, aren't you?" With his patented hangdog expression and slouch, the cowering, head-scratching Fetchit attempts to ingratiate himself by pulling out a whisk broom to clean Baxter's desk and brush his suit. Finally, he mumbles, "You need someone can do the shim-sham shimmy with words and feet?" Amused by Shaw's barely audible singing, and a dead-pan, slow-motion tap and juba patting routine, Baxter consents to give him a job guarding his office. With a sly trickster grin (and a subtle allusion to both his own plight and the nation's economic woes), Fetchit mutters, "Yessuh, nobody can get by now no how 'cause . . . last few years I . . . I jes been barely gettin' by myself."[9]

Carolina, which paired the actor with newcomer Anita Brown as domestic servants, received mixed notices from the mainstream press. But Fetchit, in a more substantial role, and Lionel Barrymore were generally applauded. "It should also be mentioned that the sloth of sloths, Stepin Fetchit, lends his dusky presence to the film," Mordaunt Hall wrote in the *New York Times.* "And his dislike of anything savoring of speed or work affords many a good laugh." *Variety* also lauded the actor's return, although his insistent mumbling still rankled their reviewer: "Stepin carries the burden of comedy. He's still funny in action, but continues to be incoherent in speech." Even in the Negro press, some grudgingly praised his performance. "Black, slow, big-eyed and Ubangi lipped," one critic gibed, his work in *Carolina* "was especially noteworthy." Soon after its release in February, however, the nostalgic tearjerker set off a mild furor in the black community that lasted until the summer.[10]

The film was set in the 1800s, and Barrymore, as Bob Connelly, a crusty Old-South bigot, is heard screaming racial insults at black servants on several occasions. Fetchit, Brown, and others playing plantation hands accept the barbs without objection. The intensity of the confrontations is so heightened that, in fact, Fetchit's role very often slips from the comedic to the dramatic. Despite the stereotypical makeup of his character, Scipio, he is required to act. And he is up to the task. It was his mesmerizing nonverbal reactions to the verbal abuse that most likely led to Barrymore's high regard for him as an actor.

Connelly's slurs and the Negro characters' passive response to them infuriated many critics and fans. "I think such pictures as 'Carolina,' which was shown recently in a local theater, ought not to be filmed because they reflect on colored people and permit the use of too many epithets," one letter writer offered. "Barrymore, the white star, made many bad cracks about us such as 'black trash,' 'slave obey your master,' and 'nigger.' I think we can well afford to do without such alleged artistic contributions."

Another irate filmgoer went so far as to pen an anonymous note to the "wooden heads" running the studio, threatening reprisals in the form of Negro servants airing the dirty laundry of their white employers.[11]

Fetchit had found himself at the center of another controversy. On this occasion, however, his only contribution to the dispute was accepting a plum role in a major picture and *not* complaining about the dialogue or his role. And if entertainment writers for the Negro press finally waffled a bit on the issue, it was with good reason. In the midst of an upsurge in black actors' employment that followed a severe cut shortly after the Depression began, many were fearful that criticism would set off a studio backlash that would ultimately harm Negro entertainers.

"Colored people are hot potatoes. We don't know what to give them so we stay hands off," a studio executive asserted in March. "If we do a picture which we think should please them they raise a howl and say we are showing them in a bad light and they boycott the picture. If we show them in a favorable light we never get a peep of approval, so consequently, we don't know whether they are satisfied or not."[12]

The *Afro-American,* which published numerous letters condemning *Carolina,* juggled the situation by running a feature article based on one letter writer's opposing opinion. "This picture purported to shame a decadent Southern white aristocrat that persists in living in the slave traditions of a hundred years ago," the fan wrote; "the colored man was only shown as he really is in such an environment."[13]

Lionel Barrymore's claim that Fetchit was twice as good an *actor* as Bert Williams also placed the comic actor at the center of an uproar involving fans, the press, and members of the black entertainment community. After all, Flo Ziegfeld of the *Ziegfeld Follies* had touted Williams as "one of the greatest comedians" he ever employed, "in fact, one of the greatest in the world." Early in 1934, the black press examined the pros and cons of Barrymore's claim more or less impartially. Defenders of the beloved *Follies* star (who had died twelve years earlier) and his legacy were far more outraged and outspoken about the comparison than were Fetchit supporters.

"Imagine Stepin Fetchit being better than Bert Williams," the *Amsterdam News* theatrical writer Romeo L. Dougherty fumed. "I spit with scorn."[14]

But, perhaps out of deference to Fetchit, most writers took no definitive stand. While clearly favoring Williams, Charles Bowen of the *Afro-American* offered one of the most balanced assessments of the dispute. "Real comedians are born rather than made. The subtle and elusive art of being funny may be the heritage of the lowly clown as well as that of a trained and sensitive actor," he wrote. "The ability to translate the natural and infectious humor of Negro people into acceptable presentation for the stage is a difficult task and one which many comedians fall short of.

"Bert Williams at whose shrine we all worship had the keenness of the average person of West Indian descent together with the training and education which the Islander of class usually attains.

"Some people deprecate the lazy slothful type which Stepin Fetchit portrays. During Bert Williams's time, there were those who objected to the role of the silly looking black man which Bert created," he continued.

"Bert Williams had a masterful and beautiful influence molding his life, that of the late Lottie Williams, his wife. She undoubtedly exercised great power over his personal life and habits. If Stepin Fetchit should be enveloped by some similarly effective influence, who shall say that we yet may not be hailing him as the exponent of a new idea in the protection of comedy. Perhaps this is what aroused Mr. Barrymore's admiration."[15]

In short, class and, more precisely, an aversion to Fetchit's extravagant, often rowdy off-screen life had been subtly added to the equation. Ultimately, it was the stark contrast between the performers' lifestyles that inspired much of the passion with which admirers weighed in to defend their favorite. Williams was clearly seen as more of a credit to the race than Fetchit; even Booker T. Washington, the pragmatic Tuskegee Institute founder and Negro spokesman, had declared that the actor did more for the race than any contemporary black man. A classical-music buff and avid reader who was known to quote Friedrich Nietzsche on occasion, Williams was esteemed for his dignified deportment as well as his stage achievements. On the other hand, while Fetchit was admired for his breakthrough as the first black movie star, his brawling, hell-raising, and much-ballyhooed reputation as the Central Avenue Bad Boy was a source of embarrassment. Without doubt, that reputation shaded estimates of his comic ability for many of his contemporaries.

During the spring of 1934, the gossip-hungry press covered Fetchit's good behavior with nearly as much attention as they had his notorious past. Typically, the stories were accompanied by colorful, if sometimes exaggerated, accounts of his former outrageous high jinks.

"Stepin Fetchit has grown up. The Negro comedian, recently brought back to Fox Films, has played roles in three recent pictures without making a single miscue," the *New York Post* reported. He "went Hollywood" at the peak of his career, the story continued, "owning three automobiles, employing as many liveried chauffeurs with epaulets topping off a sandy uniform, boasting fifty suits of clothes, living in the finest home in the 'colored' colony and entertaining like a prince. . . . Besides he insisted on directing any scene in which he played. After four years of repentance and reflection, he is back in the fold and watching his step. He drives his own flivver, lives in a modest room, is saving his money, or, rather, the studio is saving it for him."[16]

"Gone are the days" when Fetchit's excesses, like having a caddy accompany him "over a miniature golf course," make news, the *Chicago Defender* declared. "They are keeping that boy so busy that he couldn't get into mischief if he wanted to."

"Natives fear that the old boy may become too civilized for these parts if his manners keep developing," the *Baltimore Afro-American* gibed. "Others are glad to see Step acting more soberly than in the good old days when alley fights and high powered Lincolns went hand-in-hand."[17]

It is difficult to suppress the suspicion that in some mainstream press stories the overzealous crowing at the actor's return to the fold had as much to do with seeing an uppity Negro put back in his place as with true concern over his well-being or success. Stories hinting at his "childish" extravagance and the need for a paternalistic studio overseer abounded. In the context of Hollywood's opulence, one wonders, for instance, what negative connotation owning the finest home in the "colored colony" or "entertaining like a prince" could have outside of the early-twentieth-century racial transgression of overstepping one's societal niche—becoming "too big."

In March, after completing three films, Fetchit earned a "recess" from his work at Fox during which he visited his wife and son in Arizona. He also began a stage tour that took him to New York for an appearance at the 14th Street Academy of Music and, back on the coast, to northern California. With the release of two new pictures and another in the can, the actor was quickly reestablishing his nationwide popularity, and the tour, which played in both large and small venues, reportedly attracted enthusiastic audiences. The *Chicago Defender* reported that in early April, at a stop in Marysville, California, a small lumber-mill town with "a considerable Colored population, he was the idol of the town."[18]

Back in Hollywood, Fetchit began work on *The World Moves On,* an epic romance and antiwar drama directed by John Ford with Madeleine Carroll and Franchot Tone in the starring roles. On the set, Fetchit was a model of punctuality and good behavior. When the film was completed in mid-May, Fox executives were evidently pleased with his conduct; word spread that he was being considered for leading roles in several new projects. *Skeeter,* the sequel to *Hearts in Dixie* that the actor had pitched for years, was among them. And according to one Negro press entertainment writer, an even bigger project was on the table. Announcing that "Step's option" had again been extended, in her "Hollywood Hot-Cha" column, Fay Jackson aired speculation that the "initial production of Ted Butcher, associate producer at Fox, will feature the shuffling comedian as a Harlem lad who attempts to be the Lindbergh of his race by planning an air flight to Africa."[19]

Rumors about future leading roles were circulating on the lot as well as on Central Avenue when Fetchit announced that he would travel to New York to appear at a May 26 benefit for the NAACP Defense Fund at the Apollo Theater. "Fox Studios will do everything to help make the affair a success," he told *Amsterdam News* editors, adding that "he was bringing along the good will of the performers in California." It was to be the actor's first cross-country airplane flight, and friends reported that he endured some soul searching and preflight jitters. Upon arriving in New York, however, the actor apparently felt perfectly at ease. Perhaps too much so.[20]

The gala event boasted a lineup that included many of the nation's best black performers; among them were Ethel Waters, Bill Robinson, Etta Moten, the Jimmie Lunceford orchestra, Aida Ward, W. C. Handy, the Hall Johnson Choir, Cab Calloway, and Fats Waller. Even among this formidable group, as Hollywood's reigning Negro star, Fetchit was given a grand reception.

"Bedecked in a light checked suit with tails, of a combination morning-afternoon-walking suit, be-spatted and wearing an 18-karat grin, the inimitable Stepin Fetchit, movie comedian, stepped magnificently from the metal cabin of a T.W.A. passenger airplane in Newark, N.J., on Thursday, in which he had just flown from the West Coast," a reporter observed. "A squadron of motorcycle police escorted the King of Laughs up to Harlem," where he checked into Mrs. Lottie Joplin's lodging home on 138th Street, "a hangout for Harlem actors." Soon after arriving, he was escorted to a series of soirées and introduced to many of the city's stage "big shots."[21]

According to the *New York Amsterdam News*, the May 26 midnight performance attracted a "standing room only" crowd, estimated to number between 1,600 and 2,300, who witnessed a "sensational" show. The benefit's organizers reported that $1,000, which included a $100 contribution from California brought by Fetchit, was raised for the civil rights organization. Within a week, however, the event's luster faded somewhat when questions arose about the amount of money turned over to the NAACP. As one suspicious critic wrote: "I am sorry that it took about a thousand dollars worth of work and plenty of space, to say nothing of fifty thousand dollars worth of performers to raise $900." Ultimately, the event was tarnished by accusations that, while nearly all entertainers (Step included) had not been compensated, Ethel Waters, a friend of the promoter, had surreptitiously received payment.[22]

Rumors of skullduggery by the benefit's organizers gave the event something of a black eye, but during the show Fetchit's boozy and unruly performance had apparently created even more of a stir. Some accounts of the evening skimmed over the actor's stage antics, reporting simply that he had tried to "hog the show." But Fetchit's most persistent media critic, the *Baltimore Afro-American*, ran a feature story detailing the snafu.[23]

In an article entitled "Why Can't Stepin Fetchit Behave?" Ralph Matthews admitted that Fetchit had "conducted himself fairly well" since his return to Hollywood, but attributed his behavior to the studio's vigilance. "The Fox company took no chances with his temperament and appointed a white bodyguard to keep an eye on him day and night and see to it that he was delivered to the studio on time so that no time and money would be lost by his misconduct while off the lot."

Although Fetchit had "been a model citizen" in Hollywood, Matthews opined, he "seized his recent visit to Harlem to release some of the pent-up desires he has been suppressing" and "almost spoiled" the Apollo benefit show. The columnist supported the claim with an account by fellow *Afro-American* writer Louis Lautier, who had attended the affair. According to Lautier:

> At the benefit performance, Fetchit went on plastered. He did his number, then had Bill (Bojangles) Robinson, the ace dancer, bring him a chair. Stepin sat down.
>
> The audience thought it was a gag. A vocalist came on and tried to sing. He began making funny faces. The audience giggled. Photographers caught him in comical poses. The vocalist gave up.
>
> Other actors came and tried to lead Stepin off the stage, but he would not go. Finally, Lucky Millinder, leader of the Mills Blue Rhythm Band, came on, introduced another act—and then said: "All of us are here in this benefit, and even the queen of the stage, Ethel Waters, has come here to do what she can and does not try to hog the show."
>
> Stepin went to the front of the stage and asked who wanted to hear him say something about Greta Garbo. Some drunks in a box said they would. The rest of the audience hissed.
>
> "You don't want to hear me," said Stepin. "I didn't come here to put on a show; I came here to have a good time."
>
> He then lay down on the stage and said: "This is something you have never seen before; you have never seen an international actor go to sleep before."
>
> Jimmie Johnson, the pianist—called to take a bow—would not come out, but Bubbles of Buck and Bubbles came out and played.
>
> Jimmie Lunceford and his Cotton Club Orchestra were announced. By this time, Stepin had made a general nuisance of himself. Lucky Millinder grabbed him and held him until a curtain was dropped, screening him off from the audience. Then, Lunceford and his crew went on with the show.[24]

The flap over his Apollo Theater antics didn't appreciably affect Fetchit's popularity in Harlem. A few days later, he appeared without incident at the annual Lafayette Theater fund-raiser for the Harlem branch of the Children's Aid Society and, according to press reports, received "as big an ovation as George M. Cohen [*sic*] (the original Yankee Doodle Boy)" and "a host of others who made up the best array of talent seen at a midnight special show in many years." Guests at that benefit included performers Adelaide Hall, Harpo Marx, and the chorus line from Lew Leslie's *Blackbirds*, as well as Bill Robinson and bandleader Lucky Millinder, who apparently held no grudge over the Apollo affair.[25]

Fetchit's misstep in Harlem may have indicated that he was beginning to feel the pressure of studio-imposed restrictions on his behavior. The narrow path they had demanded the actor walk may, as some critics suggested, have begun to loom more as a tightrope. Or, as he said, he may have been just letting off steam and having fun. But removed from the studio's vigilant surveillance, he had indulged himself and briefly reverted to his former grandstanding behavior. During his stay in New York, there were other indications that the restraint he had shown since returning to Hollywood was becoming more difficult to maintain.

While being interviewed at a Harlem rooming house, Fetchit appeared to vacillate between his newly adopted responsible, sober self and the persona of the irreverent scamp that it had displaced. It is worth noting that, as with the press conferences of Muhammad Ali some forty years later, interviews with Fetchit were often turned into pure theater. And like Ali, who was often surrounded by an entourage that included Boudini Brown—a combination stooge and booster—Fetchit frequently faced the press with his valet or court jester at his side. His June interview with a *New York World-Telegram* reporter provided a typical example of the theatrics. The actor answered questions while lounging in a purple dressing gown and yellow flannel cap. When he became too exhausted to respond to questions, his valet chimed in with a stream of colorful tall tales about his employer's past. Between naps, Fetchit reaffirmed that, yes, he was a changed man.

"I don't cut up no more," he said, "I work hard. Every time I come to New York, I go down to St. Andrews Roman Catholic Church, way down behind the Municipal Building and load up inspiration. That's where I get my inspiration. I go down there and store up." He rose to demonstrate a lively new dance, but settled instead for a less taxing slow tap or soft shoe that he called the grind. Slumping back into his seat and yawning, he again closed his eyes as his valet took charge. When asked about losing his money in the crash, however, he suddenly perked up and flashed a glimpse of the former irrepressible spirit. "That's a lie," he blurted. "I wrote a song about it. The name is 'If I'd Saved My Dough Like You Told Me to I'd Lost It Just the Same.' I spent my dough like the fool I was and had some fun. Got no regrets.

Plenty more where that come from." Then, according to the *Telegram* reporter, "drowsiness overcame the actor."[26]

Fetchit returned to Hollywood to begin shooting *Judge Priest* with Will Rogers and Hattie McDaniel a few days after his Lafayette Theater appearance. Back on the Coast, little was made of his indiscretions in New York, and he quietly returned to work. A few days later, a reporter noted that Step "had watched his conduct and deportment so carefully" since his return to Fox last year that he had only been late on the set one day. According to director John Ford, the actor apologized, saying, "Mr. Ford, I'd have been here in plenty of time, but I forgot my make-up box and had to go back."[27]

Fetchit did, however, refute published reports that he would appear at a proposed NAACP benefit in Los Angeles. The decision was partially a consequence of his experience at the Apollo Theater but was also based on his increasingly aggravated relationship with Clarence Muse, who was actively involved in the Coast fund-raiser. In a telegram to *Amsterdam News* editors, he declared that he would have nothing to do with the affair. "I am one hundred per cent for this cause without having to associate with people out here that I don't associate with," he spewed.[28]

The pioneer black actors' relationship had hit rock bottom and would remain so for the duration of their careers. By the end of the year, the dispute had grown so intense that the men not only refused to appear at the same function together but also avoided all chances of bumping into one another. They were said to have "spots" checking on each other's whereabouts to assure that no accidental meetings occurred.

On the set of *Judge Priest,* Fetchit appeared with another black performer who would soon not only threaten his reign as the film colony's top Negro actor, but ultimately eclipse him. When he first met Hattie McDaniel, Fetchit was reportedly a little leery of her acting ability, and, as might have been expected from the keenly competitive actor, somewhat standoffish. But, "no sooner did they start rehearsal than he recognized the actress in her and expressed himself as highly pleased," Harry Levette wrote. "His pleasure was increased when he learned of her long stage, radio and victrola record experience."

Levette claimed that the picture's superstar, Will Rogers, director

John Ford, and "droll dark star" Fetchit all expressed admiration for McDaniel's work. "If Hattie should have felt any resentment at Step's cool welcome," the columnist added, "she had an opportunity to take it out on him in the play for she had to berate him going and coming for his low-down, trifling laziness around the mansion of their employer, Judge Priest."[29]

In the biography *Hattie,* Carlton Jackson wrote that McDaniel "stole" some scenes from Fetchit, "a fact that caused ill ease between the two in later years." Indeed, since during the shooting the actress's role was expanded and an additional song inserted for her, Fetchit may well have been annoyed by the attention she received as well as by her strong screen presence. Still, Fetchit was also allowed to stretch his comic performance in this film. In addition to the expected evasiveness and stylized malingering, he is given space for some verbal wit. "Why aren't you wearing shoes?" Rogers asks in one scene. "I'll save 'em in case my feet wear out," Fetchit replies.[30]

Fetchit and McDaniel did not become fast friends, but the rift between the performers never assumed the magnitude of the public clashes Fetchit had with actors Clarence Muse or Bill Robinson. Besides, during the summer of 1934, Fetchit was preoccupied with a much more serious matter.

Dorothy Stevenson Perry's health was rapidly deteriorating. Advised of his wife's condition, the actor surprised nearly everyone with the care and attention he lavished on her. He "calls her up every day," a Los Angeles journalist wrote, "sends her presents and sees that his baby is given perfect care. He is trying to win back the support of the girl who had to quit him when he 'went Hollywood.' "[31]

Despite the stress of his wife's illness, Fetchit quickly began work on a new picture. He joined Helen Morgan, Ned Sparks, and Spencer Tracy on the set of *Marie Galante,* a spy thriller involving a plot to destroy the Panama Canal. An interesting footnote to that shoot was that screen legend Spencer Tracy, something of a hell-raiser and Bad Boy himself in his youth, held up production for two weeks when he went AWOL. The incident received little coverage in the press, and Tracy quietly returned after agreeing to pay Fox $25,000 to reimburse their losses. The actor repeated the no-show on the set of his next picture, *Helldorado,* in which Fetchit also appeared.[32]

In early September, after *Marie Galante* was completed, Fetchit traveled to Arizona to visit his ailing wife. The former actress and chorus girl insisted on returning to the Los Angeles area, where she would be closer to friends and family. Just two weeks after her return, she died at Monrovia Hospital. Her death left the normally cavalier actor in shock. According to one press observer, when funeral services were held on September 25, at St. Patrick's Catholic Church on 34th Street near Central Avenue, "filmland's lackadaisical madcap comedian was a very quiet, very sad man."

The all-night requiem drew several hundred show-business and motion-picture personalities as well as family and friends; both the honorary and actual pallbearers were drawn from the ranks of the city's Negro entertainment elite. As with many Hollywood funerals, the tragic event was turned into something of a media circus.

A "touch of the Hollywood spectacular was added to the funeral by Fox newsreel photographers who shot scenes from every possible angle," a reporter wrote. Flashbulbs flared and cameras followed Step's every move, recording the actor "posing as chief mourner, holding his wife's hand, bending over her in a last farewell, following her remains to the grave."

When the services ended and the procession made its way to Calvary Cemetery, Fetchit and his four-year-old son Jemajo purposefully avoided watching the lid of the pink casket being closed or its final lowering into the grave. "We left the casket at the grave yard," he said, "setting right up on top of the ground the way you see it in the picture, all covered with flowers."

"There was no sadness at Dorothy's funeral," Fetchit said after the services when he sat for an interview. "There was sincerity and sorrowness [*sic*]. But no sadness."

In his own roundabout manner, he struggled to accept the tragedy and use it as positive motivation for his craft. "I've been on probation," he said. "Probation to myself. And I've stuck to my aims. Dorothy died just at the end of that probation. I think I have proved a good husband and father and I've done my work at the studios.

"Now I'm back on top, right where I started, improved my mistakes and willing to buckle down for real hard work. I'm an artist that somehow or other, I've always thought, ought to be in the world by myself. I have the inspiration of family life and a child to back me up. It takes some people a long time to find things out. Maybe Dorothy's death has something to it."

Then, according to one journalist, "the sad funny man shuffled on out uptown where he was to look over scripts for three major productions in which he was to be cast: 'Bachelor of Arts,' 'The Heldorado' [*sic*], 'One More Spring.' "[33]

CHAPTER TWELVE

After Dorothy Perry's death, the studio offered to look after Fetchit's "artistic" side by offering either "a trip East," where he could rest, or a strenuous schedule, which would allow him to throw himself into his work and possibly forget. Fetchit opted for the latter, and for the next four months he was among Hollywood's busiest actors. His behavior was reportedly impeccable during this time of self-reassessment and mourning.

On the surface, his return to motion pictures appeared to be on course. He had not only regained his status as the industry's highest-paid Negro actor, but (upon renegotiating his contract earlier in the year) was also the only Negro actor "on the regular payroll of a studio"—a key contractual distinction that separated stars from featured players, who were paid only while working.[1]

There had been some talk of discord between Fetchit and Hattie McDaniel on the set of *Judge Priest*. But, rumors aside, the performers had clicked when they appeared together. Each had tremendous personal magnetism and, in this picture, they were perfect complements, creating an electric presence.

One might have assumed that McDaniel's energy and robust, in-your-face presence would have overshadowed Fetchit's stylized lethargy and evasiveness, but the unique style of each actor actually underscored and highlighted the other's talents. Given more leeway than usual, Fetchit stretched out to display his lazy-man comedy shtick more humorously than in any film since *Hearts in Dixie*. As Jeff

Poindexter, he meets Rogers, the judge, when he is brought to court for stealing chickens. Rogers, however, is more interested in the bait he uses when fishing than in his thievery. They become lie-swapping, angling buddies, a leisurely kinship that enhanced the picture's romanticized version of Old South racial relations.

Fetchit snaps out of his carefree languor only when twitted by McDaniel's badgering; and the hilarious confrontations between the two charismatic cinema heavyweights compelled attention. It was the comic equivalent of a ring encounter between a brash, aggressive knockout artist and a shrewd, methodical counterpuncher. In some ways (without casting aspersions on either actor's effectiveness), the screen pairing generated the excitement and drama George Foreman and Muhammad Ali produced during their legendary "rope-a-dope" encounter.

When released in October, *Judge Priest* was a box-office hit as well as a critical success. After attending the opening at Radio City, a *New York Times* reviewer called it "a thoroughly delightful sentimental comedy," which "shows American humor at its best." McDaniel was praised for her musical sequences with Rogers, who was lauded for his work "in one of the happiest roles of his screen career." It was Fetchit, however, who received the loudest plaudits for comedy. "That cloudy streak of lightning, Stepin Fetchit," the critic wrote, "is riotous as the judge's man of all or no work."[2]

"Rogers is type-perfect," *Photoplay* declared, adding that "indispensable local color is provided by Hattie McDaniel and Stepin Fetchit in some grand scenes and music." A *Variety* review praised Rogers for "the best performance of his career" and noted that "most of the comedy" was contributed by him and Stepin Fetchit, "a natural foil to the Rogers character." In retrospect, film historians upheld the picture's credibility. Donald Bogle called it a "poetic, romanticized piece of Americana, with two charismatic black performers surfacing from the background to grab attention whenever/wherever they can."[3]

Judge Priest unquestionably advanced the stock of both its featured black players. McDaniel would increasingly be cast in more substantial parts and, some eight years later, attained stardom with her role in *Gone With the Wind,* for which she became the first Negro to win an Academy Award. Fetchit, who was billed equally with Rogers in many mainstream theaters, profited because the picture reaffirmed his box-office appeal and justified the faith that Winfield Sheehan and director John Ford had shown in him. It was among his best screen performances, and after its release the actor most likely felt that "leading" roles that he had been promised were nearer at hand.

Release of *Marie Galante* in November, however, did not help his cause. The espionage thriller, set in the Panama Canal zone and starring Spencer Tracy and the French actress Ketti Gallian, received only fair-to-middling reviews. And Fetchit's minor comic role as a waiter in a seedy nightclub generally elicited only one-line mentions. Still, between October 1934 and January 1935, the actor was rushed into another film with Rogers and slight, supportive comic roles in three new pictures.[4]

The first assignments were *Bachelor of Arts*, a romantic comedy set on a college campus, and *Helldorado*, a drama set in a West Coast ghost town. They were followed by a more substantive part in *The County Chairman*, in which he was reunited with Rogers in another folksy, rural comedy. He then took the part of a zookeeper in director Henry King's surprisingly whimsical *One More Spring*, a look at a group of characters struggling to survive the Depression.

Fetchit was rarely seen on Central Avenue and for the most part avoided promotional appearances during this time. In one of the few interviews he granted, it appeared that the actor had undergone a profound change with regard to revealing something other than the "stage" persona he usually presented to the mainstream press.

A *Los Angeles Times* reporter was able to coax him into momentarily stepping out of character during an interview for the article "Dr. Jekyll and Mr. Hyde Had Nothing on Stepin Fetchit," a title that was far more revealing than even the writer may have realized. Although he admitted that "me talkin' plain like this won't tie up with the way the studio sells me," Fetchit agreed to answer questions about his rumored interest in the arts, recitals, concerts, and such, as well as queries about the direction he hoped his career would take. "It's time for the public to appreciate me more," he said, referring to the man as opposed to the character. "Then the little things I do will seem big to them, you understand?"

"You can't detect nothin' but my character when you see me on the screen. I plays my part, and that's how it should be. It's not customary for me to have too much to say; not all at once anyway, because then people would be sayin', 'This Stepin Fetchit, who does he think he is?'

"The character is goin' to change gradually, so gradually they won't be aware of it. Otherwise they'll say I'm getting smart, and that won't do nohow."

Even as Fetchit indicated that he intended to alter the slow-witted character he had made famous, he demonstrated that, in his mind, fame and acceptance by the studios and the public were linked to their impression that the listless character he played on-screen was an actual reflection of his real life. Distrustful of whites and increasingly wary of being deemed too clever, too uppity, Fetchit was not prepared to entirely drop his trickster façade. On the other hand, when asked, he unhesitatingly affirmed his love for the fine arts and his determination to gradually change his screen image.

"I'm happy when I'm alone," he insisted. "I used to have a chauffeur, but no more; sittin' up front there, not sayin' a word. . . . I had to get rid of him; I couldn't think. Now I go to these concerts and things, and I can think, saturatin' myself in 'em.

"That's what I want you to write about me, so they'll know what I'm like. You got to show the soul of somethin'."[5]

By mid-January, Fetchit had finished *Bachelor of Arts,* and, reportedly, the studio insisted he take some time off to rest. Since returning to Hollywood, he had completed eleven films in little over a year and never complained. "Production heads worked him a little too hard in 1934," one reporter wrote, adding that "there is as much difference in the wild spendthrift playboy Step of 1928 and '29 and the present quiet, hard-working actor as in night and day."[6]

In February, Fetchit began a combined cross-country publicity tour and vacation that took him to Kansas City, Chicago, Memphis, Miami, New Orleans, and New York. He had gotten over his fear of airplanes, and, when asked about his favorite recreation, he quickly confessed that, like his pal Will Rogers, it was flying. During his holiday, he had ample opportunity to savor it.

Interviewed during a stopover in Kansas City, the dapper, apparently relaxed Fetchit spoke freely about his comeback and a variety of other subjects. His latest film with Rogers, *The County Chairman,* was faring well at the box office and had received mostly glowing reviews. When queried about his relationship with Rogers, "America's greatest living humorist," Fetchit said neither of them tried to "recite" the script the way it was written; they studied it and tried to be spontaneous before the cameras. "You see," he said, "the reason a lot of movie players never reach stardom is because they are afraid to be themselves and try to do what the director and the script says to be and do."

In the same interview, he offered a rare public opinion about race. "The way I believe the race problem is going to be solved is not by figures or oratory but one of these days we are going to wake up and find ourselves at the top and we won't know how we got there. Take the white man for instance, you see him figuring and studying and worrying and jumping out of windows when [things] go wrong. But that ain't the way. Take the lilies out in the field, they don't worry or toil," he said. "If the Lord takes care of the lilies out in the fields and the birds in the air, well, why won't He take care of us."[7]

In an interview for a *New York Times* story presumably done at about the same time, Step reportedly told the correspondent, "If you put anything I says in the papah, it might be wise to kind of transpose it into my dialeck." The printed response to the question of how he and Rogers worked was, "Paht of the time, he surprises me. Paht of the time I surprises him. But mos' of the time we surprises each other."[8]

During a stop in Chicago, he advised his old friends at the *Defender* that before leaving Los Angeles he had accepted roles in two pictures, *Steamboat Round the Bend* and *Kentucky Colonel*, both with Will Rogers. He also "virtually" admitted that "changing times must be considered if one is to continue at the top," suggesting that he was serious about modifying his stage character. Describing him as "movieland's funniest human being," the paper reported that "Step visited all the spots" while in town. "He spent several hours with Duke Ellington" and "visited with Louis Armstrong, whom he likes plenty." When a theater manager asked if he would accept a local booking, Fetchit flashed a telegram from Fox, which read: "Remember, that you are on a pleasure trip and due back here in five weeks."[9]

Arriving in New York, Fetchit spent a few days with friends before heading south, supposedly to rest, visit family, and do some research for the new Rogers films. He flew back to New York in early March.

During a brief stay, he spent most of his time hobnobbing with show-business buddies. He made official publicity appearances at events like a Motion Picture Club luncheon where the actors Walter Connolly, Constance Cummings, and Noah Beery were also guests. And prior to leaving for the West Coast, he appeared at the Brooklyn Keith-Orpheum Theater; during the weekend engagement, it was reported that cheering "early morning crowds jammed the box office and street anxious to see the funny man." In April he returned to Los Angeles.[10]

Back at home with his son, Fetchit relaxed for a short time, as shooting for *Steamboat Round the Bend* had been delayed. Instead, he was cast as Warner Oland's sidekick, Snowshoes, in *Charlie Chan in Egypt.* By this time, reviews of his latest films were in, and, while they were uneven, his position as Hollywood's premiere Negro actor seemed secure.

The innocuous *Bachelor of Arts,* based on John Erskine's autobiographical novel about his experience at Columbia College, received scant critical attention. *Helldorado,* which featured Ralph Bellamy, Madge Evans, and Richard Arlen, who took the lead role when the no-show Spencer Tracy was dumped, was released in January. The *New York Times* called it "a uniformly entertaining picture" and asserted that "a word or two might be added in praise of the lugubrious Mr. Fetchit and his younger edition (son) one Lucky Hurlic." The *Times*'s Andre Sennwald deemed *One More Spring* "a wryly amusing and warmly sentimental screen comedy" about the consequence of the Depression and noted that there were excellent bits, including "Stepin Fetchit as the zoo keeper."

The County Chairman had also been released in January; *Variety* pronounced it an example of "homely American humor" and noted that Fetchit "is again prominent as the slow-footed, dull-witted comedy relief, his bungling" accounting for many of the plot turns. Allan McMillan of the *Chicago Defender* asserted that "the lanky comedian completely stole the show" from Rogers. That may have been an overstatement, but in their third screen appearance, the Rogers-Fetchit team had sparkled. The chemistry between the two was palpable. In this film, some of the paternalism seen in *David Harum* had been eliminated, and the two actors projected the kind of on-screen camaraderie displayed by some latter-day interracial screen teams. In fact, the movie was a precursor of black-white buddy films in which—inspired by the Bill Cosby–Robert Culp pairing in the hit TV series *I Spy* (1965–1968)—Richard Pryor, Eddie Murphy, Gregory Hines, Danny Glover, and others appeared as sidekicks with white actors. And while many critics lambasted the subordinate part Fetchit played in *The County Chairman,* as with more recent films, the thirties Fetchit-Rogers roles merely reflected mainstream America's prevailing racial assumptions and restrictions during that era. Remarkably, the movie suggests that Rogers both understands and admires Fetchit's leisurely approach to life.[11]

During his absence from the film capital Fetchit received a surprising endorsement from the veteran black entertainment writer Chappy Gardner. "After watching the work of Stepin Fetchit on the screen for some time," Gardner wrote in March, "I am convinced that his artistic comedy delivers the greatest blow against race prejudice in America. All the preaching from the many church pulpits has not had the effect of easing up this ugly national feeling as has the work of this very fine actor.

"Fetchit preaches the greatest and most beneficial sermon to the white and black alike. The screen has carried the work of Fetchit into the home and heart of everyone. Audiences admire the character roles. They rush to see him, laugh at him, and leave the theaters thinking and talking about him. His name has become a universal by-word. Thousands of people working as servants thru-out the U.S. find much of the hardships taken from their jobs the next day all because their bosses and madams have been to see Stepin Fetchit and like him."

The article concluded with a nod toward Will Rogers and Twentieth Century-Fox. "Color prejudice fades when this boy acts," he wrote. "Will Rogers, a Southern gentleman from Oklahoma, lends a big hand in dispelling race feeling by calling on Fetchit and giving him the chance to exercise his acting ability. Fox studios too must be credited for having the nerve to take the lead in which a black actor might have the opportunity to help rub out prejudice."[12]

Gardner not only countered the growing sentiment among blacks that Fetchit's roles and popularity were detrimental to race progress but also must have elevated the actor's appeal to Rogers and executives like Winfield Sheehan at Fox. For Fetchit, who began work on *Steam-*

boat in May, the story vindicated his own position and may have even postponed his decision to alter his stage character.

During this time, the media ran numerous stories that were spoon-fed by press agents and, as one paper reported, "calculated to bring the droll comedian into the good graces of a suspicious public." For his part, Fetchit assumed a quiet, reclusive demeanor that surprised many Hollywood cronies. There was an air of mystery about his hermitlike lifestyle, and the radical change elicited comparisons to the elusive Greta Garbo. When questioned, the suddenly taciturn actor usually only offered the solemn reply, "I'm a great artist."[13]

"Step is almost stealing 'Garbo's thunder for exclusiveness,'" one columnist wrote. "He is seldom, if ever, seen at nite clubs; doesn't make any appearances at benefits; throws none of the old parties that got him talked about in the papers; goes to work on the dot and leaves on the dot." The reason, according to the reporter, was his son, Jemajo, or Little Step. Fetchit was apparently showering his son "Jem," who lived in a separate apartment and was attended by a nurse, with attention as well as many of the luxuries available to a wealthy movie star. News stories indicated that Fetchit was grooming the child, "an adorable, well mannered youngster with much of his pappy's dry humor," for pictures. Some press reports, like one written by the actor's close friend Elsie Roxborough, oozed with sentimentality, portraying the youngster as a precocious music lover who proudly insisted that his daddy was not "the laziest man in the world"; for Jemajo, he was "Stronger'n Pop Eye."[14]

Fetchit's place at the top of the heap of black actors seemed secure early in 1935. In addition to his hefty salary for theater engagements, Fetchit was being paid upward of $2,500 per week by Fox regardless of his work schedule. With the exception of Clarence Muse and stage stars like Ethel Waters, Fats Waller, and Bill Robinson, who were brought in for musical cameos or specific projects, few of Fetchit's peers earned more than $35 to $75 a day. Closer scrutiny of Fetchit's circumstances during this period, however, would have revealed hints of problems in the actor's personal life as well as on the set.[15]

As with most actors, Fetchit's hectic schedule made it difficult to sustain a stable father-son relationship. Jemajo, even at four years old, had expressed a desire to travel with his dad, "who was always flying off somewhere." Despite an apparent affection for the child, Fetchit eventually passed responsibility for Jemajo's upbringing along to his sisters and the boy's grandmother. The duties of a single parent, as his own father had discovered, were not readily integrated with the life of an entertainer. Nor was single parenthood easily compatible with the life of a wealthy young bachelor.

During the year, his reputation as a playboy had escalated with reports of his escorting various companions to recitals by such singers as Daniel Haynes as well as to the Symphonies Under the Stars series at the Hollywood Bowl. In addition, there were rumors about an affair with the beautiful Detroit socialite and writer Elsie Roxborough, which he denied. Fetchit insisted that his relationship with Roxborough, daughter of former Michigan state senator Charles E. Roxborough, was purely professional. "We need writers of color with a good educational background," Fetchit said, adding that he was using his influence to "have her placed in a Hollywood studio."[16]

In addition, formidable competition for the relatively few parts available to black actors was surfacing. In a plum role for which Fetchit had been considered, Bill Robinson, the nation's foremost black stage performer, had teamed with Shirley Temple in *The Little Colonel* earlier in the year. The film was a smash box-office hit. And based on fan mail received at the studios, Fetchit and Robinson, along with Clarence Muse and newcomer Jeni Le Gon, were running neck and neck as fan favorites among Negro audiences. And of course, Willie Best, the actor who initially had been recruited because of his resemblance to Fetchit, was always available at considerably less cost if the actor faltered.[17]

In April, it was announced that Robinson had been chosen to team with Will Rogers in the remake of *In Old Kentucky,* another film for which Fetchit had been considered. Reportedly, Robinson was selected because Fetchit was still at work on *Charlie Chan in Egypt* with Warner Oland on the Fox lot. Step, however, apparently resented being replaced. Although he had written glowingly about Robinson in his *Defender* column, Robinson's assignment to the picture seems to have poisoned the relationship between the two performers. Shortly afterward, Fetchit reportedly "snubbed" Robinson by refusing a studio request to have his picture taken with him and declining an invitation to attend Robinson's birthday party in the Casina de Paree on the Fox lot—an event at which reportedly nearly "every star, producer and executive of the studio" was present.[18]

The celebration, which was compared to a lavish birthday bash "Louis B. Mayer gave Marie Dressler," had Will Rogers as its chief speaker. The humorist applauded Robinson's film work as well as his stage preeminence. "I don't mind admitting that Robinson stole a picture from me. Back in vaudeville days, he always stole the show. Nobody wanted to follow him," Rogers said. "Old Step hasn't done well by me either, but Bill is not only the greatest dancer of his era, he has surprised everybody by coming to Hollywood and turning out to be a real fine actor."[19]

The Fox comic star was no doubt irritated by the doting attention that Robinson received and the magnitude of the affair. And while the anticipation of that alone may have prompted his refusal to attend, the presence of Clarence Muse at the event would have been sufficient reason. Fetchit later downplayed the incident, explaining that "I got more publicity by staying away than if I had been there." Despite the disclaimer, the rivalry between the superstars would soon erupt into a full-scale feud that neither the actors nor Fox studio could deny.[20]

As Fetchit neared completion of *Steamboat Round the Bend* and began contemplating his next film in June, he was still adhering to his reclusive lifestyle and no-nonsense work ethic. If he was concerned about being toppled from his number one rank as the premiere Negro motion picture actor, his anxiety may have been temporarily lessened by Bill Robinson's on-set difficulties.

Although "Bojangles" scrupulously maintained a gracious, ever-cheerful public image, like Fetchit he had risen to fame after a rough-and-tumble apprenticeship as a street-corner dancer and carny performer. He was "a very complex person" who was known to frequently carry a pistol, according to his old friend, ardent admirer, and fellow hoofer Honi Coles. "He'd give you anything under the sun, but he'd have to tell everybody," Coles said. "He had that kind of ego. [Bill was] the soul of generosity, but a card player and poolroom man," and his "pride was intense." During the spring of 1935, the more combative side of his personality reared itself. The dancer reportedly had some differences with Will Rogers while shooting *In Old Kentucky* and later became involved in a full-scale shouting match with the production manager over the staging of a dance sequence on the set of *Hooray for*

Love. Robinson later threatened to have his scenes in the picture deleted, prompting speculation that a "new era of sepia screen 'bad boys'" had arrived.[21]

In early August, while Fetchit was on loan to Paramount for a supportive role in *The Virginia Judge*, however, America was shocked by reports that Will Rogers and the pioneer aviator Wiley Post had died when the latter's plane crashed in Alaska. The tragic accident saddened the nation, and throughout the country fans mourned "equally the loss of two of its idols." Memorial services were held nationwide, and, at Rogers's funeral in California, thousands gathered to pay their respects to the beloved homespun humorist. "Rogers will be remembered because his wisdom and philosophy appealed to folks," his biographers wrote. "His humor made them laugh—and think; when he spoke, he spoke the language of the people."[22]

Black Americans reacted to Rogers's death with as much intensity as mainstream America. Only a month before his death, the humorist had spoken at the Second Baptist Church in Los Angeles and apologized for an unfortunate use of a racial epithet on his radio show, vowing that the accident would not be repeated. Word of his unusual display of concern over alienating Negro fans and heartfelt remorse had not only impressed the congregation but also reaffirmed his unique relationship with the Negro community across the nation.

Will Rogers's "infectious humor" struck a "responsive chord in the souls of the Negro," Harry Levette wrote shortly after the actor's death. "Not even at the death of a President have Western Negroes shown deeper sorrow at the passing of a member of the white race." Levette praised the humorist for his casting Negro bit players in nearly all of his movies during the past few years and applauded his use of feature players in "parts as to almost rival his own." Rogers, he asserted, was determined to let the "world see the Negro's talents and abilities."

Levette also rightly pointed out that Stepin Fetchit's comeback and newfound acceptance in Hollywood was largely due to Rogers's taking the actor under his wing. Fetchit had been assigned key roles in four films with Rogers after returning to Hollywood, and, when released, each was a critical and box-office success. The actors obviously liked one another and their lighthearted rapport translated into an on-screen chemistry that made them a huge draw for both white and black audiences.[23]

Fetchit, no doubt stunned by the tragedy, was among the first of a long list of Negro performers and celebrities to publicly express condolence over the death of the cowboy comedian. As he may have suspected, the tragic accident would have a significant effect on the course of his Hollywood career. When Winfield Sheehan, one of the actor's staunchest Fox supporters, abruptly left after Rogers's death, Fetchit lost another crucial ally at the studio.

Back at work on *The Virginia Judge* set, Fetchit was involved in an unusual accident. While shooting a carnival scene, he was hit with a genuine pool ball instead of a prop during a "hit-the-dunce-and-win-a-cigar" sequence. He suffered a gash in his forehead but continued the scene the next day. Little was made of the incident at the time, and the picture proceeded on schedule. Although the film mirrored the small-town setting and parochial Southern political backdrop seen in *Judge Priest* and *The County Chairman*, when contrasted with those Rogers-Fetchit projects, the picture pales. It is one of Fetchit's most embarrassing films.[24]

When *Steamboat* was released in September, most critics took the opportunity to comment on Rogers's posthumous appearance and capsulize the popular humorist's illustrious career. Mr. Rogers, "amid the understanding direction of John Ford," *New York Herald Tribune* critic Richard Watts, Jr., wrote, "was at his best." Calling the picture a "likably sentimental and modestly colorful saga," Watts also praised the Fox stock company players, including Fetchit, as being "of great assistance." The *Chicago Defender* cited Fetchit for his "grand performance."[25]

After completing *The Virginia Judge,* Fetchit was assigned a role in Fox's *The Littlest Rebel,* a Civil War drama starring box-office gold mine Shirley Temple and featuring Bill Robinson in the role of Uncle Billy, a coachman and loyal servant.

Given the tension and growing rivalry between Fetchit and Robinson, the mixture was a recipe for disaster. Shooting had barely started when Fetchit began complaining about hearing problems and headaches. His disruptive behavior became unbearable to producers when he delayed a scene by loudly insisting on softer lights or a stand-in because of his condition. He was abruptly "dismissed" from the project; Willie Best was quickly brought in as a cut-rate replacement for Fetchit in the role of John Henry, a timid slave. The press immediately surmised that the old unpredictably, quirky Stepin Fetchit had resurfaced.

During the following weeks, rumors swirled about the actor's status at the studio, and the *Baltimore Afro-American* ran a story with the headline "Stepin Fetchit Through in Films." In this instance, the paper might have taken note of a scene in Fetchit's recent movie *Charlie Chan in Egypt,* in which Warner Oland as the sage detective quips, "Theory, like most sunglasses, obscure fact." While there was little doubt that the actor had irritated Twentieth Century-Fox boss Darryl Zanuck, the announcement that his studio contract had been terminated was premature. Still, after the on-set run-in, Fetchit left for the East Coast and an extended theatrical tour; he refused to comment on the Fox situation.[26]

Some reports rightly insinuated that the actor's real bone of contention on the shoot was sharing the limelight with Bill Robinson, whose popularity was steadily increasingly. To that extent, the incident reflected the egocentric, star-fixed side of Fetchit's personality. For the black press, however, the rift between the two superstars presented a ticklish dilemma. Few journalists were willing to take sides in the dispute, praising one actor to the detriment of the other.

With the exception of the *Afro-American,* even in articles celebrating Robinson's rise to film prominence, Negro commentators carefully qualified their remarks to avoid jeopardizing Fetchit's career during his absence from Hollywood.

An October 1935 *Chicago Defender* story, for example, claimed that Bill Robinson was "the most popular Race player ever to hit filmland" and documented the admiration that studio executives and established stars had for the tap dancer. "This article is not written to say that Bill Robinson has replaced the other Race players in Hollywood," the writer added. "Bill is replacing no one—he is occupying a spot Hollywood created for him, and has wanted him to accept for years."[27]

During the fall of 1935, Fetchit threw himself into a whirlwind tour with stops in several major northeastern cities. In early October, he appeared in Boston, sharing top billing with the Noble Sissle Orchestra at the Boston Theater. He received loud praise from critics, and news reports claimed that the actor was "not the least bit worried about" the "flareup and disagreement" that cost him his job in Hollywood. A week later, he opened on Broadway at the Roxy Theater and, in an unusual gesture for the era, management openly encouraged Harlem residents to attend the "special gala presentation." The high level of promotion along with close organizational ties between the Roxy and the studio-owned Brooklyn Fox Theater prompted further speculation about Fetchit's status with Fox studios. If a split between Fox and the "high salaried movie actor" did occur, a *New York Amsterdam News* concluded, "then it must have been patched up."[28]

Apparently, although it had not been made public, some reconciliation had occurred, and if studio executives needed reassurance about Fetchit's popularity or box-office appeal, his highly praised stint at the Roxy Theater must have reassured them. While in New York, the actor was also heard on *Rudy Vallee's Varieties,* a nationally broadcast radio show, and appeared at the Majestic Theater with such stars as Phil Baker and Milton Berle at an American Federation of Actors benefit hosted by Vallee. After leaving New York, however, Fetchit's successful Eastern tour was marred by a series of bizarre incidents that recalled his temperamental excesses during the late twenties and early thirties.[29]

In November, he was rounded up with over six hundred employees and guests (including many black and white celebrities) when Philadelphia police raided several of the city's top after-hours joints for selling illegal whiskey. A week later, appearing in Baltimore, he was accused of assaulting his valet and actor James Parker when they arrived late for a scheduled performance. After a sensational appearance at Fays Theater in Philadelphia, where he "smashed the seemingly unbreakable" attendance records of Duke Ellington, Fats Waller, and Louis Armstrong, Fetchit opened with top billing for a week's engagement at the Apollo Theater in New York; according to the local press, he "was well received by large audiences." During his appearance, however, he was accused of attacking Philip Kauchers, a white process server who had ventured backstage to attempt serving a summons based on the Baltimore assault suit. In addition, a few days after the Apollo theater incident, he was again accused of assaulting Parker. The young performer, described as a "stooge" in Fetchit's act, claimed that during an argument after they left the Cotton Club his boss had hit him with an alarm clock.[30]

As with many of the actor's brushes with the law, the media frenzy surrounding court proceedings turned the incidents into a theatrical carnival—a cross between a Max Sennett slapstick comedy and Pigmeat Markham's "Here Come the Judge" routine.

The actor was arrested on December 11 after the Apollo incident and reportedly was an overnight "guest at the 135th Street station"; with "every Negro policeman attached to the station" stopping by to see him, reports claimed that even Step had a difficult time sleeping. The next day, he appeared in a Harlem courtroom to face charges on the process-server assault case. "Course I didn't do it," he told the judge. "Imagine a friend of Will Rogers's doing a thing like that." When the judge realized that the defendant was the famous picture star, he smiled and quipped, "Get the gallows ready."

After being released on $1,000 bail, the dapper performer left the court surrounded by three women and wearing "dark glasses, a flaring overcoat of white and black horse checks, tightly belted at the waist, a chromatic necktie and a hat jammed down on his face." Pushing through a "phalanx of photographers," he piled into a cab and rushed to a Washington Heights court to deal with Parker's charges.

Fetchit denied having anything to do with the fracas.

"When I got home my alarm clock was missing," he drawled, "Well, I leaned over the banister to ask this feller about it and I saw a girl hitting him."

When his lawyers called the "girl" to testify, she broke down and admitted hitting Parker with the clock. The magistrate had no choice but to throw the case out, and, according to a press report, "Stepin Fetchit thereupon oozed, opining that he'd go home for a little nap."[31]

The following week, he was also cleared of assault charges involving Philip Kauchers. The actor appeared in court with seven witnesses who testified that he was in his dressing room when the alleged attack took place. A Fetchit lookalike employed as an understudy in his stage act also testified that on the night of the encounter he was wearing Fetchit's robe. When the legal papers were mistakenly handed to him, he explained, a scuffle took place but he didn't sock the man. The magistrate, noting the remarkable resemblance between Step and his employee, dismissed the case. Before Kauchers could attempt serving the original summons for the Baltimore suit, Fetchit hurriedly fled the court and, days later, left the city.[32]

He headlined a benefit show at Chicago's Regal Theater with Benny Goodman before reporting for a holiday engagement in Pittsburgh. Asked about his court battles during this time, Fetchit seemed unfazed by the media circus. "I do not object to a little adverse publicity," he coyly replied. "Somehow people sort of expect me to do odd things and I don't like to disappoint them."[33]

While in Pittsburgh, Fetchit seemed relaxed and at ease with himself and, during an interview with a local reporter, reflected a rarely seen pensive side of his personality. "Folks may think I ain't just right," he mused. "I don't mind what they think, and I make no secret of the fact that I don't crave a whole lot of bustle on or off the stage. But I do as much brain work as the average man." The actor went on to explain that, unlike some race acts who allowed themselves to be billed beneath inferior white acts, he had always demanded proper billing and pay. He also insisted that many of his troubles in Hollywood were due to behind-the-scenes battles over the business side of entertainment.

"Under the skin, Mr. Perry is not funny, amusing." He is "an earnest student of racial problems and progress," the writer adjudged. "They may laugh at him on the stage, but he doesn't permit himself to be laughed at when he is talking business."

Fetchit refused to discuss his recent studio problems, saying only that he had quit work because after being hit on the head with a billiard ball he could not stand the glare of the klieg lights. But "he did not deny" that a recent "burst of temperament had a business angle."

"Friends of the comedian who claim to be 'in the know,'" the interviewer concluded, "insist that as soon as some more figures are added to the lazy man's contract, he will truck on back to Hollywood and forget his headache."[34]

After leaving Pittsburgh in early January, Fetchit traveled to Washington for an appearance at the Howard Theater. Reportedly, during the engagement the president's secretary promised to arrange a meeting with Franklin D. Roosevelt, who was one of the actor's biggest fans. FDR was forced to postpone the meeting for a week, however, and due to prior commitments, Fetchit had to cancel. In mid-January, the actor flew back to Los Angeles for a scheduled meeting with Fox executives and a post-Christmas visit with his son.[35]

Although details of Fetchit's discussion with Darryl Zanuck and other Fox executives were not revealed, the actor was not immediately assigned to a new picture. It is clear, however, that Fox was not anxious to sever contractual ties. Despite his widely publicized escapades on the East Coast, Fetchit had demonstrated that he was still a fan favorite and valued financial asset at the studio.

Steamboat Round the Bend was still playing in theaters and was among the studio's most profitable films. It had grossed nearly $1.5 million by January and was expected to exceed $2 million in receipts. Fetchit still reigned as the best-known and most popular black player in films. In fact, his sleepy-eyed character had peaked in national popularity, and again vied with radio's Amos and Andy as the entertainment world's most widely recognized Negro comic character.

The frequency with which Fetchit was caricatured in animated cartoons of the period indicates the worldwide popularity and near-mythological status of the character he created. The use of blacks in cartoons had spiraled with the introduction of sound movies, and caricatures of famous Negro personalities in cartoons reached an all-time high in the mid-1930s. Cab Calloway, Louis Armstrong, Eddie "Rochester" Anderson, and, later in the decade, Hattie McDaniel were among the favorites. No one, however, was seen as frequently as Step.

"The most popular black caricature used by animators," Henry T. Sampson wrote in *That's Enough, Folks*, "was that of comedian Lincoln Perry, aka, Stepin Fetchit. His drawling, shuffling, lazy, dim-witted screen persona was known and loved by movie audiences all over the world." Even during periods of inactivity, when he was not seen in feature films, as in early 1936, facsimiles of Fetchit's comic stage and screen character were visible in cartoons, which were shown in movie houses before feature films. As Sampson pointed out, "animators used it to depict the quintessential black man in many cartoons."

In *Who Killed Cock Robin?* for example, a Fetchit-like caricature appears as a crow in porter's garb at the Old Crow Bar. He is among a group of suspects brought in when the love-smitten Cock Robin (Bing Crosby), infatuated with buxom Jenny Wren (Mae West), is shot by an arrow outside the bar. "I ain't don nothin'—I ain't seen nothin'—I don't know nothin' at all," the crow whines repeatedly as he and the gaggle of feathered bar denizens are clubbed by police and herded into court. All ends well when it's discovered that Cock Robin has been felled only temporarily by Cupid's bow. The film was nominated for an Academy Award as the best short subject of 1935.[36]

The use of Fetchit's image as a symbol of the dull, indolent, perpetually confused Negro prototype, however, was a double-edged sword. Even as it heightened his visibility and affirmed his popularity and success, it foreshadowed his demise. The complex racial implications of the caricature aside, Fetchit was being boxed into an indelible one-dimensional role that allowed no variation. Like the "It Girl" Clara Bow, Fetchit's contemporary, and such later phenoms as George (Superman) Reeves and Tiny Tim, the actor was fast becoming a captive of his own image and success.

There were indications, as witnessed by his comments to reporters concerning altering his screen image, that Fetchit was aware of the situation. And it is probable that his wrangling with Fox was centered as much on the roles he was offered as on salary. The studio had shown no real interest in either offering more serious roles or financing the all-black features that Fetchit had proposed, however, and seemed content with confining the actor to the timorous caricature that still sold tickets.

Meanwhile, still unable to agree on an acceptable vehicle for his next movie appearance, Fetchit spent much of his time with his son, Jemajo, during his return home in January and February. One report claimed that having been away during the holidays, the actor had "virtually bought out a toy store" during a shopping spree with his son. Without a new picture assignment, however, Fetchit returned to the stage. By March, he was back on the East Coast appearing at the Howard Theater in Washington.[37]

After flying to Los Angeles for another conference with Fox and a short visit with his son in early April, Fetchit returned to New York, where he was booked into Loew's State Theater for another successful engagement. "Harlem is pouring into the theater in a way to set a new high for attendance," a *Chicago Defender* reviewer noted. His "slow-motion" act "provides a constant flow of laughter" and lends "much gayety to the diverting Easter entertainment," a New York critic added.[38]

Boosted by his Broadway success, Fetchit arrived on the West Coast in May to begin preparing for an appearance at the California Pacific International Exposition in San Diego. The following month, after an absence of over half a year, he returned to Twentieth Century-Fox and began shooting *36 Hours to Kill*, a crime melodrama in which much of the action takes place aboard a train. He was cast as Flash, a lethargic, inept porter, in a stock comic-relief role. Sam McDaniel appeared in an uncredited role as a waiter. Together, as was the custom in Hollywood pictures, they provided the humorous black backdrop with which the film's central action was contrasted.

At the studios, nothing had changed.

CHAPTER THIRTEEN

When Fetchit began shooting *36 Hours to Kill* in 1936, Ralph Cooper—the actor, dancer, and emcee who had hosted the Apollo Theater's Amateur Night—was also on the Fox lot. He had been hired as a replacement choreographer on the set of *Poor Little Rich Girl*, which starred Shirley Temple, and would remain in Hollywood for five years working as an actor and writer. After accepting bit parts in two Hollywood pictures, Cooper declined further roles in studio films. Instead of trying to buck the system, he turned to writing and starring in independently produced black-cast pictures such as *Dark Manhattan* (1937) and *The Duke Is Tops* (1938).

Step had headlined the Apollo bill several times during the past few years, and Cooper counted the star among his friends. "There were a lot of laughs," he later wrote. "I had a ball on the Fox lot. And a big reason it was such a delightful experience was Step. He was a fabulous character."

According to Cooper, Fetchit had abandoned his Spartan ways and partially reverted to his former flashy Hollywood lifestyle when he returned that summer. He arrived every morning in "two Cadillacs," Cooper wrote. A valet and footman rode in one, along with a large supply of "near beer, which [Fetchit] drank like water all day"; Step insisted that the beer made him drowsy and helped him get into character. The footman would open the door to the actor's car and set a footstool in place; the valet carried "a gold hanger from which was draped the raggedy costume Step would wear" during shooting that day.

Each morning Fetchit would emerge complaining about being required to arrive at 7 a.m. when he did not start working until two in the afternoon. It "happened every day," Cooper avowed. "It was my guess that the studio did it on purpose, just for laughs in the morning."

But the jokes were not exclusively on Fetchit. The actor professed a hatred of telephones, for instance, and for a time refused to have one installed in his home. When studio executives realized the aversion was a ploy to ensure selective unavailability, according to Cooper, they inserted a clause in his contract requiring that he install and maintain a phone. At Fetchit's insistence, they paid the bill. His relationship with studio boss Darryl Zanuck reportedly involved other cat-and-mouse games.

"Zanuck was a very smart fellow," Cooper wrote, "but he couldn't keep up with the subtle workings of Step's mind." Fetchit sometimes employed a manager and agent, for example, but he preferred negotiating his own contracts. It was a rare undertaking at a time when black performers' business affairs were nearly always handled exclusively by white representatives. In his dealing with Zanuck, Cooper claimed, Fetchit would listen to the mogul's proposals or suggestions, then tell him that he had to confer with his manager, Mr. Goldberg. After considering the proposal himself, the actor would return and disagree or agree, saying Mr. Goldberg either declined or "gave the go-ahead."

Finally, Zanuck's patience wore thin, and he demanded a face-to-face meeting with Mr. Goldberg. When he persisted, Step smiled, shook his head, and said, "Well, Mr. Zanuck, I guess you had to find out some day. I'm Mr. Goldberg."

For laughs, Fetchit apparently continued the gambit even after admitting that Mr. Goldberg was actually his alter ego. "Everyone realized the joke that Step was running," Cooper wrote. "He was mocking the widely held assumption that behind every successful black man there had to be an all-powerful white figure, a manager or agent or banker who called all the shots and controlled the performer's life like he was a puppet." For Fetchit, temper outbursts, orchestrated tardiness, even inventing a mythical white adviser, were parts of an arsenal of sly ruses used to take control of his own career and attempt pressuring the studios into meeting his demands for better roles and higher pay.

Step "was one actor who bent the system to work for him," Cooper wrote. "If you didn't want to mug wide-eyed and scared and act the fool, there was no room for you in the big studios." He "played dummies all his life," but "after I got to know him, I realized what a great actor he really was. Actually, that was his downfall."[1]

Certainly, with regard to the popularity of his lazy-man screen character and his unerring portrayal of the comic figure, it led to his being rigidly type-cast in the role. After finishing *36 Hours to Kill* during the summer, Fetchit was assigned a role in *Dimples,* which featured Shirley Temple, by then the number one cinema box-office draw. Although Bill Robinson did not appear on-screen, at the child star's insistence "Uncle Billy" had been called in to choreograph her dance sequences. And while that may or may not have irritated the actor, his minor, tightly reined, and uncredited part as Cicero surely affirmed his suspicions that Fox was not eager to expand his roles.

Fetchit seemed less focused on career than on outside business and recreation during the summer of 1936. He had recently begun purchasing investment property, and he told the press that he was planning a little theater development in Los Angeles. The proposed name was "Harlemwood," a little bit of "Harlem in Hollywood," he explained. Primarily, however, he seemed to be concentrating on his social life.[2]

There were continuing rumors about his relationship and possible engagement to Elsie Roxborough. Despite frequently being seen in each other's company, however, both denied any romantic link. She claimed to be collaborating with the actor on a play about his life. The true nature of the relationship notwithstanding, Fetchit had begun entertaining in grand fashion in his luxury Los Angeles apartment, and Roxborough was frequently among the high-profile guests.

As Fetchit's relationship with Roxborough, a confirmed member of the Negro upper crust, suggests, by 1936, the face of Hollywood's motion-picture Negro had gradually begun to shift, both on- and off-camera.

On-screen, Louise Beavers and Hattie McDaniel had spiced familiar maid depictions with a new, more aggressive and spirited twist. And Bill Robinson added a cheerful effervescence and light-footed nimbleness to servant roles. While he usually portrayed a kindly Uncle Tom type, the parts often blurred distinction between Southern cinema fantasy and his real-life status as a secure theatrical superstar. The changes were slight, but they provided a noticeable alternative to prior portrayals of overtly submissive, downtrodden retainers and slaves.

Behind the cameras, the changes were more obvious. During the early thirties, the somewhat rowdy black industry pioneers—many of them hard-bitten hustlers or rogues who had clawed their way to marginal positions in the studios—had begun falling by the wayside. The success, wealth, and universal appeal of a new elite group of black entertainers prompted the Negro middle class to welcome a select few top performers into their ranks. An alliance between black artists and upwardly mobile Negro professionals had gradually begun taking shape.

"Time was when theatrical troupers were excluded from the category of 'society folk.' Indeed, old-time show people will remember many an occasion when they were refused admittance even into colored lodges in some cities and towns of this country," a reporter had observed in 1932. Citing the rise of educated, "cultured and distinguished" artists, and a "growing enlightened attitude" among the middle class, the writer claimed that "the artist of the theater has taken his proper, dignified place in society."

The story was written on the occasion of a party held in honor of Duke Ellington and attended by prominent West Coast "doctors, lawyers, school teachers and intellectuals of the race" as well as such notables as Clarence Muse and the white artist James Blanding Sloan. As the item suggested, such affairs had become more commonplace in the film capital. During the summer of 1936, Fetchit's lavish parties reflected the change. He was no longer hosting the wild, often drunken and rowdy bashes that provided reams of copy for gossip columns back in 1929; news and photos of his soirées were suddenly appearing on the society pages of black newspapers.[3]

Fetchit "entertains weekly" at his "palatial apartment," and guests "are among some of the outstanding folk of both races," the *Chicago Defender* claimed. The actor regularly topped off exotic meals with so-called letters from home (sliced watermelon) served by his Chinese servants and, for a rooftop beach party, had barrels of sand delivered to his building to create the proper ambiance. The affairs, according to one report "were the last word in uniqueness and lavishness."[4]

In August, *36 Hours to Kill* was released to primarily favorable reviews. A *New York Times* reviewer gave the "melodramatic gangster" film a thumbs-up. "The episodes aboard a train, where a considerable part of the action takes place," the reviewer added, "are made all the more pleasant by the presence of Stepin Fetchit, that streak of brown lightning, as a blundering porter."[5]

Despite a few positive notices, Fetchit's part as Flash was formulaic and required no stretch of his acting or comic abilities. He was as immobile as ever, but there was reason to suspect that the lethargy was inspired as much by boredom as by any real interest in the predictable role.

Fetchit found time for a quick trip to New York during the summer. While there, it was later revealed, he spent considerable time with the young teenage dancer and singer Winnie Johnson, who was featured in *New Faces of 1936*. Johnson, the daughter of Harold "Monk" Johnson, a former catcher for Negro baseball teams in Pittsburgh and New York, was a member of the chorus line at the Cotton Club, where she had initially caught the actor's eye. Her stunning looks also attracted producers' attention, and she was selected for a "stellar" part in *New Faces.* Although little was written about the relationship until the following year, Fetchit had apparently been smitten immediately by the young showgirl. He returned to New York whenever his movie schedule permitted.[6]

Back in Hollywood, Fetchit opened at the Orpheum Theater in late September. It was a rare Los Angeles stage appearance, and, coming on the heels of his successful Eastern tour, it generated an unusual amount of interest. One critic immediately announced that in his new show Fetchit was "slower and even funnier than ever." Entertainment writer Harry Levette followed with a rave review in his "Thru Hollywood" column. "Stepin Fetchit was a seven days scream on the Orpheum stage last week, stopping every performance with the capacity audiences rolling in the aisles at his characterization of the world's laziest man," he wrote. "Step wrote his own act, designed its setting," and "proved that he is not a type but an intelligent comedian of the Charlie Chaplin caliber."

Levette went on to describe Fetchit's "side-cracking" use of a small boy as an attendant or stooge who caters to all his lethargic quirks: shoving an easy chair under him after the slightest exertion, putting the phone to his ear when it rang, or taking a bow following a finale in which the suddenly enlivened comic flashed a contrasting, fleet-footed dance display. "Twentieth Century Fox was highly pleased with the reception the fans gave him all week," Levette added. "They admit that this will add to his drawing power in the several pictures they have planned for him this season."[7]

Following his Orpheum appearance, Fetchit began shooting *On the Avenue,* a musical with a backstage Broadway theme that starred Dick Powell, Alice Faye, and Madeleine Carroll. Near year's end, he was cast in *Love Is News,* a romantic comedy starring Tyrone Power and Loretta Young. Again, Fetchit's conduct on the set of each picture was beyond reproach.

The actor's apparent determination to toe the studio line and cooperate with Fox honchos was also reflected in a rare appearance at a studio function in early December. He was among scores of Fox stars—including Joan Blondell, the Marx Brothers, Tyrone Power, and studio boss Darryl Zanuck—who attended the gala premiere of *Lloyd's of London* at Carthay Circle in Hollywood. Surprisingly, he appeared as a staid model of sobriety—the ultimate company man. Reserved and low-key, he showed up in a tailored, conservative gray suit, matching brown shoes and tie, and was modestly receptive when welcomed "with encouraging squeals of mirth."[8]

In February, shortly after completing *Love Is News,* Fetchit left the West Coast for a four-week stage tour in the East.

He was appearing at Loew's State Theater when the *New York Post* ran a feature story that, as usual, highlighted his eccentricities. "Mr. Fetchit of the perpetual revery, or whatever that fog is which surrounds him, will be in town for a few days to kick off a month of personal appearances," the writer announced.[9]

During the interview for the story, the actor laced his usual lazy-man promotional shtick with tongue-in-cheek barbs directed at his detractors as well as the producers and writers who selected his roles and wrote the dialogue for his screen roles. " 'Course, Ah really work pretty hard anyway," he reportedly joked, "sleepin' in some of the uncomfortable positions Ah do, like standin' up, or bendin' over a broom." Shifting to a more serious note, he added an unusual critical stinger. "Sometimes those script writin' men come to me and say Ah ain't readin' their lines clear enough. Most of the time they ought to be glad Ah ain't."[10]

While in New York, Fetchit also made an impromptu visit to Radio City Music Hall, where *On the Avenue* was showing and, as was his habit, spent much of his time savoring Harlem nightlife with friends. He was frequently accompanied by the stunning teenager Winnie Johnson.

In March he returned home to Los Angeles and began filming *Fifty Races to Town,* a romantic comedy starring Don Ameche and Ann Sothern; once again he was assigned a minor role as a comic diversion. Apparently, all went well during the shoot. But abruptly after the film was completed in April, he left Hollywood and began an extended stage tour. He would not work at a motion picture studio for more than a year and a half.

Unlike his previous ousters from the movie colony, Fetchit's departure in 1937 did not result from any on-set laxity or brush with studio bosses. It appears to have been entirely voluntary. It is likely, however, that his self-imposed exile was part of a strategic attempt to force Twentieth Century-Fox to either cast him in more substantial roles or sweeten his contract. It does not seem coincidental that Fetchit's abrupt decision to begin a long tour in April occurred just after Fox picked up the option on Bill Robinson's contract, signing him to an annual "long term" deal with the promise of several feature roles.[11]

Even though dissatisfied with his roles, Fetchit was at the peak of his popularity on-stage and in pictures. And it appears that he was betting that, along with his worldwide appeal and box-office success, the emblematic status of his screen character as *the* accepted popular representation of the Negro assured that the studio, as it had in the past, would pursue him. It was a risky bet for any actor under a Hollywood studio system that made or broke stars as it saw fit. Few were surprised when Twentieth Century-Fox called his bluff and went on with business as usual.

Fetchit was correct, however, about his appeal as a stage attraction. And for over a year, he would travel the country as one of America's most popular headline stage acts, even as his personal life veered through a series of mishaps and bizarre twists.

The problems began in late April while he was appearing at the

Earle Theater in Philadelphia. On Sunday, April 25, while in New York visiting friends, the actor's Lincoln Club Coupe swerved out of control and crashed into a pillar under the Eighth Avenue el after its left front tire blew out. Fetchit was pulled from the wreck unconscious and rushed to Harlem Hospital, where initially he was reported to be in critical condition and suffering from a fractured skull. He was later moved to a private hospital and the diagnosis changed to a mild concussion.[12]

During his convalescence, it became apparent that the rumored relationship between him and Winnie Johnson was as serious as some maintained. The teenage entertainer "was reported to be a constant visitor to his bedside."[13]

By mid-May Fetchit had recovered sufficiently to resume his theatrical tour, and on the twenty-first he returned to the Earle Theater to finish his engagement. En route to the West Coast in June, he informed *Chicago Defender* editors that he was handling his own bookings and acting as his own manager. While he intended to rest for a time, Fetchit said that he "expected to make two pictures" and would appear for a limited engagement at the Golden Gate Theater in Hollywood.[14]

Fetchit appeared at the Golden Gate, but his talks with Fox did not pan out. There was no formal announcement of a split with the studio, but by the fall Fetchit had returned to the East to continue his theatrical tour. While booked at Fox's Fabian Theater in Brooklyn, he also quietly resumed his affair with Winnie Johnson.

And on October 9, shortly after another narrow escape in an auto accident, Fetchit and Johnson reportedly eloped. The couple drove to Connecticut where, a news story averred, "the marriage was performed in secrecy."[15]

There was an air of mystery about the marriage from the outset, as Fetchit, Johnson, and her family were initially reluctant to confirm the union. There were also rumblings about the age disparity between the nineteen-year-old ingénue and the thirty-six-year-old actor. Suspicions about the nature of the relationship were heightened when, immediately after eloping, Fetchit continued his tour while Johnson remained behind in New York.[16]

Since Twentieth Century-Fox had not officially terminated his contract, Fetchit was presumably being paid by the studio during this time. He had personally arranged some appearances in November and

December, however, and may have felt compelled to fulfill them. During the fall of 1937 and winter of 1938, he did return to New York to visit his wife when his schedule permitted and reportedly called every evening. Without motion-picture work, he seemed intent on demonstrating that he remained a headline theatrical draw. The hard work was rewarded, and his act flourished.

From November 1937 to the spring of 1938, he continually played before capacity crowds. A lukewarm *Variety* review of a Columbia, Ohio, appearance with the Erskine Hawkins Orchestra billed as the *Harlem Hit Parade*, however, reflected the era's assumption of "second-class" status and ho-hum regard for most black comedic and theatrical fare. The critic seemed thoroughly unimpressed, dismissing the revue as "typical colored entertainment." Fetchit, he noted, kept "his audience well amused with his drawl" and "lazy bones pantomime." The show flourished, nonetheless, as black and white audiences were typically far more enthusiastic. During an Orpheum Theater date, where Fetchit appeared for the "first time" on a downtown Memphis "theater stage before a mixed audience," more than five hundred fans were turned away and the show broke an attendance record recently set by Duke Ellington and his orchestra.[17]

With the exception of a few road scrapes caused by Fetchit's notorious lack of attentiveness behind the wheel of his car and the minor hassles typically experienced by a touring entertainment troupe, the *Harlem Hit Parade* revue proceeded without incident until mid-February. After the record-smashing Orpheum Theater appearance, however, an apparently minor disagreement between Fetchit and his chauffeur ignited a bitter public squabble that sent the tour and Fetchit's career into a gradually quickening downward spiral.

Following the initial Orpheum date, the Fetchit-Hawkins revue agreed to return to Memphis for a three-day appearance later in the month. On the way to Little Rock, Arkansas, for an interim engagement, however, Fetchit had an argument with his chauffeur and apparently discharged him on the spot. The driver left Fetchit's car and got into the bus with the Hawkins band members. When the troupe's road manager refused to remove the chauffeur from the bus as Fetchit requested, the actor got behind the wheel of his car and sped off.

The Little Rock engagement was kept, but Fetchit was apparently still stewing; three days before the scheduled Memphis encore, he abruptly left town. "Every effort was made to locate him," an ANP story reported, but when the troupe was unable to contact him, local talent was hired as a replacement. Hours before the curtain of the first show, the troupe received a wire stating that Fetchit would not be able to return to Memphis because he had been involved in an auto accident. Orpheum management subsequently lodged a hefty suit against the AWOL actor.[18]

Fetchit and the *Harlem Hit Parade* revue returned to the Orpheum in the spring and the lawsuit was dropped. But the actor was apparently infuriated by the way the story was handled in the Negro press, and, during the spring, his long-simmering anger over the manner in which some black journalists portrayed him reached a boiling point. His widely publicized outburst would have far more serious implications than the Memphis fiasco itself.

"I don't see why there should be a difference between the Negro press and myself," he ranted during an April interview in Memphis. "After all, I am definitely Negro news. Now whether some colored writers want to see me in pictures or not doesn't matter as my real following is 90 per cent white, and the Negro public has had very little to do with my universal success on the stage or in pictures." He amplified the remarks with claims that only a few Negro newsmen actually knew him and the suggestion that his celebrity status had elevated him to a position that was beyond both the understanding and access of "the colored press."[19]

Fetchit, of course, knew full well that such black entertainment writers as Harry Levette and Chappy Gardner had supported his career, deflecting criticism of his stage character and even defending some of his more outrageous off-screen antics. But his temper had gotten the better of him. His rambling diatribe had careened into a broad-stroke denunciation of the Negro press and, in an attempt to brace the claim, a rash, indirect swipe at the black audience which, in reality, constituted the bulk of his fan base.

Fetchit did have several vocal adversaries among the Negro press corps. Entertainment writers such as Ralph Matthews of the *Baltimore Afro-American* did not conceal an apparent disdain for the actor's lifestyle and loathing of the character he played. Some eagerly leapt at any chance to denounce or ridicule him, and consistently challenged all claims that he was either a legitimate or representative black star. Their views, in some ways, reflected the opinions of those sportswriters and fans who vigorously contended that the ostensibly humble, more accommodating newly crowned heavyweight champion Joe Louis was a more fitting representative of the race than his controversial and outspoken predecessor Jack Johnson.

After Fetchit's rise to prominence, Matthews had written several stories with titillating banner headlines such as "Why Can't Stepin Fetchit Behave?" And coincidentally, at about the time of the Memphis incident, he published a feature story on Clarence Muse and Bill Robinson which claimed that, until Robinson's arrival, "Muse was the biggest name in the profession on screen, stage and radio so far as Hollywood was concerned." The article went on to glowingly describe the actors' stable home lives, cultural interests, and genteel pursuits, as well as to list and commend their involvement in civic and charitable matters. Fetchit emerged as a mere footnote in the piece. The proud, publicity-minded, and admittedly egotistical comic actor most likely viewed the article as a slap in the face.

One can only conjecture that Fetchit's brash, ill-conceived rant was inspired by a combination of professional and personal anxieties that temporarily fogged his understanding of why he had risen to the top. There is no doubt that he had crossover appeal, but, in general, his comedy attracted black and white audiences for entirely different reasons. Many blacks were perfectly aware of the running in-joke ("puttin' on old massa") that Fetchit deliberately enacted on stage and screen. They were laughing at what he *purposefully intended* doing. Many whites, on the other hand, laughed at what to the uninformed *appeared* to be a confirmation of a venerable Negro stereotype. For most blacks, it was ironic farce; for many whites, it was sociological verity.

Despite his theatrical success and the popularity of the *Harlem Hit Parade* tour, Fetchit was apparently frustrated by his ongoing battle for better roles and more equitable pay in the film industry—equitable, for him, meaning pay commensurate with what white artists received.

By the spring of 1938, the actor's ongoing negotiations with Twentieth Century-Fox had broken down; presumably no longer under contract, he was actively pursuing picture deals with other studios. Fetchit left Hollywood "because of his unwillingness to work for the salaries offered Race players," a critic wrote of his career a year later. "Of all the movie players Step is the one and only one who refuses to talk business with producers who seem to forget the value of a man when he happens to be a member of the Race. That drove Step from pictures before and threatens to keep him out."[20]

Fox was apparently again backing away from long-term contracts with Negro performers in 1938, and during that time the studio even cut its contractual ties with the once-hot Bill Robinson.[21]

Meanwhile, Fetchit was dealing with some nagging personal problems. Beneath the hoopla and glitzy publicity surrounding his reported marriage to a glamorous, fast-rising teenage stage star, the actor's extended theatrical tour and prolonged separation from his wife had raised eyebrows, and rumors of marital discord began circulating in the press as well as among the Harlem theatrical crowd. And while unpublicized as yet, his furlough from the West Coast and the picture industry was severely straining relationships with his son, Jemajo, who had moved in with his maternal grandmother. Fetchit tried to maintain a confident, positive façade, but behind the scenes the public image of a doting father and happy newlywed had begun unraveling.

Soon after the Memphis outburst, Fetchit shot off a telegram to the *Chicago Defender,* his staunchest ally among the Negro press, criticizing the entertainment editor's description of the organizational hierarchy of the *Harlem Hit Parade* tour. He objected to the paper's announcement of an upcoming appearance which stated that "Erskine Hawkins and his Bama State Collegians" would appear in Chicago and then added that Fetchit headed the entertainment staff "traveling with Hawkins' unit."

"Kindly try and show your dislike for me in some way other than abusing my name by allowing it printed as in your last issue in the employment of people whom I employ," Fetchit wrote. "I can see no other reason than your dislike of me that would allow your paper to print things about me so detrimental when you have been advised better."

Fetchit's overzealous complaint about the incident seemed gratuitous. And, in fact, the minor row was seemingly forgotten when, in May, he and Hawkins arrived in Chicago. It was, however, another example of his increased sensitivity to minor slights, petulance with regard to the Negro press, and near-obsessive concern with star treatment and billing.[22]

While Fetchit and Hawkins were playing Chicago's Oriental Theater, the actor received word that his young wife had given birth to a son. The eight-pound, fourteen-ounce boy was born at New York's Community Hospital on May 21, 1938. When a telegram arrived near the end of the evening's last show, Step hurriedly finished his closing number. Later that night, celebrating with friends on Chicago's South Side, he apparently put career and personal problems aside. According to one writer, the proud father "was as good at announcing his own news as was Paul Revere." He even called Walter Winchell's office to assure that the event received national media attention.[23]

Before arriving in Chicago, Fetchit had announced that if the child was a boy he would be christened "Gilesa," which like his first child's name was an acronym for three religious icons. Mrs. Perry would have no part of it, however, and in his absence named the child Donald Martin Perry. Initially, it was reported that the actor was so upset by his wife's disregarding his wishes that he decided to fly to Hollywood and pursue film work without returning to see the child. Rumors of marital discord immediately intensified. Several days later, however, he arrived in Harlem for a brief visit with his family.[24]

His wife, it was claimed, thought the name Gilesa sounded "girlish" and the child might be teased as he grew older. Still, after consulting with her husband, she offered to change it according to his wishes. Fetchit declined.

"Winnie didn't like the name Gilesa, and she has the right to change it," he said, "but he'll always be Gilesa to me, savvy." Later, Fetchit appeared to have embraced the alternate name and reconciled with his wife. "He apparently feels that there couldn't be a better name than Don Fetchit," one writer claimed.[25]

That particular incident was soon laughed off and attributed to Fetchit's legendary eccentricity. But throughout the summer and fall, rumors continued to circulate about marital problems between the glamorous young performer, often described as "one of Harlem's most attractive personalities," and a temperamental husband who was nearly twice her age.[26]

Meanwhile, Fetchit rejoined the *Hit Parade* troupe and headed west on a reorganized tour for engagements in Oklahoma and Kansas.

When the troupe suddenly disbanded in Kansas, Fetchit continued to the West Coast, where he was to negotiate the contract for a role in a proposed Paramount remake of the 1927 silent film *The Patent Leather Kid.*

He arrived in Hollywood by train from Newton, Kansas, in late June after over a year's absence and was reportedly welcomed by friends and admirers. His refusal to answer questions about his wife and child, however, again stoked rumors about family discord. When asked about his career, he was more forthcoming. Fetchit claimed that he was tired of life on the road and explained that his planned Southern theatrical tour had been canceled because of "poor business" due to the "intense heat in the South." According to one writer, however, some believed "he had been assured a place at one of the leading studios."[27]

Although details of their discussions were undisclosed, Fetchit and Paramount apparently were unable to reach an agreement about a new project. *The Patent Leather Kid* project was dropped, and weeks later the actor quickly accepted the role of Casper, a bumbling houseman, in Universal Pictures' comic romp *His Exciting Night,* which starred veteran actor Charles Ruggles. The film was completed by the end of the summer, and Fetchit returned to New York to visit his family and begin another brief theatrical tour.

While he was in New York, rumors of a looming rift between the Perrys resurfaced. A daily-newspaper story suggested that at one point Fetchit "had been looking high and low for his wife," but when questioned by a Negro press reporter, Winnie Johnson replied with a curt "No comment." She also refused to answer queries about why she was still working, saying, "It's simply that I like to keep my business to myself."[28]

Fetchit quietly returned to Hollywood in October. Soon after his arrival, it was announced that he and Hattie McDaniel had accepted parts in a new Hal Roach project, *Saturday's Eve,* which was distributed by Paramount. "The third time is a charm," a Hollywood scribe wrote, referring to Fetchit's previous "returns" to the screen. Noting that the actor had recently completed a "splendid role" in Universal's *His Exciting Night,* the reporter added that "Sepia Hollywoodia" was watching and wondering how Step would "do on his third trip to the films."[29]

Fetchit returned to New York to fulfill several contracted dates for stage appearances before beginning the picture in early November. The film, which was released as *Zenobia,* was a vehicle for Oliver Hardy, who was venturing out on his own and trying his hand at straight comedy while temporarily estranged from his partner Stan Laurel. Set in the late nineteenth century, the story centered on a country doctor who, after treating a circus elephant, is unable to rid himself of the huge, overly affectionate beast. Fetchit and Hattie McDaniel were cast in predictable comic servant roles as Zero and Dehlia.

The appearance of McDaniel and Fetchit in the middling farce marked a decisive crossroads in their careers; as McDaniel ascended, Fetchit was precipitously declining. Just as the production was being wrapped up in January, it was announced that McDaniel had won the coveted role of Mammy in the upcoming Civil War spectacular *Gone With the Wind.* She would go on to win an Academy Award in the blockbuster Margaret Mitchell vehicle and, despite some protests over the roles she inevitably played, establish herself as a formidable screen personality and, later, a television star. Upon completing *Zenobia,* Stepin Fetchit found himself in limbo.[30]

His flamboyant reign as the nation's most popular and best-known black motion picture actor had come to a virtual halt.

CHAPTER FOURTEEN

Stepin Fetchit's difficulties in Hollywood films during the 1940s resulted, in part, from the trifling, hypnotically compelling character that he imprinted on the screen. Quite simply, times were changing, and the current of popular opinion regarding comic images of blacks was shifting. The trickster-derived "Laziest Man in the World" shtick—which was the cornerstone of Fetchit's stage act and had been continually reprised in pictures—collided head-on with a concerted, rapidly intensifying effort to upgrade the black image in films. Multiple forces combined in the effort to expunge all traces of the comic stage darky from public view; they included the Negro Actors' Guild of America, some of Hollywood's more outspoken white liberals, far-left and socialist news organs, segments of the black press, and rights organizations such as the NAACP.

In addition, Fetchit's ouster was hastened by the hard line he took in negotiations with studios, a succession of high-profile legal wrangles and clashes with theatrical managers and producers, his problematic, scandal-ridden personal life, and his increasingly erratic, hell-raising encounters backstage and off-camera.

After completing *Zenobia* in 1938, he prepared to return to New York to reunite with his family and begin a series of local theatrical dates. Before leaving Hollywood, however, he was involved in another minor scrape with the law. The actor made headlines when he was hauled into court to answer what appeared to be a nuisance suit brought by two men who alleged that they suffered injuries when a car "owned" by Fetchit collided with theirs.[1]

The case was apparently dismissed, and, back in New York, Fetchit returned to Loew's State Theater for a successful week's engagement in February. Immediately afterward, he opened as the headline act at the Riviera Theater in Brooklyn and played to packed houses.

Fetchit's return to New York also appeared to have put to rest rumors concerning his marriage. A front-page photograph of the apparently happy couple holding son Donald appeared in the *Chicago Defender,* and the *Amsterdam News* and *Afro-American* also ran photos and blurbs indicating that Winnie Johnson was thrilled at the actor's return to the city. "Despite rumors of rifts during the last two months," one report claimed, "all seems to be harmony in the Fetchit family." The reports of marital bliss, however, did not mention that during Fetchit's absence the actor's young wife had been living with her parents in their Sugar Hill apartment on St. Nicholas Place and remained there after he returned and took up residence on 138th Street.[2]

During the spring, Fetchit quickly demonstrated that where money and work were concerned he was as contentious and demanding as ever. In March, at about the same time that the newlyweds and their son were being pictured as a contented theatrical family, the actor abruptly walked out on his Riviera Theater engagement after a dispute over salary. He issued a "no-pay-no-work" ultimatum, and, when the theater management declined to pay until the date was completed, Fetchit refused to go on despite the threat of a breach-of-contract suit.[3]

The following month, he began a scheduled thirty-one-day western tour, which was to end in Hollywood, where he intended to resume motion-picture work. The tour opened at Chicago's Oriental Theater with Fetchit heading an "all-star" troupe that he had organized.[4]

The initial engagement would set the tone for a tour that reaffirmed his audience appeal but, from Chicago to the West Coast, cut a swath of farcical rowdyism that one might expect to see in a slapstick TOBA comedy skit. The outlandish encounters began on Easter Sunday with a widely publicized backstage clash over Tabasco sauce and a steak dinner.

A Negro delivery boy claimed that, when he delivered a steak ordered from a local restaurant, Fetchit was dissatisfied with the meal and had two of his "stooges" attack him. Fetchit was charged with disorderly conduct and brought to court. Charges were dismissed, however, after he appeared before a judge, denied the attack, and offered an alternate explanation of the conflict.

When the meal was delivered, Fetchit said, he reached for his Tabasco sauce. The delivery boy, apparently offended by the breach of condiment etiquette, attempted to snatch the steak back. One of Step's assistants "got rid of him in a hurry." The next day, the assistant went to the restaurant to order a steak with sauce and was "clubbed" by two restaurant employees, Fetchit claimed. At the hearing, where the assistant appeared with his head wrapped in bandages, the judge quickly dispatched the complaint. "I think it's even," he said. "Case dismissed." Later in the month, while appearing in Sioux Falls, South Dakota, Fetchit sued the restaurant for $100,000 but received no compensation. Still, reports of the burlesquelike encounter made the headlines in newspapers across the country.[5]

During a Fargo, North Dakota, appearance in May, Fetchit was arrested for provoking a "one-man-riot" in a residential area and spent the night in jail. He insisted that his loud temper outburst was provoked by a homeowner's refusal to permit him to retrieve his overcoat, a photograph, and $100 that he had left inside the house. He pled not guilty and was given a "60-day suspended sentence at 'hard labor.'"[6]

Fetchit's plans for a Hollywood return after a month on the road apparently went no smoother than his spring theatrical tour; he was again unable to come to terms with the studios. Frustrated, he announced that he "would stay out of Hollywood and make only legitimate stage appearances." He resumed an extended summer road tour, during which both audience and critical response were mixed. Frequently, critical notices depended on whether reviews came from mainstream or Negro newspapers. An early July appearance at the Pix Theater in Portland, Oregon, for instance, was a sellout according to a *Baltimore Afro-American* report, and Fetchit was asked to "give extra shows to meet the heavy response." The exact same act was panned by *Variety* when the actor appeared at the Roxy in Salt Lake City, Utah, later in the month. The "colored film star, spotted next to closing, offers little in talent as a singer or shuffle dancer," the critic claimed; "he continually resorts to emitting guttural sounds and Harlem double-talk, which went over Roxy pew-holder's heads."[7]

When the actor returned to New York in August, he faced new problems. The government questioned his reported income and challenged some items listed as deductions on his tax return. Fetchit had listed quantities of beer as a deduction, for instance, explaining that it was an essential item "needed to keep him lazy enough to continue as a star in movies and on stage." The IRS was not amused.

On a more positive note, it was also reported that Fetchit was "booked for appearances on Broadway in two outstanding plays." The actor explained to a reporter that his recent inability to come to terms with Hollywood producers was linked to "his unwillingness to work for the salaries offered race players." He had turned down movie contracts that did not pay what he was "in the habit of making." And while reiterating that he was prepared to pursue the production of his own films, the actor said that he expected to return to the West Coast in the fall "to do three pictures that would make him the highest paid Race player in Hollywood."[8]

Fetchit had been approached with offers of roles in two Broadway plays: Erik Charell's proposed musical based on *A Midsummer's Night Dream,* which was to feature a score written by Benny Goodman, and John Shubert's musical comedy *Three After Three.* In addition, he made arrangements to appear in a star-studded revue at the Cotton Club at Broadway and 48th Street (where it had moved in 1936) costarring with his old friend Louis Armstrong.[9]

The opening date for the revue was shifted several times as Armstrong's manager Joe Glaser and Fetchit's "office" haggled with club manager Herman Starks over conflicting contractual obligations and, presumably, salary since the club was experiencing some financial difficulties. Management also announced that it intended to cut big-budget production numbers and to pare its famed chorus line. Amidst this chaos, a vaudeville version of the revue, the *Cotton Club Parade,* starring Fetchit and Armstrong, opened at the Golden Gate Ballroom on Lenox Avenue on October 19.[10]

From all appearances in early fall 1939, the volatile actor had once again put his career and personal life back on course.

According to Lula Jones—who as a child lived in the 75 St. Nicholas Place apartment building in which Winnie Johnson and such celebrities as Jimmie Lunceford and Buck Clayton resided—Fetchit regularly visited his "wife" and son during this time. "He was warm and very funny," she recalled, "always kidding around, falling down and making us laugh. The children in the neighborhood loved him, and he seemed to love kids. He'd take us down to the corner drugstore for ice cream of, sometimes, all the way downtown for outings."

In early November, the *Amsterdam News* published a photograph of "the beauteous Wini Johnson" with a caption that trumpeted the performers as one of Negro entertainment's most glamorous celebrity couples. Mrs. Perry, who is "one of the Cotton Club beauties and had a stage and nightclub reputation second to few," the item exclaimed, is "happy that papa Step is back in town and near the family hearth."[11]

Days after the photo appeared, however, Lincoln and Winifred Johnson Perry had, according to press accounts, "gone their separate ways." Johnson told a reporter that she saw her husband only when he visited their baby. She insisted that she would keep the child but gave no reason for the split. Fetchit also refused to comment on her claim. News of the separation and the couple's refusal to provide details shocked and confused friends, fans, as well as many in the entertainment community.[12]

In addition, a serious behind-the-scenes rift surfaced between Fetchit and Cotton Club manager Herman Starks. Fetchit objected to cutbacks in the presentation and had voiced his opinions to Starks in no uncertain terms; apparently in protest, he conveniently missed several *Cotton Club Parade* shows at the Golden Gate. In late October, some sources reported that he had insisted on having a chorus line behind him. "Working in a floor show without girls is like working in a kitchen minus utensils," he said later. "It just cannot be done." He also voiced more self-indulgent requests, such as having management "build him a special dressing room containing a bath and kitchen." Before the show opened on Broadway, the disagreement had spiraled into a full-blown, highly publicized quarrel.

Then, in a letter that was reprinted in part or its entirety by several newspapers, Fetchit laid out specific conditions under which he would appear at the Broadway club. The demands, according to one news source, "exploded like a bombshell" and stunned downtown show folk:

> Mr. Herman Starks:
>
> This is to advise that it will necessitate you to furnish me with a Chinese girl singer and very light straight man for support of my original song presentation during my engagements at the Cotton Club.

Also you are to furnish the following props and costumes: a white French phone with a fifty-foot cord and a proper plug-in connection, and battery telephone bell to ring continually offstage; also, a minstrel covered chair, and tamborine [*sic*]; a small piano and stool; a green low-back overstuffed parlor chair; a collapsible service tray and tea wagon; two school desks; a prop pinto horse.

Also three microphones—a long, short and table microphone, all connected for use; three school girl costumes for the Dandridge Sisters and a school teacher's outfit for principal to be selected; a minstrel outfit for me and an interlocutor's outfit for principal to be selected; a Philip Morris uniform and maid's outfit for the Chinese girl.

Also a French artist's beret and jacket for me; and two new song arrangements each week, the music and word material I will furnish and their arrangements furnished by you; also a Will Rogers outfit and makeup for a straight man.

During my engagement I can be the only one allowed to talk other than the straight man and all other acts must have fast moving routines and songs. You must furnish a new Cotton Club book to include printed matter I have in collection with these song presentations and my picture must be printed among the Cotton Club stars on the upstairs bar lobby wall in place desired by me.

"Nota bene"—and nota bene that nota bene!—"These props, costumes, printing matter, art work and arrangements with all principals is absolutely necessary, with rehearsals at least three days before my opening. So let's get going if I am to open as we desire Wednesday.

Regards, STEPIN FETCHIT[13]

Although Starks's reply to Fetchit's letter was not publicized, one can assume that he was not pleased with the detailed and somewhat extravagant requests. As one writer ironically noted, "Stepin Fetchit, the black glacier, may be deliberate but he is also thorough." The show opened as planned on the first of November with Fetchit and Armstrong backed by a veteran lineup of variety acts, an abbreviated Cotton Club Girls chorus line, and the young comedy duo Stump and Stumpy. Few of the perks that Fetchit demanded were supplied, and tensions between the irascible star and Starks steadily mounted. Within three weeks, Fetchit's Cotton Club stint was terminated.[14]

Wild rumors circulated about a brawl that had occurred backstage at the Cotton Club, some indicating that Fetchit had hurled bricks at the crew. The comedian denied the allegations.

"Sure I had a fight with Herman Starks, manager of the place," Fetchit said, "but the story that I tossed bricks at half of the Cotton Club crew is entirely false. My trouble was with Starks only and we had our troubles out and then everything was straight." He again explained that his act depended on the right props and "assistants," and, pressed about the brick-tossing allegations, quipped, "Figure it out for yourself. Where would a guy find a brick in the Cotton Club." Relieved at having removed himself from the situation, he later told reporters, "You don't know how glad I am to get out of there." A *Chicago Defender* news item wryly observed, "The two men won't miss each other much."[15]

The Cotton Club bill for the week of November 29 did not list Fetchit as a costar; Louis Armstrong was the lone feature attraction. The club's financial woes continued, however; and by June 10, 1940, the legendary cabaret had shut down.

By December 1939, Fetchit was appearing in Boston with the road company of *Three After Three,* which starred the French actress Simone Simon. The show was scheduled for a January premiere at the Ethel Barrymore Theater.

In Boston, Fetchit appeared surprisingly lighthearted. In a letter to *Chicago Defender* editors, he made light of a proposed abbreviated role in the movie *Tongues a Wagging,* which he had turned down. He had "only two words to say, one in each of the first and last few minutes of the screening," he wrote of the picture project. The producer thought I might be "finished with my first line by the time the last one was due to be flashed." In similar fashion, he joked about a critic's response to his role as Chesterfield, the butler, in *Three After Three.*

In the second act, his character starts to tell the other players that a cab is waiting for them, but by the time he finishes, the cab has run out of gas. Then he begins to apologize for being so slow, but before he is through, the curtain comes down and patrons file out. In a rarely heard deprecative jest, Fetchit revealed that one critic had written that the latter bit "was easy on both my vocal cords" and the audience's since they were "fortunate to flee from hearing distance."[16]

It appeared that he had not only come to terms with critics who denounced and satirized his dawdling, lazy-man speech pattern but, in fact, embraced the criticism as a kind of wrongheaded recognition of his comedy approach. If so, he had no doubt beamed at the *Times* review of his last movie, *Zenobia,* published earlier in the year. Calling the picture an "antebellum costume romance in slapstick," the reviewer wrote, "As for Stepin Fetchit, he is getting as stylized as James Joyce; it is now almost impossible to form any idea of what he is trying to say."[17]

While rehearsing for *Three After Three,* Fetchit met with a New York reporter and elaborated on his minimalist approach to comedy. Asserting that his mumbling was deliberate, he deconstructed a line from the play to demonstrate how he would deliver it. As written, the line had his character, Chesterfield, saying, "You know dat cahr we ain't got? Where I got it parked I got to move it from de fire-plug so we don't get a ticket." The only "important words," Fetchit insisted, were "car," "ain't," "parked," "fire-plug," and "ticket." He had reduced the speech to five words, which with his slurred, molasses-like delivery required nearly as much time to utter as the original phrase. He insisted that the technique, which he called "audible pantomime," was the key element in his distinct stage and motion-picture portrayals. Although he did not make the claim, the actor's emended version may simply have been an attempt to avoid delivering the original nonsensical lines.

"When I was in pictures, people wrote from England and other countries to say they couldn't understand me—would I please talk plainly?" he explained. "But I didn't, or else I'd lose my lazy-bones character. The same would happen if an English cockney character or an excitable Italian talked plainly for the benefit of American audiences—there'd be no personality left."[18]

At this juncture in his career, Fetchit obviously still had supreme confidence in his highly stylized characterization. In contrast to previous statements indicating that he was considering altering the character to fit changing times, he now seemed determined to adhere to his unique style of comedy.

His confidence as well as his apparent ease and satisfaction with his role in *Three After Three* was quickly dampened, however, as the show struggled on the road. And while he was only marginally at fault, Fetchit's six-month tour with the musical comedy ultimately evolved into a headline-grabbing fiasco that matched the Cotton Club encounter in terms of bad press. The musical had been scheduled to open on Broadway in January with the title *Walk with Music,* but bad notices forced producer John Schubert to postpone the premiere and keep the show on the road for more rehearsals and "extensive revisions."

Trouble reared during an engagement in Toronto early in the year with a minor scrape with customs officials. Fetchit was accused of purchasing three suits and, in an attempt to avoid paying duty, reporting only one. Meanwhile, in Detroit and Chicago, *Walk with Music* was "blasted by critics." The comic was among the few bright spots acknowledged by reviewers. "It is hardly believable that a musical comedy with such headliners as these could be so poor," one critic wrote, adding that "Fetchit kept the audience in an uproar each time he appeared behind the footlights."[19]

After the Detroit engagement, Fetchit's temperament reared itself again and he quit the show after a dispute with John Shubert. Actor Tory Brown was brought in as a replacement when the company regrouped in preparation for its May or June Broadway opening.[20]

At about the same time, Fetchit's public image suffered another blow when his nine-year-old son Jemajo "charged through his grandmother" that he had been "discarded" and "abandoned" by his father. The child sought and received permission to legally change his name to Robert Lee Strange.[21]

In May 1940, just prior to the Broadway premiere, Fetchit rejoined *Walk with Music* and a revised cast, which featured Kitty Carlisle, Mitzi Green, and Jack Whiting. But the patchwork play—despite what most considered an excellent, upbeat score featuring the lyrics of Johnny Mercer and the music of Hoagy Carmichael—was generally panned by critics.

In a lukewarm review that praised Carmichael's music, the *New York Times* critic Brooks Atkinson noted that "liking Stepin Fetchit is an acquired taste which this column has not yet mastered."[22]

Fetchit "withdrew" from the production "by mutual agreement with the management" in early July, and the show closed later that month. The reservations about Fetchit's performance to which Atkinson referred, however, reflected a dilemma with which many other movie- and theatergoers, black and white, were increasingly wrangling. Fetchit's dogged commitment to the stylized, near-surreal portrayal of the slothful character that had catapulted him to fame and served him for more than a decade was increasingly meeting resistance from mainstream theatrical managers and critics.

The comic characterization still appealed to an older, hard-core base of black fans, and Fetchit remained a popular attraction at TOBA theaters and black-circuit clubs. But younger black audiences were tiring of the rural, folk-derived comic shtick. With the United States' entry into World War II and Negro soldiers' participation in the struggle, a new generation of Negroes would completely disavow the indirect, conniving challenge to white authority that Fetchit's character represented. Black leaders and returning servicemen would demand America's overt recognition of their rights and equal status under the law. Its possible rewards notwithstanding, the venerable trickster ploy was rapidly losing credence in the black community.[23]

Recognizing and seeking to exploit the trend, NAACP executive secretary Walter White began a crusade to rid the motion-picture screen of "subservient, dim-witted, craven, eye-rolling" Negro caricatures in the early 1940s. It was, of course, not the first effort to pressure Hollywood studios to alter the predominantly servile, farcical image of Negroes in pictures. The black press had encouraged letter-writing campaigns by filmgoers during the thirties, and individual artists initiated their own protests. The fan letters had been largely ineffectual; for the most part producers ignored them, using the correspondence to compile a list of Negroes' favorite stars. But there had been such small isolated victories as the cast of *Hallelujah!* successfully lobbying to change objectionable bits of dialogue, Louise Beavers's previously cited lobbying to have the word "nigger" deleted from the script of *Imitation of Life*, and a similar demand by Hattie McDaniel when she accepted a role in *Gone With the Wind*. Most efforts, however, had been futile. NAACP protests after the release of *Birth of a Nation* in 1915, for example, had been ignored.

White's campaign was more successful because of its timing (the backdrop of a war against Hitler and his racist ideals) but also because of the support of such prominent film stars as Humphrey Bogart and John Garfield and both the black and mainstream press. His efforts began when he met the Republican presidential candidate Wendell L. Willkie prior to the 1940 election. Willkie expressed sympathy for

White's cause and, after being defeated by Roosevelt in November, he supported and helped rouse national concern for the crusade. In 1942, White and Willkie attended a luncheon with Darryl Zanuck, Walter Wanger, and other elite studio executives to discuss the issue.

"Restrictions of colored to roles with rolling eyes, chattering teeth, always scared of ghosts, or to portrayals of none-too-bright servants," White told the executives, "perpetuates a stereotype which is doing infinite harm." He also suggested that repetitious portrayals of "mentally inferior" Negroes, "lacking in ambition," were a major cause of the sparse opportunities offered blacks in America and throughout the world. Like the esteemed civil rights leader W. E. B. Du Bois, White was essentially lobbying for a severe cutback in the comic portrayal of Negroes in pictures or, at the very least, the increased representation of black professionals. There were Negro maids, servants, and sharecroppers, he admitted, but "there are also Negro artists, doctors, lawyers, scientists, teachers, businessmen, and others who have made and are making very material contributions to their own and the country's advancement."[24]

It was not a fresh argument, and, as before, for the studios there was the bottom-line reality of the popularity of comedy and concern for alienating the Southern white constituency with images of successful, serious blacks. Still, Zanuck, Wanger, and others agreed to seriously consider rectifying the problem, promising to attempt to liberalize their depiction of Negroes in accordance with changing times. Although many saw it as a victory, the immediate attention and verbal consent that White elicited from producers angered and stirred a backlash among some in the Negro film community. They resented an outsider stepping in and initiating negotiations that directly affected their livelihood without their consent or input. In August, near the same time White met with studio executives, a group of black performers met at the home of Hattie McDaniel to discuss the problem. Leigh Whipper, Ernest Whitman, Nicodemus Stewart, Lillian Randolph, Mantan Moreland, and Clarence Muse were among the participants. The topic of discussion was the growing pressure they felt as they attempted to satisfy the demands of both the studios and civil rights leaders.[25]

Animosity between White and a hard-core cadre of Negro actors, spearheaded by Muse and McDaniel, steadily intensified during the early forties. The gist of their dispute was that White, in courting studio bosses in the attempt to exact change, gave the impression that it was the black actors who perpetuated the screen image of the ever-grinning darky. The Fair Play Committee argued that it was the producers and the scripts they offered which dictated on-screen stereotypes, and that, instead of cozying up to white studio executives, White should have been pressuring them, not the black actors.

"What do you want me to do? Play a glamour girl on Clark Gable's knee?" McDaniel exploded. "When you ask me not to play the parts, what have you got to offer in return?" During this time, she offered the now-famous quip, "Hell, I'd rather play a maid than be one."[26]

Clarence Muse also emerged as an important spokesman for the actors' point of view. "How can some outside person fight the cause of the artists by conferring with producers only, leaving to the sidelines the very person for whom they're fighting?" he asked, adding that White's "purpose" was noble "but his formula bad." The actor's statement, which appeared in several Negro newspapers, argued that White's approach had led to a general assumption that rectifying the presentation of blacks in films required eliminating all dialect and replacing dark-skinned Negroes with light-skinned or mulatto actors. "The boys with their hair straightened will have a better social picture outlook and all the pictures should have Negro lawyers, doctors and architects—and above all—don't have them too black," he wrote. "This is the reaction being broadcast throughout Hollywood."

Muse went on to suggest that since, realistically, African Americans often had menial jobs, spoke in dialect, and were dark-skinned, the emphasis should be placed on scripts that give those characters some noble attributes and show them as ambitious, law-abiding Americans.[27]

The comic actor Mantan Moreland also weighed in against what, to some performers, was a misdirected approach by White (a self-imposed "Mr. Fix-It") and the NAACP. "I admit there's a big job for these guys to do but they should start with the man on the street," Moreland sarcastically told a Negro press reporter. He suggested that White appoint "deputies" to patrol the streets of black communities and reprimand people who didn't "conduct themselves decently," were "loud in theaters," wore "conspicuous clothes," or cursed. "He could start the ball rolling," the comedian said, "by improving the status of colored in every town and city where the NAACP has an organization for advancement."[28]

Despite dissent among actors, the combined pressure of the NAACP, the actors' own Fair Play Committee, and progressive forces in the white film community gradually began to effect some noticeable change. That shift was probably hastened in 1943 by deadly race riots that erupted in Harlem and Detroit, underscoring the critical status of American race relations. A liberal drift in American social policies later in the decade—witnessed by President Truman's executive order demanding "equality of treatment" in the armed forces—also helped expedite the subtle shift to more fully drawn or representative Negro characters in motion pictures during the forties.

Although change evolved slowly and, in fact, spawned new arguments over what the proper image of the Negro should be, an immediate benefit was the production of two black-cast musicals that employed the talents of some of black America's most illustrious entertainers. MGM's *Cabin in the Sky* and Twentieth Century-Fox's *Stormy Weather* were both released in 1943.

Cabin in the Sky was based on a successful Broadway play that depicted black life in an imaginary setting and pitted the forces of heaven and hell against each other in a battle to claim the soul of an average working man. Eddie Anderson played Little Joe, the black Everyman, and Ethel Waters was cast as his loyal wife. Lucifer's henchmen were portrayed by Louis Armstrong, Mantan Moreland, Rex Ingram, and Willie Best; and Lena Horne was cast as the sexy enchantress who attempts to lure Joe away from his wife. The plot, however, was little more than scaffolding for a series of dazzling dance and musical numbers; Joe and his wife are the only characters who rise above obvious caricature. *Cabin* was highlighted by a raft of dazzling musical numbers that featured the principals as well as a dance number by John Bubbles and the music of Duke Ellington and the Hall Johnson Choir. As striking was the film's near-absence of straight-out comedy and all traces of the familiar grinning darky stereotype.

While *Stormy Weather* was laced with comedy throughout, it also largely avoided servile, lazy, or inept stage Negro stereotypes. The picture was supposedly based on the lives of black entertainers Noble

Sissle and Jim Europe, but instead centered on a romance between Bill Robinson, playing himself, and Lena Horne. And as in *Cabin,* the real focus was the parade of high-profile black entertainers who light up the screen. Joined by the Katherine Dunham Dance Troupe, Fats Waller, Ada Brown, Cab Calloway, and a sensational young dance team, the Nicholas Brothers, Horne and Robinson presented a series of jazzy, show-stopping musical numbers that allowed viewers to ignore the makeshift plot.

The comedy, of a type heretofore rarely seen outside black honky-tonks, variety shows, theaters, and the occasional independent race movie, was provided by old stalwarts Flournoy Miller, Johnny Lee, and the Fetchit act-alike Nicodemus Stewart. The film was notable for its hip, urban ambiance and the spontaneous humor that flowed naturally from that overriding spirit. Even Stewart's portrayal of a slow-talking darky character was elevated by its controlled, urbane tone.

The films marked another milestone in the depiction of blacks in motion pictures, and, although there would be some backsliding and wrong turns, during the next few decades the black presence in Hollywood films would gradually begin to reflect the diverse reality of black life.

Ironically, the two films not only had roles in which Stepin Fetchit might have easily been cast, but were also manifest examples of the kind of black-cast motion pictures for which he had vainly lobbied during the thirties. Fetchit, however, was far removed from the Hollywood scene by the time the studios decided to experiment with alternate portraits of black American life. His exile was largely the result of his assertive dealings with the studios and the recklessness or, some would argue, perfidy displayed in his professional life.

One crucial event in Fetchit's fall from grace with fans and theater and movie producers had occurred in 1940. The actor had fallen on lean times after his knotty encounters with the Cotton Club management and the producers of *Walk with Music.* Those highly publicized run-ins had prompted many theatrical producers to adopt a hands-off policy. His increasing antagonism with the Negro press contributed to his decline during this period because his appearances at small nightclubs and second-tier black venues were virtually ignored by the media. And since his salary demands and refusal to accept minor, supporting comic roles in studio pictures had alienated producers, Hollywood was not knocking at his door.

When Walter White began lobbying for more equitable representation and better roles for Negro actors, he was advised that Eddie Anderson, Louise Beavers, Mantan Moreland, Hattie McDaniel, Sam McDaniel, and Stepin Fetchit topped the list of performers who appeared in objectionable roles. Fetchit had not appeared in a film since 1939, however, so much of White's criticism was aimed at the others. But even in his absence, the exiled entertainer remained a conspicuous *symbol* of the demeaning screen presence that protesters targeted.

Estranged from his wife, financially pressed, and unable to command the big-time theatrical engagements he once enjoyed, Fetchit had been cast aside. He had nowhere to turn except the TOBA circuit. For nearly a year and a half, he took to the road, beating the bushes in seedy nightclubs and cramped black theaters where, only two years before, the presence of the cinema's most popular star would have been unimaginable.

His activities were largely unreported during this period. But according to the vocalist and trombone player Leon "Peewee" Whittaker, whose band played carnivals in the South, he and Fetchit toured the Southeast in the fall of 1940. They were booked by Sam Dorsey, who owned a chain of theaters catering to Negroes. "He tried to take me back to California with him to make some records," Whittaker claimed. "I got as far as Lake Charles. He begged me to go out there with him." Whittaker wanted to stay in the East and declined the invitation, but he later regretted his decision. "I would have been somewhere if I had went on out there," he said.[29]

In January 1941, Fetchit's appearance in the annual National Vaudeville Artists performance at New York's Palm Garden was widely reported and seemed to indicate an upturn in his fortunes; Olsen and Johnson, Henny Youngman, and Ethel Waters also performed at the event. During the western swing that followed his appearance in New York, however, Fetchit was barely able to make ends meet. In February he began bankruptcy proceedings. That spring, according to later reports, his manager was unable to secure bookings at credible venues, and Fetchit sued him. During this time, Fetchit hired the young pianist

Gerald Wiggins, who had been recommended by Art Tatum, as an accompanist. In September, while making dual appearances at the Jefferson Inn and the Silver Slipper in Detroit, Fetchit sued the Inn's theater manager, claiming he had been promised four days' booking but had been paid for only one. The manager countersued and won, contending that the actor "was such a poor box office draw" he had paid him a "full week's salary after four days" and given him his "walking papers."

The incident provoked more speculation that the actor's show-business career was finished. "When a performer reaches the stage that he is paid the week in advance, he'd better give up the ghost," an acerbic *Afro-American* item reported, posing the rhetorical question, can it "be that Fetchit is just plumb nowhere?"[30]

Fetchit's motion-picture prospects must have darkened along with his frame of mind when in 1942 it was announced that the week of January 26 was being celebrated as "Willie Best Week" in many black communities across the country. "The young rolly-eyed actor who has taken everyone by storm" was reportedly being honored by fans and theater managers. With reports of Fetchit's demise circulating in the black press, the news that Best—who blatantly imitated the lazy-man shtick—had usurped the niche that he had carved out and popularized in Hollywood must have crushed him.[31]

In early April 1942, however, "after many a try," Fetchit finally secured an engagement in a "sepia first class show" in New York. He was contracted to costar with Ethel Waters and the Les Hite band at the Brooklyn Strand Theater.

"It was like pulling up the musty curtains on the stage of a theater which has long been deserted but suddenly signs of life begin to creep in," Dolores Calvin wrote of his appearance. "It was like a ghost returning to make sure that he was not forgotten. So it was when the curtain unfolded and there stood Stepin Fetchit." Calvin went on to describe how, following his "marriage" to Winnie Johnson, Fetchit's career had plummeted. She alleged that after two years of second-rate bookings the "aging" performer was "becoming a fadeout."[32]

At this stage in his career, a return to motion pictures seemed unlikely. Bill Robinson, Mantan Moreland, Hattie McDaniel, Willie Best, Louise Beavers, Eddie Anderson, and the beautiful young starlet

Dorothy Dandridge had surpassed him as the top-drawing black actors. Despite the disappointment of his recent theatrical tour, the stage now loomed as his best opportunity in show business.

Almost immediately, however, a new scandal arose that would scuttle even that promising vehicle.

CHAPTER FIFTEEN

In March 1941, Winnie Johnson had quietly filed suit for child support, but warrant officers had been unable to catch up to Fetchit for over a year. His high-profile appearance at the Brooklyn Strand Theater, however, provided a perfect opportunity for his arrest. Shortly after the opening, Fetchit was reportedly hauled off the stage, hustled into court, and held on $500 bail.

"We were working at the Brooklyn Strand. The house band was Les Hite's band from Los Angeles," Gerald Wiggins said. "The army took his [Hite's] piano player, and the police took Stepin Fetchit off the stage." Wiggins replaced the pianist in Hite's group and traveled to California; Step went directly to jail.[1]

Because he either refused to or could not afford to make bail, Fetchit remained behind bars for over two weeks. When released, however, he delivered a bombshell announcement that shocked nearly everyone.

"I've got the biggest story of the week, but I want you to be sure and get everything I say," he told a group of newsmen. "Listen fellows, I am not, have never been and never will be married to Miss Winnie Johnson."

When dumbfounded reporters asked for an explanation, he elaborated on the claim.

"I mean just this," he said. "Winnie and I were never married. It was all a publicity stunt. I also want you and everybody else to know that that is not my baby. Winnie knows the baby isn't mine but she's trying to be smart."[2]

Johnson immediately confirmed the couple's four-year matrimonial hoax but insisted that the child, Donald Martin Perry, was Perry's. After the actor was released, a special sessions court hearing was convened in May. When his attorney, State Senator Joseph Esquirol, "found a default in the complaint," arguing that Johnson's petition had been filed too late, Fetchit was initially cleared of paternal responsibility. The actor immediately left for an engagement in the Midwest, but in June, after Johnson claimed that the child was about to become a public charge and welfare authorities stepped into the case, he was ordered to return to New York for another hearing.[3]

Fetchit's denial of paternity and, in the eyes of many, abandonment of the popular chorus girl and her child immediately created adverse publicity for the actor. Some pals reportedly "nixed" him immediately after he aired his charge. And as the case proceeded, with claims and counterclaims escalating on both sides, it quickly developed into a major scandal and media spectacle.[4]

"I don't want him to support me," Johnson insisted, "I only want him to take care of our baby." For his part, Fetchit claimed that he "was only trying to help the kid out of a tough situation."[5]

Later, Fetchit expanded his account of the origin of the alleged ruse. He told reporters that he had been reluctant to reveal details because he and Johnson had "promised" not to tell anyone about their "secret vow." According to Fetchit, they had known each other for about six years. "When she advised me of the blessed event," he insisted, "I told her I'd say I was the father, if she would come and live with me as my wife. She agreed and that was the end of our marriage ceremony."[6]

A throng of curious reporters gathered to witness the proceedings when the litigants appeared in Manhattan's special sessions court for a final hearing in June. Fetchit's slow-motion movements, drowsy-eyed expressions, and laconic responses reportedly kept onlookers gawking. "It was good matinee," one reporter offered, "four times the justices threatened to clear the courtroom because of laughter." It was also pointedly acrimonious, as Fetchit's attorney blistered Johnson with questions about her sex life in the attempt to support his client's claim. Among the prominent names offered as the possible father were the black composer and producer Donald Heywood, for whom it was alleged the child was named, and Curt Horrman, a wealthy white sportsman, with whom Johnson had been seen in public on several occasions.

"The pretty mother and actress" denied having an affair with Heywood and claimed that there had never been an "intimate relationship with the white sportsman," insisting that he was "a friend of the family."

Fetchit "knew there was no affair between my daughter and Horrman," Winnie's father, Howard Johnson, added. "Horrman came here and she went out with him just as she went out with J. J. Shubert and other wealthy whites. These trips were always of a business nature."

In support of Winnie Johnson's claim of Fetchit's fatherhood, Bill Robinson was called to testify that the comic had introduced Johnson to him and said that she was his wife.[7]

Fetchit countered by admitting he had introduced Johnson to Robinson as "Mrs. Stepin Fetchit." But, he insisted, "that's not a legal name. That's a phoney name." When asked why he hadn't denied reports of the couple's elopement, Fetchit replied: "Well, I wanted the people out West, where I was popular, to think I was a married man, and the people in the East, I wanted them to think I was good for Winnie."[8]

When all of the evidence was in, the court decided in favor of Johnson and ordered Fetchit to pay $12 a week for the child's support. Court justices, however, stipulated that the temporary award would depend on the "Corporation Counsel's investigation to determine whether the Negro actor could pay more." Fetchit's attorney claimed that his client was making only "$100 to $350 a week when he could find work" and had made only $2,000 the previous year. He also claimed the actor owed the IRS $50,000.[9]

As both Johnson and Fetchit suggested, the alleged union was a hoax. There is no record of a marriage between Lincoln Perry and Winifred Johnson in either Connecticut or New York in 1937. And if, as suggested, it was concocted for publicity purposes, then both participants got more than they expected.

Johnson, who was appearing in Ed Sullivan's *Harlem Cavalcade*, was embraced even more avidly by fans. She remained the darling of Harlem dancers and went on to a moderately successful career on Broadway. Later, the beautiful young star joined Duke Ellington's band as a vocalist. She toured with Ellington and later married, then divorced, Dr. Middleton H. Lambright, the dean of the South Carolina Medical College in Charleston. Her son took the name Donald Martin Lambright.

Fetchit also received abundant publicity. Unfortunately, it was overwhelmingly adverse. The high-profile face-off with Johnson, a favorite in Harlem as well as with big-time theatrical producers, had given the impression that he was either a publicity-seeking charlatan or a cad. In either case, it almost certainly further damaged his pursuit of more prestigious New York stage engagements. In Hollywood, Fetchit had managed to make himself even more of an outcast.

His decline and public ignominy, however, had not reached rock bottom.

During the fall of 1942, he returned to the road with renewed determination to make a comeback. He had signed on with the high-powered theatrical manager Joe Glaser and, booked in midwestern theaters, the tour was increasingly successful. Aware of his image problems, by 1943 he and Glaser had arranged for the actor to entertain servicemen during personal appearances at Camp McCoy, near Sparta, Wisconsin. During the summer, however, Fetchit found himself involved in another scandal.[10]

On July 8, during an engagement at the Regal Theater in Chicago, policemen entered his room at the Vincennes Hotel and found him with sixteen-year-old Juanita Randolph, the daughter of a local musician and an aspiring performer. According to police, Randolph opened the door of the bathroom and walked out wearing a pair of the actor's pajamas. Reportedly, Fetchit immediately yelled, "It's a frame-up."[11]

Randolph, who according to her mother had not been home in three days, initially signed an affidavit alleging that she and Fetchit had twice been intimate. The claim was shocking even at a time when entertainers frequently dated and married teenage showgirls. Fetchit denied the allegation, insisting that he had met the girl but did not even know she was in his room. After being charged with contributing to the delinquency of a minor, he was released on bail to await trial on July 13 in domestic court. He later gave the press his version of the story.

Fetchit claimed that Randolph had approached him backstage at the Regal Theater three days earlier, identifying herself as a reporter who wanted to interview him. After he agreed to talk with her, she revealed that she was seeking a job in his stage act. "She told me she was 23 years old," he said. He also insisted that there had been no physical contact between them, claiming that when she arrived with friends two days later she was wearing the same clothes she had worn when they met. Her friends left, Fetchit said, and he thought Randolph had also gone. When the police knocked, she opened the door to his bathroom holding the pajamas.

At first it appeared to be a typical "he said, she said" scenario, but the proceedings quickly veered into the kind of travesty that the public had come to expect with Fetchit. First, news was leaked that Randolph was suspected of bringing similar charges against the dance team of Joyner and Foster the year before. Then, at the trial before Judge Joseph Hermes, Randolph recanted her affidavit, thus supporting Fetchit's version of the encounter. When she refused to verify her previous statement, she was charged with contempt of court and remanded to a juvenile facility. She was released within a week, but after numerous motions by his attorney Emmett Moynihan, Fetchit was sentenced to a thirty-day term in the Bridewell House of Corrections.[12]

With Fetchit behind bars on what appears to have been inconclusive evidence, the case took another bizarre turn. Rumors began circulating that the actor had somehow managed to substitute a lookalike or stooge in his cell and was actually on the West Coast. The trial judge vowed that the prisoner was Fetchit, saying he had seen "him in a Will Rogers picture," but one prosecutor speculated that a "switch may have occurred between felony court and Bridewell." An investigation followed and the mystery was solved when the actor's fingerprints were matched with the prisoner's. Fetchit's agent had tried to inject some reason into the farce from the beginning, telling authorities that his client did not have a brother or a double. "He's written me three letters from his cell," he said. "Stepin's always trying to fool people and that's what got him into jail, trying to fool people."[13]

Following the Randolph affair, the forty-one-year-old performer returned to the road. Dismissed as a has-been, an over-the-hill relic whose particular brand of comedy was no longer tolerable, he abruptly vanished from the national spotlight.

He would get one more chance in Hollywood, but by the time he next appeared in a major studio picture, World War II had ended, "I

Like Ike" was a national refrain, America was ensnared in a knotty conflict in Korea, and the nation was inching toward a school desegregation crisis that would ignite the civil rights movement.

Despite the drive for the elimination of degrading, stereotypical comic roles, in the forties Hollywood churned out a series of B-pictures featuring craven, inept Negro caricatures—the "slew-footed, liver-lipped, swivel-eyed cretins" that novelist and *Pittsburgh Courier* columnist George S. Schuyler decried. Studios may have struggled to find scripts that offered more representative, diverse roles for Negro actors, but there was apparently little difficulty in finding parts for old-school comedians like Best and Mantan Moreland. During the 1940s alone, the two actors displayed their particular brand of eye-rolling, fainthearted buffoonery in nearly 150 motion pictures.[14]

Meanwhile, the embattled Fetchit crisscrossed the country in near obscurity. Generally, he appeared in juke joints, burlesque houses, cabarets, and the type of seedy small black clubs that, in the 1950s, performers like Lenny Bruce and Redd Foxx dubbed "toilets" and comedienne LaWanda Page would describe as "the kind of place where, if you ain't home by nine o'clock at night, you can be declared legally dead." By the mid-forties, the continued use of the tagline "Famed Movie Comic" must have begun striking a hollow, ironic note in the ears of even his most ardent fans.

Fetchit had essentially become a second-tier, vagabond entertainer who, like marginal performers in today's oldie shows, wrings as much currency as possible from nostalgia and the echo of bygone fame. Even that endeavor was greeted with disfavor by some fans and critics. After being released from jail in 1943, for instance, he reportedly made an attempt to restore his image by entertaining an all-black army unit in support of the war effort. According to the late producer and writer Matt Robinson, the appearance was a disaster. "Step said he got a few laughs when he talked about his movie career but was booed by some soldiers the minute he set foot on the stage," Robinson said. "Whenever he tried his lazy-man thing, the audience got quiet. He worked his way through the performance, but it was the last time he appeared at an army camp."[15]

Some critics were equally firm in their repudiation of Fetchit's stylized comedy. "Folks of the stage and movies always rated Step the 'laziest' of actors," the *Afro-American* theatrical editor wrote in 1943. "He cashed in on his characterization to the dismay of those seeking to have colored[s] portrayed in healthier roles. They don't have to worry now, the axe has fallen on Step."[16]

In November 1943, appearing at a South Side Chicago cabaret after serving his term at Bridewell, he announced that he was broke and owed millions. Reportedly, he had $140 in assets and debts of $3.9 million. In addition to a large IRS debt, he claimed that he owed $1 million to the lawyer who represented him in the 1942 paternity suit and another million to Joe Glaser for releasing him from his contract. Some four years later, Fetchit would file bankruptcy papers.

Still, the doggedly determined artist would not abandon his quest for a comeback. Even while he appeared in small town burlesque houses or second-rate urban theaters in the Midwest and South, and occasionally surfaced at such premier venues as Harlem's Apollo Theater, he desperately sought a return to Hollywood. "Why you'd think I was the one that started this war I been doing awful," he wrote in a plaintive entreaty for work sent to director John Ford in February 1945. "I've never seen so much suffering with good health in all my life."[17]

His vacillating theatrical career and current outcast status in Hollywood notwithstanding, Fetchit joined other actors in speaking out against the crusade to eliminate so-called demeaning comic types from the screen. In a controversial 1945 interview, he passionately argued that the character he portrayed was not detrimental to Negro progress. He agreed that "pictures should not offend," but blasted the attempt to limit screen portrayals of Negroes only to selected, approved sorts. "There are as many types of colored people as there are types of white people," he asserted. "Hollywood takes one colored man, these days, and dresses him up in fine clothes. He's supposed to represent colored people generally, but what about the thousands of other types? How will they be represented?"

"People laugh at the things I do," he continued, "but I'm more of a humorist than a comic."

"I do the character like any other great actor would. You dig my character from the cut of my hair . . . from the clothes I wear and from everything I say or do. I am an original looking man to start with and I try to look as dumb as I can when I'm acting. I look as if I'm always trying to get out of something, but you see that I have a soul and I'm thinking fast."

And while adamantly insisting that "Stepin Fetchit is no Uncle Tom role," he asserted that "I don't see why a certain type of colored character should be kept off the screen. Our newspapers are all wrong when they jump on so-called 'Uncle Tom Roles.'" As the *Afro-American* reporter left, he added, "I guess you better come back again soon . . . there'll be a lot of people who won't like this interview and I'll have to answer them."[18]

In pressing his point, Fetchit ignored the fact that rational protesters were lobbying for more diversity, not a distorted or skewed representation of solely exemplary black characters who did not reflect the masses. Finally, however, it was his remarks in defense of Southern protocol and his questioning of the goal of blacks' struggle for equal rights that most riled critics.

Calling himself a "perfect Southerner," he expressed concern over offending white Southerners' sensibility, suggested that—since "when a Southerner changes, he is sincere"—under Truman, who "was from the South," race relations would improve, and wondered aloud about the underlying intent of the drive for social equality. "Are they struggling to get on top so they can wreak vengeance on whites? If this is so, then it's dangerous."[19]

Responses to the interview, as he anticipated and may have even desired, were loud, widespread, and overwhelmingly acerbic.

One of the more virulent attacks came from the *Daily Worker,* a Communist Party newspaper. Describing Fetchit as the creator of "the internationally frowned on caricature of a Negro who shuffles through one menial task after another in a half-sleep, half-awake imbecilic dream world," columnist David Platt zeroed in on the actor's remarks concerning the fight for equal rights. His view, Platt wrote, was a mirror image of the philosophy of John E. Rankin (an ultraconservative Mississippi congressman and, some assert, Nazi sympathizer). Claiming that the actor had been "poisoned," Platt added that it was no longer just Stepin Fetchit who "bows and scrapes before his superiors" but also his creator, Lincoln Perry.[20]

On balance, it should be added that Fetchit also asserted that if everyone were Catholic there would be no race problem, adding that "some of the justice of Communism could be well mixed with the Catholic religion. Then everything would be all right."

During the latter half of 1945, it appeared that the critical responses to that interview and the struggle to revive his career were taking their toll. While appearing at the Earle Theater in Philadelphia shortly afterward, for instance, a newsman reported that, although Fetchit was as talkative as ever, the normally dapper actor had let his personal appearance visibly slip. "Garbed in a pair of green riding britches and a torn brown coat," Fetchit attributed his unkempt room, scattered personal belongings, and appearance to "studied indifference"; a tactic, he explained, that Will Rogers had adopted to give fans the impression that he was unconcerned about clothes. The reporter, however, subtly suggested that the glaring disarray appeared to be a reflection of Fetchit's sinking spirits and stalled career.[21]

Financially strapped and with no hope of a quick end of his lockout in Hollywood, Fetchit was forced to put his pride aside and turn to the independent black movie industry that he had previously spurned. His first effort was *Big Timers,* a low-budget, surprisingly tame and ineffective picture that matched Fetchit with Jackie "Moms" Mabley. It was produced by Robert M. Savini's Astor Pictures. Although Fetchit seemed particularly uninspired in this film, in the context of an all-black cast his slow-talking, lazy-man routine was clearly not offensive. With no white backdrop to accentuate a racial interpretation, Fetchit's character is simply seen as a cartoonish exaggeration, which is what he always insisted was the goal. Still, the patchwork plot—revolving around the antics of a group of guests and workers in a Harlem hotel—and the almost amateurish production undermined the project.

Jack and Dave Goldberg's *Miracle in Harlem,* which was released in 1948, garnered more attention. A combination musical and gangster film, the picture was regarded as something of "a technical landmark in the history of race movies."[22]

As Swifty, a handyman in a black-owned candy store, Fetchit stumbles through his chores, removes his hat to deliberately massage his head when perplexed, and mumbles incoherently in the attempt to unravel the simplest equation or complete ordinary tasks. Again, his portrayal looms in stark contrast to almost identical parts he played in mainstream movies surrounded by white actors.

In an entirely black setting, he comes across *purely* as a comedian. The cryptic, obsequious racial overtones of his poignant interpretation of the malingering Negro, which embarrassed many black viewers, evaporate, and the audience views the character as he intended, as a doleful clown. In this context, it is easier to see that the carefully orchestrated buffoonery is of itself benign. Fetchit emerges not as a racial symbol but as a skilled artist, and we laugh at his apparent ineptitude, even feel a sense of superiority. But we also glimpse that, well, perhaps total dedication to labor is not all it's cracked up to be. The shadowy influence of race is removed and, with it, nearly all of the unwarranted overtones of denigrative stereotypes.

In one scene, Fetchit has the following exchange with a black detective:

FETCHIT: This the place that I'm looking for, headquarters, man?

LIEUTENANT: What do you want?

FETCHIT: Well, you see . . . I, uh, I'm suppose to know what I want . . . uh—

LIEUTENANT: Sit down!

FETCHIT: I'll put my hat here (to himself). Uh . . . I was supposed to . . . (searching clothes)

LIEUTENANT: What are you nervous about?

FETCHIT: I ain't exactly nervous. I just generally falls to pieces 'round polices. It's much more worst than nervous, Captain yo' honor.

LIEUTENANT: Lieutenant, not your honor.

FETCHIT: Well, Lieutenant Not Your Honor, uh . . . the law generally is and I usually ain't.

Later, when the detective questions Fetchit about a murder, viewers see how his overt obtuseness was often used as a diversion:

LIEUTENANT: What do you know about handling a knife?

FETCHIT: I knows lots about a knife but I ain't goin' tell you. But I know I cain't eat my mash potatoes without a knife—

LIEUTENANT: Stop the foolishness!

FETCHIT: I ain't foolin', Mister, 'cause I have to have a fawk for everything I eat. If I cain't fawk it, I cain't . . . uh, I just don't bother with it myself.[23]

The type of manipulation and deceit displayed in the scene revealed as intentional wit by the concluding off-color rejoinder, was central to Fetchit's humor. And given the opportunity, he displayed it masterfully. His performance in the film was positively noted, even though the picture was not generally reviewed well. A *Variety* reviewer praised Fetchit for producing "laughs as the slow-moving handyman," but called the film "predictable."[24]

In 1948, Fetchit's carefree, prankish nature was still restrained, and according to the former actor and filmmaker William Greaves, who had a lead role in *Miracle,* on the set the actor was focused and businesslike. "He was quiet and a little standoffish," Greaves recalled. "He kept to himself and seemed very serious about what he was doing. It was in that context that I realized how talented he was. His actual persona off-screen was not this idiot that we were used to seeing. But it was okay for him to act that way in *Miracle in Harlem,* because it was a black cast movie and other people were portraying lifestyles that contrasted with the comic character he played."[25]

Miracle was followed by the comedy-musical short *Richard's Reply,* which was released in 1949. Produced by Robert M. Savini and distributed by All-American Pictures, the film was an example of the raft of musical and comedy shorts featuring prominent black entertainers that surfaced in the forties. Produced for distribution in theaters within black communities and usually ignored by mainstream critics, these pictures were often the only unadulterated record of the era's black ethnic comedians.

Richard's Reply was a comic scenario based on Dusty Fletcher's famed stage bit and popular song "Open the Door Richard." In the original bit, Richard is never seen; he is the silent, uncooperative roommate who ignores the inebriated Fletcher's pleas to let him into their apartment. "Open the Door Richard," with its catchy lines and Fletcher's acrobatic slapstick portrayal of a drunk attempting to gain access to his room with a ladder was among the era's classic routines, ranking with Pigmeat Markham's "Here Come the Judge" as a favorite on the black-circuit stage tour. It was also the basis for several hit recordings in the late forties, and in subsequent years over two-dozen versions of the song were released.

Richard's Reply cuts back and forth from external shots of the flustered Fletcher attempting to gain entry to the apartment to internal bedroom shots where Fetchit, in nightshirt and sleeping cap, portrays the unresponsive Richard. It was perfect casting since Fetchit was asked only to stay in character and deliver a monologue that approximated his stage routine.

The short opens with Richard in bed: "I was laying here dreamin' everybody was tryin' to wake me up. . . . Why I have such a dream like that? I ain't bothering nobody, just tendin' to my own business, doin' nothin', restin' up." With Earl Bostic and his orchestra providing a jazzy musical background and singer Flores Marmon attempting to rouse Richard from his nap with seductive overtures over the telephone, the comic dialogue continues. "Who's that on the phone? My roommate's downstairs knocking, tell'um I hear'um, Jones. Rave all he wanna, but tell'um I'm sure. I ain't goin' open that door." The drowsy Richard then questions Marmon: "What size hair is you got?" and quips, "I sorta recognize yo' voice but yo' breath sound like you been eatin' a onion." Exhausted, he finally announces, "Right now, I'mo finish a little nap I started week befo' last. I ain't goin' open that door."[26]

The short offers what is perhaps the best example of Fetchit's humor or "audible pantomime" available in pictures. In its tone and spirit, it vividly captures his style, deceptive wit, and near-perfect timing. It is an extremely funny short feature.

Fetchit's spirits and prospects were on the rise in the late forties. In addition to the three black-cast pictures, a January 1947 appearance at the Apollo Theater with Mantan Moreland and Dizzy Gillespie received a rare positive notice in *Variety*. "Harlem's hothouse of rebop comes this week with one of its better bills and grabs a nice payee send-off all around," the reviewer wrote. "Great favorites in this house, Stepin Fetchit and Mantan Moreland close with some fast running patter that gives Fetchit, despite his long absence from the screen, somewhat the best of it."[27]

Soon, rumors of another return to Hollywood began surfacing. In 1949, for example, there were reports that Hollywood producers were considering making a film about the life of Satchel Paige, the ageless Negro League baseball player who the Cleveland Indians had signed the previous year. Considered the best pitcher ever to play in the Negro Leagues, Paige had built a legendary reputation when facing white Major League players in the 1930s and early '40s. Fetchit bore more than a slight resemblance to him. In addition, *David Harum* had been rereleased and was playing in theaters nationwide. The actor was being introduced to a new, younger audience, and producers may have thought it was the perfect time to bring him back to the screen.

"Film moguls have decided the slow-moving comic would be just the actor to portray the role of the great Cleveland pitcher. . . . Satchel Paige has done a lot for baseball," one reporter asserted. "We hope to see his life story told on the screen. And who is better able to do so than Step, the guy who helped make Will Rogers famous."[28]

Months passed and the Paige story was put on hold by the studios as Fetchit worked the TOBA circuit. In July 1951, however, to the surprise of his detractors, it was suddenly announced that the comic actor was being recalled to Hollywood to appear in *Sudden Fear*, an RKO picture starring Joan Crawford. "The minute people see me again," Fetchit beamed to a reporter, "I'll be right back where I was in 1937. I left it good . . . I was on top."[29]

Despite his enthusiasm, as with the Satchel Paige project, initial reports of his being cast in *Sudden Fear* were premature. The film was shot without him; Crawford was nominated for an Academy Award as Best Actress in the RKO thriller. Meanwhile, Fetchit continued a theatrical tour that took him to the Midwest and Southwest.

Within weeks, however, another opportunity arose. Universal Pictures contacted him and offered a part in the new action film *Bend of the River.* He immediately accepted. In addition, on October 15, 1951, while performing in Oklahoma, he quietly married thirty-five-year-old Bernice Sims, who was variously described as a former showgirl and a "prominent church worker." The wedding took place without the ballyhoo and publicity that attended his previous "marriage," but clearly Fetchit had found a more mature mate who could help settle his unruly temperament and support him during the wildly vacillating career turns to come. Reportedly a strong, practical woman, while Sims was tolerant of Fetchit's ego and eccentricities, she was neither overwhelmed by his celebrity nor reluctant to point out his faults. The actor had found a partner who could both deal with his shifting moods and support his still-ambitious career goals. Their union would emerge as the actor's most rewarding and enduring relationship, they remained companions until Sims's death in 1985.[30]

Shortly after the ceremony, the newlyweds traveled together to the West Coast. In this, his fourth comeback, Fetchit's arrival in the film capital was greeted with little or no fanfare. The trip was financed in part by millionaire Herman Pagels, a retired St. Louis businessman and longtime admirer of the actor's work. Pagels was reportedly providing $100 a week plus incidental cash to Fetchit and his wife when they arrived in Hollywood. The couple moved quietly into a "small unadorned second-floor apartment on Los Angeles' West 38th Street" as Fetchit began shooting on the Universal Studios lot.

Although his boisterous optimism and ego seemed to have been tempered, Fetchit did return to films with high expectations. He wanted to be received well enough to win a crack at more serious roles, he told an *Ebony* magazine reporter. His goal was "portraying famous Negroes" like Satchel Paige or acting in films that depicted the Negro masses more authentically. "There's a need to bring the right recognition to the average Negro—the porter, shoe shine boy and steel mill worker," he said. "I want to bring that about. It has never been done before, but I think I can do it."[31]

Universal pictures executives had other ideas about Fetchit's future in films, however; and during filming on and around the Columbia River in Oregon, the director Anthony Mann called him aside to elaborate. "You have a great thing to do in your role in this picture. Not only from a personal standpoint but from the consideration of the Negro people as well," Mann exhorted. "You have to prove that comedy can be done without offense to your people. We picked you because we felt that the role could only be handled by an artist with your capabilities."[32]

Fetchit's response to Mann's pep talk was not recorded, but in his role as Adam, the riverboat captain's assistant, the actor visibly moderated some of the more fawning or obsequious aspects of his cinema character. In fact, despite some harsh critical reactions to his portrayal, there is little in this film to embarrass anyone from a racial standpoint. Fetchit and Chubby Johnson (the captain) leave Jimmy Stewart and his cohorts halfway into the picture; and when they depart laughing, with arms around each other's shoulders, there is a sense of honest camaraderie between them. The "comic" aspect of Fetchit's role is limited to his mild carping at the captain and some beneath-the-breath rumblings about the danger they face during the boat trip. Still, Fetchit's very presence seems to have upset some critics.

Bosley Crowther of the *New York Times*, for example, called the picture "a present for Western outdoor fans," but opined that "we are sorry to note that Stepin Fetchit is back to play a clownish stereotype." On the other hand, while the *Variety* reviewer agreed that it was "a strong outdoor feature," he found that "Stepin Fetchit and Chubby Johnson, riverboat operators, and the others come through with excellent support."[33]

Overall, reactions to Fetchit's return did not provoke any undue outcry and were positive enough to warrant an offer of another role; during the summer of 1952 he began work on the Argosy Productions film *The Sun Shines Bright*. The picture was directed by Fetchit's old friend John Ford and based on three stories by Irwin S. Cobb, the author whose tales had also inspired *Judge Priest*. Fetchit was called upon to reprise his role as the judge's handyman and pal Jeff Poindexter. Despite Ford's presumed noble intentions, the film was a throwback to Old South depictions of traditional paternalistic racial relations, which, with the civil rights movement about to begin, was as stale and curdling to black Americans as rancid cream.

Most reviewers pounced on the film with well-justified liberal outrage. It is "hard to imagine a more laborious, pedantic, saccharine entertainment package," the *Times* critic wrote. He was particularly upset at the inclusion of a lynching scene that had been cut from the 1934 version of *Judge Priest*. "After parading a handful of Negroes to and fro in quaking servitude," he added, "the picture foists an inexcusable synthetic sequence about a near lynching." As to Step, he noted that the actor was "still dancing attendance on his Honor twenty years later" and "seems more bent than ever." *Variety* did concede that "Stepin Fetchit's extremely languid comedy" provided "a chuckle here and there."[34]

Fetchit's role in *The Sun Shines Bright* confirmed that in Hollywood he was only being considered for near-obsolete, throwback roles of the stooped, shallow, comic Negro. The Jeff Poindexter role was a disaster for an actor seeking to establish himself in a new light or create a new image. From all indications, however, it was not truly a choice. He had been rigidly typecast. Fetchit had announced his intent to pursue better roles after completing *Bend of the River* in an *Ebony* magazine article, and at around the same time, he reiterated those goals in a conversation with his pal Louis Armstrong.

Armstrong, an incurable collector of nearly everything, was known for recording conversations with friends. And before *The Sun Shines Bright* went into production, he taped a conversation with himself, Fetchit, and some other friends in a Los Angeles hotel room.

As they kibitzed and shot the breeze about race, women, and sex in the trumpet player's room, the chat briefly turned serious. "You always think you're before a camera," Armstrong says to Step. "Every move you make, boy. You just a born movie star, you know that?"

"Yeah, I hope so. But it ain't payin' off now," Step moans.

"Why?"

"I got to get in another type of business."

"Well, you told me that you didn't even wanna work, you know," Armstrong says. "I asked that boy out at Fox, what's old Step doin' out at Fox. 'Stepin Fetchit,' he say, 'I ain't seen him for years.' And I thought you came in to work for Fox."

"Naw . . ."

"I think you should go out there . . . any studio you get a contract with, Step. You should stay before your movie audience."

"Pictures ain't having such a good time lately."

"Not so bad," Armstrong interrupts. "They talkin' 'bout takin' $800 out of my salary for tax, shit. They ain't said what they goin' pay me, and they takin' $800 for tax."

" 'Cause you makin' so much," Step laughs.

"But you said they wasn't doin' so good."

"I do all right in pictures, don't worry," Step says. "I got it all covered. I know what's happening."

"I just want to see you do all right, Step."

"You're doin' the life of Satchel Paige, aren't you?" one of the other men in the room asks.

After Fetchit assures them that he expects to get the role of Paige, there is a roar of approval and laughter.

"Now that's goin' be a picture. Yeah, that's goin' be nice," Armstrong says. "It's goin' be a gas. See what I mean . . . see what I'm talkin' 'bout. That's why you were born, man. You were born for that fuckin' character."

"When we do Satchel Paige, that's when I retire," Step says.

"Damn, if Satchel Paige was just a little younger, he could do the life of Stepin Fetchit," Armstrong laughs.

"I'm goin' do that one myself," Steps says.

"Naw, I'm goin' reduce to do that one."

"How you goin' get tall?" Step laughs.

After a little more banter, Fetchit decides to leave and agrees to return the next night with his wife. "I'm goin' bring my wife up here," he says, then warns, "Don't say nothin' 'bout me, though."

"Don't worry, man. You got a Cadillac there."

"Yeah, I don't know what I did, but I sho got a Cadillac," Step says before leaving.[35]

The conversation not only reflected the entertainers' rather raunchy wit and irreverent attitudes but also affirmed the genuine respect the two men had for one another and underlined Fetchit's determination to get at least one substantial noncomic movie role.

Partially surviving through the largesse of his patron, Herman Pagels, Fetchit and his wife remained in Los Angeles for a year or so after completion of *The Sun Shines Bright.* He continued lobbying for the lead role and peddling a screenplay (the rights of which he owned) based on the life of Satchel Paige. Despite his coaxing and cajoling, however, the Satchel Paige story was never made and producers offered no other serious role. While in Los Angeles, Fetchit also performed locally unveiling a revamped nightclub act, which featured some new, timelier, standup comic material as well as original songs that he had written.

During an appearance at the Zanzibar Club in Santa Monica in 1953, Fetchit's estranged son, Jemajo Perry, who still lived and worked in Los Angeles, went to see his father perform. "They didn't want me down there," Jemajo said during an interview in Los Angeles, "but I went to see him anyway. I was thrilled. Despite the bad feelings, I was proud of him. He danced, sang, joked, and played the piano, and the audience loved it. That's when I realized that my father was a genius comedian, a great performer." Although father and son didn't immediately mend their differences, years later the two would establish a tentative reconciliation.[36]

While on the West Coast, Fetchit was also visited by Charles Austin, the nephew of the actor's childhood friend Dr. Wheelock Bisson. Young Austin, an aspiring musician and, later, a conductor and teacher, had met Fetchit when he stopped in Memphis for a performance at the W. C. Handy Theater and visited Dr. Bisson in the late 1940s. During the early fifties, Austin, who was then twenty-four years old, lived with Fetchit and his wife in Los Angeles.

"Step was something," Austin recalled during a recent interview. "It didn't matter that times were bad, he always acted like a big star. We went to all the clubs out there, even segregated ones like the Crescendo, where they didn't allow blacks. Step would just walk right in and they didn't say a word. They loved him out there, and they treated him like a movie star. People like Eddie Fisher, the singer who married Elizabeth Taylor, treated him like royalty and offered support. We also hung out with Redd Foxx and Slappy White, who were working as a team in those days, and Step borrowed a lot of their jokes for his new act.

"There was no one like him," Austin continued, "he was funny, charming, and could talk a man out of his shirt before anyone know what happened. Had the priests at the parishes giving *him* money. He was always hustling. In L.A., he even talked a car dealer out of a car. It was a big red Cadillac, and Step got it for no money down—never paid a penny. He used to hide it during the day and drive my old beat up Dodge so they didn't repossess it. Yeah, he was one of a kind."

Frustrated with his inability to find work in pictures, Fetchit had moved to Memphis to try his hand at songwriting. "He even collaborated with David Raskin, who wrote the music for *Laura*," Charles Austin said. The songs were never released, however, and by 1955 Fetchit had moved back to Chicago and returned to the stage. His activities were largely unreported, and his reputation as an elite performer gradually faded. But the notoriety and associated stigma of the character he created would continue to shadow African American entertainers.[37]

There would be only two more motion pictures, both cameo appearances, and one last hurrah as he again briefly claimed the national spotlight in a final shrill, desperate defense of his reputation. Even in decline, however, the wily old-timer would demonstrate that he still had a few tricks up his sleeve.

CHAPTER SIXTEEN

During Fetchit's return to Hollywood in the early fifties, there was a brief upsurge of excitement among old-time stage and motion-picture comics. In 1951, *The Amos 'n' Andy Show,* that perennial radio favorite, debuted on television with an all-black cast. It was a major breakthrough with regard to the exposure of black performers in the relatively new medium.

While liberally interlaced with familiar vaudeville bits and slapstick or sight gags that might be seen on numerous TV sitcoms or variety shows of the period, it was exclusively focused on African American life, and its humor flowed from familiar attitudes shared by the era's lower-stratum black folk. Most often it contrasted the harebrained schemes of Kingfish and his Mystic Knights of the Sea Lodge cohorts with the day-to-day lives of a generally respectable group of Harlemites. Kingfish's conniving typically involved the willing complicity of Algonquin J. Calhoun, a bogus lawyer (played by Johnny Lee, Step's old partner), and Lightnin', the lodge's dim-witted, slothful handyman (played by Nicodemus Stewart). The gullible Andy Brown (played by Spencer Williams) was usually the target of Kingfish's larcenous shenanigans.

In addition to Lee, Stewart, and Williams, the show featured many of Fetchit's old stage and screen cronies. Tim Moore (as Kingfish), Lillian Randolph (Madame Queen), and Sam McDaniel (in frequent guest appearances) were all part of a close-knit fraternity of veteran performers who had survived what the producer, playwright, and sitcom writer

Matt Robinson called "the sow belly circuit" and gone on to marginal fame and success on the stage or screen.[1]

The show, with its splendid cast of stage-savvy, multitalented performers, was not only excruciatingly funny but, regrettably, also represented the last gasp of authentic or traditional black humor in the mainstream media for nearly two decades. Its initial success and popularity notwithstanding, *Amos 'n' Andy* was doomed from the outset.

By the fifties, the drive to erase all so-called negative images of comic Negroes from the media had reached its peak. Gradually more and more African Americans had come to support the position of the NAACP and other civil rights organizations. Even though, in *private*, many blacks laughed uproariously at the studied buffoonery of the old-school comedians, they had come to see it as a *public* embarrassment. The black middle class was expanding, and, having acquired stable, secure jobs, its members were anticipating fulfillment of the mid-forties' liberal promises. Sensitivity was at its height, and many African Americans regarded traditional black stage humor as objectionable—an archaic reminder of a past in which uneducated and downtrodden blacks were spotlighted as the norm. Comic exaggeration and frivolity aside, the cry for increased media representation of successful, serious African Americans grew louder.

And in 1951, shortly after *Amos 'n' Andy* debuted on TV, the NAACP launched a campaign to cancel both the television and radio versions, claiming they were insulting to African Americans. The civil rights organization published an article entitled "Why the Amos 'n' Andy Show Should Be Taken Off the Air" and listed seven reasons. Among them were claims that the show supported a belief "among the uninformed and prejudiced that Negroes are inferior, lazy, dumb and dishonest"; that "every Negro" was portrayed as "a clown or crook"; that "Negro doctors" and "lawyers" were shown as "quacks and thieves" or ignorant, unethical "cowards"; and that "Negro women" were portrayed "as cackling, screaming shrews in big-mouth closeups." The article argued that "an entire race" of 15 million Americans was "being slandered each week by this one-sided caricature." The merits of those claims notwithstanding, television producers took note of the outcry, and at the end of the 1953 season the show was dropped; ironically, the radio version and its original white creators remained on the air until the sixties.[2]

The cancellation of *Amos 'n' Andy* had a broad-sweep effect on black entertainers in television as well as motion pictures. In 1953, for instance, *Beulah*, which variously featured Ethel Waters, Hattie McDaniel, and, in its final season, Louise Beavers in the title role, was also canceled. By 1955, several other shows featuring blacks as menials were scratched; they included *The Great Gildersleeve* with Lillian Randolph and *My Little Margie* and *The Stu Erwin Show* with Willie Best. The most prominent of a handful of survivors was Eddie "Rochester" Anderson of *The Jack Benny Show*, which lasted until the early sixties. Frustrated by increased protests or wearied by the controversy, television executives apparently took the path of least resistance; they eliminated black characters or pulled the plug on nearly every show that featured a servile black comic role—which is to say, there was a virtual blackout.

By the mid-fifties, comic roles for blacks all but disappeared from the Hollywood screen as well. The careers of Willie Best and Mantan Moreland offer dramatic illustrations. After being seen in 150 motion pictures during the forties, they appeared in a single film each in the fifties. Best's film career came to an abrupt end, and he died in 1962 at age forty-six. Moreland was rediscovered in the mid-sixties and had cameo roles in seven pictures before his death in 1973.

Stepin Fetchit, despite the relatively good reviews he received for his performances in *Bend of the River* and *The Sun Shines Bright*, fared no better. In fact, the latter picture, with its atavistic Old South theme and fawning, happy-go-lucky darkies, reestablished his dubious connection to a suddenly defunct genre. Efforts to move beyond the trifling, lethargic character he had indelibly imprinted in films or to find work in noncomic roles fell on deaf ears. His former success and nationwide popularity, combined with the mythical status of his name, were prohibitive hurdles.

Shifting social values and the accelerated drive for equal rights had sounded the death knell for Stepin Fetchit and nearly all of the old-school black stage comics. Some, like Moms Mabley and Pigmeat Markham, would survive on the "chitlin' circuit," a string of theaters and clubs that catered almost exclusively to black audiences, before being rediscovered by the mainstream in the 1960s. Most would fade into oblivion as a group of younger, more articulate stand-up comedians burst onto the scene.

Slappy White, Redd Foxx, and Nipsey Russell were among the first wave, and, by the sixties, Godfrey Cambridge, Dick Gregory, Bill Cosby, and Flip Wilson would bring African American humor back into stage prominence. In pictures, comic blacks remained conspicuously absent until the seventies.

With the early-fifties radical revamping of the black image in mainstream entertainment, most of the early-twentieth-century movie clowns were instantly relegated to marginal status as curios, vestiges of a bygone era. It was a devastating turn of events for performers who had only years before tasted fame and fortune and, as household names, basked in the mass adulation of their peers and fans. For an entertainer as assertive and proud as Stepin Fetchit, the descent was particularly crushing.

During the late fifties, Fetchit and his wife returned to Chicago and, for a time, dropped out of sight. Ignored by the press and regarded as pariahs in some circles, Fetchit and a raft of old-school performers (Pigmeat, Mantan, Butterbeans, Snowflake, Dusty, and Moms) could only wait and nourish the faint hope that the tide would turn—that somehow the curtains would once again rise for a type of performance artistry that had been a staple in America for nearly a century. Meanwhile, like Fetchit, most were forced to scrounge for one-night bookings on the black theatrical circuit or in obscure, second-rate mainstream venues.

"Stepin Fetchit is traveling the back roads of show business," a scoffing, where-are-they-now-type magazine piece noted in the fifties. "He 'carpet bags' his talents—along with screening of scenes and clips from his old movies—for one-night stands in one-horse towns." The article went on to recite a long list of past scandals and mock the comic's defense of his stage character, ridiculing hyperbolic assertions such as Fetchit's claim that he had done more for his people "than anyone, including Booker T. Washington."[3]

Indeed, negotiating most of his own bookings and accepting whatever was offered, Fetchit continued beating the bushes in small midwestern and Southern towns throughout the late fifties. He played seedy nightclubs, or "toilets," and mostly obscure burlesque houses where he shared billings with strippers ranging from Gypsy Rose Lee to relative unknowns like Heaven Lee and the exotic Akiko O'Toole. Considering his outspoken past, at the outset he was surprisingly reticent about the events that had hastened his fall from the showbiz "parlor" to its shoddy bargain basement. Initially, there were no outbursts or accusatory harangues directed at the NAACP or civil rights activists. He seemed to have humbly accepted his eclipse as a star and reconciled himself to the meager status of a second-tier performer. Some recalled that during this time he seemed dispirited and reclusive.

Comic Tim Moore's niece, Julie McCowan, met Fetchit briefly on two occasions around 1959. "He was a friend of my uncle," she said, "and he knew my father, Tim's brother."

"The first time I saw him, he stopped by our house in Rock Island [Illinois] because he had car problems," she said. "He was on his way to an engagement somewhere in the area." It was late and he needed assistance finding a mechanic, so he stopped to ask for help. "He was with a driver, but he came to the door and slumped down in a chair while my father made some calls. He didn't say much, but we knew he had been a big movie star," she said. After her father helped him find a mechanic, he left. "He seemed to be off in his own world."

"About a year later, I saw him again," she said. "He was in town staying at the Fort Armstrong Hotel downtown. He was performing at a local club, I don't remember which one, but it may have been the Fort Theater, which was right across the street from the hotel. A lot of black performers appeared there, including the Mills Brothers, Butterbeans and Susie, Ella Fitzgerald, and the Ink Spots. My father called him, and we arranged to stop by the hotel to see him.

"When we got there, at first he wouldn't come to the door. Finally, he opened it just a little and peeked out. He left, then came back and just handed me and my father a couple of autographed photos. He didn't say much, and he looked tired and irritated. It was very strange—like something was on his mind or he didn't really want to be bothered. I didn't understand it because I knew that he had known my father very well. I guess he could have just been tired, but I remember being upset. At the time, I thought he didn't seem very nice."[4]

Despite his lagging spirits and restrained demeanor in the late fifties, the moody artist was apparently fuming internally. And when critics turned up the heat in the mid-sixties, he would unleash a torrent of invective. In the interim, reports of his activities surfaced only sporadically in the press.

In 1959, while headlining the *Flamingo Follies* revue at the Faust Club, a burlesque house in Peoria, Fetchit seemed to take a stoic, philosophical view of life as an exiled Hollywood star. "People all think I'm broke," he told a *Variety* stringer. "I'm a showman but I don't live a show life." Then, apparently responding to a question about the nation's intensifying racial crisis, he declaimed: "It's no disadvantage to be colored. If this were true, God wouldn't have created me so. You're as great as the next person. You've just got to realize it." The writer, noting that the comic was "down a bit, but not out," reported that he "scored" with his singing, dancing, and "lazy man" act.[5]

Despite his claim of not being broke, it soon became apparent that Fetchit was having serious financial problems. That situation may well have provoked his decision to change his age, adding ten years, during the early sixties. Acquaintances such as Matt Robinson have suggested the change was an attempt to elicit sympathy at a time when his public image had sunk to its lowest point. But it is just as likely that the wily actor shifted his age to expedite eligibility for Social Security and health benefits. Given his proclivity for and delight in duping the public, the trickster scam is as reasonable as the former explanation. At any rate, in the early sixties Stepin Fetchit's reported birth date suddenly changed from 1902 to 1892. No one noticed or seemed to care that from the late fifties to the early sixties a former internationally known motion picture star had aged ten years. Reporters continually marveled at his youthful appearance.

In 1961, reports surfaced that Fetchit had begun a Southern junket. En route to Miami, he appeared at the Star Lite Club in Kissimmee, Florida. According to Charlie Cotton, the club owner, that appearance was arranged at the last minute by Fetchit's friend, the comic Jack Carter; Cotton expressed surprise that the "black movie star" would play his club and added that Fetchit "was quite a hit."[6]

Later in the year, the recently aged "68-year-old" entertainer was interviewed while appearing in Waukegan, Illinois. Perhaps provoked by increasingly scarce bookings and lower salary offers, he had begun aggressively defending his reputation and past film work. "For no particular reason I'm still identified with a movie role I did more than 30 years ago," he told a *Variety* reporter. "I've changed the material in my act 20 times since then. Why I've been in show business for 50 years—don't you think I'd have enough business sense to change my act with the times?"

The comic did not mince words concerning his detractors either. He said he was not insulted by being called an Uncle Tom, calling the original Harriet Beecher Stowe fictional character a man with a "soul" who was an "integrationist and a social reformer—something that all of these eggheads today seem to have forgotten."

Displaying far more spirit than he had a few years earlier, he claimed that his "worst enemies" were "imitators" of his "old movie character. I changed and they didn't, but they're still judging me on the carbon copies." The comic also disputed the claim that Dick Gregory was the first black comedian to bring topical humor to white audiences, insisting that he presented social commentary at the Orpheum Theater in Memphis as early as 1932, and was "still doing it."[7]

The assertion that he began using topical humor in 1932 is, of course, far-fetched. The few available descriptions of his act at that time indicate that his stylized slow-motion dance and "audible pantomime" were the focus of his humor. The only variation noted by reviewers was his occasional patter about movies and the roles he played on-screen. By the sixties, however, Fetchit had begun adapting to rapidly changing times and was enlivening his patented languid, snail-like movement, dreamy, deadpan expression, and slow, incoherent drawl with occasional topical quips.

He never entirely abandoned the slumbery routine that had catapulted him to fame, however; a typical performance included some variation of the following bit.

> *"I'm so lazy, even when I walked in my sleep I used to hitchhike. My head was so bald I used to comb it with a spoon. People say, 'How'd you get in pictures?' I say, 'Well, when I was a kid I always wanted to be somethin', course I didn't want to do nothin' to be it. I used to go 'round trying to get a job doin' nothin', but everywhere I went they either wanted me to do somethin' or else they didn't wanna give you nothin' for it. So I kept tryin' til I growed up, then I seen this man in California makin' a picture and I say, 'Mr., you want somebody to do nothin',' and they say, 'Yeah.' So I been busy working ever since. Yeah, and I work up to the place where the less I have to do, the mo' I make. Tryin' to make as much as I can, so when I get old I can rest."*[8]

"The first fifteen minutes of my act is getting to the middle of the stage," he told a reporter. "And when I leave I am wheeled off in my chair. I even had a fellow come out and wave my hand good-bye to the crowd."

Working in seedy burlesque houses and midwestern nightclubs during the sixties and seventies, however, Fetchit added some contemporary gibes:

> *"Negroes vote 20 or 25 times in Chicago. They don't try to cheat or nothin' like that. They tryin' to make up for the time they couldn't vote in Mississippi. When you in Mississippi you have to pass a test. Nuclear physics—in Russian. And if you pass it, they say, 'Boy, you speak Russian? You must be a Communist—you can't vote.'"*

> *"You know how we travel in the South? Fast. At night. Through the woods. On top of the trees. That's right! And in Vietnam—flat on the ground."*

> *"My wife and I were just voted the good-neighbor award, we even went out and burned our own cross."*[9]

The quips obviously didn't have the bite of Gregory's sixties social satire, nor were they offered with a rapid-fire Henny Youngman delivery. But they demonstrated that Fetchit was not completely mired in the "white man's Negro" mind-set for which he was often denounced by detractors.

His transition, however, went unnoticed by critics and movie producers. In one sense, it was a matter of having been too good at enacting the lazy-man character. In addition, his knack for publicity and his early insistence that distinctions between his personal life and stage character be minimized had conveyed the impression that he truly was the trifling stage Negro he portrayed. Even for younger audiences who knew nothing of his past, accepting the on-stage transition of a stooped, languorous relic of bygone vaudeville buffoonery (typically dressed in vestigial coonskin coat and rakish skimmer) into a hip, spry social commentator required an imaginative leap of immense proportions. In the minds of most Americans, in and out of show business, Lincoln Perry the man and Stepin Fetchit the character were one and the same.

Fetchit was well aware of the public's entrenched mistaken perception and, during the sixties, futilely railed against it. At the same time, he pressed on with the attempt to reestablish himself in mainstream entertainment. In April 1964, for instance, he wrote Mike Todd, Jr., requesting a role in his upcoming show at the World's Fair.

Addressing Todd as "Mr. Mike," Fetchit requested a part in the impresario's "America Be Seated" presentation at the fair, emphasizing that he would be entertaining and "particularly acceptable" to all guests and patrons. "I always keep working without any lengthy commitments," he wrote, "so that when the right thing came along I'd be able to accept." Noting that he had a "gentleman's agreement" to appear at a Battle Creek, Michigan, supper club, Fetchit assured Todd he "could join him at once" with "instant presentation of song and dance and comedy."[10]

Fetchit was not asked to join the show.

Shortly afterward, however, it became clear that the comic was not only desperately seeking employment in a legitimate, world-class production but was also seriously ill when the letter was penned. By the end of April, Fetchit would be snatched from the anonymity of chitlin'-circuit and burlesque-house bookings when the press discovered that he was a charity-ward patient in Chicago's Cook County Hospital.

As with all tales of the decline of the once rich and famous, there was immense public interest and, perhaps, even covert delight in witnessing the abject decline of an internationally known celebrity. The story was picked up by most major mainstream newspapers and often run with banner headlines. "Stepin Fetchit Shuffles to Charity Ward," the *Philadelphia Daily News* chimed. Reports revealed that Fetchit was suffering from a prostate disorder and that an operation was pending; most offered a brief summary of the actor's sudden rise to fame, his grandiose reign at the top and equally rapid decline and descent into poverty. Despite the humiliating circumstances and seriousness of the illness, Fetchit seemed in good spirits.[11]

"Me and Charles de Gaulle," he laughed, referring to the French president's prostate problems, "only look at all that money de Gaulle has. I wouldn't be here if I had it."

Asked about his glory days in Hollywood, Fetchit estimated that he had made $2 million, but, he said, "When you give away all your money you've got to go in debt. I had assets of $146 when I filed for bankruptcy in 1947." Of his more recent experiences, he said, "I do stand-up—no takes from the old movies; that age is gone. The movies don't entertain anymore. There's no more show business." Still, he admitted that working "in small night clubs in smaller towns" didn't pay very much.[12]

The feisty entertainer's ego had not been deflated, however, he used the occasion of renewed attention to announce that he was still "the funniest Negro comedian alive." In a similar vein, he took another swipe at Dick Gregory, then the hottest black wit on the comedy scene. "Gregory is nothing but show business," he carped. "If he wants to preach, he should become a preacher."[13]

Fetchit seemed to have recovered rapidly and was discharged from the hospital in May. He was back on the road by the end of the summer and, in October, surfaced in the entourage of the newly crowned heavyweight champion Muhammad Ali, who had announced his conversion to the Nation of Islam, or Black Muslims. The actor accompanied Ali to the Chicopee, Massachusetts, training camp where the fighter began preparation for his May 1965 return bout with former champion Sonny Liston. When Malcolm X was assassinated at Harlem's Audubon Ballroom in late February, tensions within the camp mounted steadily.

After John F. Kennedy's assassination in 1963, Malcolm had characterized the slaying as an instance of "chickens coming home to roost" and had been suspended by Black Muslim leader Elijah Muhammad. The charismatic orator soon formed his own group, the Organization of Afro-American Unity, which vied in popularity with the Muslims. Relations between Malcolm and the Nation of Islam had become increasingly volatile. Suspicions about the Muslims' involvement in Malcolm's death had spurred rumors that armed supporters of the slain leader were headed to Chicopee to avenge his death by assassinating Ali, the Nation of Islam's most visible and popular representative. The FBI and, of course, Muslim supporters were there to protect Ali. By most accounts, it was literally an armed camp. In that tense atmosphere, Fetchit's laconic humor no doubt provided some much needed relief.[14]

Assuming the role of camp jester and cheerleader, which was later filled by Boudini Brown, who coined the "float like a butterfly, sting like a bee" chant, Fetchit was given the unofficial title of "strategic adviser" and purportedly taught Ali some of the ring tricks that Jack Johnson had shown him. In May, after Ali kayoed Liston in Lewiston, Maine, with what many observers called a "phantom" blow in the first round, the champion attributed the knockout to the "anchor punch" that Fetchit had passed on to him. Many were skeptical of the legitimacy of both the knockout and the supposed origin of the punch that floored Liston—and with regard to the latter, the doubt was justified. Both Muhammad Ali and Fetchit were consummate self-publicists; few black celebrities were as adept at or took more delight in toying with or bamboozling the media. With that in mind, one can also reasonably assume that the widely reported claim that Fetchit converted to the Muslim faith was, like his supposed marriage to Winifred Johnson, a ruse. The actor remained a practicing Catholic and was seldom seen without his rosary beads. In the 1980s, he denied having made any religious conversion.[15]

The friendship between Ali and Fetchit shocked some. Ali's outspoken militancy was seen as diametrically opposed to the actor's presumed subservience by many observers. "It would be difficult to find a more incongruous situation than the Clay-Fetchit association," a contemporary writer opined. "The world's perhaps most famous and most arrogant Negro, Cassius Clay, has among his entourage the Negro who probably had done more than any man to label his race with all the things Clay isn't." The writer, like most other black and white observers, grossly underestimated the complexity of both men. Unlike most others, Ali was apparently astute enough to recognize that despite the servile character he portrayed, Fetchit was a proud, assertive black man. And Fetchit no doubt admired the champion's flamboyance and mischievous nature, which in some ways mirrored Jack Johnson's as well as his own.[16]

Despite the similarities and mutual respect, there were some deep-seated differences. Ali had at the time embraced the Nation of Islam and proclaimed his allegiance to a philosophy that insisted on black independence, which in the sixties was regarded as a call for racial separatism. Fetchit was a lifelong Catholic who repeatedly aired the view that the races should be united and claimed that his movie character had hastened that unification. It was around this time that he claimed that "preachers and politicians are separating people rather than bringing them together." Despite the apparently genuine affection and regard the two men shared, Fetchit was finally as misplaced among Ali's menacing, dark-suited entourage as a Saint Bernard among pit bulls. They soon parted ways but remained friends.

After his brief whirl in the spotlight with Ali, Fetchit again returned to the black-circuit theatrical tour and small-town burlesque houses. For a time, he and his wife lived in the two-story home of friends and entertainers Jodie and Susie Edwards (better known as Butterbeans and Susie), who unlike their prodigal house guest had been far more temperate with their show-business earnings.

According to Honi Coles, the renowned tap dancer who was part of the vaudeville team of Coles and Atkins as well as a longtime stage manager at the Apollo, the comedy duo's hospitality was not unusual. "Susie and Butter were great people," Coles said. "During lean times a visiting entertainer could always find a plate with greens and cornbread at their house."

And, as Coles pointed out, times were very lean for Fetchit during the mid-sixties. "He was strange," Coles said. "I knew him when he was near the top of the game, a star, and, later, when he was on the outs. He was always kind of moody—you know, up and joking then distant, far away. But when things went downhill, he seemed to withdraw completely. Step and Butter went way back though, and when Step got down on his luck and he fell out of favor, well, he turned to his old friend."[17]

In the mid-sixties, with the civil rights movement gaining momentum and the nation's attention riveted on daily, televised confrontations between nonviolent protesters and billy club–wielding Southern sheriffs with fire hoses and snarling attack dogs, Fetchit once again faded quietly into the shadows. During a decade that witnessed the assassination of John F. Kennedy, Malcolm X, Martin Luther King, Jr., and Bobby Kennedy, the fate of an aging former black movie star seemed inconsequential.

Still, a few more "Where Are They Now?" pieces surfaced, and Fetchit predictably rose up to defend his image and contribution to the evolution of black entertainment. "I went in and kicked open the door in Hollywood," he told a *Newsweek* reporter in 1967. "I went in the back door so now Sidney Poitier can come in the front door." The actor also echoed his long-standing claim that he had been ousted by the studios in the late thirties because he refused to accept any more demeaning roles. Amid the chaos, violent racial clashes, and increasingly militant posture of the black community in the mid-sixties, his protestations were either drowned out or rejected as the self-serving grousings of a cultural relic.[18]

The stint with Ali and its accompanying publicity had rekindled memories of the former star in some circles, however, and early in 1968 when NBC-TV executives began searching for a project for the fast-rising comic Flip Wilson, Fetchit was rumored to be a candidate for a costarring role in a new sitcom. It seemed that the old-school comic had been rediscovered by industry insiders. But Fetchit was suddenly thrust onto center stage for an entirely different reason.

On July 2, CBS began airing a nationally televised seven-part documentary series entitled *Of Black America.* The first segment, "Black History—Lost, Stolen, or Strayed," was narrated by the young comic phenomenon Bill Cosby.

"The tradition of the lazy, stupid, crap-shooter, chicken-stealing idiot was popularized by an actor named Lincoln Theodore Monroe Andrew Perry," Cosby noted during a sequence on black images in the media. "The cat made $2 million in five years in the middle of the thirties and everyone who ever saw a movie laughed at Stepin Fetchit." In effect, the show placed blame for the popular acceptance of the lazy, inarticulate, craven comic Negro squarely on Fetchit's shoulders.[19]

The comic had been forewarned about the documentary's theme when clips from his old pictures were used to promote the show, and he had hired an attorney with the Chicago law firm of Cooper & Wallace. Shortly after the broadcast, he demanded a retraction and began an aggressive campaign to defend himself and rebuild his image. He accused the network, and the show's producers and sponsors, of slander—"taking me, a Negro hero, and converting me into a villain." Insisting that he was "a credit to the [film] industry," Fetchit told reporters he wanted "equal time to refute the show, to repair the damage to my business enterprises, and to repair my position in the history of show business."

A letter sent to CBS president Frank Stanton by his lawyer reiterated the request. "Stepin Fetchit's name and picture were used to advertise the series" in advance, the attorney wrote, and he asked that his client "be granted equal time to correct the distorted portrayal of his position in the movies."[20]

CBS, of course, refused the request for equal time or, for that matter, any air time to refute the show's claims. Fetchit, however, seemed genuinely hurt. CBS "called the character I created the epitome of the black man who sold out his people, and in a single program I was judged and found guilty in front of millions of people," he said during a press conference in Chicago. "They're making me a villain," but "if it wasn't for me there wouldn't be no Sidney Poitier or Bill Cosby or any of them."[21]

Using the newly acquired publicity platform the incident provided, he also lobbied for a return to films or television. "I'm generally doing all right, I'm no pauper," he insisted when queried about his career and financial status. "I've been writing." He also admitted that the CBS program had unfortunately been aired just as he was making a comeback and listed some of his projects: "television specials, feature pictures, a book—my life story—and lectures."[22]

Certainly, during the summer of 1968 a television sitcom featuring Stepin Fetchit and Flip Wilson was being contemplated. And in early fall, after a fifteen-year absence, the comic returned to Hollywood to appear in a comedy skit on Wilson's NBC-TV special. The sequence, according to the *Los Angeles Times,* was being viewed as a pilot, which "could later be developed into a weekly series, which would restore Fetchit's career in a big way."[23]

The skit was aired on Wilson's 1968 variety special *Flip Out with Flip*—an edgy, mildly risqué comedy special that reflected the irreverent political and social satire of the late sixties and generally mirrored the quick-take, one-liner blackout format popularized on television by *Rowan and Martin's Laugh-In.* The Fetchit-Wilson skit stood out in that it ran for an uninterrupted twenty minutes and was clearly intended to develop the characters portrayed. Fetchit was cast as the owner of the "Jackson & Jackson Swap Shop," a ramshackle Harlem secondhand or antique store, and Wilson played his son, a rash, ambitious youth determined to leave the ghetto, move downtown, and become a lawyer.

The skit was laced with one-liners and wisecracks typical of the era's sitcoms. When Wilson reveals his collegiate aspirations, for instance, Fetchit cracks, "Didn't you forget something?"

"What?" Wilson demands.

"High school!"

The chemistry between the comedians was unique, however, and, reflecting the sixties' assertive race consciousness, Fetchit, as the surly, conniving shop owner, displayed no trace of the inept, confused character he had played in films. In contrast, he was cast as an articulate, proud black man determined to redirect his son's impulsive assertiveness.

In an edgy climactic encounter, the son's apparent militancy and disrespect for his father's old-school ways are subtly reversed, and Fetchit emerges as the voice of reason and true race consciousness.

Wilson rants that he is "talking about making it . . . getting some respect" and insists he will be "the black Perry Mason."

"You just goin' be another white man with a black face," Fetchit snaps. "You better listen to your old man and stay here where you belong."

"Here we go again," Wilson shoots back. "Ole Uncle Tom telling it like it ain't. Yessuh, boss. Stay in your place, boy, white folks don't like no uppity niggers. Well, kiss my NAACP card."

Fetchit rails at the label "Uncle Tom" and chides the son with a spiel that a militant civil rights spokesman might have voiced.

"You better hush up, boy. If you want respect, make something of yourself right here. This is where we need green power . . . right here is where we need a criminal lawyer because the worst crime around here is being black. So now if you want to carry your sad, ugly, ignorant self downtown, go ahead. I'll get along without you just fine—every day."

"All of a sudden I come home and it sound like Adam Clayton Powell is in town," Wilson says as he stops at the door.

It was strong stuff for a TV sitcom in the sixties—both poignant and funny. After the father and son were reconciled at the conclusion, it was evident that the impish young comic and veteran film and stage star clicked as a sitcom duo. Most impressively, Fetchit had effectively shucked the stooped-shouldered, dim-witted image that had overtly marked his film character and shown that he could persuasively portray a dignified, sensible modern-day black man. It was to no avail, however; adverse publicity following the CBS special and apparent temerity on the part of TV executives doomed the prospective sitcom.[24]

Wilson went on to stardom on *The Flip Wilson Show* (1970–1974), the first successful nationally televised, black-hosted variety show in TV history. And in 1972, *Sanford and Son,* featuring father and son owners of a Los Angeles junkyard, debuted on NBC with Redd Foxx and Demond Wilson in the lead roles; it became one of television's most successful sitcoms. "According to Fetchit," a *Jet* magazine writer reported, "as a result of the CBS presentation, he was not given the starring role in another television show, Sanford and Son, that was being groomed for him and comedian Flip Wilson."

Wilson, who had worked the chitlin' circuit himself and was a great admirer of Fetchit and other old-school comedians, later expressed regret over the incident. "The timing was a disaster," he said during a 1980 interview at his Los Angeles home. "I hit it off with Step and we worked well together. I didn't agree with the decision to drop him, but there wasn't much I could do. The tide had turned against him, and nobody wanted to take a chance."[25]

Fetchit's disappointment went far deeper, of course. The dashed opportunity haunted him for the remainder of his life.

"It was to have been the twilight success of my life," he said later. "But the producers couldn't afford to have Flip associated with me since that show decided I was 'the epitome of the black man who sold out his people.' "[26]

Despite his disappointment over the scuttled sitcom project, Fetchit waged an extensive publicity campaign in an effort to return to mainstream entertainment while in Hollywood in 1968. He insisted, however, that he was not "trying to erase the image of the bumbling character" he created.

"I see no harm in it," he said. "Just because Charlie Chaplin played a tramp doesn't make tramps out of all Englishmen and because Dean Martin drinks that doesn't make drunks out of all Italians. I was only playing a character, and that character did a lot of good."[27]

On another occasion, he focused his anger on leftist groups whom he felt were twisting the minds of a younger generation of blacks, by encouraging their disrespect for the past. Young Negroes "are taught to ignore anything old-time," he said. "It's the same as if the Jewish people would ignore Moses because he didn't bring them through the Red Sea in Rolls-Royces or Cadillacs. Young people are taught by phony leftists to only recognize the things they are doing today."[28]

During the late 1960s and early '70s, he began lashing out at civil rights leaders and the black power movement. He blamed the increased ridicule of and attacks on the screen character he created, as well as his Hollywood ouster, on militant blacks. His rhetoric, however, was not only ill timed but was becoming noticeably more histrionic and strident. "Me and the civil rights movement don't get along, because they are all phony organizations. I go around advising people who they have fooled. I call all of the civil rights leaders—*all* of them—nothin' but, ah, playin' both ends *and* the middle," he told an Iowa radio talk-show host. "They're the worst things that ever happened to anybody. And half of them, ah, a majority of them, has foreign interests—un-American interests. That goes for the NAACP, Martin Luther King, and any bunch of them that you can name that are posing as out for the interests of the Negro."[29]

During an interview with a *Los Angeles Times* writer, he railed that early in his career he had "defied the laws of white supremacy" and demanded first-class citizenship. "I had to defy a law which said Negroes were supposed to be inferior. I was a militant, in fact, I was the first militant. But I did it the right way," he said. "I gave the Negro first-class universal citizenship to point to. I did the job."

Fetchit also sounded off against well-intentioned white liberals who supported the militant movement. "They are either stupid or don't have the best interests of the Negro at heart," he raged. "Instead of trying to unify blacks and whites and play down the differences between blacks and whites they are separating us."[30]

His rambling, unfocused diatribes, which were repeated whenever possible and to whomever would listen, naturally only worsened the situation. While his outspoken interviews, press conferences, and public appeals may have found a welcome audience among conservative bigots and newsmen looking for controversy, they infuriated many blacks who had previously supported him. They also alienated white liberals within the film industry who might have sympathized with his plight.

The CBS-TV special and Fetchit's aggressive defense of his reputation had severely damaged his already flagging market value as even a nostalgic curio. For many he had suddenly become a confirmed emblem of inferiority—and as a touchstone for the era's heated racial debate, he was untouchable. By 1969 he had returned to Chicago's

South Side. Still vehemently protesting the inequity of his depiction on the CBS documentary, he resumed his makeshift schedule of occasional engagements at small-town clubs and theaters. Within months, however, while performing in a small club in Louisville, Kentucky, he was once again drawn into the headlines. This time the catalyst was a deadly tragedy that occurred on the Pennsylvania Turnpike.

In April, Donald Martin Lambright, the disputed son of Fetchit and Winifred Johnson, killed three people, including his wife, and wounded fifteen other motorists before fatally shooting himself on the turnpike. Lambright, reportedly a member of a militant black-separatist organization, was said to have been disturbed by the assassination of Martin Luther King, Jr. He was "very sensitive to infringement on the freedom of all people," his uncle avowed, "and almost paranoid about race relations."

Although there was no supportive evidence, some hinted that Lambright's militant extremism was an attempt to compensate for his father's widely publicized image as "the White man's Negro." When contacted about the tragedy, Fetchit admitted that he was Lambright's father, but wisely avoided the issue, saying, "I can't understand it, he was such a cool, calm and intelligent boy." He offered his regrets to Lambright's mother and the victims' families and said that he had not seen his son in two years.[31]

Following the turnpike incident, Stepin Fetchit again slipped into obscurity. He was forced back into the seamy clubs, lodges, and strip joints that provided his only source of income. The pain and humiliation still lingered, however, and the comic was not yet ready to abandon the struggle to salvage his past or return to the limelight.

In June 1970, the actor took the fight to another level. He filed suit in the Indianapolis United States District Court citing the Columbia Broadcasting System, Twentieth Century-Fox Film Corporation, the Xerox Corporation, and the Indiana Broadcasting Corporation as defendants. The complaint accused the program of "pretending to relieve racial tensions through education and understanding, by slurring an entire generation of Negro Americans as inept and by subtly encouraging black militancy as a solution to present Negro problems." It also alleged that prior to the broadcast Fetchit "enjoyed an image as one of the first accepted Negro movie stars of the United States and was considered a talented comedian who made a definite contribution toward black progress in America and prepared the way for acceptance by the public of Negro actors and actresses who followed."

Fetchit asked for $25,000 in actual damages and $2,975,000 in punitive damages for malice, invasion of privacy, and defamation of character.[32]

In September 1972, the suit was blocked when the U.S. District Court ruled that the program constituted "fair commentary on a public figure"; the decision was immediately appealed by Fetchit's lawyers. Finally, in October 1974, the Supreme Court rejected the appeal and upheld the lower court decision. The actor's defamation complaint had been dismissed. "If any justices sympathized with [Lincoln] Perry—and none indicated a desire to hear his case," a news item noted, "they may have felt the time was not ripe to consider the issues he raised."[33]

In this instance, Fetchit may have lost the war, but he did win a battle. Publicity surrounding the suit and his appeals to newspapers across the country had aroused enough interest in Hollywood for the actor to be called to the West Coast for a role in *Cutter,* a 1972 NBC-TV *Mystery Movie.* Peter DeAnda was cast as Cutter, a black Chicago detective, "a la Shaft," who was hired to find an African American pro quarterback who had been kidnapped. Fetchit had a comic role as a laconic shoe-shine man. It was to be a continuing part, but the film did not make the network's regular schedule. Fetchit remained in Hollywood, however, and eventually found work in two more films.

His first appearance occurred more or less by accident. While awaiting the outcome of the Supreme Court decision, he often hung out with show-business friends like the comedian Slappy White. In 1973, White was preparing to shoot the Matt Robinson–produced film *Amazing Grace* with Moms Mabley and Butterfly McQueen. "Step showed up uninvited" on the set one day "as Slappy White's 'dialogue' coach and stayed on to become chief comic kibitzer," a *New York Magazine* writer claimed. And according to Robinson, who had met Fetchit at a poolside party at White's house, once on the set, Fetchit immediately began lobbying for a part in the picture.[34]

"When Slappy White introduced me to him, I didn't even know he was alive," Robinson recalled. "I talked to him and one day decided it would be a piece of history if I put him in this film. I told him, 'Step, you got this one line—you do this.' Afterward, Step would come in with this long sheet of paper and start talking: 'I see where we could do some more.' Every day it was something else. I began to understand how he got as far as he did—he worried people to death. Finally, like myself, they must have said, 'All right! I surrender. Just do it, we'll see how it works.' "

That "pestering determination," Robinson later wrote, probably fueled the comic's early success in motion pictures.

"One can imagine him then, calling up and calling on every executive at Twentieth Century-Fox, relentlessly talking, leaning into their faces, lecturing, cajoling, singing, dancing, laughing" until he was given a contract, Robinson said. During the *Amazing Grace* shoot, Fetchit kept on pushing to expand his part, and when Slappy White joined in lobbying for more lines, Moms Mabley jokingly offered her old vaudeville friends some advice. "Well, let'um put on a dress and be Grace," she said.

At one point, Fetchit urged that if Robinson could "do a two-minute sequence of me playing my new composition, 'Hank Aaron Home Run 715,' and then cut to a stock shot of an integrated Las Vegas audience, this picture would have a universal touch to it." Robinson resisted the pressure and, ultimately, Fetchit's role was limited to a cameo appearance at the opening of the film. The producer and comic remained friends, however, and Robinson would later write a critically well-received play, *The Confessions of Stepin Fetchit,* centered on Fetchit's life.[35]

The film, shot in Los Angeles and New York, was finally a vehicle for the venerable Moms Mabley. In her first and only feature Hollywood film, she had the title role of Grace, a feisty octogenarian who intervenes in a Baltimore mayoral race and turns the city's politics around. Released in August 1974, the movie received middling reviews but did well at the box office in urban areas. *Variety,* for instance, called it a "weak lowercase item for less discriminating blacks"; as in that review, most notices simply cited Fetchit for his cameo return to pictures. It remains a cult favorite, however, among devotees of African American comedy.[36]

The reunion of the legendary group of old-school comics must have pleased Fetchit, and when he returned to Chicago in 1974, he was no doubt anticipating a decision in his suit against CBS. When its dismissal was announced in October, Fetchit was crushed. He had failed in the attempt to reestablish his career and reputation. Still, he routinely contacted newspaper columnists and feverishly bent the ear of practically anyone else who would listen with protest of his public vilification in the television documentary. According to his wife Bernice, however, a spark had been extinguished. His obsession with the wrongful smear and his place in cinema history intensified, and, as he had on previous occasions, the comic reportedly withdrew. He focused his attention on his autobiography and a proposed TV documentary of his life.[37]

Hollywood summoned Fetchit for the last time in 1975. Along with more than sixty other former film stars, he was called for a cameo appearance in Paramount's farcical *Won Ton Ton, the Dog Who Saved Hollywood.* Set in the 1920s, the picture starred Bruce Dern, Madeline Kahn, and Art Carney, and spoofed the silent-film era when animal stars like Rin Tin Tin were major moneymakers in the industry. Fetchit was cast in the role of a dancing butler and asked to perform his "Stepin Fetchit" dance routine. It was an appropriate curtain call since his brief scene recalled his stage act and sequences from his first Hollywood picture, the silent film *In Old Kentucky.* It was in that film, released more than fifty years earlier, that his distinctive dancing and "flying feet" had initially been noted.[38]

After completing the picture in October 1975, the actor returned to Chicago, where he still resided in the South Side home of Jodie Edwards. During the fall and winter, he accepted only a handful of engagements in and around the Chicago area. Early in 1976, his spirits were lifted somewhat when the versatile entertainer Ben Vereen expressed an interest in portraying him on-screen. Fetchit visited Vereen at the Plaza Hotel in New York, where the performers reportedly discussed the film project. During the New York visit, he was introduced onstage at one of Vereen's performances and received a five-minute standing ovation.

"Step was very happy" after the visit, a friend wrote, "because of Vereen's interest in doing his life story." It would have given him an opportunity to dramatize his life experience and climb to the top of the movie industry from his own perspective, a project for which he had continually lobbied. When no progress had been made on the proposed movie by spring, however, Fetchit stoically accepted the disappointment, resuming the slow-paced daily routine that he had adopted.[39]

At age seventy-three (still claiming to be eighty-three), he no longer needed his acting skills to affect the famed lazy-man routine. Increasingly, he spurned engagements, staying at home and turning to his collection of clippings and photographs for comfort; he could not alter current estimates of his achievements, but he could on occasion block them out by revisiting the past. Even so, puzzled perhaps by the fury and evident rancor of his critics, he was often drawn to more negative write-ups, those containing the most devastating indictments. Seething internally each time he scanned them, he often stormed to the telephone and resumed the dogged attempt to discredit his accusers and revive his reputation.

On the morning of April 21, 1976, Fetchit was engaged in that daily ritual when he suffered a massive stroke.

According to Matt Robinson, who subsequently interviewed friends and family, Fetchit "was reading an article that, typically, blamed him for every black problem this side of slavery" at the time of the edema. When his wife discovered him unconscious on their bedroom floor, he was rushed to the emergency room. Paralyzed on his left side, with jaw immobile and mouth agape, Fetchit remained on the critical list for several days and for weeks was unable to speak or communicate. The stroke had done what critics and detractors had been unable to do throughout his career—silence the feisty, outspoken actor.[40]

CHAPTER SEVENTEEN

While recuperating at Michael Reese Hospital, Fetchit was showered with letters and calls from fans and admirers. The hospital was also swamped with visitors who either knew or simply had heard of the legendary star. "Step has thousands of old friends coming to the hospital each day," Winnie Johnson, the comic's ex-paramour and mother of his second child, wrote. "They are regular people from the neighborhoods, guys from the corner drug stores, persons from senior citizen homes, postal workers, cab drivers, nurses from the hospital compound and the doctors, too."[1]

A stream of entertainers and celebrities also stopped by to pay their respects. They included Jack Carter, Ben Vereen, Muhammad Ali, and John Wayne, who had been friends with Fetchit for nearly five decades, as well as many of the old "sow circuit" performers with whom Fetchit had worked. President Ford was among those who sent messages.

"Old Step! Remember me?" Wayne reportedly asked the comic. Unable to speak, Fetchit simply moaned in reply. "That's okay, Step. You know we all love ya," the actor encouraged, adding that "we had a lot of fun together" before he left.[2]

Wayne's "words seemed to have brightened Step's whole life in seconds," Winnie Johnson wrote. And indeed, for an entertainer who had basked in the nation's applause and adulation for almost half a century, then fallen into disgrace and near-obscurity, the response of fans and friends must have been uplifting. The outpouring of affection and respect for his achievements was exactly what the actor had been seeking in his furious struggle to clear his name. During the early days of his recuperation, his wife, Bernice, his sister Marie Carter Perry, as well as Winnie Johnson (who had apparently resolved past differences with the actor) and a host of friends, were constantly at his side.

After Bernice insisted that doctors examine her husband's jaw, they discovered that it had been broken. An operation repaired the injury and, with restored mobility, the gap-mouthed disfigurement was eliminated but the comic's speech was permanently impaired by aphasia. As he slowly improved, the swarm of attention slackened and the press lost interest in the story. Within months, the actor was moved to a Chicago nursing home. Visitors eventually dwindled and were limited to his wife, his sister, old friends like Jodie Edwards (Butterbeans) who lived nearby, and the occasional appearance of such show-business cronies and celebrity associates as Louis Armstrong and Muhammad Ali.

There was a belated bow to Fetchit's legacy in African American film history by the NAACP in 1976. Their Hollywood chapter granted him a Special Image Award in recognition of his contribution to the evolution of black films. For the bedridden actor, however, the unexpected honor may not have been as highly regarded as it was intended to be. As Step might have said, it was "a day late and a penny short."

With the upsurge of more militant demands for equal rights in the streets and the debut of so-called blaxploitation films dominating the Negro presence in films during the seventies, old-time vestiges of Hollywood's plantation days like Stepin Fetchit were far removed from most moviegoers' minds. Even megastar Sidney Poitier was losing his appeal with African American audiences, who insisted on more assertive black images in films. In fact, with the release of Melvin Van Peebles's quirky and much-underrated *Sweet Sweetback's Baad Asssss Song* in 1971, for a time nothing less than gritty action films with macho heroes played by Jim Brown, Jim Kelly, Robert Hooks, and Fred Williamson or superheroines played by Pam Grier seemed to appeal to mass black audiences. In Fetchit's absence, it should be noted, the film industry had finally dared to bring the story of the comic's old Bad Boy buddy Jack Johnson to the screen (a project for which Fetchit had lobbied for decades); a cinema adaptation of the Broadway hit *The Great White Hope* was released in the early 1970s with James Earl Jones in the lead role.

Meanwhile, Fetchit languished in a nursing home that was rapidly becoming unaffordable, and his wife began searching for an alternate living space. By 1977, George L. Bagnall, president of the Motion Picture Country Home and Hospital in Woodland Hills, California, got word of the actor's predicament. He invited Fetchit to take up residence at the convalescence home, and, later in the year, Bernice and Fetchit made the trek from Chicago.[3]

Bernice, described at the time by writer and family friend Matt Robinson as a woman "whose Southern voice is never raised, whose sight is impaired but whose dignity is intact," brought her husband to California. Although ailing herself, she moved "a man whose weakened bladder, paralyzed side, and impaired speech would have imposed a serious problem for a team of paramedics," Robinson wrote. Fetchit, according to his wife, made the trip even more difficult.

"He was screaming on the plane to make his star demands understood, constantly having to be wheeled to the rest room, and yelling unintelligibly to the driver who took us out to Woodland Hills," she told Robinson.[4]

Once situated, like many furiously independent retirees, the still irascible comic did not adjust easily to life in a nursing home. Bernice initially stayed in Watts while Fetchit settled into one of the sixty-two suites, or one-room apartments, in the facility's lodge; during the eighties, when her health worsened, she moved into the home with her husband. At the outset, however, she visited once each week, taking a two-hour bus ride from Los Angeles to shave Step, dress him, lay out and arrange his clothes, pick up and return freshly washed laundry, and, according to Robinson, "be abused."

Fetchit, Robinson wrote, continually yelled at her, the nurses, and administrators, "all of whom he assumes to be in his employ." It was the temperament of a star, and at Woodland Hills—where the likes of Buster Keaton, Bruce Cabot, Eddie "Rochester" Anderson, Norma Shearer, Larry Fine of the Three Stooges, Herbert Marshall, and Johnny Weissmuller resided before their deaths—the outbursts were not unusual. Weissmuller, for instance, had roamed the hallways at night, screaming at other residents and reprising his bellowing Tarzan yell until transferred to another facility. Such behavior was tolerated, up to a point, by administrators at Woodland Hills whose motto was and still is We Take Care of Our Own. That care extended to footing the bill for indigent residents, a hospitality that Fetchit and other fallen stars gladly accepted.[5]

Woodland Hills is a beautiful, spacious facility that, in addition to the lodge in which Fetchit resided, offers more than 50 cottages, or one-room flats, with small gardens, and a 175-bed hospital. The grounds, dotted with citrus and palm trees, provide a calm, serene atmosphere for its 300 residents, all of whom are former entertainers or TV and movie studio technicians. But for Fetchit and many of the other formerly celebrated, high-profile entertainers, the biggest problem was tedium. With only an occasional visitor other than his wife and sister, Fetchit reportedly spent most of his time in his room watching television or marking off days on several calendars that hung from the walls.

"A small percentage of the people here are loners, and we simply fail to get them involved," then-executive director Jack Staggs said. "Besides his paralysis, Mr. Perry is suffering from a disease no medication can cure—boredom."[6]

During his stay at the Country Home, other awards trickled in, and some may have temporarily offset the tedium of nursing-home living and even quelled the comic's thirst for recognition that he felt was long overdo. In February 1978, for instance, during Black History Month, the Oakland Museum Association announced that the comic had been inducted into the Black Filmmakers Hall of Fame. But even that honor was announced with caution, and the apparent wish to avoid any controversy that may have been stirred up by the induction. "It is our intention," said Mrs. Norvel Smith, spokesperson for the museum, "to pay a much deserved tribute to the early filmmakers who have paved the way in films for the successful careers of the stars of today."[7]

In February 1980, when Matt Robinson and I visited Step at the Country Home, the comic was lively and energetic, his spirits apparently lifted by the sight of visitors. Ten minutes after we arrived and met him in the visitors' lounge, he left, then hobbled back with an armload of frayed clippings and photographs retrieved from a huge suitcase he kept tucked in a corner of his room. For an hour or so, he struggled to make himself understood and occasionally scratched out notes on a small pad to either answer questions or support his claims and accusations. Bouncing up and down in his seat or vigorously nodding his head when a point was made, even in his late seventies and partially crippled, the *man* bore little resemblance to the halting, mumbling, perpetually baffled *character* that I had seen him play in films, or the wry, laconic, near-somnolent character he reportedly played onstage. Still energetic and vibrant, his face alternately lit up with intensity or an impish grin. Louis Armstrong's observation that Step was "born to be a star" assumed even more impact when I recalled that face-to-face meeting.

It was also apparent that, like some latter-day, sable Don Quixote, he was still jousting with windmills and shadows. The entire conversation that day centered on his desperate attempt to justify his career, refute his detractors, and establish his credibility and contribution to performance arts in motion pictures. As it turned out, the frantic efforts were unnecessary. With regard to his comic brilliance, on that day he was preaching to the choir.

The entreaties and arguments might have been persuasive for many others, however, had they bothered to listen. Unfortunately, by the 1980s not many were either concerned or listening. Coverage of Fetchit's activities after his stroke had been so limited that by the early eighties many Americans assumed he was dead. By then even his image had been excised from many of the motion pictures in which he originally starred, and most of his films were banned from television screenings. The character he created, along with most movies in which he appeared, had become museum pieces, seen only at rare film festivals and, for the curious and determined, by request at the Library of Congress or other archival institutions. He had been so consummately swept under cover—the result of a more assertive African American's embarrassment from and insistent dismissal of the character he portrayed and white liberals' desire to be politically correct—that except for family, show-business friends, movie buffs, and rare die-hard fans, he was literally a forgotten man.

But while the man may have slipped into obscurity, the legend—his emblematic status as a symbol of slavery and black America's powerless past—was rapidly expanding. Stepin Fetchit's name had been codified as a symbol of what, among many African Americans, was the era's worst sin: scraping or bowing before the white man. In the eighties vernacular, it had become a synonym for "turncoat," "house nigger," and "Tom," that is, practically any heretic who did not demonstratively display unquestioned allegiance to black assertiveness and resistance to even the mere appearance of white control.

Curiously, it was not because any extensive, focused campaign had been waged against the man. The villainous symbolic image was shaped more subtly, a result of the allegorical resonance of his stage name and the indelible visual impact of his film roles being gradually absorbed into the national consciousness. Outside of the CBS special, in which he had been accused of popularizing the comic image of the "lazy, stupid, crap shooter, chicken stealing idiot," few critics cited him except in passing reference from the mid-1940s to the 1970s. Most forties protests targeted comic screen images, but by then Fetchit's Hollywood career was basically finished; criticism was aimed primarily at Mantan Moreland, Hattie McDaniel, and Willie Best. By the early fifties, with black comic roles a rare commodity in motion pictures, television's *Amos 'n' Andy Show* and *Beulah* were the prime targets of organized protest. And following the deprecatory CBS documentary in 1968, although a few articles mocked his shrill attacks on the civil rights leaders, Fetchit's image or rare stage performances seldom drew criticism from the black press. It simply ignored him. Mainstream pundits were far more critical.

After the fifties, nearly all reflections of old-school Negro performers' overtly accommodating guises were pilloried by liberal mainstream critics. The effort was almost always a well-intentioned attempt to support the civil rights movement and African Americans' struggle to erase negative images that, because white America had accepted them as accurate representations of the race, had bedeviled blacks during the first half or the century. Reviews by *Variety*, the *New York Times*, the *Los Angeles Times*, and other mainstream media outlets commonly denounced Fetchit's appearances as racially offensive throwbacks and, as dictated by the fashion of the era, assumed that it was not only the expected but also the correct thing to do. Bosley Crowther's review of *Bend of the River* in 1952, in which he wrote, "We are sorry to note that Stepin Fetchit is back to play a clownish stereotype," was a typical example of the new, accepted identification of Fetchit and most all of the old black motion-picture comics with racial inferiority.[8]

• • •

For Lincoln Perry, who battled various ailments and was in and out of the Country Home's hospital during the eighties, the struggle came to an end in 1985. In January his wife, who had moved into the convalescence home, died after a long illness. Two months later, he was hospitalized with heart problems. And on November 19, Perry died of pneumonia and congestive heart failure.

The funeral services, held at St. Agatha's Catholic Church in Los Angeles, were reportedly attended by only "50 friends and relatives." While admittedly most of the comic's old show-business cronies were either sick, dead, or dying, it was a strikingly sparse and anticlimactic turnout for the funeral of an actor who some had deemed "the father of black movie stars." The absence of prominent film stars and entertainers of the eighties was conspicuous. Family members among the mourners included Perry's sister Marie Carter and first son Jemajo Perry.[9]

Eulogies were delivered by Sunny Craver, an actor who Perry had met and assisted in 1956; Hosea Alexander, a church deacon, and family members. Alexander noted that the actor "took pride" in the fact that he was the first black movie star. And Craver, one of the comic's longtime friends, insisted that, far from being a detriment to the black struggle, Perry was one of its earliest advocates.

"He taught me not only to be a good entertainer and to take pride in what I do, but he also taught me to be black and to be proud of the fact that I was black," the actor said. During the fifties, Perry had secured the actor's job in a theater production, Graver recalled, by convincing the director that the actor's role was essential. He also praised Perry's generosity, supporting the comic's claim that most of his money was lost because he "gave it away."

"I once saw him hand a producer $30,000 in cash," Craver said. "The producer asked for a loan, but Stepin Fetchit said, 'I won't lend it to you, I'll give it to you.'"

"We have to draw distinctions," Craver advised, "between the character Stepin Fetchit and the man."[10]

Perry was buried at Calvary Cemetery.

Lincoln Perry had passed away quietly, unnoticed by nearly all who were not frequent obituary-page readers. The character he created and popularized, however, had been indelibly etched into the public mind.

The name Stepin Fetchit retained the negative connotation that had led middle-class black Americans to blanch with embarrassment and a good part of white America to assume, or perhaps hope, it represented the true soul of black men. For most, it would be forever identified with filmland's infamous, servile "coon" image, and for many it became the standard by which that image was measured.

"Fetchit was the embodiment of the nitwit Black man," David Pilgram, a Ferris State University professor of sociology wrote in his 2000 essay "The Coon Caricature."

"He was portrayed as a dunce" who was incapable of correctly pronouncing a "multisyllabic" word. "Scratching his head, eyes bulging," he "portrayed the coon so realistically that Whites thought they were seeing a real racial type." Although Fetchit was elected to the Black Filmmakers Hall of Fame, his legacy, according to Pilgram, was that would "always be remembered as the lazy, barely literate, self-demeaning, White man's Black."[11]

That assessment had been so thoroughly imprinted in the public mind by the 1980s that Stepin Fetchit, the man and character, had been subsumed into the category of racial epithet. (Interestingly, like many critics, Pilgrim may have confused the comic with contemporaries Mantan Moreland and Willie Best, since he describes Fetchit as displaying the "bulging" eyes those funnymen made famous. In contrast, Fetchit's eyes were nearly always half-closed.) No matter, as the slip indicates, the term "Stepin Fetchit" had emerged as a catchword for all subservient movie clowns. It had become a synonym for "racial inferiority" and "toadying" not just on the street but also among writers and politicians and other ostensibly educated groups.

In 1981, for instance, the black newspaper columnist Carl Rowan expressed contempt for black economist Thomas Sowell and his conservative politics by comparing him to "Stepin Fetchit" and "Aunt Jemima." In Washington, Texas democrat Henry B. Gonzalez made news by calling a fellow black member of the House the "Stepin Fetchit of the Reagan administration" after they tangled over budget cuts in 1989. And in 1990, a white teachers' union leader labeled the black superintendent of schools in California's Centinela Valley Union High School District a "Stepin Fetchit" when he opposed administrative changes suggested by a predominantly white union. Today the term

"Stepin Fetchit," like "Uncle Tom," is defined as a racial epithet, a synonym for "degrading racial stereotypes" by several on-line sites.[12]

As "Stepin Fetchit" gradually became accepted as a colorful derisive term instead of the stage name of Hollywood's first black motion picture star, Lincoln Perry receded further into the shadows. His stage and screen achievements were effectively eclipsed by generally skewed, after-the-fact racial and political interpretation of his stage and screen character.

Occasionally, a few more temperate voices spoke out against the injustice. Most often the dissenters were actors or comedians, performers who had been in the trenches during a repressive era. Before his death, for example, Jester Hairston, the composer and actor best know for supporting roles on *Amos 'n' Andy* and (as Rolly, a wisecracking deacon) the late-1980s sitcom *Amen,* offered the view of a performer who had been there and worked alongside Perry. "We had a hard time then fighting for dignity," Harris said in 1978. "We had a lot of legitimate beefs, not just myself but Bert Williams and Bill Robinson and, yes, Stepin Fetchit—but we had no power, we had to take it, and because we took it the young people today have opportunities."[13]

When asked what he thought of the appropriateness of *Saturday Night Live*'s use of racial humor in 1978, the comic Garrett Morris passionately defended the old-school comedians and their right to be heard.

"Well, I feel two things," he said. "First, I wonder why reporters never ask Gilda [Radner] about Irish humor. Racial humor is the point of the show, man. Why pick on me? We're trying to do what comedy has done all along—satirize society's soft underbelly. I don't think we'll ever be there with black humor in this country till blacks can laugh at Stepin Fetchit the way whites can laugh at W. C. Fields. I mean, you can draw no other conclusion from the comedy of W. C. Fields than that of a statement on middle-class child-haters and alcoholics. But you don't see people going around saying, 'Hey, we can't have that on the air.' "[14]

Flip Wilson, a friend and admirer of Perry, also viewed him from a more liberated perspective. "Look, everything is right for its time," the late comic said. "Step had perfect timing. He was right on time. His humor was only insulting if you were uptight. Whatever degree of insult you might see in it, it is still a very, very vital part of our history—and it was funny. It exposed who we really were and what the times were really like. You have to accept it as fact."[15]

Unfortunately, later generations don't usually consider the biases or circumstances that shaped the reputations of past cultural icons. We tend to view them through a black-and-white lens that obscures intermediate shadings and skews our assessment by imposing current standards on behavior that evolved from vastly different conditions. Once established as villains or heroes, in knee-jerk fashion, they are routinely either tarred with opprobrium or whitewashed with reverence. Moreover—historical fact and the realities of bygone eras notwithstanding—African Americans have been reluctant to recognize the merit of behavior that remotely smacks of passive resistance or "Tomism," even though the tact was at one time an accepted, effective, even necessary, means of diverting racial oppression and attaining one's own ends.

Still, on those rare occasions when Perry's movies were exhibited, a few open-minded younger viewers who witnessed his work for the first time were impressed. After viewing *Hearts in Dixie* at a Los Angeles film festival in 1988, for instance, Charles A. Johnson, a black, twenty-four-year-old West Coast journalist, was astonished at his reaction to Perry's screen character. "For years, it seems, I had heard that Fetchit perpetuated the lie that blacks are shiftless and lazy, that he was a sell-out. No black actor that I know of has had worse press from people who have never seen his movies."

But, Johnson wrote, "Nobody ever mentioned to me that Stepin Fetchit was *funny.*

"I didn't even have time to become righteously indignant before I was laughing out loud at Fetchit's philosophically lazy character who was 'too tired from rest.' It would be an insult to his artistic touch to say any comic actor could have carried off this totally absurd creation—a mix of childlike innocence, grown-up goldbricking and a dramatic and comic timing you could set your watch by.

"As to his threat to the industriousness of future generations of blacks, or anyone else desperate enough to choose a 59-year-old cartoon character as a role model," he concluded, "it seems as diabolical a threat as Charlie Chaplin's 'Tramp' is to white children."[16]

In retrospect, no one can deny that the sole focus on dense, kowtowing, inarticulate black servants (even happy, semiarticulate ones, for that matter) in pictures was an issue that needed addressing. But to blame and, often, ostracize the actors who portrayed them was as senseless and misdirected as berating Carroll O'Connor for portraying the bigot Archie Bunker or mocking Negroes for obediently picking their masters' cotton during slavery. The real villains were America's racist caste system and studio executives who refused to elevate morality above profit and confront the Southern lobbyists and audiences who insisted on perceiving Negroes as inferiors. The most just solution would have been to demand representation of serious, ambitious, middle-class blacks to balance portraits of comical, uneducated ones. Walter White and other rights leaders were aware, however, that such a request during the 1930s and early 1940s would have been fruitless.

Of the actors who portrayed characters fitting the "coon" image in early films, Lincoln Perry was undoubtedly the most famous and, during his heyday in the late 1920s and mid-1930s, the most popular. Outside of his ascendancy and preeminence, however, his selection as the prime example of the demeaning stereotype was not only arbitrary but also flagrantly unjust.

There is little doubt that for white Americans who were inclined to believe it, he helped confirm racist stereotypes of blacks as, on one hand, slow, lazy, and stupid, and, on the other, as garish spendthrifts. But he did not invent the stereotypes, and it's preposterous to assume that they would have eroded or vanished without his presence. Moreover, there were hundreds of lesser, mostly unheralded or now forgotten comics whose acts were far more reprehensible and who were perfectly willing to accept any roles that Perry declined. He continually argued that he portrayed the soul of his character while his imitators sunk to "yes'sah, boss" stereotypes.

In fact, if Perry had been Irish, English, Italian, or Jewish instead of black, he probably would have been remembered and hailed, along with Charlie Chaplin, Harold Lloyd, and Buster Keaton, as one of the finest performers to emerge in Hollywood's Golden Age of Comedy. Portraying the same character in a different place, at another time—even currently, in the twenty-first century with its dubious license to wallow in crude humor and play the fool with impunity or, at least, without social outcry—Perry may well have been honored as a masterful satirist.

It could easily be argued that the comic image Lincoln Perry projected was not nearly as harmful, deleterious, and degrading as the images projected by many of today's black comedians, rap artists, and even television sitcom stars. There is one crucial difference, however; he and the hundreds of lesser-known or now-forgotten old-school comedians and entertainers who worked in the picture industry had no choice. Today's black performers have vast options and still often opt for routines or projects that are mired in either salacious or degrading stereotypes. And except for an occasional complaint from insistent critics of demeaning portraits of blacks in the media, like Bill Cosby, detractors are noticeably silent.

Moreover Perry's public excesses were no more extravagant, gaudy, or buffoonish than the nouveau riche motion-picture stars who partied wildly and lived like kings during Hollywood's Golden Years. His spirited self-indulgence was no more a reflection of the Negro's so-called gaudy tastes, as many claimed, than it was a symptom of the era's fashion. Moreover, compared to the extravagant living of some twenty-first-century TV and movie stars, rap artists, and entertainment moguls, black and white, Perry's prodigal excesses in some ways seem prudent.

His tainted legacy notwithstanding, Lincoln Perry was not only one of the most talented comic actors to emerge in early-twentieth-century America, but also one of the era's most colorful individuals. In addition, he was among its most confounding and unpredictable.

He portrayed an overtly cowering, fainthearted lackey with such verve that he was frequently misjudged as being one, while off-camera he was an assertive, demanding egotist and manipulator. Moody, sometimes introverted and evasive, he was also an outgoing, insistent prankster. Ostensibly a devout Catholic, he was known to be a rowdy hell-raiser and frequent womanizer. At times a race-conscious journalist and agitator who fought for the rights of blacks in the film industry, when attacked by race leaders and militants, he became a blistering critic of a social movement that, in his eyes, had betrayed him.

Lincoln Perry was clearly an enigma. But an even greater puzzle, perhaps, is why as one of a few of the era's black actors who consistently fought to improve his roles and put his career on the line to do so he would be labeled by many observers and critics as the chief culprit in demeaning the black image.

The answer lies partially in his vivid, near-surreal presence on the screen. A haunting, unsettling aura surrounded the character Perry portrayed and continually reprised in motion pictures. Even though in mainstream films the character's rebellious, folk-inspired subversiveness (avoiding unrewarded labor by pretense and sham) was subverted and, ultimately, perverted, Perry played the part with such mesmerizing vagueness that he literally commanded the screen. The actors—including Lionel Barrymore, Warner Baxter, and Will Rogers—who admitted that he stole nearly every scene in which he appeared had justifiable cause. His tantalizing slow movements, provoking pauses, quizzical expressions, and slurred, molasses-like, almost indecipherable speech, literally forced viewers to watch him—to pay strict attention. In the end, most audiences were hypnotized by his performance. Perhaps most riveting and disturbing is that after viewing a scene in which Stepin Fetchit appears, it is difficult to determine whether it was comedy or ultra realism, in effect, tragedy. In that sense, Perry was absolutely correct when he insisted he portrayed the "soul" of his character.

He was without doubt a brilliant character actor, even though the *character* he portrayed gradually fell into disfavor and was detested by many. In addition to his on-screen brilliance as a comic actor in roles that allowed him to stretch beyond brief houseboy and porter portrayals, the comic's off-screen behavior contributed to his alienation from both the white and black film communities.

His aggressive demands for star treatment, better roles, and a salary equivalent with that of white actors irked many studio executives and led others to label him a troublemaker or outright uppity Negro. There was little attempt to support him when the tide turned and critics attacked the character he played, even though Fox and other studios had reaped huge profits from the films in which he appeared.

For blacks, Perry's quirky, evasive personality and refusal to conform to the middle-class standards they expected from a Negro star was a source of continued irritation. Even as his rise to fame opened doors for other actors and resulted in higher pay for feature players and extras, his wild publicity schemes, unpredictability, and flamboyant, Bad Boy behavior irritated many fellow actors as well as nearly all middle-class blacks. At bottom, Perry was simply not the well-behaved, model citizen that the black community would have chosen as a representative of the first black movie star. For that ideal model of respectability, they would have to wait for the 1950s and the emergence of the suave Sidney Poitier.

Lincoln Perry was, however, a bold representative of a more surreptitious, rural African American tradition, one that had allowed black Americans to survive and reach a point where even thinking about true middle-class acceptance and respectability was possible. And, as he alternately cajoled, then slow-walked and shim-sham-shimmied his way through the briar patch of America's early-twentieth-century racism to claim motion-picture stardom, his association with that tradition became clearer.

In addition to being a consummate actor and comic, he was—in the tradition of sly rural blacks who survived daily humiliation and sporadic violence by their wits and what has been called shrewd humility—a crafty trickster.

"Bred en bawn in a briar-patch, Bred en bawn," Br'er Rabbit yelped as he scampered to freedom after hoodwinking Br'er Fox with woeful entreaties to beat him, skin him, do anything except "fling me in dat briar-patch."

It is likely that Lincoln Perry had a similar outcome in mind when he penned his patented folk ditty, then shambled onstage to dance and sing it: *"The Step 'n' Fetchit! Step 'n' Fetchit! Turn around, stop and catch it . . . Turn around, stop and catch it . . ."*

Finally, even after changing times and a traumatic social upheaval banished him from Hollywood movies, few did *catch* on to or truly comprehend the wily rebellious nature of the early twentieth century's so-called dancing fool.

NOTES

Chapter One

1. "Biographies of Your Favorite Stage Stars," *Chicago Defender,* April 7, 1934.
2. Joseph McBride, "Stepin Fetchit Talks Back," *Film Quarterly,* Summer 1971.
3. Harold Cruse, "1920's–1930's–West Indian Influence," in *The Crisis of the Negro Intellectual: From Its Roots to the Present* (New York: William Morrow, 1968), pp. 115–46.
4. McBride, "Stepin Fetchit Talks Back."
5. Herbert Howe, "Stepin's *High-Colored* Past," *Photoplay,* June 1929.
6. Matt Robinson, "Stepin Fetchit, Why Do They Call You Stepin Fetchit?" unpublished essay, 1979, author's files.
7. "Stepin Fetchit Seen as a 'Bert Williams,'" *Los Angeles Times,* January 9, 1929.
8. Lawrence Gellert, "Bert Williams: Philosophical Tidbits Gleaned from His Songs and Stories," an unpublished Works Project Administration Research Paper, n.d., p. 8.
9. W. C. Handy, *Father of the Blues* (New York: Da Capo Press, 1991), p. 33.

Chapter Two

1. Elisabeth Goldbeck, "Step Tells All," *Motion Picture Magazine,* July 1929.
2. Matt Robinson, "Stepin Fetchit, Why Do They Call You Stepin Fetchit?" unpublished essay, 1979, author's files.
3. Joseph McBride, "Stepin Fetchit Talks Back," *Film Quarterly,* Summer 1971, p. 25.
4. Robinson, "Stepin Fetchit."
5. In 1923, a circus called the Siegrist-Silbon Shows was acquired by Carl J.

Sedlmayer, who combined the names "Royal" for Canada and "American" for the United States and began advertising it as the "Most Beautiful Show on Earth."

6. Joseph Mitchell, "Stepin Fetchit, Negro Film Actor, 'Too Sleepy to Show New Dance Step' . . . ," *New York World-Telegram,* June 2, 1934.
7. Tom Fletcher, *100 Years of the Negro in Show Business!* (New York: Burge & Co., 1954), p. 207. The "medicinal" tonics sold at the medicine shows were often alcohol-based or laced with codeine, a drug that was placed under governmental regulation by the Harrison Act of 1914.
8. Romeo L. Dougherty, "Things Theatrical," *New York Amsterdam News,* October 12, 1934; "Biographies of Your Favorite Stage Stars," *Chicago Defender,* April 7, 1934.
9. Herbert Howe, "Stepin's *High-Colored* Past," *Photoplay,* June 1929.
10. W. C. Handy, *Father of the Blues* (New York: Da Capo Press, 1991), pp. 179–80.
11. Mel Watkins, *On the Real Side: A History of African American Comedy* (Chicago: Lawrence Hill Books, 1999), p. 175.
12. Carlton Jackson, *Hattie: The Life of Hattie McDaniel* (Lanham, Md.: Madison Books, 1990), p. 16.
13. Tom Fletcher, *100 Years,* pp. xvii, 13.
14. Ibid., p. 57.
15. Ethel Waters and Charles Samuels, *His Eye Is on the Sparrow* (New York: Pyramid Books, 1972), pp. 164–70.
16. Watkins, *On the Real Side,* p. 367.
17. Howe, "Stepin's *High-Colored* Past."
18. David Levering Lewis, *When Harlem Was in Vogue* (New York: Knopf, 1981), p. 13, source of quote unspecified.
19. Richard Schickel, *D. W. Griffith: An American Life* (New York: Simon & Schuster, 1984), pp. 268–70.
20. After becoming ill while doing location shooting, Lucas died less than a year after the film was completed. Some contend that Bill Foster—a Chicago press agent, sportswriter, and occasional producer and actor—made the first black motion picture, *The Railroad Porter*; it was reportedly "an imitation of Keystone comic chases completed perhaps three years before *The Birth of a Nation.*" Still, there is little doubt that the appearances by Lucas and Williams were the first in which established black stars played leading roles.
21. Thomas Cripps, *Slow Fade to Black* (New York: Oxford University Press, 1997), p. 80.

Chapter Three

1. Ethel Waters and Charles Samuels, *His Eye Is on the Sparrow* (New York: Pyramid Books, 1972), p. 77.
2. Clarence Muse, "Muse Hits TOBY," *Afro-American* (Baltimore), August 18, 1928.
3. "Lincoln Perry's Letter," *Chicago Defender*, October 8, 1927.
4. Herbert Howe, "Stepin's *High-Colored* Past," *Photoplay*, June 1929.
5. Ruby Berkley Goodwin, "When Stepin Fetchit Stepped into Fame," *Afro-American* (Baltimore), July 6, 1929.
6. "Lincoln Perry Writes," *Chicago Defender*, December 4, 1926.
7. James Dennison, *Scandalize My Name: Black Imagery in American Popular Music* (New York: Garland Publishing Co., 1982), p. 427.
8. Alain Locke, "Should the Negro Be Encouraged to Cultural Equality," *Forum* 78 (October 1927): 508. In his essay collection *The New Negro* (1925), Locke contended that the mass migration of blacks to urban centers had eradicated outworn concepts of Black Mammies, Sambos, and Uncle Toms that had previously defined Negro life and were often used to justify repression. The complexity of city life had created a community of blacks who were forced to deal with an urban environment and created a New Negro. "Interest in the cultural expression of Negro life," Locke wrote, "heralds an almost revolutionary revaluation of the Negro."
9. James Weldon Johnson, *Along This Way: The Autobiography of James Weldon Johnson* (New York: Atheneum, 1968), p. 328. The influx of downtown thrill-seekers to Harlem led James Weldon Johnson to write: "At these times, the Negro drags his captors captive. On occasions, I have been amazed and amused watching white people dancing to a Negro band in a Harlem cabaret; attempting to throw off the crusts and layers of inhibitions laid on by sophisticated civilization; striving to yield to the feel and experience of abandon; seeking to recapture a taste of primitive joy in life and living; trying to work their way back into that jungle which was the original Garden of Eden; in a word, doing their best to pass for colored."
10. Matt Robinson, "Stepin Fetchit, Why Do They Call You Stepin Fetchit?" unpublished essay, 1979, author's files.
11. Joseph McBride, "Stepin Fetchit Talks Back," *Film Quarterly*, Summer 1971, p. 26; author interview with Matt Robinson, c. February 1980.
12. "Lincoln Perry's Letter," *Chicago Defender*, February 19, 1927.
13. Ibid., February 5, 1927.
14. Ibid., February 25, 1928.
15. Ibid., September 29, 1928.
16. Ibid., November 5, 1927.
17. Ibid., March 19, 1927.

18. Ibid., May 14, 1927.
19. Ibid., May 21, 1927.

Chapter Four

1. "Remembering 47th Street," Internet document, 47th Street quote from interview with Timuel L. Black; Jervis Anderson, *This Was Harlem* (New York: Farrar, Straus & Giroux, 1982), p. 142, source of Calloway quote unspecified.
2. From condensed Internet version of *Central Avenue Sounds: Jazz in Los Angeles,* Clora Bryant et al., eds. (Berkeley: University of California Press, 1987).
3. Bette Yarbrough Cox, *Central Avenue—Its Rise and Fall* (1890–c. 1955) (Los Angeles: BEEM Publications, 1996), pp. 267–68.
4. "Lincoln Perry's Letter," *Chicago Defender,* July 9, June 18, and June 11, 1927.
5. Ibid., May 21, 1927.
6. Ibid., July 9, July 30, July 23, and June 18, 1927; Buddy Brown, "Coast Dope," *Chicago Defender,* June 11, 1927.
7. "Lincoln Perry's Letter," *Chicago Defender,* June 4, 1927.
8. Ibid., June 4, and June 18, 1927; Billy Tucker references, June 4, June 18, and July 23, 1927.
9. Leonard Maltin and Richard W. Bann, *Our Gang: The Life and Times of the Little Rascals* (New York: Crown, 1977), p. 278; Thomas Cripps, *Slow Fade to Black* (New York: Oxford University Press, 1997), p. 130; Sul-Te-Wan quote from interview with Cripps.
10. Cripps, *Slow Fade to Black,* p. 112.
11. Ibid., pp. 102–103; "Greetings of the Season from the Colored Stars of Screenland," *California Eagle,* December 21, 1928.
12. "Many Actors, Singers in Film," *Afro-American* (Baltimore), March 29, 1930; Herbert Howe, "A Jungle Lorelei," *Photoplay,* July 1929.
13. Margaret McKee and Fred Chisenhall, *Beale Black and Blue: Life and Music on America's Main Street* (Baton Rouge: Louisiana State University Press, 1981), p. 48.
14. Carlton Jackson, *Hattie: The Life of Hattie McDaniel* (Lanham, Md.: Madison Books, 1990), p. 21; Geraldyn Dismond, "Movies Stars Came in by 'Back Door,'" *Afro-American* (Baltimore), September 21, 1929. Beavers began as a minstrel-show singer but was employed as silent film star Leatrice Joy's maid when she arrived in Hollywood in the early twenties. Until the early thirties, McDaniel often worked as a maid in wealthy Los Angeles households to supplement her meager earnings from extra work at the studios and her $5-per-week role as Hi-Hat Hattie on KNX radio's popular weekly variety show, *The Optimistic Do-Nut Hour.*

15. Cripps, *Slow Fade to Black,* p. 112.
16. Donald Bogle, *Toms, Coons, Mulattos, Mammies, and Bucks: An Interpretive History of Blacks in American Films* (New York: Viking 1973), p. 111, source of Tucker quote unspecified.
17. Thomas Cripps, *Black Film as Genre* (Bloomington: Indiana University Press, 1978), p. 26.
18. Author interview with Honi Coles, 1979. By 1927, Micheaux had released over a dozen silent films. Among them were *Within Our Gate* (1920), a controversial antilynching film; *The Symbol of the Unconquered* (1921), an indictment of the Ku Klux Klan; racial uplift movies like *Birthright* (1924); and *Body and Soul* (1924), which introduced Paul Robeson to the screen. The latter, a scathing attack on unscrupulous jackleg preachers, is the only surviving example of Micheaux's silent-film work.
19. Robert Oberfirst, *Al Jolson: You Ain't Heard Nothin' Yet* (New York: A. S. Barnes, 1980), p. 83.
20. "Lincoln Perry's Letter," *Chicago Defender,* July 9, 1927.
21. Ibid., July 30, 1927.
22. Ruby Berkley Goodwin, "When Stepin Fetchit Stepped into Fame," *Afro-American* (Baltimore), July 6, 1929.
23. Matt Robinson, "Stepin Fetchit: Why Do They Call You Stepin Fetchit?" unpublished essay, 1979, author's files.
24. "Lincoln Perry's Letter," *Chicago Defender,* August 13, 1927.

Chapter Five

1. *Journal of The Society of Motion Picture Engineers* 48, no. 4 (April 1947), Part 2, "The Work of Case and de Forest"—1911–1925; Part 3, "Commercialization of Movietone by Fox," from the journal's Internet site.
2. Thomas Cripps, *Slow Fade to Black* (New York: Oxford University Press, 1997), p. 220.
3. James Weldon Johnson Memorial Collection, Beinecke Library, Yale University, August 15, 1929; Geraldyn Dismond, "Movie Stars Came in by 'Back Door,'" *Afro-American* (Baltimore), September 21, 1929.
4. Dorothy Manners, "Enter the Dixies," *Motion Picture Classic,* February 1929.
5. Cripps, *Slow Fade to Black,* p. 219.
6. Buddy Brown, "Coast Dope," *Chicago Defender,* September 10, 1927.
7. "Carolyn [*sic*] Snowden Starring in Pictures," *California Eagle,* September 23, 1927.
8. "Lincoln Perry's Letter," *Chicago Defender,* September 17, 1927.
9. Bette Yarbrough Cox, *Central Avenue—Its Rise and Fall (1890–c. 1955)* (Los Angeles: BEEM Publications, 1996), p. 31.

10. "Lincoln Perry's Letter," *Chicago Defender*, October 8, 1927.
11. Ibid., October 15, 1927.
12. Ibid., November 26, 1927.
13. Ibid., November 5, 1927.
14. "Film Reviews," *Variety*, December 21, 1927.
15. "Lincoln Perry's Letter," *Chicago Defender*, January 14, 1928.
16. "Coast Dope," *Chicago Defender*, September 10, 1927.
17. Clora Bryant et al., eds., *Central Avenue Sounds: Jazz in Los Angeles* (Berkeley: University of California Press, 1998), p. 34.
18. "Lincoln Perry's Letter," *Chicago Defender*, October, 29, 1927.
19. Lawrence Gellert, "Bert Williams: Philosophic Tid-bits Gleaned from His Songs and Stories," unpublished Works Project Administration Research Paper, n.d., p. 8, New York Public Library, Schomburg Center for Research in Black Culture; William McFerrin Stowe, Jr., "Damned Funny: The Tragedy of Bert Williams," *Journal of Popular Culture* 10, no. 1 (Summer 1976).
20. Charlene Regester, "Stepin Fetchit: The Man, the Image, and the African-American Press," *Film History* 6 (1994): 502, 518.
21. New York Public Library for the Performing Arts, Stepin Fetchit clips, c. December 1940, newspaper source unidentified.
22. Ruby Berkley Goodwin, "When Stepin Fetchit Stepped into Fame," *Afro-American* (Baltimore), July 6, 1929.
23. "Lincoln Perry's Letter," *Chicago Defender*, December 31, 1927.
24. "Talking Shorts," *Variety*, September 4, 1929; Thomas Cripps, *Slow Fade to Black*, p. 205.
25. Cripps, *Slow Fade to Black*, p. 207, quotes from *New York Amsterdam News*, August 13, 1930.
26. "Lincoln Perry's Letter," *Chicago Defender*, May 12, 1928.
27. Ibid.
28. Ibid., May 26, 1928.
29. Hal Erickson, All Movie Guide, www.allmovie.com.

Chapter Six

1. "Lincoln Perry's Letter," *Chicago Defender*, September 29, 1928.
2. Ibid.
3. Ibid.
4. Ibid., October 13, 1928.
5. Ibid., November 10, 1928.
6. Mordaunt Hall, "The Screen," *New York Times*, February 18, 1929; "Film Reviews," *Variety*, February 18, 1929.
7. Donald Bogle, *Blacks in American Films and Television* (New York: Fireside, 1988), p. 105.

8. "Chas. Gilpin Here to Make 'Lonesome Road,'" *California Eagle,* November 2, 1928.
9. "Shooting Begun on 'Hearts in Dixie,'" *California Eagle,* November 30, 1928.
10. "Lincoln Perry's Letter," *Defender,* November 10, 1928.
11. Thomas Cripps, *Slow Fade to Black* (New York: Oxford University Press, 1977), p. 238, trade paper and date unspecified.
12. "Greetings of the Season from the Colored Stars of Screenland," *California Eagle,* December 21, 1928; "Stepin Fetchit Seen as a 'Bert Williams,'" *Los Angeles Times,* June 9, 1929.
13. "Jas. B. Lowe, Robt. Muse Considered for 'Hearts in Dixie,'" *California Eagle,* December 21, 1928.
14. Cripps, *Slow Fade to Black,* pp. 162, 237–38; *Ebony,* September 1972, p. 50.
15. "Actor Too Proud to Work in Films with Own Race," *Chicago Defender,* December 28, 1928.
16. Maurice Dancer, "I Didn't High-Hat Colored Players," *Pittsburgh Courier,* February 2, 1929.
17. "Fox Studios Completes Retake Scenes," *California Eagle,* February 15, 1929.
18. Fox advertisement, *Motion Picture Classic,* April 1929.
19. Cripps, *Slow Fade to Black,* p. 237; Turner Classic Movies Internet review by Kerryn Sherrod and Jeff Stafford.
20. Cripps, *Slow Fade to Black,* p. 244.
21. "Vidor Hopes Film Will Vie with Best," *New York Amsterdam News,* January 16, 1929; Kevin Brownlow and John Kobal, *Hollywood: The Pioneers* (New York: Knopf, 1979), p. 196.
22. Daniel L. Haynes, "What 'Hallelujah' Means to the Negro Race," *California Eagle,* February 15, 1929.
23. Cripps, *Slow Fade to Black,* p. 246, news quotes from the *Charleston Gazette,* December 9, 1928, and New York Public Library for the Performing Arts, clips.
24. Ibid., Parsons quote from New York Public Library for the Performing Arts, clips.
25. Eva Jessye, "The Actors in 'Hallelujah' Didn't Get Enormous Salaries," *Afro-American* (Baltimore), July 5, 1930.
26. Ibid.
27. Cripps, *Slow Fade to Black,* p. 243.
28. Jessye, "The Actors."
29. Ibid.; Dorothy Manners, "Enter the Dixies," *Motion Picture Classic,* February 1929.
30. Jessye, "The Actors"; July 5 and "The Truth About Hallelujah," July 12, 1930.

31. J. Winston Harrington, "Harlem Folks Claim Jim Crow Move in Hallelujah Showing," *Chicago Defender,* August 24, 1929; James Gow, "Harlem First Night," *New York Amsterdam News,* August 28, 1929.
32. Mordaunt Hall, *New York Times,* February 28, 1929.
33. Thomas Cripps, *Slow Fade to Black,* p. 242, quotes from sample clips in George P. Johnson Collection, UCLA, including Los Angeles, Cleveland, and New York newspapers.
34. "Sylvester Russell's Review," *Pittsburgh Courier,* July 27, 1929; "'Hearts in Dixie' Opens in New York," *Chicago Defender,* March 16, 1929; *Chicago Whip,* May 18, 1929; Maurice Dancer, *Afro-American* (Baltimore), March 9, 1929.
35. Cripps, *Slow Fade to Black,* p. 242.
36. "Film Reviews," *Variety,* March 6, 1929; Mordaunt Hall, "The Screen," *New York Times,* February 28, 1929; "Stepin Fetchit Seen," *Los Angeles Times,* June 6, 1929; "Sylvester Russell's Review," *Pittsburgh Courier,* July 27, 1929; "'Hearts in Dixie,'" *Chicago Defender,* March 16, 1929; Donald Bogle, *Blacks in American Films and Television* (New York: Fireside, 1988), p. 431, source of Muse quotation unspecified.
37. "The Picture Parade," *Motion Picture,* June 1929, p. 60; "The Shadow Stage, A Review of the New Pictures," *Photoplay,* March 1929, p. 55.
38. Robert Benchley, *Opportunity,* April 1929.
39. Peter Noble, "The Coming of the Sound Film," an excerpt from Noble's book *The Negro in Film* (London, 1948), reprinted in the *International Library of Negro Life and History: Anthology of the American Negro in the Theatre,* compiled and edited by Lindsay Patterson (New York: Publishers Co. 1968), p. 248.
40. Hall, "The Screen," *New York Times,* August 21, 1929; Cripps, *Slow Fade to Black,* p. 242, quotes from New York Public Library for the Performing Arts and New York Public Library, Schomburg Center for Research in Black Culture, clip files.
41. Ralph Matthews, "'Hallelujah' Could Have Been Filmed Right in Baltimore," *Afro-American* (Baltimore), May 31, 1930.
42. Cripps, *Slow Fade to Black,* p. 106.
43. "Southern Attitude Kills Negro Progress in Films," *Afro-American* (Baltimore), May 17, 1930.
44. "No More Colored Casts–Fox," *California Eagle,* May 30, 1930.
45. "Southern Attitude Kills Negro Progress in Films."
46. Elisabeth Goldbeck, "Black—*and Potentially* Blue," *Motion Picture Classic,* p. 70.
47. In 1967, McKinney died in New York; she was fifty-four years old. In 1978, she was elected posthumously to the Black Filmmakers Hall of Fame.
48. Muse, who was inducted into the Black Filmmakers Hall of Fame in

1973, survived and sustained himself nicely as a character actor, adviser, writer, and composer. His best-known song was "When It's Sleepy Time Down South," the classic jazz ballad that became the theme song for Louis Armstrong's big band in the 1930s. He also collaborated with Elliot Carpenter in writing the music for *Spirit of Youth* (1938), an independent race film that dramatized the life of heavyweight champion Joe Louis. Muse's screenwriting credits include *Way Down South* (1939), a surprisingly tame plantation musical considering that it was written with the black activist and poet Langston Hughes; and *Broken Strings* (1940), a race film dealing with a young musician's dilemma about playing classical European music or jazz.

Chapter Seven

1. Clora Bryant et al., *Central Avenue Sounds: Jazz in Los Angeles*, (Berkeley: University of California Press, 1998), p. 9; Bette Yarbrough Cox, *Central Avenue—Its Rise and Fall* (Los Angeles: BEEM Publications, 1996), pp. 35–36.
2. Elisabeth Goldbeck, "Step Tells All," *Motion Picture Magazine*, July 1929.
3. "Lincoln Perry's Letter," *Chicago Defender*, October 13, 1928; *California Eagle*, advertisement for the Apex Club, December 21, 1928; Cox, *Central Avenue*, pp. 267–68.
4. Herbert Howe, "A Jungle Lorelei," *Photoplay*, July 1929.
5. "Theatrical Weekly Finds Race Show Biz Is Poor," *Chicago Defender*, January 10, 1931.
6. "Mosby's Apex Nite Club a Permanent Fixture," *California Eagle*, November 21, 1930; Harry Levette, "Behind the Scenes with Harry," *California Eagle*, August 28, 1931.
7. Levette, "Behind the Scenes with Harry," *California Eagle*, October 31, 1931; Jim Haskins, *The Cotton Club* (New York: Random House, 1977), pp. 29–30.
8. Levette, "Behind the Scenes with Harry," *California Eagle*, August 28, 1931.
9. Cox, *Central Avenue*, p. 258.
10. Joseph McBride, "Stepin Fetchit Talks Back," *Film Quarterly*, Summer 1971, p. 24.
11. Harry Levette, "Behind the Scenes with Harry," *California Eagle*, August 22, 1930.
12. Harry Levette, "Gossip of the Movie Lots," *Afro-American* (Baltimore), September 2, 1933.
13. Herbert Howe, "Stepin's *High-Colored* Past," *Photoplay*, June 1929.
14. Ibid.
15. Herbert Howe, "A Jungle Lorelei," *Photoplay*, October 1929.

16. "Fetchit Returns," *New York Times,* November 26, 1933; "Stepin Fetchit Comes Back," *Ebony,* February 1952.
17. Robert Sklar, *The Plastic Age* (New York: George Braziller, 1970), p. 1.
18. Bruce Catton, "The Restless Decade," from *The Twenties,* an Essandes Paperback Edition of the American Heritage Special Issue, p. 5.
19. Ibid., p. 6.
20. Kenneth Anger, *Hollywood Babylon* (New York: Dell, 1981), pp. 103, 108.
21. Ibid., p. 101, source of quote unspecified.
22. Stepin Fetchit, "Perry Writes to Clear Up Many Rumors," *Chicago Defender,* December 27, 1930.
23. McBride, "Stepin Fetchit Talks Back," pp. 22, 23.
24. Elisabeth Goldbeck, "Step Tells All," *Motion Picture Magazine,* July 1929; Herbert Howe, "Stepin's *High-Colored* Past," *Photoplay,* June 1929.
25. Louis R. Lautier, "Is Stepin Fetchit the Equal of Bert Williams? Lionel Barrymore Says Yes; Eddie Cantor, No," *Chicago Defender,* March 17, 1934; "Can Lazy Bones Stepin Fetchit Come Back?" *Afro-American* (Baltimore), February 3, 1934; Goldbeck, "Step Tells All."
26. "Can Lazy Bones Stepin Fetchit Come Back?"; Lautier, "Is Stepin Fetchit the Equal of Bert Williams?"
27. Goldbeck, "Step Tells All"; author interview with Keter Betts, October 2003; Ruby Berkley Goodwin, "When Stepin Fetchit Stepped into Fame," *Afro-American,* July 6, 1929.
28. Goldbeck, "Step Tells All."
29. "Step and Fetchit Makes the Grade in Peoria as a Song and Dance Man," *Variety,* October 28, 1959; "Stepin Fetchit Comes Back," *Ebony,* February 1952.
30. Goodwin, "When Stepin Fetchit Stepped into Fame."
31. "Stepin Fetchit Calls His Film Image Progressive," *New York Times,* July 24, 1968.
32. *Negro Historical Bulletin,* June 1951, pp. 205–6, quotations from *New York Times*—news article, July 12, 1910, and editorial, July 13, 1920.
33. Howe, "Stepin's *High-Colored* Past."
34. "Fetchit Returns," *New York Times,* November 26, 1933.
35. Goldbeck, "Step Tells All."
36. "Negro Screen Comedian Will Marry Today," *Los Angeles Times,* June 27, 1929.
37. Goodwin, "When Stepin Fetchit Stepped into Fame."
38. "Stepin Fetchit and 'Bubbles' Battle for Public," *Afro-American* (Baltimore), July 6, 1929.
39. Author interview with John "Bubbles" Sublette, October 1979.
40. "Say Fetchit Jilted Her; Sues for $100,000," *Afro-American* (Baltimore), July 13, 1929.

41. "Negro Actor Compromises Suit for Balm," *Los Angeles Times*, August 7, 1929; "Actor Must Pay $5,000 Damages," *New York Times*, August 8, 1929.
42. Goodwin, "When Stepin Fetchit Stepped into Fame"; "Stepin Fetchit Seen as a Bert Williams," *Los Angeles Times*, June 9, 1929.
43. "Film Reviews," *Variety*, May 1, 1929.
44. Ibid., May 29, 1929; "The Shadow Stage," *Photoplay*, July 1929; "The Picture Parade," *Motion Picture Magazine*, September 1929.
45. Mordaunt Hall, "The Screen," *New York Times*, May 27, 1929.
46. Goodwin, "When Stepin Fetchit Stepped into Fame."
47. "Reviews," *Variety*, August 21, 1929.
48. Ralph Matthews, "Movie Comedian Expects God to Help Him Keep His Wife," *Afro-American* (Baltimore), May 16, 1931.
49. McBride, "Stepin Fetchit Talks Back," p. 23.
50. "Film Reviews," *Variety*, August 21, 1929; Hall, "The Screen," *New York Times*, October 5, 1929.
51. "Film Reviews," *Variety*, September 11, 1929; Hall, "The Screen," *New York Times*, September 9, 1929.
52. "Stepin Fetchit to Tour Country," *Pittsburgh Courier*, December 21, 1929.
53. Harry Levette, "On the Movie Lots," *Afro-American* (Baltimore), November 23, 1929.

Chapter Eight

1. "Star Stays Up Late to Get Sleepy," *Pittsburgh Courier*, January 18, 1930; "Stepin Fetchit," *Philadelphia Tribune*, January 16, 1930.
2. "Stepin Fetchit Gets Big Contract from Columbia," *Pittsburgh Courier*, January 25, 1930.
3. " 'Stepin' Failed to 'Fetchit,' So Now He's Out in the Cold Again," *Pittsburgh Courier*, February 8, 1930.
4. "Fetchit Out, Muse In," *Afro-American* (Baltimore), February 22, 1930.
5. "Stepin Fetchit Gets Big Contract from Columbia"; "Movie Comedian Expects God to Help Him Keep His Wife," *Afro-American* (Baltimore), May 16, 1931.
6. "Can't Keep a Good Man Down," *Pittsburgh Courier*, February 22, 1930.
7. "Perry Writes to Clear Up Many Rumors," *Chicago Defender*, December 27, 1930.
8. Mordaunt Hall, "The Screen," *New York Times*, February 8, 1930.
9. "Can't Keep a Good Man Down."
10. Leonard Maltin and Richard W. Bann, *Our Gang: The Life and Times of the Little Rascals* (New York: Crown, 1977), p. 115.
11. Ibid.; publicity photograph of Stepin Fetchit and Farina, *Afro-American* (Baltimore), March 1, 1930.

12. Frankye-Marilyn Whitlock, "Coast Breezes," *Chicago Defender,* April 5, 1930.
13. "Aged Actor Dies," *Afro-American* (Baltimore), March 29, 1930.
14. "Chased into a Chicken Coop, Says Colored Comedian," *Los Angeles Times,* April 7, 1930; "Stepin Fetchit's Easy Ways Will Get Him Down," *Pittsburgh Courier,* April 12, 1930.
15. Herbert Howe, "A Jungle Lorelei," *Photoplay,* July 1929.
16. Elisabeth Goldbeck, "Black—*and Potentially* Blue," *Motion Picture Classic,* April 1930.
17. Howe, "A Jungle Lorelei."
18. Harry Levette, "Behind the Scenes with Harry," *California Eagle,* October 24, November 21, 1930.
19. Ibid., October 16, 1931; Goldbeck, "Black—*and Potentially* Blue"; Elisabeth Goldbeck, "Step Tells All," *Motion Picture Magazine,* July 1929.
20. "Stepin Fetchit's Lazy Drawl Big Hit in Chicago," *Pittsburgh Courier,* May 10, 1930.
21. "Playhouses and Playfolk," *Afro-American* (Baltimore), May 24, 1930.
22. "Fetchit Balks When Salary Is Withheld,"*Afro-American* (Baltimore), June 7, 1930.
23. Ibid.
24. Jervis Anderson, *This Was Harlem: 1900 to 1950* (New York: Farrar, Straus & Giroux, 1982), pp. 242–43, date of *Tribune* article unspecified.
25. "Black Belt's Nite Life," *Variety,* October 16, 1926.
26. Anderson, *This Was Harlem,* p. 235, source of quote unspecified.
27. Ibid., p. 309, Savoy quotation from *Ebony* magazine, 1946, month unspecified.
28. Ibid., p. 173, date of quote unspecified.
29. Ibid., p. 170, source of quote unspecified.
30. "Stepin Fetchit at the Lafayette," *New York Amsterdam News,* June 11, 1930; "At the Lafayette," *New York Amsterdam News,* June 18, 1930.
31. "Film Reviews," *Variety,* July 2, 1930; *New York Amsterdam News,* August 27, 1930.
32. "Bill Can Sprint Yet," *Afro-American* (Baltimore), July 12, 1930; "The Big Fight with Demsey at Douglas," *New York Amsterdam News,* July 9, 1930.
33. "Fetchit Doubles Up," *Afro-American* (Baltimore), July 12, 1930; "Theatrical Notes," *New York Times,* June 27, 1930; "Legit Names Crowding in for Brief Stays," *Variety,* July 2, 1930.
34. "Fetchit Doubles Up."
35. Robert A. Hill, *The Marcus Garvey and UNIA Papers,* vol. 1, *1826–August 1919* (Berkeley: University of California Press, 1983), pp. xxxv–xxxvii, xii.

36. Anderson, *This Was Harlem*, pp. 123–25.
37. "Stepin Fetchit Busy Working in New York," *Chicago Defender*, July 5, 1930.
38. *Chicago Defender*, July 19, 1930.
39. "Theatrical Notes," *New York Times*, September 13, 1930; "New Acts," *Variety*, September 17, 1930.
40. "Troubles Come Fast for Film Funny Man," *Afro-American* (Baltimore), November 15, 1930; "Stepin Fetchit's Baby Named from Bible" and "First Photo of Stepin Fetchit, Jr.," *California Eagle*, October 24 and November 7, 1930.
41. "Son Born to Mrs. Fetchit in New York," *Chicago Defender*, September 20, 1930.

Chapter Nine

1. Harry Levette, "Behind the Scenes with Harry," *California Eagle*, October 10 and November 21, 1930.
2. "Troubles Come Fast for Funny Man," *Afro-American* (Baltimore), November 15, 1930.
3. Ibid.
4. Levette, "Behind the Scenes with Harry," December 12, 1930.
5. Ibid.
6. "Fetchit Disliked Role Given Him in 'The Prodigal,'" *Chicago Defender*, June 13, 1931.
7. Mordaunt Hall, "The Screen," *New York Times*, June 27, 1931.
8. Charlene B. Regester, "Stepin Fetchit: The Man, the Image, and the African American Press," *Film History* 6 (1994): 510, *Defender* quote from Clifford W. MacKay, "Going Backstage with the Scribe," *Chicago Defender*, December 13, 1930.
9. "Perry Writes to Clear Up Rumors," *Chicago Defender*, December 27, 1930.
10. "Stepin Fetchit Preaches a Xmas Sermon to Actors," *Afro-American* (Baltimore), December 27, 1930.
11. Ibid.
12. Harry Levette, "Gossip of the Movie Lots," *California Eagle*, February 13, 1931; "Stepin Fetchit at Tivoli," *California Eagle*, April 3, 1931.
13. Levette, "Behind the Scenes with Harry," April 24, 1931.
14. "Stepin Fetchit's Wife Threatens Divorce Suit," *California Eagle*, April 24, 1931.
15. "Movie Comedian Expects God to Help Him Keep His Wife," *Afro-American* (Baltimore), May 16, 1931.
16. Ibid.; "Fetchit Blames 'Friends' for Marital Rifts," *Chicago Defender*, May 9, 1931.
17. Levette, "Behind the Scenes with Harry," June 12, 1931.

18. MacKay, "Going Backstage with the Scribe," June 20, 1931; Levette, "Behind the Scenes with Harry," June 19, 1931.
19. "Comedian Just Caveman," *New York Herald Tribune,* August 26, 1931.
20. "Stepin Fetchit's Wife Enters Divorce Suit: Says Brutality Replaces Comic Role in Home," *Chicago Defender,* August 29, 1931.
21. Joseph Mitchell, "Stepin Fetchit, Negro Film Actor, 'Too Sleepy to Show New Dance' . . . ," *New York World-Telegram,* June 2 1934; Fay M. Jackson, "Pink Casket for Wife of Movie Comic," *Afro-American* (Baltimore), September 29, 1934.
22. "Stepin Fetchit Will Play Cafe in September," *Chicago Defender,* August 29, 1931; Charlene B. Regester, "Stepin Fetchit: The Man, the Image, and the Afro-American Press," *Film History* 6 (1991): 511, quote from Ralph Matthews, "Looking at the Stars," *Afro-American* (Baltimore), May 20, 1933.
23. "Footlights," *Chicago Defender,* November 29, 1930; MacKay, "Going Backstage with the Scribe," April 25, 1931; "Little Edgar 'Blue Boy' Connor Here," *New York Amsterdam News,* December 14, 1932.
24. Thomas Cripps, *Slow Fade to Black* (New York: Oxford University Press, 1997), pp. 106–108.
25. Scenes from *The Smiling Ghost,* Warner Brothers (1941).
26. Hal Erickson, All Movie Guide, www.allmovie.com.
27. Cripps, *Slow Fade to Black,* p. 108, Best quote from *Silhouette,* George P. Johnson Collection, UCLA; Ibid., p. 268.
28. "Biographies of Your Favorite Stage Stars," *Chicago Defender,* April 7, 1934.
29. "Sans the Footlights (Or Even the Stage), " *Chicago Defender,* September 3, 1932.
30. "Step Is Star in This Film," *Chicago Defender,* November 25, 1933.
31. Joseph McBride, "Stepin Fetchit Talks Back," *Film Quarterly,* Summer 1971, p. 22.
32. Frankye M. Whitlock, " 'Fetchit' and Muse in Near Fist Battle," *Chicago Defender,* September 5, 1931.
33. "Step Seeks Players for His New Picture," *Chicago Defender,* October 31, 1931; Regester, "Stepin Fetchit," p. 511, quotation from "Stepin Fetchit to Produce Own Film," *Chicago Defender,* September 19, 1931.

Chapter Ten

1. *New York Times,* April 22, 1934.
2. "Afro Readers Say," *Afro-American* (Baltimore), February 15, 1930.
3. Melvin Patrick Ely, *The Adventures of Amos 'n' Andy: A Social History of an American Phenomenon* (New York: Free Press, 1991), pp. 173–79.
4. Joseph McBride, "Stepin Talks Back," *Film Quarterly,* Summer 1971, p. 22.

5. Donald Bogle, *Toms, Coons, Mulattos, Mammies, and Bucks* (New York: Viking, 1973), p. 134.
6. Harry Levette, "Behind the Scenes with Harry," *California Eagle,* June 24, 1932; Harry Levette, "Plenty of Work for Movie Stars Now," *California Eagle,* September 3, 1932.
7. Louis R. Lautier, "Louise Beavers Wouldn't Use Epithet in 'Imitation of Life,'" *Afro-American* (Baltimore), March 2, 1935.
8. Charlene B. Regester, *Black Entertainers in African American Newspaper Articles, 1909–1950: An Annotated Bibliography of the Chicago Defender, the Afro-American (Baltimore), the Los Angeles Sentinel and the New York Amsterdam News* (Jefferson, N.C.: McFarland & Co., 2001), vol. 1, p. 94; "Two Film Stars on Royal Bill This Week," *Afro-American* (Baltimore), April 16, 1932; "Stepin Fetchit Is Starred in Radio," *Chicago Defender,* August 20, 1932; Regester, *Black Entertainers,* p. 104.
9. "Stepin Fetchit's Show Closes," *California Eagle,* October 21, 1932; *Variety,* New York Public Library for the Performing Arts, clips, article date and title unspecified.
10. "Stepin Fetchit, Lazy in Speech, Is Rather Smart," *Chicago Defender,* March 4, 1933; Levette, "Behind the Scenes with Harry," March 3, 1933.
11. "Stepin Fetchit, Lazy in Speech, Is Rather Smart"; Errol Aubrey Jones, "Hear Fetchit and Heywood to Join in Show," *Chicago Defender,* July 15, 1933, source of quote unspecified.
12. Ralph Matthews, "Why Can't Stepin Fetchit Behave?" *Afro-American* (Baltimore), June 23, 1934.
13. "Can Lazy Bones Stepin Fetchit Come Back?" *Afro-American* (Baltimore), February 3, 1934; "Fetchit Arrested for Speeding," *Afro-American* (Baltimore), July 22, 1933; Jones, "Hear Fetchit and Heywood."
14. Charles Bowen, "Bert Williams or Stepin Fetchit, Which Was the Greater Comedian?" *Afro-American* (Baltimore), January 27, 1934; "Lost! One Film Star; Name, Stepin Fetchit," *Chicago Defender,* October 28, 1933; Harry Levette, "Gossip of the Movie Lots," *Afro-American* (Baltimore), September 2, 1933.
15. "Fetchit Back in Movies Again," *Afro-American* (Baltimore), August 19, 1933. "Fetchit has been given another chance," the article reported, "despite the disastrous endings of his previous two tickets."
16. "Fetchit Returns," *New York Times,* November 26, 1933; "Stepin Fetchit with Us," *Los Angeles Times,* October 18, 1933.
17. Levette, "Gossip of the Movie Lots," September 2, 1933, date of *Los Angeles Examiner* article unspecified; "Stepin Fetchit Is Back in the Films," *Chicago Defender,* September 2, 1933.
18. Levette, "Gossip of the Movie Lots," September 2, 1933.
19. Matthews, "Why Can't Stepin Fetchit Behave?"

20. "Stepin Fetchit Is Star in This Film," *Chicago Defender,* November 25, 1933.
21. Harry Levette, "Stepin Fetchit Is Sure Movies Rule," *Chicago Defender,* December 23, 1933.
22. Joseph Mitchell, "Stepin Fetchit, Negro Film Actor, 'Too Sleepy to Show New Dance . . .'" *New York Herald Tribune,* June 2, 1934.
23. Telephone interview with Sidney Bloomberg from his San Francisco home.

Chapter Eleven

1. "Lost! One Film Star; Name, Stepin Fetchit," *Chicago Defender,* October 28, 1933; "Stepin Fetchit With Us," *Los Angeles Times,* October 18, 1933.
2. Harry Levette, "Behind the Scenes with Harry," *California Eagle,* November 10, 1933, January 19 and January 12, 1934.
3. Charles Bowen, "Bert Williams or Stepin Fetchit, Which Was the Greatest Comedian?" *Afro-American* (Baltimore), January 27, 1934; Louis Lautier, "Is Stepin Fetchit the Equal of Bert Williams? Lionel Barrymore Says Yes; Eddie Cantor, No," *Chicago Defender,* March 17, 1934; "Can Lazy Bones Come Back," *Afro-American* (Baltimore), February 3, 1934.
4. "Fox Re-Signs Stepin Fetchit for Bigger and Better Roles," *Variety,* April 10, 1934; "Stepin Fetchit's Work Wins Him New Contract with Fox," *Chicago Defender,* April 21, 1934; "Stepin Fetchit Sets Record," *California Eagle,* January 19, 1934.
5. Fay M. Jackson, "Hollywood Lowdown," *Afro-American* (Baltimore), December 13, 1933.
6. "Fox Re-Signs Stepin Fetchit for Bigger and Better Roles"; "Stepin Fetchit's Work Wins Him New Contract With Fox."
7. Fay M. Jackson, "Hollywood Gossip," *Afro-American* (Baltimore), March 10, 1934; Mordaunt Hall, "The Screen," *New York Times,* March 2, 1934.
8. "Film Reviews," *Variety,* April 24, 1934; "Who's Who This Week in Pictures," *New York Times,* April 22, 1934; "The Shadow Stage," *Photoplay,* June 1934.
9. Scenes from *Stand Up and Cheer,* Fox Film Corporation, 1934.
10. Mordaunt Hall, "The Screen," *New York Times,* February 25, 1934; "Film Reviews," *Variety,* February 20, 1934; Jackson, "Hollywood Gossip."
11. "Defends Fetchit in Role Played in 'Carolina,'" *Afro-American* (Baltimore), July 7, 1934; "Afro Readers Say," *Afro-American* (Baltimore), April 28, 1934; "Hit Use of Word 'Nigger' in Fox Film of the South, 'Carolina,'" *Chicago Defender,* March 31, 1934.
12. Ralph Matthews, "If You Want Better Movies Just Write a Letter," *Afro-American* (Baltimore), March 17, 1934.

13. "Defends Fetchit in Role Played in 'Carolina.'"
14. Lautier, "Is Stepin Fetchit the Equal of Bert Williams?"; Bowen, "Bert Williams or Stepin Fetchit"; Romeo L. Dougherty, "My Observations," *New York Amsterdam News,* January 3, 1934.
15. Bowen, "Bert Williams or Stepin Fetchit."
16. Donald Bogle, *Blacks in American Films and Television: An Illustrated Encyclopedia* (New York: Fireside, 1988), p. 390, *New York Post* quote c. spring 1934.
17. "Stepin Fetchit's Work Wins Him New Contract With Fox"; Harry Levette, "Coast Codgings," *Chicago Defender,* May 12, 1934; Fay Jackson, "Hollywood Hot-Cha," *Afro-American* (Baltimore), May 12, 1934.
18. Levette, "Coast Codgings," April 28, 1934.
19. Jackson, "Hollywood Hot-Cha."
20. "Stepin Fetchit Here for the Apollo Benefit Show," *New York Amsterdam News,* May 26, 1934; Fay M. Jackson, "Hollywood Lowdown," *Afro-American* (Baltimore), June 9, 1934.
21. "Fetchit in New York for Benefit," *Chicago Defender,* June 2, 1934.
22. "Apollo Theater Has a Sensational Week," *New York Amsterdam News,* June 2, 1934; Romeo L. Dougherty, "My Observations," *New York Amsterdam News,* June 9, 1934.
23. Henri De La Tour, "Splendid Array of Talent at Lafayette," *New York Amsterdam News,* June 2, 1934.
24. Ralph Matthews, "Why Can't Stepin Fetchit Behave? *Afro-American* (Baltimore), June 23, 1934.
25. De La Tour, "Splendid Array of Talent at Lafayette."
26. Joseph Mitchell, "Stepin Fetchit, Negro Film Actor, 'Too Sleepy to Show New Dance,'" *New York World-Telegram,* June 2, 1934.
27. Levette, "Behind the Scenes with Harry," July 6, 1934.
28. Dougherty, "My Observations," June 9, 1934.
29. Harry Levette, "Stepin Fetchit Moves O.K. Under Girl Boss," *Chicago Defender,* July 7, 1934.
30. Carlton Jackson, *Hattie: The Life of Hattie McDaniel* (Lanham, Md.: Madison Books, 1990), p. 23.
31. Matthews, "Why Can't Stepin Fetchit Behave?" quotation, Fay Jackson.
32. "Spencer Tracy Laid Off Again," *Variety,* October 2, 1934.
33. Fay M. Jackson, "Pink Casket for Wife of a Comic," *Afro-American* (Baltimore), September 29, 1934.

Chapter Twelve

1. Fay M. Jackson, "Pink Casket for Wife of a Comic," *Afro-American* (Baltimore), September 29, 1934; Ralph Matthews, "Black Movie Stars Made by Mailman," *Afro-American* (Baltimore), March 17, 1934.
2. "Presenting Dr. Rogers," *New York Times,* October 12, 1934.

3. "The Shadow Stage," *Photoplay*, December 1934; "Film Reviews," *Variety*, October 16, 1934; Donald Bogle, *Blacks in American Films and Television: An Illustrated Encyclopedia* (New York: Fireside, 1988), p. 123.
4. Andre Sennwald, "The Screen," *The New York Times*, November 21, 1934. Andre Sennwald noted that "Helen Morgan, Ned Sparks and Stepin Fetchit provide amusing sketches in a Panama café."
5. Philip K. Scheuer, "Dr. Jekyll and Mr. Hyde Had Nothing on Stepin Fetchit," *Los Angeles Times*, December 16, 1934.
6. Harry Levette, "Coast Codgings," *Chicago Defender*, January 26, 1935.
7. L. Herbert Henegan, "Stepin Fetchit Tours South to Get Atmosphere for New Film," *Afro-American* (Baltimore), April 13, 1935.
8. John C. Moffitt, "Mr. Fetchit in Kansas City," *New York Times*, February 24, 1935.
9. Hilda See, "Comedy King of Movies Talks of New Picture He's Making," *Chicago Defender*, February 16, 1935.
10. "Screen Notes," *New York Times*, March 7, 1935; "Stepin Fetchit at Brooklyn Theater," *Afro-American* (Baltimore), March 16, 1936.
11. "Film Reviews," *Variety*, April 17, 1935; "The Screen," *New York Times*, January 7, 1935; Andre Sennwald, "The Screen," *New York Times*, February 22, 1935; "Film Reviews," *Variety*, January 22, 1935. Allan McMillan, "Hi Hattin' in Harlem," *Chicago Defender*, January 4, 1936.
12. Chappy Gardner, "C. Gardner Praises Stepin Fetchit's Work on Screen," *Chicago Defender*, March 16, 1935.
13. Fay M. Jackson, "Stepin Fetchit Through in Films, Hollywood Report," *Afro-American* (Baltimore), October 12, 1935.
14. Fay M. Jackson, "In Hollywood," *Afro-American* (Baltimore), May 18, 1935; Elsie Roxborough, "Stepin Fetchit Eyes Film Berth for His Young Son," *Chicago Defender*, April 27, 1935.
15. Douglas W. Churchill, "Facts and Frills from Hollywood," *New York Times*, May 3, 1935.
16. Nellie Dooling, "I May Be Lazy, but I Ain't No Fool," *Pittsburgh Courier*, January 4, 1936; Ralph Matthews, "Friendship Just Platonic but She Will Go to Hollywood," *Afro-American* (Baltimore), November 30, 1935.
17. Jackson, "In Hollywood."
18. Harry Levette, "Coast Codgings," *Chicago Defender*, May 25, 1935; "Bill Robinson Gets Chance in 'Old Kentucky'" and "Step Refuses to Pose with Bojangles," *Afro-American* (Baltimore), April 27, 1935.
19. Fay M. Jackson, "Bill Robinson Honored in Hollywood," *Chicago Defender*, June 15, 1935.
20. Jackson, "Stepin Fetchit Through in Films, Hollywood Report."
21. Author interview with Honi Coles, August 1979. "Bojangles Sore About

the Way His Film Was Cut," *Afro-American* (Baltimore), May 18, 1935; Fay M. Jackson, "Hollywood," *Afro-American* (Baltimore), July 6, 1935.

22. Bryan B. Sterling and Frances N. Sterling, *Will Rogers: A Photo-Biography* (Dallas: Taylor Publishing Co., 1999), pp. 223, 226.
23. Levette, "Coast Codgings," August 24, 1935.
24. Press Sheet and Sales Catalogue, *The Virginia Judge,* 1935.
25. Richard Watts, Jr., "On the Screen," *New York Herald Tribune,* September 20, 1935; "Stepin Fetchit Clicks in Last Will Rogers Picture," *Chicago Defender,* September 14, 1935.
26. Jackson, "Stepin Fetchit Through in Films"; "Stepin Fetchit Again Fired by Fox Film Group," *Afro-American* (Baltimore), September 28, 1935.
27. "Hollywood Takes Bill Robinson in Arms," *Chicago Defender,* October 19, 1935.
28. "Stepin Fetchit Not Troubled by Fiasco," *New York Amsterdam News,* October 19, 1935; "Stepin Fetchit a Hit in Boston," *Afro-American* (Baltimore), October 19, 1935; "Stepin Fetchit at Roxy Friday," *New York Herald Tribune,* October 15, 1935; "Droll Stage Comedian Billed Here," *New York Amsterdam News,* October 5, 1935.
29. "Today on Radio," *New York Times,* October 24, 1935; "Entertainment Aids Actors Federation," *New York Times,* November 4, 1935.
30. "Stepin Fetchit Is Taken by Pa. Cops in Liquor Raids," *Afro-American* (Baltimore), November 16, 1935; "Stepin Fetchit Crowns Valet, Lands in Jug," *Afro-American* (Baltimore), November 23, 1935; "Fetchit to Head Bill at the Apollo Theater," *New York Amsterdam News,* December 7, 1935; "Fetchit Hit in 'Lazy Town' at the Apollo," *New York Amsterdam News,* December 14, 1935; "Stepin Fetchit Beat Him, Says Process Server," *New York Herald Tribune,* December 13, 1935; "Why Can't Stepin Fetchit Stay Out of Trouble?" *Afro-American* (Baltimore), December 21, 1935.
31. "Stepin Fetchit Snaps to Life—Jailed on Fighting Charge," *New York Evening Post,* December 12, 1935; "Stepin Fetchit Beat Him, Says Process Server"; "Fetchit Stars in 2 Courts," *New York Evening Journal,* December 12, 1935.
32. "Stepin Freed by Stooge in Sock Charge," *New York Daily News,* December 18, 1935; "Stepin Fetchit Wins in Court and Is Freed," *Chicago Defender,* January 4, 1935; "Stepin Fetchit Freed," *New York Times,* December 18, 1935.
33. Matthews, "Friendship Just Platonic."
34. "Stepin Fetchit and Benny Goodman to Headline Show at Regal," *Chicago Defender,* December 14, 1935; "Stars That Shine," *Chicago Defender,* January 4, 1936.
35. Jai Butti, "Films," *Afro-American* (Baltimore), January 25, 1936.
36. Henry T. Sampson, *That's Enough, Folks: Black Images in Animated*

Cartoons, 1900–1960 (Lanham, Md.: Scarecrow Press, 1988), pp. 161, 216–17; *Who Killed Cock Robin?* Walt Disney/United Artists, 1935.

37. "Hollywood Lowdown," *Afro-American* (Baltimore), January 4, 1936; "Step Finds Encores Too Taxing," *Afro-American* (Baltimore), March 21, 1936; "Tour Means Two Checks for Fetchit," *Afro-American* (Baltimore), March 28, 1936.
38. "Stepin Fetchit Loew's Headliner," New York Public Library for the Performing Arts, Stepin Fetchit clips, April 13, 1936, source of article unspecified; "News of the Stage," *New York Times,* April 11, 1936; Chappy Gardner, "Harlem Helps Broadway Welcome Stepin Fetchit," *Chicago Defender,* April 18, 1936; "State Bill Headed by Stepin Fetchit," *New York American,* April 11, 1936.

Chapter Thirteen

1. Ralph Cooper, *Amateur Night at the Apollo* (New York: HarperCollins, 1990), pp. 124–28.
2. Harry Levette, "Coast Codgings," *Chicago Defender,* November 2, 1935; "Stepin Fetchit Plans 'Harlemwood' Theater," *New York World-Telegram,* June 20, 1936.
3. David Arlen, "Hollywood's '400' on Parade," *New York Amsterdam News,* April 13, 1932.
4. "Movie Comic Entertains Friends," *Chicago Defender,* September 5, 1936; "Stars Frolic at Fetchit's All-Day Party," *Chicago Defender,* August 15, 1936.
5. T.M.P., "Screen," *New York Times,* August 15, 1936.
6. St. Clair Bourne, "Two Stars Elope," *New York Amsterdam News,* October 16, 1937.
7. "Stepin Fetchit Big Stage Hit in Los Angeles," *Chicago Defender,* October 3, 1936; Harry Levette, "Thru Hollywood," *Chicago Defender,* October 24, 1936.
8. Frank Nugent, "Dateline Hollywood," *New York Times,* December 6, 1936.
9. Irene Thirer, "'Harder You Work, Less You Get'—Stepin Fetchit," *New York Post,* February 5, 1937; "News of the Stage," *New York Times,* February 26, 1937.
10. Thirer, "'Harder You Work, Less You Get.'"
11. "Fox Studios Buy Contract Option of Bill Robinson," *Chicago Defender,* April 24, 1937.
12. "Stepin Fetchit Hurt in an Auto Crash" and "Stepin Fetchit Improves," *New York Times,* April 26 and 27, 1937; "Stepin Fetchit Hurt as Auto Hits 'El' Pillar," *New York Herald Tribune,* April 26, 1937; Alan McMillan, "Stepin Fetchit Is Near Death from Automobile Smashup in New York," *Chicago Defender,* May 1, 1937.

13. Bourne, "Two Stars Elope."
14. "Fetchit to Finish Philly Date, Crash Interrupted," *Variety,* May 19, 1937; "Stepin Fetchit Up; Off to West Coast for Rest," *Chicago Defender,* June 5, 1937.
15. "Fetchit in a Hurry for Once—He Elopes," *Afro-American* (Baltimore), October 16, 1937; "Stepin Fetchit Heir to Arrive in New York," *Afro-American* (Baltimore), May 21, 1938.
16. "Stepin Fetchit Crashes His Car; Unhurt," *Chicago Defender,* October 16, 1937; Bourne, "Two Stars Elope"; "Fetchit in a Hurry for Once—He Elopes."
17. "Stepin Fetchit at Philly's Nixon," *Chicago Defender,* November 27, 1937; "Stepin Swingit" and "Fetchit in Band Role in South," *New York Amsterdam News,* January 22 and February 5, 1938; "Erskine Hawkins' Band to Play 'Chi's' Oriental May 20," *Chicago Defender,* May 7, 1938; "Harlem Hit Parade," *Variety,* April 20, 1938; "Stepin Fetchit Outdraws Duke," *Afro-American* (Baltimore), February 12, 1938.
18. "Stepin Fetchit Walks Out on Stage Show in Memphis," *New York Amsterdam News,* February 19, 1938.
19. "Stepin Fetchit Raps at Press," *New York Amsterdam News,* May 7, 1938; James H. Purdy, Jr., "My Real Following Is White, Says Step," *Afro-American* (Baltimore), April 30, 1938.
20. "Stepin Fetchit and U.S. Split on Income Taxes," *Chicago Defender,* August 12, 1939.
21. Lillian Johnson, "Light and Shadow," *Afro-American* (Baltimore), October 14, 1939.
22. James J. Gentry, "An Open Letter to Stepin Fetchit," *Chicago Defender,* May 14, 1938.
23. "Step Now a Proud Papa!" *New York Amsterdam News,* May 28, 1938.
24. "Stepin Fetchit Agrees to Wife's Choice of Names," *New York Amsterdam News,* June 18, 1938; "Step, Wife Argue on Baby's Name," *Afro-American* (Baltimore), June 18, 1938; "Winnie Liked 'Donald Martin' and 'Donald Martin' It Will Be," *Pittsburgh Courier,* June 18, 1938.
25. "Step's Wife Didn't Want Her Boy's Name to Sound Girlish," *Afro-American* (Baltimore), June 25, 1938.
26. "With Step Back in Town, She's Happy," *New York Amsterdam News,* November 4, 1939.
27. "Fetchit Back in Hollywood After a Year," *Chicago Defender,* June 25, 1938.
28. "No Comment—Mrs. Fetchit," *Afro-American* (Baltimore), September 24, 1938.
29. Lawrence F. LaMarr, "Stepin Fetchit Set for Paramount Pix," *New York Amsterdam News,* October 22, 1938.
30. "Gets Coveted Role in 'Gone With Wind,' " *New York Amsterdam News,* January 21, 1939.

Chapter Fourteen

1. "Stepin Fetchit Has to Settle Lawsuit," *Chicago Defender,* February 11, 1939.
2. "The Stepin Fetchit's Celebrate," *Chicago Defender,* March 11, 1939; "When Baby Hollers, Step Steps," *New York Amsterdam News,* March 11, 1939; "The Fetchit Family," *Afro-American* (Baltimore), March 11, 1939.
3. "Fetchit Does Famous Walkout," *Chicago Defender,* March 11, 1939.
4 "Stepin Fetchit at the Oriental," *Chicago Defender,* April 15, 1939.
5. "Fetchit Wins by a Head," *New York Daily News,* April 13, 1939; "Stepin Fetchit Freed After Steak Attack," *Chicago Defender,* April 22, 1939; "Stepin Fetchit Planning 100-G Suit in Sauce Case," *New York Amsterdam News,* April 29, 1939.
6. "Step's Back in Trouble," *New York Amsterdam News,* May 6, 1939.
7. "Stepin Fetchit and U.S. Split on Income Taxes," *Chicago Defender,* August 12, 1939; "West Likes Fetchit," *Afro-American* (Baltimore), August 8, 1939; "Roxy, Salt Lake City," *Variety,* July 26, 1939.
8. "Stepin Fetchit and U.S. Split on Income Taxes."
9. "News and Gossip of the Rialto," *New York Times,* July 19, 1939; "News of the Stage," *New York Times,* October 27, 1939; "Stars Galore in New Cotton Club Revue," *Chicago Defender,* October 14, 1939.
10. "Stars Galore in New Cotton Club Revue" and "Stepin Fetchit in Rehearsal for Big Show," *New York Amsterdam News*, November 4, 1939.
11. Author interview with Lula Jones of East Elmhurst, N.Y., January 2005; "With Step Back in Town, She's Happy," *New York Amsterdam News,* November 4, 1939.
12. "Say Stepin Fetchit, Wife Have Separated," *Chicago Defender,* November 11, 1939.
13. "'They Exaggerated My Trouble' Says Fetchit," *Chicago Defender,* November 25, 1939; "Fetchit Doesn't Like Slumming," *Variety,* October 25, 1939; "Stepin Fetchit Upsets the Gay White Way," *New York Amsterdam News,* November 18, 1939; New York Public Library for the Performing Arts, Stepin Fetchit clips, c. October 1939; the source and date of article, and exact date of letter, unspecified; Jim Haskins, *The Cotton Club* (New York: Random House, 1977), p. 154.
14. New York Public Library for the Performing Arts, Stepin Fetchit clips.
15. "'They Exaggerated My Trouble' Says Fetchit"; The Scribe, "Stepin Fetchit Is Glad to Be Off Broadway," *Chicago Defender,* December 16, 1939.
16. "An' Here's a Letter from Stepin Fetchit to Editor," *Chicago Defender,* January 6, 1940.
17. B.R.C. (Bosley Crowther), "The Screen," *New York Times,* May 15, 1939.

18. "Stepin Fetchit Calls Self 'An Audible Pantomimist,'" New York Public Library for the Performing Arts, Stepin Fetchit clips, date and source of article unspecified, c. winter of 1939–1940.
19. "Stepin Fetchit Stars in Very Poor Play," *Chicago Defender,* March 2, 1940.
20. "Stepin Fetchit, Late, Delays Show Opening," *Chicago Defender,* March 23, 1940; "News of the Stage," *New York Times,* March 13 and May 20, 1940; "Fetchit Fetches Self Out of Play," *Afro-American* (Baltimore), March 23, 1940; "Stepin Fetchit Is in Trouble Again" and "Equity Drops Charges Against Actor Stepin Fetchit," *Chicago Defender,* April 13 and April 27, 1940.
21. "Stepin Fetchit's Disowned Son Seeks to Change Name," *New York Amsterdam News,* April 13, 1940; "Stepin Fetchit Is in Trouble Again."
22. Brooks Atkinson, "The Play," *New York Times,* June 5, 1940.
23. "Saroyan Ready to Try Out Play," *New York Times,* July 4, 1940.
24. "Film Executives Pledge Better Roles for Colored in Pictures," *Afro-American* (Baltimore), August 8, 1942; *Variety,* June 17, 1942, New York Public Library for the Performing Arts, clips, date and article title unspecified.
25. Thomas Cripps, *Slow Fade to Black* (New York: Oxford University Press, 1997), p. 376; Carlton Jackson, *Hattie: The Life of Hattie McDaniel* (New York: Madison Books, 1990), pp. 100–101.
26. Hedda Hopper, "Hattie Hates Nobody," *Chicago Tribune,* December 14, 1947.
27. Clarence Muse, "Muse Presents the Other Side of the Film Picture," *Pittsburgh Courier,* September 12, 1942.
28. "Colored Actors Portray Life as It Is, Says Famed Comedian," *Afro-American* (Baltimore), August 21, 1943.
29. Liner Notes for "Since Ol' Gabriel's Time: Hezikiah and the Houserockers," from the Internet.
30. Bankruptcy listings, *New York Times,* February 5, 1941; Dolores Calvin, "They Do Come Back Is the Story Written by Stage and Screen's Famous Comedian Stepin Fetchit," *Chicago Defender,* April 11, 1942; "Stepin Fetchit Loses in Non-Showup Act," *Afro-American* (Baltimore), September 13, 1941.
31. "'Willie Best Week' Scheduled to Start at Loew's Brevoort," *New York Star Amsterdam News,* January 24, 1942.
32. Calvin, "They Do Come Back."

Chapter Fifteen

1. "Stepin Fetchit Held on Charge of Paternity," *New York Amsterdam Star News,* April 4, 1942; Clora Bryant et al., eds., *Central Avenue*

Sounds: Jazz in Los Angeles (Berkeley: University of California Press, 1998), p. 313.

2. "Winnie Admits Stepin Fetchit Is Not Husband," *New York Amsterdam Star News,* April 18, 1942.
3. "Step, Winnie Still Tiffing Over Child," *Chicago Defender,* May 23, 1942.
4. "Step' Fetchit Shuffles into Court Friday," *New York Amsterdam Star News,* May 9, 1942.
5. "Winnie Admits Stepin Fetchit Is Not Husband"; "Step' Fetchit Shuffles into Court Friday."
6. "Winnie Admits Stepin Fetchit Is Not Husband."
7. "Stepin Fetchit Must Pay," *Afro-American* (Baltimore), June 20, 1942.
8. "Bill Robinson Testifies in the Stepin Fetchit's [*sic*] Battle," *Chicago Defender,* June 20, 1942.
9. "Fetchit Ordered to Support Child," *New York Times,* June 12, 1942.
10. "Stepin in Cell, Breaks a Date," New York Public Library for the Performing Arts, Stepin Fetchit clip file, source unspecified, n.d.
11. "Police Surprise Stepin Fetchit in Hotel, Seize Him in Juvenile Delinquency Case," *Chicago Sun,* July 9, 1943; "Stepin Fetchit and Girl Taken in Hotel Raid," *Afro-American* (Baltimore), July 17, 1943.
12. "Police Nab Stepin Fetchit with Girl, 16, in Hotel" and "Stepin Fetchit Accuser Gets 8-Month Jail Term," *Chicago Defender,* July 17 and July 24, 1943; "Girl in Stepin Fetchit Case Gets Jail Term" and "Actor Begins 30-Day Term at Bridewell," *Afro-American* (Baltimore), July 24 and October 2, 1943; "Stepin in Cell, Breaks a Date."
13. "Fetchit 'Stand-in' Myth falls Down Under Probe," *Afro-American* (Baltimore), October 23, 1943.
14. George Schuyler, "Views and Reviews," *Pittsburgh Courier,* September 5, 1942.
15. Author interview with Matt Robinson in Los Angeles, c. February 1980.
16. E. B. Rea, "Encores and Echoes," *Afro-American* (Baltimore), August 14, 1943.
17. "Stepin Owes Millions," *New York Times*, November 13, 1943. John Ford Collection, Indiana University, letter from Lincoln Perry dated February 16, 1945.
18. Michael Carter, "Stepin Fetchit," *Afro-American* (Baltimore), May 26, 1945.
19. Ibid.
20. David Platt, *Daily Worker,* May 28, 1945.
21. "Stepin Fetchit's 'Indifference,'" *Afro-American* (Baltimore), June 30, 1945.
22. Donald Bogle, *Blacks in American Films and Television: An Illustrated Encyclopedia* (New York: Firestone, 1989), p. 151.
23. From *Miracle in Harlem,* Herald Pictures/Screen Guild Productions, 1948.

24. "Film Reviews," *Variety,* August 11, 1948.
25. Author interview with William Greaves in New York, Summer 2003.
26. From *Richard's Reply,* Astor/All-American Pictures, Robert M. Savini, c. 1949.
27. "Reviews: Apollo, N.Y.," *Variety,* January 22, 1947.
28. "Talk of 'Satchel Paige' Film with Stepin Fetchit Starred," *Chicago Defender,* October 29, 1949.
29. "Stepin Fetchit Returns," *New York Times,* July 7, 1951.
30. Author interview with Matt Robinson in Los Angeles, c. February 1980.
31. "Stepin Fetchit Comes Back," *Ebony,* February 1952.
32. Ibid.
33. Bosley Crowther, "The Screen in Review," *New York Times,* April 10, 1952; "Film Reviews," *Variety,* January 23, 1952.
34. H.H.T., "The Screen in Review," *New York Times,* March 17, 1953; "Film Reviews," *Variety,* May 6, 1953.
35. Collected tapes from Armstrong's home, Louis Armstrong Archives, Queens College.
36. Interview with Jemajo Perry, Los Angeles, January 2006.
37. Telephone interview with Charles Austin at his Miami home, March 28, 2006.

Chapter Sixteen

1. Author interview with Matt Robinson, Los Angeles, c. February 1980.
2. W. A. Low and Virgil A. Clift, *The Encyclopedia of Black America* (New York: McGraw-Hill, 1981), p. 104.
3. "Do You Remember Stepin Fetchit," *Negro Digest,* November 1950.
4. Telephone interview with Julie McCowan, March 19, 2003.
5. "Stepin Fetchit Makes the Grade in Peoria as Song & Dancer at Cafe," *Variety,* October 28, 1959.
6. "Charlie Cotton, the Man Who Brought Star Lite to the City," *Orlando Sentinel,* July 4, 1990.
7. "Stepin Fetchit, Now 68 and 50 Yrs. in Show Biz, In Re Ofay Audiences," *Variety,* September 27, 1961.
8. Radio performance and interview by Warren Bolt, Clinton, Iowa, spring 1967.
9. "Where Are They Now?" *Newsweek,* November 20, 1967; Joseph McBride, "Stepin Fetchit Talks Back," *Film Quarterly,* Summer 1971.
10. Typed letter sent to Mike Todd, Jr., at Ritz Carlton Hotel in Boston, April 18, 1964; offered on Internet auction by Houle Rare Books and Autographs, Los Angeles.
11. "Stepin Fetchit Shuffles to Charity Ward," *Philadelphia Daily News,* April 30, 1964.
12. "Stepin Fetchit of Films Now a Charity Patient," *New York Times,*

May 1, 1964; "Stepin Fetchit Shuffles to Charity Ward"; "Stepin Fetchit in Charity Ward," *New York Post,* May 2, 1964.

13. "Stepin Fetchit Shuffles to Charity Ward."
14. Richard Durham, *The Greatest: My Own Story* (New York: Random House, 1975), pp. 120–22.
15. "His Cake and He'll Eat It, Too," photo caption, *New York Herald Tribune,* October 29, 1964; Melvin Durslag, "Did Stepin Fetchit Alter Ring History?" *Los Angeles Herald Examiner,* November 22, 1985.
16. Richard Lamparski, *Whatever Became of . . . ?* (New York: Crown, 1967), pp. 184–85.
17. Author interview with Honi Coles, New York City, 1979.
18. "Where Are They Now?"
19. From *Of Black America,* "Black History—Lost, Stolen, or Strayed," Columbia Broadcasting System and 20th Century-Fox Corporation, July 1968.
20. "Stepin Fetchit Calls His Film Image Progressive," *New York Times,* July 24, 1968.
21. "Irked Fetchit Returns to Defend His Image," *Los Angeles Herald-Examiner,* July 26, 1968.
22. "Stepin Fetchit Calls His Film Image Progressive."
23. Aleene MacMinn, "Records, TV: Stepin Fetchit, 76, Stages Comeback," *Los Angeles Times,* October 25, 1968.
24. From *Flip Out With Flip,* NBC-TV, 1968.
25. "$3 Million 'Fetchit' Suit Goes to Trial Sept. 18," *Jet,* August 24, 1972; author interview with Flip Wilson, Los Angeles, November 1979.
26. Delmarie Cobb and Antoinette Marsh, "The Father of Black Movie Stars," *Black Stars,* c. December 1979.
27. MacMinn, "Records, TV."
28. "Obituaries: Stepin Fetchit, 83, Dies; Pioneer Black Film Actor," *Washington Post,* November 21, 1985.
29. Radio performance and interview by Warren Bolt, Clinton, Iowa, spring 1967.
30. MacMinn, "Records, TV."
31. "Turnpike Gunman Kills 3 and Himself—Near Harrisburg" and "Turnpike Slayer Was Termed a Paranoid," *New York Times,* April 6 and 7, 1969; Michael Seiler, "Stepin Fetchit, Noted Black Comic of '30s Dies," *Los Angeles Times,* November 20, 1985.
32. "Stepin Fetchit Says He Was Defamed on TV Series About Blacks," *New York Times,* July 20, 1970.
33. John P. MacKenzie, "Supreme Court Rejects Appeals of 'Stepin Fetchit,' 800 Others," *Washington Post,* October 16, 1974.
34. Mark Jacobson, "Amazing Moms," *New York Magazine,* October 14, 1974.
35. Author interview with Matt Robinson, Los Angeles, February 1980;

Matt Robinson, "Stepin Fetchit, Why Do They Call You Stepin Fetchit?" unpublished essay, 1979, author's files; Jacobson, "Amazing Moms."

36. "Film Reviews," *Variety,* July 17, 1974.
37. Author interview with Matt Robinson, Los Angeles, February 1980.
38. "Pictures: Stepin Fetchit Cameo," *Variety,* October 14, 1975.
39. Wini Johnson, "Ailing Stepin Fetchit Buoyed by Admirers," *New York Amsterdam News,* May 22, 1976.
40. Robinson, "Stepin Fetchit"; author interview with Matt Robinson, Los Angeles, February 1980.

Chapter Seventeen

1. Wini Johnson, "Ailing Stepin Fetchit Buoyed by Admirers," *New York Amsterdam News,* May 22, 1976.
2. *New York Post,* April 27, 1976.
3. Delmarie Cobb and Antoinette March, "Stepin Fetchit: The Father of Black Movie Stars," *Black Stars,* c. December 1979.
4. Matt Robinson, "Stepin Fetchit, Why Do They Call You Stepin Fetchit?" unpublished essay, 1979, author's files.
5. Ibid.; David Hart, "Oldtime Hollywood Alive, Well in Retirement at Country House," *Chicago Tribune,* December 1985.
6. Cobb and March, "Stepin Fetchit."
7. "Stepin Fletcher [*sic*] Named to Hall of Fame," New York Public Library, Schomburg Center for Research in Black Culture, Stepin Fetchit clips, unidentified Atlanta, Georgia, newspaper, February 1978.
8. Bosley Crowther, "The Screen in Review," *New York Times,* April 10, 1952.
9. Michael Molinski, "Domestic News," United Press International, November 20, 1985; Cobb and March, "Stepin Fetchit."
10. Molinski, "Domestic News."
11. Dr. David Pilgram, "The Coon Caricature," October 2000, at www.ferris.edu/news/jimcrow/coon/.
12. Henry Allen, "Hot Dispute and Cool Sowell," *Washington Post,* October 1, 1981; Dean Murphy, "String of Racial Incidents Led to Student Walkout," *Los Angeles Times,* March 8, 1990; Bill McAllister and Chris Spolar, "The Transformation of HUD: 'Brat Pack' Filled Vacuum at Agency, *Washington Post,* 1989; see www.wordiq.com or www.free-definition.com.
13. Joseph McLellan, "From 'Bwana' to Chorister," *Washington Post,* August 22, 1978.
14. "Gospel, Mozart and 'Saturday Night' Satires," *Washington Post,* February 18, 1978.
15. Author interview with Flip Wilson, Los Angeles, November 1979.
16. Charles A. Johnson, "Hollywood Signs: A Young Perspective on Two Old Black Movies," *Los Angeles Times,* March 13, 1988.

INDEX

BLUES LEGACIES AND BLACK FEMINISM

by Angela Y. Davis

From one of this country's most important intellectuals comes a brilliant analysis of the blues tradition. Davis examines the performances and lyrics of Ma Rainey, Bessie Smith, and Billie Holiday as articulations of an alternative consciousness at odds with mainstream American culture. She demonstrates how the roots of the blues extend beyond a musical tradition to serve as a consciousness-raising vehicle for American social memory. A stunning, indispensable contribution to American history, as boldly insightful as the women Davis praises, *Blues Legacies and Black Feminism* is a triumph.

Women's Studies/African American Studies • 0-679-77126-3

HER DREAM OF DREAMS

by Beverly Lowry

Madam C. J. Walker is an American rags-to-riches icon. Born to former slaves in Louisiana in 1867, she went on to become a prominent African American businesswoman and the first female self-made millionaire in U.S. history. The story of her transformation from a laundress to a tremendously successful entrepreneur is both inspirational and mysterious, as many of the details of her early life remain obscure. In this superior biography, Beverly Lowry's abundant research fleshes out Walker's thinly documented story and frames it in the roiling race relations of her day.

Biography • 0-679-76803-3

KING OF THE WORLD

by David Remnick

In 1964, when Muhammad Ali (then known as Cassius Clay) stepped into the ring with Sonny Liston, he was widely regarded as an irritating freak who danced and talked way too much. Six rounds later Ali was not only the new world heavyweight boxing champion: He was "a new kind of black man" who would shortly transform America's racial politics, popular culture, and its notions of heroism. *King of the World* does justice to the speed, grace, courage, humor, and ebullience of one of the greatest athletes and irresistibly dynamic personalities of our time.

Biography/Sports • 0-375-70229-6

TO BE YOUNG, GIFTED AND BLACK

by Lorraine Hansberry

In her first play, the now-classic *A Raisin in the Sun*, Lorraine Hansberry introduced the lives of ordinary African Americans into our national theatrical repertory. In this book, Hansberry transformed her own life story into a work that has inspired a generation of readers. It follows the author from her childhood in Chicago, through her arrival in New York, where the triumph of *Raisin* made her famous overnight, to her death at the age of thirty-four. Hansberry's autobiography rings with her voice: a black woman who was angry, loving, bitter, funny, and defiantly proud.

Autobiography/ African American Studies • 0-679-76415-1

UNFORGIVABLE BLACKNESS

by Geoffrey C. Ward

Geoffrey C. Ward portrays the most celebrated—and the most reviled—African American of his age. Jack Johnson battled his way out of obscurity and poverty in the South to win the title of heavyweight champion of the world. At a time when whites ran everything in America, he took orders from no one and resolved to live as if color did not exist. While most blacks struggled simply to exist, he reveled in his riches and fame, to the consternation and anger of much of white America. The federal government set out to destroy him, and he was forced to endure prison and seven years of exile. This biography shows Jack Johnson as he really was—a battler against bigotry and the embodiment of American individualism.

Biography • 0-375-71004-3

THE WHOLE EQUATION

by David Thomson

Acclaimed critic David Thomson masterfully evokes the history of America's love affair with the movies and the tangled history of Hollywood in *The Whole Equation*. Thomson takes us from D.W. Griffith, Charlie Chaplin, and the first movies of mass appeal to Louis B. Mayer, who understood what movies meant to America—and reaped the profits. From Capra to Kidman and Hitchcock to Nicholson, Thomson examines the passion, vanity, calculation, and gossip of Hollywood and the films it has given us.

Film • 0-375-70154-0